The Englishman's Daughter:
A True Story of Love and Betrayal in World War I

The Napoleon of Crime:
The Life and Times of Adam Worth, Master Thief

Forgotten Fatherland: The Search for Elisabeth Nietzsche

THE MAN
WHO WOULD BE
KING

THE MAN
WHO WOULD BE
KING

THE FIRST AMERICAN IN AFGHANISTAN

BEN MACINTYRE

FARRAR · STRAUS · GIROUX / NEW YORK

Farrar, Straus and Giroux
19 Union Square West, New York 10003

Copyright © 2004 by Macintyre Books Inc.
All rights reserved
Distributed in Canada by Douglas & McIntyre Ltd.
Printed in the United States of America
First edition, 2004

Grateful acknowledgment is made to the following for permission to repro-
duce the images herein:
The National Portrait Gallery, London, for the images of Joseph Wolff by
W.M.B. Measor, and Sir William Hay Macnaghten by James Atkinson; the National Army Museum, London, for the images of the Bolan Pass, Afghan irregulars, and the storming of Ghazni; © Tate, London, 2003 for the images of
Remnants of an Army, by Lady Elizabeth Butler; *Central Asia: Personal Narra-
tive of General Josiah Harlan, 1823–1841,* edited by Frank Ross, for the images
of Josiah Harlan, Harlan's sketch of Shah Shujah, and Harlan's sketch of Dost
Mohammed Khan; *Cabool: A personal Narrative of the Journey to, and residence in
that City in the Years 1836, 7 and 8,* by Sir Alexander Burnes, for the images of
View of Kabul from the East, Sir Alexander Burnes, and Dost Mohammed Khan;
France: Private collection for the images of Maharaja Ranjit Singh and three
Akalis; Private collection for the images of Fakir Aziz ud-Din and Allard's
Cuirassier; *Soldier and Traveller: Memoirs of Alexander Gardner,* by Alexander
Gardner (edited by Major Hugh Pearse), for the images of Jean-Francois Allard
and Alexander Gardner; *European Adventurers of Northern India 1785 to 1849,*
by Charles Grey, for the image of Paolo di Avitabile.

Library of Congress Cataloging-in-Publication Data
Macintyre, Ben, 1963–
  The man who would be king : the first American in Afghanistan /
Ben Macintyre— 1st ed.
    p.   cm.
  Includes bibliographical references and index.
  ISBN 0-374-20178-1 (hc : alk. paper)
    1. Harlan, Josiah, 1799–1871.   2. Afghanistan—History—19th century.
3. Afghanistan—Kings and rulers—Biography.   4. Americans—
Afghanistan—Biography.   I. Title.
DS367.H37M33 2004
958.1'03—dc22
[B]   2003061764

Designed by Jonathan D. Lippincott
Maps designed by Jeffrey L. Ward

www.fsgbooks.com

1   3   5   7   9   10   8   6   4   2

FOR BARNEY, FINN, AND MOLLY

If I want a crown I must go hunt it for myself
—Rudyard Kipling, "The Man Who Would Be King"

CONTENTS

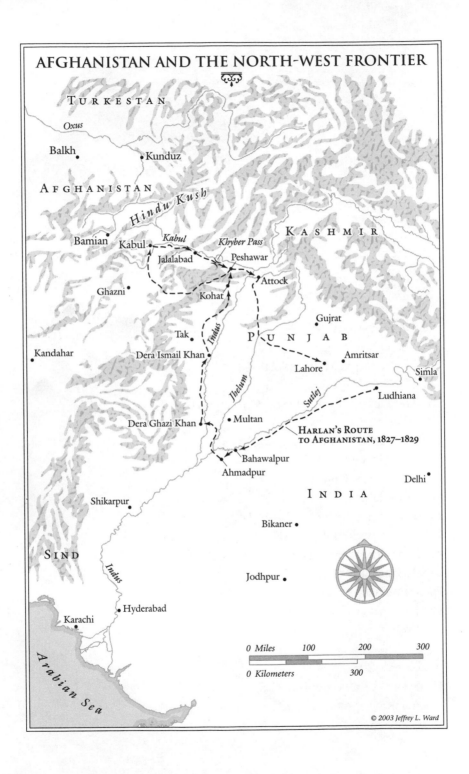

AFGHANISTAN AND THE NORTH-WEST FRONTIER

TURKESTAN

Oxus

Balkh

Kunduz

AFGHANISTAN

Hindu Kush

Bamian

Kabul

Kabul

Jalalabad

Khyber Pass

Peshawar

KASHMIR

Ghazni

Kohat

Attock

Tak

Indus

Gujrat

PUNJAB

Kandahar

Dera Ismail Khan

Lahore

Amritsar

Simla

Jhelum

Sutlej

Ludhiana

Dera Ghazi Khan

Multan

**HARLAN'S ROUTE
TO AFGHANISTAN, 1827–1829**

Bahawalpur

Ahmadpur

Delhi

INDIA

Shikarpur

Bikaner

SIND

Indus

Jodhpur

Karachi

Hyderabad

Arabian Sea

0 Miles   100   200   300

0 Kilometers   300

© 2003 Jeffrey L. Ward

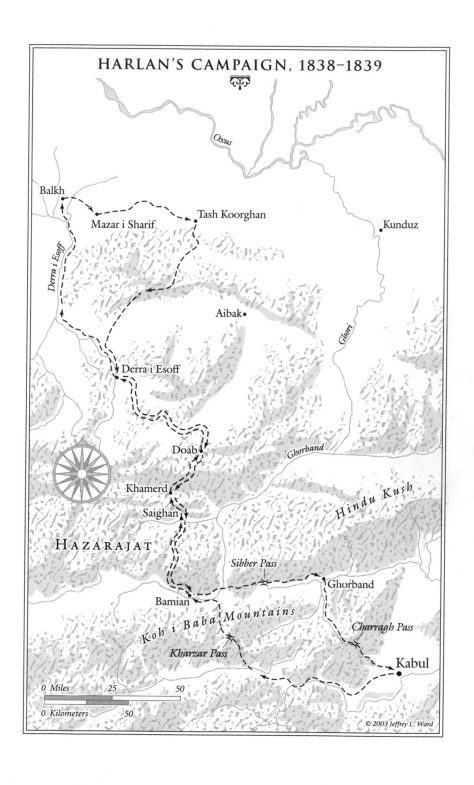

HARLAN'S CAMPAIGN, 1838–1839

Oxus

Balkh

Mazar i Sharif

Tash Koorghan

Kunduz

Derra i Esoff

Ghori

Aibak•

Derra i Esoff

Doab

Ghorband

Khamerd

Saighan

Hindu Kush

HAZARAJAT

Sibber Pass

Ghorband

Bamian

Koh i Baba Mountains

Charragh Pass

Kharzar Pass

Kabul

0 Miles   25   50

0 Kilometers   50

© 2003 Jeffrey L. Ward

PREFACE

In the winter of 1839, a conqueror, enthroned on a large bull elephant, raised his standard in the wild mountains of the Hindu Kush. His soldiers cheered, fired matchlock rifles into the air, and beat swords against their shields made of hide. Two thousand native horsemen shouted their loyalty, each in his own tongue: Afghan Pathans, Persian Qizilbash, Hindus, Uzbeks, Tajiks, and Hazaras of the highlands, descendants of the Mongol horde. Six cannons roared to salute the flag, their echoes ricocheting across the snowy pinnacles.

The commander reviewed his troops with satisfaction. Not yet forty, the face above the long black beard was already as rugged as the landscape around it. Beneath a flowing fox fur cloak he wore robes of maroon and green satin, a girdle of silver and lace, and a great silver buckle in the shape of a soldier's breastplate. His cat-skin cap was circled with gold.

Like Alexander of Macedon, who had led his army on the same mountain path twenty-one centuries earlier, the leader was called great by his followers, and his titles, past, present, and future, were many: Prince of Ghor, Paramount Chief of the Hazarajat, Lord of Kurram, governor of Jasrota and Gujrat, personal surgeon to Maharaja Ranjit Singh of the Five Rivers, the Highly Stationed One equipped with Ardour and Might, Chief of the mighty Khans, Paragon of the Magnificent Grandees, Holy Sahib Zader, Companion of the Imperial Stirrup, Nearest Friend of Shah Shoojah al-Moolk, King of Afghanistan, Chief Sirdar and Commandant of the invincible armies of Dost Mohammed Khan, mighty Amir of Kabul, Pearl of the Ages and Commander of the

Faithful. He was also known as Hallan Sahib Bahadur, victor of the battle of Jamrud, slayer of infidel Sikhs, scourge of Uzbek slavers, and was even said to have magical power. Some claimed that he was an expert alchemist who had forged a priceless talisman to make the dumb speak and conjured gold from base metal, a teller of stories in every tongue, and master in the art of intrigue. In his own language, the prince was known by other names: doctor, soldier, spy, botanist, naturalist, and poet; but also mercenary, even mountebank.

His Highness never traveled without his books, and when the guard had been posted for the night and the mastiffs howled to ward off the wolf packs in the ravines, he retired to his tent and wrote, tumbling torrents of words in a language none but he could read. In his journal he recorded: "I unfurled my country's banner to the breeze, under a salute of twenty-six guns, and the star-spangled banner gracefully waved amidst the icy peaks, seemingly sacred to the solitude of an undisturbed eternity."

For His Highness Hallan Sahib had another name and another title: Josiah Harlan, Quaker, of Chester County, Pennsylvania.

THE MAN
WHO WOULD BE
KING

PROLOGUE

In 1989, as an aspiring foreign correspondent, I was sent to Afghanistan to cover the final stages of the decade-long war between the Soviet army and the CIA-backed Mujahideen guerrillas. Afghanistan was then the crucible of the Cold War. Just as the Russians and the British had tussled for preeminence there in the nineteenth century in the undeclared war Rudyard Kipling called "the Great Game," so the United States and the U.S.S.R. fought for supremacy in the Afghan mountains at the end of the twentieth. The Soviets were losing and would soon withdraw, leaving behind fifty thousand dead soldiers and a million dead Afghans.

Having made arrangements to join one of the seven Mujahideen groups, I headed to Peshawar on Pakistan's North-West Frontier, forty miles from the Afghan border. Once a part of Afghanistan itself and the summer capital of Afghan kings, Peshawar was the principal staging post in Pakistan for the anti-Soviet insurgency. The bazaar was thronged with tough-looking Pushtuns, the Afghan warrior tribe the British knew as Pathans, many with machine guns slung casually over their shoulders. An enterprising stall holder offered to sell me a captured Soviet tank. I settled instead for the standard Mujahideen outfit, obligatory for any "resistance tour": Pathan pancake hat and dun-colored saggy pajamas, or *shalwar kamiz*, over which I wore the regulation foreign correspondent's sleeveless photographer's jacket with many unnecessary pockets. I had already grown something that might pass for a beard.

At dawn the next day a trio of armed Mujahideen knocked at the door of my hotel room and led me to a waiting jeep. For the next twelve hours we drove up the Khyber Pass, and then onto rocky tracks that wound deep into the mountains, until we finally arrived at the camp of the Mujahideen commander Gulbuddin Hekmatyar. I was too callow to know it at the time, but black-bearded Hekmatyar was the most fundamentalist of the Mujahideen leaders, a man as ruthless as he was ambitious, whose brutal shelling of Kabul in the civil war that followed killed thousands of civilians and devastated the city. The entrance to his camp was marked by a lone sentry and a large, dead vulture, impaled on a post, the first victim I had seen of the Afghan war. Over the ensuing weeks I was swept away by my own Afghan adventure. The Mujahideen fighters looked after me as one might a vulnerable and rather dim younger brother, and I filed breathless dispatches for my newspaper, with rather too much emphasis on the first person. I thought myself very dashing indeed.

Returning to Peshawar after my first stint "inside," I went to the American Club, the social hub of the Western crowd. The place was often frequented by journalists, young ones like myself, but also scarred veterans in their anecdotage, along with arms dealers, aid workers, and monosyllabic Americans who were probably spies or mercenaries. Almost everyone had stories of night skirmishes and narrow escapes, the self-inflating chaff of the war zone. We were all living out our romantic fantasies in a land that invited and nourished them.

During the day we lounged around the pool and relaxed by swimming, planning, and Kipling. The works of Rudyard Kipling were required reading, for Britain's bard of imperialism captured the wildness and wonder of the North-West Frontier like no other writer, before or since. It was in Peshawar, fresh from my first foray into Afghanistan, that I first read "The Man Who Would Be King," Kipling's timeless short story that John Huston later adapted into a film starring Sean Connery and Michael Caine. Written in 1888, when Kipling was just twenty-three and working as a journalist for the Allahabad *Pioneer*, "The Man Who Would Be King" tells the tale of a bearded adventurer, Daniel Dravot, who penetrates the remotest mountains of Afghanistan in the middle years of Victoria's reign, disguised as a Muslim holy man. Following the trail of Alexander the Great deep into the Hindu Kush, he trains a tribal army and is crowned king by the local tribesmen. Adopting the symbols of Freemasonry, he proclaims his own fake religion and is exalted as a living god until, like all who aspire to deity, he crashes to earth. It was thrilling stuff, a story of freelance imperialism in which a white man becomes a powerful potentate in a distant land, but also a cautionary tale of colonial hubris, ending in disaster. The narrator is a newspaperman, who hears the story from the adventurer's dying partner. "The Man Who Would Be King" made a profound and lasting impression on me.

Over the next few years, I made several more reporting trips to Afghanistan and twice visited Kabul, but after the Soviets retreated, the West swiftly lost interest. The defeat of the Soviet army by the Afghan Mujahideen contributed to the collapse of Communism, but as Afghanistan fractured into civil war, the country was left to slide toward fundamentalism, eventually producing Islam's most mutant form, the extremist, terrorist Taliban. Long before the rule of the mullahs, the news story had moved on—and so had I, to New York, then Paris, and finally to Washington. I returned to Britain just a few days before September 11, 2001.

In the wake of that atrocity, as America declared war on terrorism and the Taliban, I found myself writing about Afghanistan again, trawling through the histories to piece together a narrative of that broken land for my newspaper. While American "daisy cutter" bombs were blasting al-Qaida fighters out of the caves of Tora Bora and special forces were hunting through the same Afghan hills I had known a decade earlier, I was combing the stacks of the British Library. There was one name that caught my attention, deep in the footnotes of books about nineteenth-century Afghanistan: Josiah Harlan, the first American ever to enter that country. A Pennsylvania-born Quaker and Freemason, Harlan had slipped into Kabul disguised "as a dervish" in 1824, long before the British got there. The American adventurer was said to have trained an army for the amir of Kabul, crossed the Hindu Kush, and proclaimed himself a prince in the mountains. His story sounded impossibly romantic, deeply implausible, and strangely familiar. I was not the first to notice the similarity between this life and Kipling's short story. The U.S. State Department précis on Afghanistan notes that "Josiah Harlan, an adventurer from Pennsylvania who was an adviser in Afghan politics in the 1830s, reputedly inspired Rudyard Kipling's story 'The Man Who Would be King.'" Harlan's reputation would certainly have been known in Allahabad when Kipling was working there:

the novelist adapted the American Freemason and former soldier into an English Freemason and former soldier, but the parallels between the real Josiah Harlan and the fictional Daniel Dravot, Kipling's self-made king of Kafiristan, are too close to be coincidental.

There were tantalizingly few details about the life of the American, and the principal contemporary sources, almost all British, were conspicuously hostile. The first official British history of the First Afghan War (1839–42) dismissed him as "clever and unscrupulous . . . an American adventurer, now a doctor and now a general, who was ready to take any kind of service with any one disposed to pay him." Harlan published only one book in his lifetime, a polemical anti-British tract. In 1939, more than sixty years after his death, a researcher pulled together some fragments of his unpublished work, but concluded that the bulk of Harlan's writings—journals, letters, and an entire manuscript recording his adventures—had all been destroyed in a house fire in 1929.

Harlan, it seemed, was doomed to remain a fleeting and enigmatic presence in history, a figure in fiction, but not in fact. As American soldiers poured into Afghanistan at the beginning of the twenty-first century, seeking to bring order to the chaos, this unwritten half-life seemed uncannily contemporary. Harlan had taken the pioneer spirit to a completely different frontier. Here was a Wild West figure in the far wilder East, who had achieved a peculiarly American feat by voyaging over the sea to terra incognita and making himself a king. And yet, in his own country he was entirely unknown.

I extended my search to the Punjab, where Harlan had lived in the 1820s, to his birthplace in Pennsylvania, to San Francisco, where he died, and back to Kabul. Gradually Harlan's life began to take shape: in the official records of Maharaja Ranjit Singh of Lahore, in the memoirs and diaries of contemporary travelers and soldiers, and in the intelligence archives of imperial India. In a tiny museum in Chester County, Pennsylvania, I finally discovered Harlan's lost voice: in an old box, buried and forgotten among the files, was a tattered manuscript handwritten in curling copperplate, most of Harlan's missing autobiography, unnoticed and unread since his death, along with letters, poems, and drawings.

In 1842, Harlan boasted to a newspaper reporter that he had once been the prince of Ghor or Ghoree, a realm high in the Hindu Kush, under a secret treaty with its ruler. "He transferred his principality to me in feudal service, binding himself and his tribe to pay tribute for ever," Harlan was quoted as saying. "The absolute and complete possession of his government was legally conveyed according to official form, by a treaty which I have still preserved." This contract was assumed to be lost. Some claimed it had never existed. But there, yellow with age at the bottom of the box, was a document, written in Persian and stamped with an intricately beautiful oval seal: a treaty, 170 years old, forged between an Afghan prince and the man who would be king.

1

A COMPANY WALLAH

Josiah Harlan's hunt for a crown began with a letter. A grubby, much-handled, unhappy letter, it followed the young American merchant seaman from Philadelphia to Canton, China, and finally to India. The year was 1822, and the letter was written by one of Harlan's brothers back in Chester County, Pennsylvania. He had entrusted it to another seaman bound for the East in the hope that the bad news might reach Josiah before he set sail for home. After many months, the dog-eared document caught up with Harlan in Calcutta, the teeming capital of British power in India. He read it, burned it, swore that he would never return to America, and set off alone on an eighteen-year odyssey into the heart of Central Asia.

That was the way Harlan remembered it. A Byronic act of impulse prompted by a broken promise and an injured heart; but in truth his journey had started many years earlier. It began in the avid imagination of a schoolboy, in the dockside stories of the seamen, in a newly born American empire of limitless promise and adventure. It began in the mind of a youth who was born a humble Quaker but imagined himself an ancient king.

Joshua and Sarah Harlan, Josiah Harlan's parents, were prosperous, pious people of quiet pacifism and deep faith. A merchant broker, Joshua had made sufficient money in the great port of Philadelphia to buy a small farm in Newlin Township, Chester County, where he had raised a large family. There had been Harlans in the county since 1687, when one Michael Harlan, from Durham, England, had emigrated, like so many Quakers, to the New World. Devout members of the Religious Society of Friends, Joshua and Sarah were plain of dress and speech, rejected the trappings of worship, never swore an oath or drank a drop of alcohol, and passionately opposed war. They were, therefore, somewhat unlikely candidates to produce a son who would become an Oriental potentate with his own army and a taste for exotic costumes.

Josiah Harlan arrived with little fanfare on June 12, 1799, the latest addition to a brood that already included Ann, James, Charles, Sarah, Mary, Joshua, William, and Richard. Edward was born four years later. We know little of Josiah's earliest years, save that they were noisy, joyful, and scholarly, for the Quaker educational system was excellent. Josiah read widely and voraciously: Shakespeare and Burke, Pliny and Plato, histories and romances, poetry and politics, treatises on natural history, physics and chemistry.

Harlan was just thirteen when his mother died, worn out by childbirth, leaving Joshua to care for ten children. Sarah bequeathed an estate of two thousand dollars to her three daughters, but left nothing to her seven sons, who were expected to make their own fortunes—which they did in ways that show Josiah was not the only Harlan anxious to explore the world beyond Chester County. Charles departed for South America as soon as he was old enough to leave home and was never seen again; James went to sea and died aboard an English man-of-war at the age of twenty-seven; and Richard wandered the East before becoming a celebrated anatomist. (Richard's hobby was studying human crania, and he finally amassed 275 of them, the largest collection in America.) While the sons of the family were off collecting crowns of gold and bone and dying in exotic locations, the daughters remained at home: all three of Josiah's sisters would die unmarried in Chester County.

Motherless, Josiah Harlan plunged deeper into a world of imagination and learning. At the age of fifteen, one contemporary recorded, he "amused himself with reading medical books and the history of Plutarch, as also the inspired Prophets." A natural linguist, he read Latin and Greek, and spoke French fluently. Josiah could put his mind and hand to anything, whether or not the results were worth it: his poetry was poor and his watercolors were worse. Botany became a passion, and his writings overflow with observations on plants and flowers, wild and cultivated. His prose style, particularly at moments of emotion or elation, tended toward the flowery.

Above all, he steeped himself in Greek and Roman history. Many years later, an educated traveler who came across Harlan in the wilds of the Punjab found him immersed in classical literature, "in the which study I found him wonderfully well versed." Harlan's obsession with Alexander the Great dates from his earliest boyhood. He could recite long passages from Plutarch's *The Age of Alexander*, and he carried a copy of *The History of Alexander* by Quintus Curtius Rufus throughout his travels. Alexander's conquests in Persia, Afghanistan, and India were an inspiration to the young man growing up among the placid green fields of Pennsylvania, and he idealized the Macedonian conqueror: "In seven years Alexander performed feats that have consecrated his memory amongst the benefactors of mankind, and impressed the stamp of civilization on the face of the known world," he wrote. Harlan would follow Alexander from Pennsylvania to the uncharted corners of Afghanistan, and back again.

A young American in a young America, Josiah Harlan was impatient, ambitious, and utterly convinced of his own abilities. Some considered him arrogant; others thought him charming. No one ever found him boring. By the age of eighteen, he was over six feet tall, a striking, muscular, raw-boned and handsome young man with a long face, high forehead, and somewhat unsettling dark hazel eyes. He might have been the embodiment of a growing nation in young adulthood, as described by Henry Adams: "Stripped for the hardest work, every muscle firm and elastic, every ounce of brain ready for use, and not a trace of superfluous flesh on his nervous and supple body, the American stood in the world a new order of man."

Harlan grew up in the America of Thomas Jefferson, a place of infinite space and possibility. Explorers like Meriwether Lewis and William Clark had started to open up the western two-thirds of North America, but vast areas of the globe remained undiscovered and unmapped: the interior of Africa, Australia, Antarctica, and, somewhere beyond the borders of India, the mysteries of Central Asia. The very breadth of the American continent inspired faith in the potential of a world to be discovered. Walt Whitman would rejoice in the scale of the American horizon:

> My ties and ballasts leave me, my elbows rest in sea-gaps,
> I skirt sierras, my palms cover continents,
> I am afoot with my vision.

Intrepid Americans were moving west by the thousand: young Harlan, however, shed the ballast of his childhood, and headed east.

Josiah's wanderlust and his growing interest in medicine can be traced to the influence of his brother Richard. Three years older than Josiah, Richard had entered the medical department of the University of Pennsylvania, and then "made a voyage to Calcutta as a surgeon of an East India ship" in 1816. After a year at sea, Richard had returned to complete his medical degree, bringing back tales of his voyage and of the sights and sounds of India. In the spring of 1820, Joshua Harlan arranged a job for Josiah as "supercargo," the officer in charge of sales, on a merchant ship bound for Calcutta and Canton.

Before setting sail for the East, Harlan joined the secret fraternal order of Freemasons, which traces its origins to the stonemasons who built Solomon's Temple. Quite when or why the young American came to take the oath is unclear, but there was much in Freemasonry to attract a man of Harlan's temperament: the emphasis on history, on masculine self-sufficiency, and on the exploration of ethical and philosophical issues. America's Masonic lodges tended to draw freethinkers and rationalists, men of politics and action: one-third of the signatories to the Declaration of Independence, including George Washington and Benjamin Franklin, had been Masons. Joined by high ideals and a shared fealty to the lodge, Freemasons were expected to demonstrate the utmost tolerance while following a moral system clothed in ritual with allegorical symbols adopted from Christianity, the crusaders of the Middle Ages, and Islam. Like Rudyard Kipling, who would also join the organization as a young man, Harlan "appreciated Freemasonry for its sense of brotherhood and its egalitarian attitude to diverse faiths and classes."

Harlan seldom discussed his religious beliefs, but his Quaker upbringing molded him for life. Founded in England in the seventeenth century, the Quaker movement had taken deep root in America, with a credo that set its adherents apart from other Christians. Quakers—a name originally intended as an insult because they "tremble at the word of God"—worshipped without paid priests or dogma, believing that God, or the inner light, was in everyone. All of human life was sacred. "Therefore we cannot learn war anymore," declared the Quaker testimony. "The Spirit of Christ which leads us into all truth will never move us to fight and war against any man with outward weapons, neither for the Kingdom of Christ nor for the kingdoms of this world." Harlan was brought up in a spirit of religious egalitarianism: men and women were granted equal authority in meetings, Quakers declined to doff

their hats to those of higher status, and as early as 1774 the Society of
Friends prohibited Quakers from owning slaves. Quaker mysticism was
directed toward social and political improvement rather than dry theological speculation. In the course of his life Harlan would move away
from some Quaker tenets, most notably the prohibition on war, but the
religion remained central to his character and beliefs, revealing itself in
a hardy independence of thought, belief in sexual equality, deep-rooted
opposition to slavery, and a marked disinclination to bow and scrape
to those who considered themselves his superiors.

Harlan's journey to the East would last thirteen months, taking him
to China, India, and then, with a full cargo of Eastern merchandise,
back to Philadelphia. Enchanted by his first adventure on the high seas,
Harlan was preparing to set sail again, in the summer of 1821, when he
accidentally fell in love.

He never mentioned the name of his first love. He refers to her
obliquely in his writings, but was too much of a gentleman ever to di-
vulge her identity. Yet he left a clue and carried the memory of her for
the rest of his life. Among the handful of documents he left behind,
sandwiched between a miniature watercolor and a recipe for Albany
cakes, is a sixteen-line floral love poem in Harlan's handwriting, entitled
"Acrostick in explanation of the lines addressed to Miss Eliza S. on presenting a bouquet."

> Each quickening pulse in Coreopsis speaks
> Lo at first sight my love for thee was mov'd
> Iris love's messenger salutes those cheeks—
> Zephyrs! sweetly breathe where Alfers lov'd
> Althea says with passion I'm consumed
> Be wreathed the moss rose bud and locust leaves
> Emblem of love confess'd beyond the tomb—
> Thy Captive made, Peach blossoms fernéd leaves
> Heliotropes blue violet and Tulip red
> Secure devotion love its declaration—
> Whilst ecstasy from fragrant Jess'mine's bred—
> Ambrosia means love's acceptation
> In Verbena, Daisy red, Cowslip and Mignonette
> Must sense and beauty, grace, divinity set.
>
> From Marigold—that's cruelty!—abstain
> And Rose, fair lady, for it means disdain!

This style of love poetry is now, mercifully, long out of fashion, but Harlan's horticultural verse was the product of some expert pruning: reading the first letter of each line reveals the name *Elizabeth Swaim*.

The Swaims were a large, well-to-do Philadelphia clan of Dutch origin. Early in 1822, Josiah Harlan and Elizabeth Swaim were engaged, although no formal announcement was made. Harlan again set sail for Canton, telling his fiancée that they would be married when he returned home the following spring.

Eliza Swaim seems to have had second thoughts from the moment the ship left port, but for months, as Harlan slowly sailed east, he remained unaware that she had jilted him. Not until Richard's letter caught up with him in Calcutta did he discover that Eliza had not only broken off their engagement, but was now married. A decade later, Harlan was still angrily denouncing the woman who had "played him false." When Joseph Wolff, an itinerant missionary, met him for the first time in 1832, Harlan unburdened himself to the priest: "He fell in love with a young lady who promised to marry him," Wolff noted in his journal. "He sailed again to Calcutta; but hearing that his betrothed lady had married someone else, he determined never again to return to America." Harlan would stick to his vow for nearly two decades. But he would keep the love poem to "Eliza S." until he died, alongside a second floral poem, written after he had received the devastating news, as bitter as the first verse was adoring.

> How sweet that rose, in form how fair
> And how its fragrance scents the air
> With dew o'erspread as early as early morn
> I grasped it, but I grasped a thorn.
>
> How strange thought I so fair a flower,
> Fit ornament for Lady's bower,
> Emblem of love in beauty's form,
> Should in its breast conceal a thorn.

Harlan embraced his own loneliness. Henceforth, the word *solitude* appears often in his writings. He had reached out and grasped a thorn; he would never clasp love in the same way again. The broken engagement was a moment of defining pain for Josiah, but Elizabeth Swaim had also set him free. Cutting himself off from home and family, determined never to return, he now plunged off in search of a different sort of romance, seeking adventure, excitement, and fortune, caring nothing for his own safety or comfort.

Emotionally cast adrift in Calcutta, Harlan learned that the British were preparing to go to war against Burma and needed medical officers for the campaign. The jungles of Burma seemed an adequate distance from Pennsylvania and so, following his brother's example, Harlan signed up as a surgeon with the East India Company. That he did so in order to escape the mortifying memory of Eliza Swaim is apparent from a reference in his unpublished manuscript. "Gazing through a long window of twenty years," he wondered what would have happened "if, in place of entering the service for the Burma War in the year 1824, I had then relinquished the truant disposition of erratic motives and taken a congenial position in the midst of my native community and quietly fallen into the systematic routine of ordinary life—if I had sailed for Philadelphia instead of Rangoon or had I listened to the dictates of prudence, which accorded with the calculations of modest and unambitious views, and not a personal incident that occurred during my absence from home." This "personal incident" would lead Harlan into a life worthy of fiction, which, in time, it would become. From now on, he began to fashion his self-plotted saga, acutely aware of his role as the protagonist, narrator, and author of his own story. "It is from amongst such incidents and in such a life that novelists have sought for subject matter," he wrote. "In those regions, which are to me the land of realities, have the lovers of romance delighted to wander and repose and dream of fictions less strange than realizations of the undaunted and energetic enterprise of reckless youth."

Calcutta, where Harlan now abandoned ship, was the seat of British rule in India, the capital city of the Honourable East India Company. The "Grandest Society of Merchants in the Universe," "the Company," as it was universally known, was an extraordinary outgrowth of British history, an alliance of government and private commerce on an imperial scale, and the precursor of the British Raj. Chartered under Elizabeth I, by the early nineteenth century the Company could wage war, mint currency, raise armies, build roads, make or break princes, and exercise virtual sovereignty over India. Twenty years before Harlan's arrival, the

Company's governor general had become a government appointment, serving the shareholders while simultaneously acting in Britain's national interests. The Company was thus part commercial and part political, ruling an immense area through alliances with semi-independent local monarchs and controlling half the world's trade. This was "the strangest of all governments, designed for the strangest of all empires," in Lord Macaulay's words. Only in the aftermath of the Indian mutiny in 1858 would the British crown take formal control of the subcontinent.

Service with the East India Company promised adventure and advancement, and potential wealth. More immediately, for Harlan, it offered distance from Eliza Swaim, and a paid job as a military surgeon. That he had never actually studied medicine was not, at least in his own mind, an impediment. Years later, he would claim that he "had in his early life studied surgery," but what medical knowledge he possessed appears to have been entirely self-taught. A medical textbook was a part of every educated traveler's baggage, and before his first voyage to Canton, Harlan had "taken a few of his brother's medical books with him and then decided to use their contents in treating persons other than himself." The rough life aboard a merchant vessel had presented opportunities to observe and treat a variety of ailments and injuries. In July 1824, with no qualifications whatever, relying on an alloy of brass neck and steely self-confidence, Harlan "presented himself for examination at the medical board, and was appointed surgeon at the Calcutta general hospital." Calcutta was one of the most unhealthy places on earth, and with war looming in Burma, surgeons, however novice, were in hot demand.

For decades the expansionist Burmese had been steadily advancing along the eastern frontier of the Company's dominion, conquering first Assam and then Shahpuri Island near Chittagong, a Company possession. Fearing an attack on Bengal itself, the British now responded in force with a seaborne army of some eleven thousand men. On May 11, 1824, using a steamship in war for the first time, British forces invaded and captured Rangoon, but with Burmese resistance hardening, Calcutta ordered up fresh troops. Harlan had been on the payroll for just a few months when, to his intense satisfaction, he was ordered to the battlefield; if he had any qualms about violating the Quaker rules on pacifism, they were suppressed. "He was transferred to the Artillery of

Dum-Dum, and proceeded with that detachment to Rangoon" by boat. It was a most uncomfortable voyage, lasting more than a fortnight. Harlan was deeply impressed by the resilience of the native troops. "The Hindu *valet de chambre* who accompanied me consumed nothing but parched grain, a leguminous seed resembling the pea, during the fifteen days he was on board the vessel." Arriving in Rangoon in January 1825, Harlan was appointed "officiating assistant surgeon and attached to Colonel George Pollock's Bengal Artillery."

The British defeated a sixty thousand strong force outside Rangoon, forcing the enemy into the jungle, but the army was suffering numerous casualties, mostly through disease, and the Burmese showed no sign of surrendering. In February, a young English adventurer named James Brooke was ambushed by guerrillas at Rangpur and severely wounded by a sword thrust through both his lungs. Brooke would recover and go on to become Rajah Brooke, founder of the dynasty of white rajahs that ruled Sarawak in Borneo from 1842 until 1946, the best-known example of self-made imperial royalty. It is tempting to imagine that the future prince of Ghor tended the wounds of the future rajah of Sarawak, but sadly there is no evidence of a meeting between Harlan and Brooke, two men who would be kings.

That spring, the artillery pushed north and Harlan was present at the capture of Prome, the capital of lower Burma, after some ferocious hand-to-hand fighting. The Treaty of Yandaboo, in February 1826, brought the First Anglo-Burmese war to a close. After battling through two rainy seasons, the Company had successfully defended and extended its frontier, but at the cost of fifteen thousand troops killed, and thousands more injured or debilitated by tropical disease. One of the casualties was Harlan himself, who was put on the invalid list and shipped back to Calcutta, suffering from an unspecified illness.

Once he had recuperated, Harlan was posted to the British garrison at Karnal, north of Delhi, and it was there that he discovered a soul mate who would become his "most faithful and disinterested friend." Looking back, Harlan wrote that this companion "rendered invaluable services with the spontaneous freedom of unsophisticated friendship, enhancing his favours by unconsciousness of their importance. He accompanied me with unabated zeal throughout the dangers and trials of those eventful years." His name was Dash, a mixture of red setter and

Scottish terrier, a dog whose fierce and independent temperament matched Harlan's exactly. "Dash never maintained friendly relations with his own kind. Neither could he be brought to tolerate as a companion any dog that was not perfectly submissive and yielding to the dogged obstinacy and supremacy of an imperious and ambitious temper," wrote Harlan. The description fit both man and dog. "Dash had always been carefully indulged in every caprice and accustomed to the services of a valet. He was never beaten and his spirit, naturally ardent and generous, maintained the determined bearing which characterises a noble nature untrammelled by the servility arising from harsh discipline. Dash could comprehend the will of his master when conveyed by a word or a glance."

Harlan passed the time in Karnal training his puppy, cataloguing the local flora, treating the soldiers suffering from dysentery, and reading whatever he could lay his hands on. In 1815, literary London had been briefly enthralled by the publication of *An Account of the Kingdom of Caubul, and its dependencies in Persia, Tartary, and India, comprising a View of the Afghaun Nation and history of the Dooraunee Monarchy*, a colorful two-volume description of the exotic, unknown land inhabited by the Afghan tribes. The author was the splendidly named Mountstuart Elphinstone, an East India Company official who in 1808 had led the first ever diplomatic mission to Afghanistan, accompanied by an entire regiment of cavalry, two hundred infantry, six hundred camels, and a dozen elephants. The Englishman described a wondrous journey among ferocious tribesmen and wild animals, through a landscape of savage beauty. Elphinstone had been received at Peshawar with great pomp and ceremony by Shah Shujah al-Moolk, the Afghan monarch then in the sixth precarious year of his reign. Ushered into the royal presence, the Englishman had found the Afghan king seated on a huge golden throne. "We thought at first he had on an armour of jewels, but, on close inspection, we found this to be a mistake, and his real dress to consist of a green tunic, with large flowers in gold, and precious stones, over which were a breast-plate of diamonds, shaped like two flattened fleur-de-lis, an ornament of the same kind on each thigh, large emerald bracelets and many other jewels in different places." On Shujah's arm shone an immense diamond, the fabled Koh-i-Noor, or Mountain of Light.

Elphinstone's orders were to secure Afghan support against a potential Franco-Persian alliance, and his visit became an elaborate exchange of diplomatic pleasantries. The English officers were presented with dresses of honor, the Oriental mode of conferring esteem. In return Elphinstone showered the Afghan court with gifts, to the ire of the Company's bean-counters who rebuked Elphinstone for "a principle of diffusion unnecessarily profuse." In spite of the rather unseemly way Shujah gloated over his haul (he was particularly taken with Elphinstone's own silk stockings), the Englishman had described the king and his sumptuous court in the most admiring terms: "How much he had of the manners of a gentleman, [and] how well he preserved his dignity." The British mission never penetrated past the Khyber Pass and into the Afghan heartland for, as Shujah explained, his realm was deeply unsettled, with the looming possibility of full-scale rebellion. Indeed, within a few months of Elphinstone's departure, Shujah would be deposed.

Although Elphinstone had never actually seen Kabul, his *Account* was heady stuff. Harlan absorbed every thrilling word of it: the jewels, the wild Afghan tribesmen, the sumptuous Oriental display and the "princely address" of the handsome king wearing his crown, "about nine inches high, not ornamented with jewels as European crowns are, but to appearance entirely formed of those precious materials." The book's vivid depiction of the Afghan character might have described Harlan himself: "Their vices are revenge, envy, avarice and obstinacy; on the other hand they are fond of liberty, faithful to their friends, kind to their dependents, hospitable, brave, hardy, laborious and prudent."

Reading by candlelight in Karnal cantonment, entranced by what he called this "well arranged and minutely true account of Avghanistaun," Harlan dreamed of new adventures. He was growing impatient with service in the East India Company, and increasingly unwilling to follow the orders of pimply young Englishmen. One of the many contradictions in Harlan's personality was his insistence on strict military discipline among his subordinates, while being congenitally incapable of taking orders from those ranking above him. The freeborn American was also decidedly free with his opinions, and the young surgeon's outspokenness, often verging on insubordination, did not endear him to his superiors: "Harlan does not appear to have obtained a very good name during his connection with the Company's army, which he soon quitted," wrote a contemporary. One later account claimed that he was on leave when the order was issued for the dismissal of all temporary surgeons, but Harlan insisted that the decision to leave the service was his alone. Elphinstone painted a thrilling picture of princely Afghan warlords battling for supremacy in a medieval world where a warrior could win a kingdom by force of arms. "A sharp sword and a bold heart supplant the laws of hereditary descent," wrote Harlan. "Audacious ambition gains by the sabre's sweep and soul-propelling spur, a kingdom and [a] name amongst the crowned sub deities of the diademed earth." The Company, by contrast, kept subordinate princes on the tightest rein and in British-controlled India the native monarchs were little more than impotent figureheads, he reflected, feeble and supine. "Under English domination we have his stiff encumbered gait, in place of the reckless impetuosity of the predatory hero. The cane of the martinet displaces the warrior's spear."

Spurred by "the undaunted and energetic enterprise of reckless youth," Harlan was already imagining how his own bold heart and sharp sword might be used to supplant the laws of hereditary descent, and in the summer of 1826 he ended his allegiance to the British Empire. Harlan had witnessed British imperialism in action, but his own imperial impulse was of a peculiarly American sort. Thomas Jefferson himself had spoken of "an empire for liberty" and imagined the ideals of the American Revolution stretching from ocean to ocean, and beyond; the America of Harlan's youth had expanded at an astonishing rate. He had been just four years old when Jefferson doubled the nation's size by purchasing from France the Louisiana Territory west of the Mississippi, and throughout his childhood the white population had been steadily pushing westward, while scientific-military expeditions such as those of Lewis and Clark set out to determine the contours of this vast new land. The ending of the War of 1812 had cleared the way for further settlement of the Mississippi Valley, while under the Convention of 1818 Britain and the United States agreed to occupy jointly the vast territory of Oregon. A treaty with Spain the following year established America's southern border. The Indians of those territories, not to mention any French and Spanish subjects who also lived there, found themselves part of the new republican American empire. Harlan's worldview reflected this urgent, embracing outward impetus, what one historian has called "the heady optimism of that season of U.S. empire at surge tide." New lands and peoples were there to be discovered, scientifically explored, introduced to the benefits of civilization by force, exploited as a matter of course, and brought into the great American experiment. That the inhabitants did not wish to be absorbed into a greater America and preferred to govern themselves, was immaterial.

Harlan deeply admired Jefferson and retained a lifelong faith in republican values, but at the same time he considered himself a "high Tory in principles," and an admirer of "kingly dignity." America had won its independence from Great Britain just sixteen years before Harlan's birth. He never expressed nostalgia for British rule and came to loathe the more oppressive aspects of British imperialism, yet he firmly believed that sovereign power should be invested in a single, benign ruler, whether power came through democracy (as with Washington and Jefferson) or through conquest. In this sense, Harlan's imperialism resembled the original *imperium*, the authority exercised by the rulers of Rome over the city-state and its dominions. In Harlan's mind, no figure in history represented this combination of civilized expansionism with kingly dignity more spectacularly than Alexander the Great. "His power was extended by the sword and maintained by the arts of civilization. A blessing to succeeding generations by the introduction of the refinements of life, the arts and sciences, in the midst of communities exhausted by luxury or still rude in the practices of barbarism . . . Vast designs for the benefit of mankind were conceived in the divine mind of their immortal founder, the universal philanthropist no less than universal conqueror." Conquest, benevolence, philanthropy, and immortality: Harlan saw Alexander's empire, like the expanding American *imperium*, as a moral force bringing enlightenment to the savages, and he would come to regard his own foray into the wilderness in the same way: not simply as a bid for power, but the gift of a new world order to a benighted corner of the earth. It was a language of cultural emancipation that would have loud echoes nearly two centuries later.

Harlan's ideas of empire were still in their infancy when he left the roasting Indian plains and made his way to Simla, the hill station in the north where British officialdom was on retreat from the summer heat. Technically, as a civilian, Harlan was now persona non grata, since "neither British subjects nor foreigners were allowed to domicile in the interior of India without a license," but following an interview with the Governor General Lord Amherst himself, the permit was granted. Harlan chose not to linger in the Himalayan foothills. Instead, armed with his copy of Elphinstone, he headed toward Ludhiana, the Company's last garrison town in northwest India.

Ludhiana marked the westernmost edge of British control, a dusty border post where civilization, as the British saw it, ended, and the wilderness began. Beyond was the mysterious Punjab, and even farther west, across the mighty Indus, lay mythical Afghanistan: a "terra incognita," in Harlan's words. In Simla, Harlan had learned that Maharaja Ranjit Singh, the mighty independent ruler of the Punjab, had already employed a handful of European officers to train his army in modern military techniques, and might be looking for more such recruits. The Sikh king was also famously obsessed with his health. After barely a year as an army medical officer, Harlan considered himself amply qualified to work for the maharaja as either doctor or soldier, or both.

On a late summer's evening in 1826, accompanied by Dash and a handful of servants, Harlan rode into Ludhiana, caked in dust but still resplendent in his full service uniform, complete with cocked hat. Presiding over this outpost of empire was one Captain Claude Martine Wade, the East India Company's political agent and the leader of its tiny colony of Europeans. Wade's tasks were to police the border, maintain relations with the local Indian princes, and report back to Calcutta with whatever intelligence he could glean on the chaotic political situation beyond the frontier. Wade was the shrewdest of Company men, as dry and penetrating as the wind that blew off the western desert, and he observed the arrival of this unlikely young American with a mixture of interest and deep suspicion. Harlan made his way directly to Wade's residence and handed the British agent a document, signed by the governor general himself, giving him permission to cross the Sutlej, the river separating the company's domain from that of Ranjit Singh.

Cordial but reserved, Wade invited Harlan to lodge at the residence while he made preparations for his journey. The offer was readily accepted, and having dispatched a letter to Ranjit Singh by native courier requesting permission to enter the Punjab, Harlan settled down to await a reply in comfort. "I enjoyed the amenities of Captain W.'s hospitality," he wrote, noting that the Englishman "with the characteristic liberality of his country, extended the freedom of his mansion to all." Over dinner, Wade explained that he maintained "respectful and obedient subservience from the numerous princely chieftains subject to his surveillance" by playing one off against another. The English agent handled his delegated authority with ruthless skill, caring little what the local rulers did to their subjects or to each other, so long as British prestige was maintained. As Kipling wrote in "The Man Who Would Be King": "Nobody cares a straw for the internal administration of Native States . . . They are the dark places of the earth, full of unimaginable cruelty."

Harlan was impressed by Wade's cynical attitude to power, declaring him an "expert diplomatist" and "a master of finesse who wielded an expedient and peculiar policy with success." Wade, in turn, was intrigued by his energetic and enigmatic guest, who seemed to have money and who spoke in the most educated fashion about the local flora and ancient history. Many strange types blew through Ludhiana, including the occasional European adventurer, but a mercenary-botanist-classicist was a new species altogether.

Puzzled, Wade reported to Calcutta: "Dr. Harlan's principal object in wishing to visit the Punjab was in the first place to enter Ranjit Singh's service and ultimately to pursue some investigation regarding the natural history of that country." He warned Harlan that the Company could not approve of the first part of his plan, since "the resort of foreigners to native courts is viewed with marked disapprobation or admitted only under a rigid surveillance." Yet he did not try to dissuade him from heading west. In the unlikely event he survived, a man like Harlan might prove very useful in Lahore, Ranjit's capital.

Harlan's future was clear, at least in his own mind: he would join the maharaja's entourage and rise to fame and fortune, while compiling a full inventory of the plants and flowers of the exotic Punjab. Like Lewis and Clark, with American bravado and learning, he would open up a new world. The only hitch was that Ranjit Singh would not let him in. The maharaja had signed a treaty with the British back in 1809, but as the greatest independent ruler left in India, he was pathologically (and understandably) suspicious of *feringhees*, as white foreigners were called. The British were happy to let the Sikh potentate get on with building his own empire beyond the Sutlej. "Very little communication had heretofore existed betwixt the two governments," wrote Harlan. "The interior of the Punjab was only seen through a mysterious veil, and a dark gloom hung over and shrouded the court of Lahore." Which was exactly the way Ranjit Singh wanted it.

As he cooled his heels waiting for a passport that never arrived, Harlan began to form an altogether more extravagant plan that would take him far beyond the Punjab in the service of a different king, who also happened to be his neighbor in Ludhiana.

2

THE QUAKER KING-MAKER

Fifteen years earlier, Shah Shujah al-Moolk had welcomed Mountstuart Elphinstone to Peshawar, seated on his gilded throne. Now the Afghan king was an exile and Ludhiana's resident celebrity. "His Majesty might be seen almost daily in the vicinity of Loodianah in regal state," wrote Harlan. "The throng of a long procession proclaimed the approach of the King, shouting to the listless winds and unpeopled highways, as though he was in the midst of obedient subjects, with the deep and sonorous intonation of self-important command, where there was none to obey!"

The spectacle of this displaced potentate, parading the streets and demanding subservience from invisible subjects, struck the American as both touching and admirable, the display of a monarch who "never compromised his royal dignity," and never disguised his belief that his protectors and hosts were infidels and inferiors. As Harlan observed with sly pleasure, even Captain Wade, the senior British official in Ludhiana, was treated as a minion. "The forms and etiquette of his court were no less strictly preserved by the banished king than they were in the brightest days of his greatness! Under no circumstances, however urgent, would His Majesty deviate from the etiquette of the Kabul court [and] his high and mighty hauteur could not be reconciled to an interview on equal terms with another human being."

Ousted by his own brother, Shujah had fled to the Punjab in 1809, taking with him his harem and most of the Afghan royal jewelry, including the Koh-i-Noor diamond, the priceless gem originally taken from the Moguls by the conquering Nadir Shah of Persia and today a centerpiece of Britain's crown jewels. Throwing himself on the mercy and hospitality of Ranjit Singh, Shujah found himself a prisoner of the maharaja, who had fixed his acquisitive eye on the diamond. "Sentinels were placed over our dwelling," the exiled king wrote, as Ranjit gradually increased the pressure by depriving the king of the "necessaries of life," which, in the case of Shujah and his luxury-loving entourage, were very considerable. Finally, the reluctant Shah Shujah had agreed to hand over the Koh-i-Noor in exchange for five thousand rupees and a promise that Ranjit would help the Afghan monarch regain his crown. Instead of fulfilling his side of the bargain, however, Ranjit set about trying to extract Shujah's remaining treasure. Recalling his pleasant encounter with Elphinstone, Shujah resolved to make a dash for British India.

Smuggling out some four hundred wives, children, concubines, eunuchs, retainers, and others from under Ranjit's nose was no easy task, but by bribing his guards, most of the harem was successfully moved to Ludhiana. Ranjit reinforced the "bodyguard" surrounding his royal guest. "Seven ranges of guards were put upon our person, and armed men with torches lighted our bed," Shujah recorded. Finally the deposed king escaped by secretly tunneling through several walls and then wriggling to freedom through the main sewer of Lahore, arriving smelly but safe on the other side of the city wall. After a series of adventures that took him through the passes of Lesser Tibet, Shujah had eventually reached Ludhiana. "Our cares and fatigues were now forgotten and, giving thanks to Almighty God who, having freed us from the hands of our enemies and led us through the snows and over the trackless mountains, had now safely conducted us to the lands of our friends, we passed a night for the first time with comfort and without dread." Reunited with his wives and provided with a substantial home and pension by the British, Shah Shujah al-Moolk had settled into comfortable exile and immediately began plotting his return to Kabul.

The ousted king was a strange, violent, but curiously romantic figure. Astute, charming, vain, and greedy, Shujah could be unexpectedly merciful on occasion, but by inclination he was brutal, capable of the most capricious and revolting cruelty. He had ruled for just six years, but he was convinced he would one day return in triumph to Kabul. Visitors were always impressed by his poise, despite the indignities he had suffered, yet there was something mournful about him. It was said that he had been born under an unlucky star. Shujah talked a good military game but tended to balk on the battlefield at the critical moment, and despite removing the crown jewels en masse, he complained that he was almost broke. "He wanted vigour," wrote one observer. "He wanted activity; he wanted judgement; and, above all, he wanted money."

Shujah repeatedly lobbied the British for help to win back his throne, but without success. "His Majesty strenuously kept alive the impression amongst his followers and contemporaries that he was about to attempt the invasion of Kabul, sustaining their hopes and anticipations," wrote Harlan, but the British insisted on maintaining strict neutrality, at least for the time being. The exiled king argued that he did not need a British army, but British cash. "Money would readily achieve all that was necessary," he had told Captain Wade. "By the loaning of a few hundred thousand rupees, he would disseminate confusion amongst his enemies. From the diffusion of gold, he proposed to create and nourish a powerful party that should sustain his own policy and by these means, which have ever been the successful mode of controlling the Avghaun tribes, to mount again that unsteady throne."

Harlan discussed Shah Shujah's predicament with Wade, and found the British agent doubtful that the Afghan king would ever regain his crown. "We conversed together upon the future probabilities of Shah Shujah's restoration," wrote Harlan. "The subject of Russian influence was even then frequently discussed in the social circles of British India [and] the opinion of Captain W. sunk deep into my mind when he calmly observed, 'There is no possible chance for Shujah's restoration unless an ostensible demonstration of Russian diplomacy should transpire at Kabul!'" This was Harlan's initiation into the Great Game, the shadowy struggle between Britain and czarist Russia for influence and control in Central Asia. Harlan would later recall the "singular prescience" of Wade's observation. Fear of Russian encroachment would eventually persuade the British to restore Shah Shujah to his throne, with horrible consequences.

The exiled king's poignant daily cavalcade, the tales of his fabled wealth, and the wild, primitive land beckoning from beyond the Indus captured Harlan's imagination entirely. He wrote: "I had determined to indulge the spirit of adventure that then absorbed my views of life." If

the British would not return this great man to his throne, then Harlan
himself might take a hand in the restoration, perhaps winning power
and fame in the process. Europeans had forged their own kingdoms
here before, starting with Alexander the Great. The most recent self-
made king had been George Thomas, an Irish mercenary who at the
end of the previous century, with a combination of guile, good fortune,
and extreme violence, had carved out a realm east of Delhi and assumed
the title of raja of Haryana. Here were kingdoms for the making, requiring only enterprise, energy, and luck. "Every man in his own estimation is a king," wrote Harlan, "enfeafed in the royal prerogative of
divine right, with whom self is the God predominant."

Any audience with the exiled king would have to be arranged without alerting the British. Through an intermediary, Harlan sent a secret
message to Shujah's vizier, or chief counselor, outlining "a general proposition affecting the royal prospects of restoration." The king snapped at
the bait, and Harlan was summoned to a private interview in the garden
of the royal residence.

At twilight on the evening of the appointment, a figure clad in
Afghan turban and *shalwar kamiz* slipped quietly out of Wade's house
and headed in the direction of Shujah's walled compound. "I assumed
the disguise of a Cabulee," wrote Harlan, "although then unaccustomed to the role and unaddicted to the air of a native." The British had
posted a pair of guards at the gates to Shujah's residence, ostensibly for
his protection but also to spy on visitors, including the numerous local
"dancers" attending the king and his court. The soldiers had been bribed
in advance, and at a prearranged signal, they melted away. "The Indian
sentries were well trained in the amatory service of His Majesty," Harlan
remarked wryly. "The magic influence of 'open sesame' could not have
been more effective upon bolts and bars. The portals were thrown open
and I approached the small wicket gate that afforded secret egress in
a retired part of the wall."

On the other side of the gate stood Mullah Shakur, Shujah's vizier,
personal cleric, and sometime military commander. "The priest was a
short fat person," wrote Harlan. "The rotundity of his figure was ade-
quately finished by the huge turban characteristic of his class, encased
in voluminous outline by a profusion of long thick hair which fell upon
his shoulders in heavy sable silvered curls." There was a reason for the

vizier's elaborate hairdo, for Shakur's most obvious distinguishing feature was the absence of his ears. These had been cut off on the orders of
the king many years earlier, as a punishment for cowardice on the battlefield, and Mullah Shakur had grow his "flowing locks to conceal the
mutilation."

Harlan would soon discover that Shujah had an unpleasant pen-
chant for punishing his courtiers by removing ears, tongues, noses, and
even the testicles of those who had offended him, and despite his own
disfigurement, Mullah Shakur was an enthusiast for this brutal form of
chastisement. The result was an "earless assemblage of mutes and eunuchs in the ex-king's service," including one Khwajah Mika, the chief
eunuch, an African Muslim in charge of the royal harem. The king had
ordered Khwajah to be de-eared during a royal picnic, after the tent
protecting the king's wives from sight had blown down in a gust of
wind. "The executioner was of a tender conscience," Harlan wrote, and
"merely deprived Khwajah Mika of the lower part of the organ." Having already lost his manhood, the African appears to have been philosophical about the additional loss of his lobes, and unlike the mullah,
he "shaved the head and fearlessly displayed the mark of royal favour."

Earless and suspicious, Mullah Shakur eyed the American visitor
carefully. "Having assured himself by carefully scanning my features
that I was the person he expected, for my dress entirely concealed the
Christian outline, he replied to my salutation in a subdued tone and
turning about without another word, led the way into the interior."

It was the golden moment just before sunset in India known as the
time of "breathing the air," *hawa khana*, when the cooling earth exhales.
What Harlan saw in the dusk light took his breath away: a vast and perfectly tended Oriental garden in full bloom: "His Majesty's tastes and
exiled fancies sought gratification in the floral beauties of his native soil,
and the royal mind had ameliorated its misfortunes in the construction
of a garden on the model of oriental horticulture practised in the City of
Cabul. This enclosure, which was 300 yards square, included the fruit
trees, the parterres of flowers, the terraced walks and the well irrigated
soil incident to the place of his nativity, and thus the king caused to be
transplanted a part, at least, of the dominion which he had lost." Like
many expatriates, Shujah had surrounded himself with memories of
home, but he had done so in spectacular style, reproducing the gardens

of Kabul's Bala Hisar fortress, from the harem buildings to the flower beds to the pavilions, where Shujah would play chess "in the long twilight of a summer evening and contemplate with enraptured gaze those frail remembrances of his vanished greatness."

Motioning Harlan to follow, the vizier set off down a cool avenue of lime and orange trees. Many years later, Harlan recalled the delightful sensation of leaving the parched evening heat of India to enter the refreshing shade of a make-believe pleasure garden with blooming flowers, ornamental ponds, and fountains sending "cool spray, scintillating in the moonlight."

As they neared a large terrace, walled with richly embroidered cloth, the mullah touched Harlan's shoulder, indicating he should remain where he was, and slipped inside the enclosure. Household servants and slaves flitted between the trees, observing the newcomer in Afghan robes, who tried to calm his nerves by identifying the different varieties of fruit trees. Silently Mullah Shakur reappeared at Harlan's elbow, drew him toward the terrace, and lifted the flap. Inside, on an elevated banquette, sat Shujah al-Moolk, the exiled king of Afghanistan, enthroned in a vast armchair.

Harlan snapped off his best military salute. Shujah responded with a courteous nod, a few words of welcome, and a sprinkling of light compliments. Harlan had been boning up on Afghan courtly etiquette, and he struggled through the fantastically ornate language required when addressing royalty. "I replied in bad Hindoostani and worse Persian," he conceded, "for I was then but a neophyte in the acquisition of Oriental languages."

Harlan studied the exiled monarch, a stout and imposing figure in middle age with a thick, black beard dyed the color of midnight. His clothing was expensively simple, a plain white tunic of the finest muslin over dark silk pantaloons, but his headgear was priceless: a large velvet cap, scalloped at the edges, adorned in the center by a large diamond. Harlan was immediately struck by "the grace and dignity of His Highness's demeanour." Every movement, every word, was freighted with unquestionable authority. The heavy-lidded eyes radiated power and menace, but also sadness: "Years of disappointment had created in the countenance of the ex-King an appearance of melancholy and resignation." His commands were barked in monosyllables, and his servants, including Mullah Shakur, were plainly terrified, loitering in submissive attitudes, like dogs waiting to be kicked.

Courtesies over, in a mixture of languages, Harlan made the king an offer. He would travel secretly to Kabul and link up with Shah Shujah's allies to organize a rebellion. Meanwhile, Shujah should begin raising troops for an assault against Dost Mohammed Khan, the prince who had usurped his crown. Once Harlan had managed to "ascertain and or-ganise his partisans" in Kabul, he proposed to return to Ludhiana and lead the king's troops in a full-scale invasion. If all went according to plan, this would coincide with a mass uprising in Kabul, and Shah Shu-jah al-Moolk, with Harlan at his side, would return in triumph to the throne of his ancestors. Harlan even offered to provide some of the troops. "I engaged to join the royal standard with a thousand retainers," he wrote, "holding myself responsible for the command of the army and the performance of all duties connected with the military details of an expedition into the kingdom of Kabul."

If the king was surprised by this audacious proposition, he was far too clever to show it. His popularity in his homeland, he told Harlan, "far preponderated above the present leader in Kabul," and he listed the powerful supporters who would flock to the royal banner. Indeed, he would have launched such an invasion already, but the British had de-clined to promise him a safe haven in case of failure and he was con-cerned for the safety of the harem, which he could hardly take into battle. If the British government would look after his family, and prom-ise that he could return to Ludhiana if the invasion failed, then "he would instantly commence preparations for an expedition." Shujah had not yet recruited a single soldier to his cause, and already he was talking about defeat. This, as Harlan would soon learn, was typical of a man whose arrogance was matched only by his timidity.

And what, Shujah asked pointedly, did Harlan expect for himself, should this daring plan come to fruition? Harlan's response was aston-ishing. In return for restoring Shujah's crown, Harlan wanted power. Here was a young American adventurer, without references, Persian, or experience of military command, offering to retrieve Shujah's crown by recruiting a fifth column in Kabul and leading an invasion of Afghanistan; in exchange, he expected to govern the kingdom, in fact if not in name. If their joint enterprise was successful, Shujah would reign once more in

Kabul, but Harlan proposed to rule as his vizier, an Afghan potentate in his own right.

Even Shah Shujah's poise appears to have been temporarily undermined by this presumptuous suggestion, and instead of replying directly, the exiled king "broke into a poetical effusion in praise of Kabul," its music, its gardens, its trees laden with luscious fruit. "Kabul is called the Crown of the Air," he declared. "I pray for the possession of those pleasures which my native country alone can afford."

Then he fell into a reverie, and for several minutes nothing was said, as the American in the Afghan robes and the exiled king with the diamond on his head sat side by side in a garden on the edge of India. "The dead silence was undisturbed except by the trickling of water into the basin of the fountain," wrote Harlan. Finally Shah Shujah fixed his visitor with a beady stare, and spoke: "Should success attend your measures, I am ready to relinquish all political power into your hands and claim only for myself the summer and winter residences, with the fruits of Kabul and Kandahar. Heaven grant we may enjoy together the revival of those sweetly varied and luxurious hours which daily haunt my imagination and in unison participate in possession of an inheritance which fate at this moment denies to me."

The interview was over. Harlan bowed and backed out of the royal presence. His encounter with this pining potentate had moved him. "My feelings warmed into deep sympathy for the exiled monarch and I took leave of His Majesty with the confirmed determination of devoting myself to his service." Harlan was elated by the pure romance of his imagined mission, and the opportunity to invent himself as the liberator of a country oppressed by tyranny. Of course he only had Shujah's word for this, but that was enough. "I saw him [as] an exiled and legitimate monarch, the victim of treasonable practices, popular in the regard of his subjects, opposed by a combination of feudal chiefs against the hereditary ruler [they] had driven into banishment."

Harlan would eventually come to see the Old Pretender in a very different light. On closer acquaintance, Shujah "disclosed few virtues and unveiled the dark vices of an evil nature," wrote Harlan, who would eventually conclude: "In his true colours he was unparalleled in infamous debauchery." The mutilated mullah who now led Harlan away was warning enough that he was dealing with a most unpredictable man. Ears or no, Mullah Shakur had been listening intently throughout the interview, and as they walked back down the avenue of fruit trees the scarred old warrior-holy man instructed Harlan to begin military preparations and await word from Shujah on the timing of his quest. At the wicket gate Harlan bade farewell to the vizier and the two men parted, as Harlan wrote, "he to revalue with His Majesty the probabilities of success which my proposals encouraged, and I to devise additional and appropriate measures for the prosecution of castle building."

To build castles Harlan needed troops. With impressive hubris, he now ordered a Ludhiana tailor to sew him an American flag, ran it up a makeshift flagpole on the edge of town, and, without any authority to do so, began recruiting an army under the Stars and Stripes. There were plenty of native mercenaries knocking about the border station looking for work and adventure, and word soon spread that the *feringhee* was prepared to pay good money for fighting men. Local Europeans were convinced that this peculiar American planned to carve out his own kingdom, as George Thomas had done a generation earlier, an impression he did nothing to dispel. William McGregor, an English doctor posted in Ludhiana, was in no doubt that Harlan was bent on personal conquest: "He started from Ludhiana with the intention of subduing all the countries across the Sutlej," wrote McGregor, noting that Harlan had "hoisted the American flag at Loodiahana, and collected a rabble." Joseph Wolff, the wandering missionary, recorded that Harlan had left British India intending "to make himself king of Afghanistan."

Harlan had little choice but to confide in Claude Wade, and told the Englishman that Shujah had invested him with "the powers of a secret agent, in which he was commissioned and stimulated to revolutionize Avghanistan in favor of the 'true King.'" Indeed, the British agent, with his wide network of informers, was probably aware of what Harlan was up to from the moment he entered Shujah's pleasure garden. Wade, maintaining British neutrality, did not overtly encourage the scheme, while indicating that any information Harlan cared to relay about the Afghan situation would be received with great interest; unofficially, of course. The British official wrote to Calcutta: "Dr. Harlan proposed to communicate his progress to me as opportunities might offer, and should his communications contain anything of interest to the government, I shall consider it my duty to report."

Wade had another, more specific task for the young American: to determine what had happened to the last white man to reach Kabul, an explorer who had set off into the wilderness four years earlier and had never come back. The fate of William Moorcroft, horse doctor, pioneer, and British spy, was and remains one of the great mysteries of the period.

An English veterinary surgeon employed by the Company as superintendent of its stud, Moorcroft had become convinced that in the wilds of Tartary, beyond the fabled Hindu Kush, were horses of such strength and beauty that they would transform the bloodstock of the Company's cavalry. He would make three extraordinary journeys in search of the legendary Turcoman steeds, the last of which would take him to the Punjab, Ladakh, Kashmir, Afghanistan, and Bokhara—and kill him.

Moorcroft's mission went beyond horse hunting, for by penetrating the unmapped regions, he hoped to open up the markets of Central Asia and establish a British commercial presence there before the Russians did so. In 1820, he had set off on what would be an epic five-year, two-thousand-mile journey, accompanied by a three-hundred-strong entourage including another Englishman named George Trebeck, George Guthrie, an Anglo-Indian doctor, and a Gurkha guard. Moorcroft had crossed the Sutlej on inflated animal skins, traversed Sikh territory, and entered the Himalayan heights via the Rohtang pass, becoming one of the first Europeans ever to reach the remote Buddhist kingdom of Ladakh. Along the way his veterinary expertise was used to treat a variety of human ailments, most notably cataracts. From Ladakh, Moorcroft continued through Kashmir and after journeying across the Punjab plains, he had crossed the Indus into the land of the Pathans. In December 1823, Moorcroft arrived in Peshawar. Ignoring written instructions to return, Moorcroft had pressed on, through the Khyber Pass and on to Kabul. The Afghan city was going through one of its regular periods of bloody upheaval, and Moorcroft did not care to linger. Following the old trade route, he crossed the mountains, becoming the first Englishman to reach the steppes of Transoxiana since the sixteenth century.

There, however, Moorcroft fell into the clutches of Murad Beg, the khan of Kunduz, an Uzbek warlord with an unsavory reputation for slave dealing. Murad Beg did not disguise his opinion (a valid one) that Moorcroft was a spy, deserving immediate and painful death. Trebeck described Murad as "a wretch who murdered his uncle and brother, prostituted to a robber his sister and daughter, and sells into slavery women he has kept for a considerable time in his seraglio." Only after paying Murad twenty-three thousand rupees was Moorcroft able to continue his journey to Bokhara; the canny khan was perfectly well aware that he would have to come back the same way.

Moorcroft finally reached Bokhara in February 1825, at the same moment Harlan was fighting his way through the Burmese jungle. There he obtained sixty horses and turned back toward British India. At Balkh, successor to the fabled Bactrian city where Alexander the Great had built an outpost of Greek civilization, Moorcroft was once more forced to negotiate for his life with the repulsive Murad Beg. In the last entry in his journal, the fifty-nine-year-old explorer wrote of the "confusion, oppression and tyranny" inflicted by the Uzbek chief. And there, abruptly, his diary ended. Just how Moorcroft perished is unknown. Officially he died of fever, a victim of Balkh's famously pestilential climate, but there were persistent rumors that he had been poisoned, or, less credibly, that he had survived and lived out his remaining days in secret retirement in Ladakh. All of Moorcroft's possessions, including his books, notes, and journals, were promptly stolen. The rest of the party remained trapped, for Murad Beg's horsemen had sealed off every escape route. Guthrie succumbed to fever, followed by Trebeck. "After burying his two European fellow-travellers he sunk, at an early age, after four months suffering in a distant country, without a friend, without assistance, and without consolation." Extravagant rumors circulated in India that the entire party had been murdered at the instigation of Russian agents, determined to prevent British commercial penetration of Central Asia. Without even the frail protection of their British leaders, the surviving members of Moorcroft's party were captured by the Uzbeks and sold into slavery.

Moorcroft's death was announced in *The Asiatic Journal* in 1826. The East India Company was happy to forget about its ill-fated and rebellious envoy, but John Palmer, a friend of the horse vet and one of the most powerful merchants in Calcutta, was determined to get to the truth. From official documents, it appears that Palmer got wind of Harlan's plans through Claude Wade and commissioned him to find out exactly what had happened to Moorcroft and, if possible, to retrieve his plundered property. One historian has estimated that "the sum to get back Moorcroft's effects would have been between 50,000 and 60,000 rupees," a very substantial addition to Harlan's war chest.

The recruits to Harlan's expanding but motley army came in a variety of shapes and sizes: Muslims and Hindus, a number of Afghans, and even Akalis, Sikh fundamentalists who were among the most ferocious and least reliable of mercenaries, as apt to kill their commanders as the enemy. Dr. McGregor was unimpressed with the quality of these troops, and Harlan himself was well aware that he was employing a band of cutthroats loyal to his money and little else. At some expense, therefore, he recruited a troop of twenty-four sepoys, native Indian soldiers who had served in the Bengal army on whom he could place some reliance. Another former Company soldier, "a faithful hindoo of the Brahmin caste" by the name of Drigpal, was appointed *jemadar*, or native officer, in command of the sepoys. Harlan's army would be fashioned on the British model. By the autumn of 1827, he had assembled about a hundred fighting men and calculated that more could be impressed en route. What he had not yet found, and stood most in need of, was a trusty lieutenant, a native who knew the country, could maintain discipline, and possessed at least a modicum of military experience. "The time for my departure drew near," he wrote. "My camp was pitched in the vicinity of the cantonments, my followers were all entertained [employed] and the American flag before my tent door signalised the independence of the occupant."

Harlan sent a message to Mullah Shakur, informing him that the army was ready to depart, and the American was summoned back to the king's garden for "another private conference, wherein plans of action and routes of travel were devised and decided upon, and such letters received as the ex-king supposed might prove serviceable to me in the course of my movements." The vizier also handed over a large sum of money in gold and silver coin, to defray Harlan's expenses and, most important, for bribery once he reached Kabul. When this was added to the funds he had saved from his Company service and the fee for finding Moorcroft's property, Harlan believed he now had sufficient funds to start a revolution.

The date of departure was set for November 7, 1827, and as he prepared to strike camp, Harlan felt a twinge of melancholy. He was ambivalent about the British rulers of India, but he had made some close friends among them, admiring the sheer resilience and energy of men like Claude Wade. "A shadow of regret passed like a fleeting tide when I looked back upon the happy period of my residence in British India, and concern for the future began to crowd upon me in the anticipation of dangers unknown." Those dangers could hardly have been more extreme, for Harlan had set himself a series of monumental tasks: to unseat the incumbent ruler of a country famed for its savagery, at the behest of an exile with the habit of lopping off bits of his employees; to spy for the British (who would disown him completely if he was caught); and to find the property of a man who had probably been murdered by slave-dealing Uzbeks. In his spare time he intended to write a treatise on natural history.

William Moorcroft had failed to return from the wilderness, despite taking with him the Company's official seal, a unit of heavily armed Gurkhas, two light artillery pieces, and two European companions. Harlan was now proposing to follow him, with only a motley group of mercenaries and a bag of gold, on a quest inviting disaster and an exceptionally messy death. As an American, he had no imperial power to fall back on in case of difficulty. As one observer put it: "Harlan enjoyed only the protection of his abilities. They were more than sufficient." While his future appeared uncertain and in all probability brief, Harlan viewed the coming trials with almost morbid pleasure: "I had just stepped within the threshold of active life, was alone in the world, far removed from friends and home, inadequately acquainted with the language of the country I was about to visit, and surrounded by selfish and deceitful and irresponsible people in the persons of my domestics and guards—consisting of Avghauns, Hindus and Musslemen of India— with all the world in boundless prospect and none with whom to advise or consult. Completely alone, companionless and solitary, I plunged into the indistinct expanse of futurity, the unknown and mysterious, which like the obscurity of fate is invoked in the deep darkness of time."

Harlan had never been more alone, or farther from Pennsylvania, or more contented.

Two days before the army was due to depart, a most peculiar figure appeared outside Harlan's tent and demanded an audience. Tubby, barrel-chested, and at least fifty years old, the man was missing his left arm from above the elbow, one eye was partly clouded over, the other glittered with intelligence, and both were crossed in an alarming manner. The fellow's military bearing was complemented by a pair of enormous mustaches and a mighty curved saber, or *talwar*, dangling from his belt. The man offered a crisp salute with his remaining hand and launched into a bizarre prepared speech: "I have served His Majesty by flood and field, through good and evil fortune, to the footstool of the throne and the threshold of the jail. For 20 years have I been a slave to the king's service in which I lost my left hand and had nothing but the stump of my arm to exhibit in lieu of honours and wealth and dignities, which the worthless have borne off in triumph, and I am still the unrewarded, the faithful, the brave, the famous Khan Gool Khan, Rossiladar, commander of a thousand men, fierce as lions, yesterday in the service of Shah Shujah, may he live forever."

The "blear-eyed Avghaun thrust out his right arm and crossed the stump of his left upon it near the shoulder," as he declared: "This much of his salt have I eaten." Finally, he got to the point: "Here I am in the Saheb's service. May his house flourish, for the future I am his purchased slave and respect even the dog that licks his feet!"

Once Gul Khan had regained his breath, he explained that he was a Rohillah, a member of the Afghan tribe whose horse-trading enterprises in India had led to their establishing a number of small states along the north India trading routes. The Rohillahs were expert horsemen, and famous as mercenaries. Gul Khan announced that he had served for years as a soldier under the banner of Shah Shujah. "He had wandered many years with His Majesty, [and] had followed the fortunes of the ex-king when he fled from the prison to which Ranjeet Singh, after securing the Koh-i-Noor, had ignobly confined Shujah who was then his guest, had traversed the great Himalaya mountains when the royal fugitive, to escape the danger of recapture, fled from Lahore through the Kashmir and penetrating into Tibet, threaded the intricate mazes of those deep glens and unknown valleys, crossing pass after pass over mountainous routes covered with heavy forest or eternal snows and scarcely inhabited by man, the redoubt of the hyena, the leopard and the wolf, braving the rapacious brutes in his flight from the still more ferocious creature man!"

Since Shujah's arrival in Ludhiana, Gul Khan and his fellow Rohillahs had worked as mercenaries (or, more accurately, as freelance bandits) serving various princes in the surrounding areas. Declaring himself "thoroughly acquainted with the country I had before me," the Great Gul Khan now offered his services as *risaldar*, or native commander. Harlan had come across Rohillah mercenaries before and noted sardonically: "The versatility of service for which the Rohillahs are remarkable gives them pre-eminent claims as traitors to their salt, and renders them useful but dangerous and unfaithful agents."

Mulling this singular job application, Harlan enquired how Gul Khan had lost his arm. At this, the talkative Rohillah became taciturn, muttering vaguely that his injury had been "sustained upon the field of battle." The amputation remained a mystery. "He seemed averse to talk much and openly on the subject however voluble upon other matters," wrote Harlan. "I afterwards heard there were several versions concerning Gool Khan's handless limb, and some ascribed that misfortune to the royal displeasure."

"I had then no suspicion of his honour or honesty," wrote Harlan, who would later come to doubt both. There was no time to substantiate Gul Khan's claims, and for all his odd appearance, he seemed the ideal lieutenant, his band of Rohillahs a useful addition to the ranks. "This was an enterprise requiring the perseverance of a fearless and determined spirit and a knowledge of the country," wrote Harlan. "Of the two first requirements I could boast the possession. The other essential was attained by enlisting individuals who knew the language, the people and the routes. These were present through Gool Khan, and he was forthwith installed as leader of the mercenary band who followed my fortunes."

On November 17, 1827, the inhabitants of Ludhiana turned out to witness Harlan's departure: with Old Glory fluttering overhead, an American in a cocked hat rode out of town on a thoroughbred horse, accompanied by a mongrel dog, a ragtag army of mercenaries, and a one-armed bandit. The British agent also watched him go, and informed Calcutta that Harlan was planning to cross the Indus, proceed to Peshawar, and thence to Kabul itself. Claude Wade evidently did not expect to see him again.

Harlan had originally intended to take the most direct route into Afghanistan, by crossing the Sutlej, passing through the Punjab, and

entering the country via Peshawar. Ranjit Singh, however, was still refusing to grant safe passage. Harlan put the delay down to inefficiency,
but more likely the Sikh maharaja had gotten wind of Harlan's plans
and did not want a private army marching through his territory. "The
dilatory proceedings of the Punjab court quickly exhausted my patience
and in contempt of the procrastinating ruler, I determined upon taking
the route via Bhawulpore across the Indus below Mooltaun, [to] follow
up the right bank of the celebrated stream and reach Peshawar," thus
avoiding the Punjab itself.

Alexander the Great was much on Harlan's mind, for he would be
entering lands the Macedonian had conquered some twenty-one centuries earlier, although heading in the opposite direction. In 331 B.C.,
having defeated the Achaemenid monarch Darius the Great, Alexander
claimed the Persian Empire and marched eastward into Afghanistan,
founding cities as he went: Alexandria Arachosia near Kandahar,
Alexandria-ad-Caucasum north of Kabul. Then, after a grueling march
over the Hindu Kush, he had penetrated the wild lands beyond the
Oxus, building his most remote city at the northeastern limit of Persian
influence: Alexandria-Eschate, "Alexandria-at-the-end-of-the-world." As
Darius had ruled through satraps, subordinate provincial governors, so
Alexander appointed rulers in his wake to administer the expanding empire. In 327 B.C., he crossed back over the mountains and set his sights
on India, crossing the great Indus river in 326 B.C. and defeating Poros,
the local king, at the battle of Jhelum. He had then marched south,
through the lands Harlan now saw in the desert distance.

As the troop marched alongside the Sutlej—"the Hysudrus of the
Greeks," noted Harlan—its leader observed that the local people had
carved irrigation channels to cultivate patches of land on either side of
the river. "The country was made to smell like the rose," he wrote.
British engineers would eventually build a vast network of canals and
waterworks, creating a new and fertile agrarian region, but in Harlan's
time, patches of thick jungle still bordered the rivers, with scrub and
desert beyond. "Here and there we struck the desert border as we advanced, a flat surface of sand extending to the horizon without vegetation." His excitement mounting, Harlan gazed across the plain towards
"the interior of Asia, the land of caravans, the land of the elephant and
tamarisk, and the dominion of the horse."

Before leaving Ludhiana, Harlan had purchased seven saddle horses for Gul Khan and the other officers, and seven camels to carry supplies, weapons, and baggage. This included tents, a large armchair, folding chairs, tables, several dozen muskets (flintlocks and matchlocks), ammunition, gunpowder, rope, and Harlan's substantial library. For his own use, the American had selected three horses: a sleek Arab, a gray from Tartary, and "a half-English brood mare named Flora." Gentle and swift, Flora had been a gift from "a valued friend," a British army colonel, and she was Harlan's most prized possession.

Behind the camels lumbered a line of carriage cattle, bearing additional food and forage. Since he was heading into country that was sparsely inhabited and probably hostile, Harlan wrote, "supplies of all kinds—water, flour, grain, forage and frequently wood—[must] be transported with the forces." The baggage train moved with infuriating slowness. Nothing is "more certain to hamper the movements of an army than superfluous baggage or impedimenta," wrote Harlan, who had brought only a few personal luxuries, such as tea, coffee, chocolate, and spices. A plentiful supply of tobacco was stashed in Harlan's saddlebags, but in deference to Muslim beliefs, he dispensed with alcohol entirely. "Long experience, general and personal, convinces me that the interdict of Muhammad had been attended with results divinely philanthropic to the myriads of his followers," he wrote. Harlan had been raised in a strictly abstemious Quaker culture, and while he sometimes drank socially or medicinally, he regarded drunkenness with pious disapproval.

In other respects, however, Harlan wore his Quakerism lightly, too lightly for some of his brethren back in Chester County. While Harlan was marching into the unknown, news of his activities had reached home, where the Society of Friends convened a meeting to discuss the case of wandering Brother Harlan. A painful decision was reached: "Josiah Harlan, who has for many years been absent from this country, has violated our testimony against war by serving in the capacity of surgeon in an army. This meeting is of the judgement that the time has arrived when it is proper to testify its disunity with his conduct, and that he no longer retains the right of membership with the Religious Society of Friends." Harlan did not know that he had been disowned by his own church. As a Freemason, he had little time for dogmatic religion,

whether Islamic or Christian, but throughout the ensuing years of warfare and intrigue he continued to consider himself a Quaker.

There was another crucial item of luggage packed away on top of
one of the camels, which no man who would be king, or king-maker,
could do without. This was a large royal mace, described by Harlan as
"an embossed silver stick five feet long tapering from a globular head
two and a half inches in diameter." The mace was an indispensable tool
of courtly etiquette, a visible demonstration of royal clout to be carried
on ceremonial occasions by a functionary described by Harlan as the
Shaughaussy or "mace bearer" whose job, apart from looking appropri-
ately official and dignified, was to act as the conveyer of important messages. The man responsible for this function in Harlan's entourage was
one Amirullah, a cadaverous Afghan with a long beard and opinions on
everything, whose commanding figure and natural pomposity made
him ideal for the task. He would become Harlan's loyal confidant. Harlan regarded Amirullah as his mascot. Impressing local chieftains along
the route was not only good form, but a vital means of self-protection.

Harlan was determined that although his troop might look like a
posse of brigands, they would march like an army. "The movements of
my party were regulated by military discipline," he wrote. The day began at 4 a.m., when the camp was roused by a bugle call, with the march
beginning no more than an hour later. Once the sun was up, the troop
would pause for a breakfast of cold chapatis (flat bread), before resuming the march. At midday, a halt was ordered and the men would dis-
perse to prepare meals in large *dekshies*, or cooking pots, according to
their different religious traditions. After the main meal of the day, the
march recommenced, ending in late afternoon at a campsite selected by
an advance party. For his own accommodation, Harlan had obtained a
"large single poled tent," which was surrounded by "Connaughts or extensive walls of cloth with bamboo stretchers" to create a semiprivate
enclosure. The soldiers gathered for the night under a large tent without walls, while "the house servants and inferior attachés" were housed
in a third, smaller tent.

When the march was passing through inhabited areas Harlan usually led the troop on horseback, noting that "the display of dignity is
important," but at other times he adopted another form of transport
uniquely suited to the terrain. This was the *cudjawa*, or camel litter, the

closest thing available to a first-class traveling compartment: "A covered box," in Harlan's words, "provided with a cupola admitting of an upright sitting posture" and made from scarlet woolen cloth. The *cudjawa* came complete with its own heating system for winter travel, and even bathroom facilities. "The interior being lined with woollen rugs, they prove to the traveller a very comfortable contrivance . . . ample enough to allow one to keep in them a small fire, and also to perform the required necessities." Regrettably, there is no contemporary account of just how this mobile toilet operated.

"The comfortable seclusion of a Cudjawa" was a mode of travel particularly suited to a bookish man, and Harlan observed that with "a few days' experience and a supply of literature, the passenger could readily engross the measure of a long journey, continually and often agreeably varied by ever changing scenes and novel incidents which serve to enliven him in this singularly oriental and primitive mode, to cure the spirits and amuse the mind with strange reflections upon unfamiliar objects." Jolting along at about two miles an hour, Harlan had ample opportunity to reread Elphinstone and what little other literature existed on Afghanistan, and imagine the terra incognita ahead.

3

MY SWORD IS MY PASSPORT

The Afghan empire had once been powerful beyond legend, wealthy beyond words. As Harlan wrote: "During the rule of the antient regime the kings possessed countless treasures and jewels and gold, supplying the expenses of licentiousness and luxury from previously accumulated hereditary wealth. Vast sums were disbursed in the capital cities of Kandahar, Cabul and Peshour." This was the empire forged in the mid-eighteenth century by the Afghan conqueror Ahmad Shah Abdali, founder of the Durrani dynasty, who had extended his rule from Kabul to Peshawar and Lahore, and finally to Delhi, Kashmir, and Sind. He had crossed the Hindu Kush, subduing the Hazara tribes en route, and then vanquished the Uzbeks of Balkh and Kunduz, taking his realm to the border of modern Afghanistan. The death of Ahmad Shah in 1773 started the steady, bloody disintegration of his empire, and by the 1820s it had fragmented, shot through with fantastically complex internecine feuds, like veins through marble.

For as long as anyone could remember, a brutal and complicated civil war had raged in Afghanistan, punctuated by occasional interludes of tranquility. Like the Wars of the Roses, two great families, rival clans within the Durrani elite, battled for supremacy: the Saddozai, of which Shah Shujah was the leading claimant, and the Barakzai, whose paramount chief, Dost Mohammed Khan, now ruled in Kabul. The Saddozai princes fought each other, while resisting the growing power of the Barakzai clan, whose scions fought bitterly for supremacy among themselves.

The period immediately before Harlan set out for Afghanistan had seen some particularly Byzantine plotting and fratricidal violence. In 1783, Zaman Shah, Ahmed Shah's grandson (a Saddozai), ascended the throne with the support of Painda Khan (a Barakzai), who became his vizier. Nervous of Painda Khan's growing power and aware that he was plotting a coup, Zaman Shah first dismissed, then executed him. The Barakzai vizier, however, had left behind no fewer than twenty-three sons, each anxious to avenge him and take power himself. The eldest of these, Fatah Khan, immediately set about provoking a rebellion: Zaman Shah was ousted in favor of his half brother Shah Mahmud, and then blinded by having his eyeballs pierced with a lancet. This was the traditional fate of a deposed Afghan king, for a blind king was as good as dead. Shah Mahmud held on for just three years before he was deposed by another Saddozai, Zaman Shah's brother: Shah Shujah al-Moolk.

Shah Shujah was in Peshawar, opening presents from Mountstuart Elphinstone, when he learned that Shah Mahmud was up in arms once more, with the backing of the troublesome Fatah Khan. After six years as king, Shujah was himself ousted and set off on the wandering path that would eventually lead him to Ludhiana. Shah Mahmud was reinstalled, but not for long. In 1818, repeating history, Shah Mahmud became deeply suspicious of his Barakzai vizier, and Fatah Khan was put to death with an imaginative cruelty spectacular even by the exacting standards of the time. His eyes were removed with a dagger, and the top of his head was peeled off ("an operation similar to the African mode of scalping," observed Shah Shujah in his memoirs) before a slow public dismemberment. The blind vizier was led to a large tent erected for the purpose outside the western city of Herat, surrounded by his mortal enemies, and systematically murdered: ears, nose, hands, and beard were cut off and then his feet, before his throat was finally cut.

The lingering death drove Fatah Khan's many surviving brothers to a peak of vengeful fury (and temporary unity) and after a series of battles, Mahmud, the Saddozai king, was beaten back to Herat. The Barakzai brothers set about dividing up the country among themselves: four brothers held Peshawar; another five ruled over Kandahar while Dost Mohammed Khan, the ablest of them all, established himself as chief of Ghazni and gradually set about extending his rule over Kabul. Having divided up the country as completely as their brother had once been dismembered, the remaining brothers naturally now fell to fighting each other. The Barakzais were a polygamous recipe for friction, sharing a single father but divided by multiple mothers: siblings sharing both mother and father tended to be allies, while half brothers were more often at loggerheads. The bewildering confusion of plot and counterplot, blood feud coagulating on blood feud, brother against brother, king against vizier, had reduced what is now Afghanistan to a Hobbesian war of all against all, riven with feuds between interrelated warlords. One commentator said of Afghan politics: "Sovereignty was an exceedingly uncertain commodity. One moment the Amir of Kabul might be a potent monarch, in the next he might be an object of ridicule, an outcast whose life would be very precarious, if indeed it existed at all."

Elphinstone and others had painted what they knew of Afghanistan's turbulent history in the most lurid colors, and Harlan marveled at the duplicity of the various contenders, the bewildering rise and fall of the claimants. "Prince after prince in confused succession mounted the tottering throne," he wrote. "The prize was literally handed about like a shuttlecock. The king who in the battle may have dispatched a favourite son in the command of his army would probably before night find himself flying from his own troops."

Yet by 1826, a vague pattern of power had emerged from the bloody morass, with the rise of Dost Mohammed Khan as amir of Kabul, the nearest thing to an Afghan monarch. He was owed at least nominal allegiance by his restive brothers, and ruled by means of a volatile combination of dictatorship and oligarchy. As Harlan observed: "In the course of civil war distant provinces threw off their allegiance or were seized by neighbouring powers. The dominion of Cabulistan became contracted and reduced. The government was seized by an usurping dynasty and the royal family banished." Whatever Shah Shujah, lurking in Ludhiana, may have told Harlan about the man currently in power in Kabul, Dost Mohammed Khan was proving a tenacious and increasingly popular ruler. Even today, Afghans use the phrase: "Is Dost Mohammed dead, that there is no justice?" He would not be easy to unseat. Shah Shujah and Dost Mohammed Khan, the old Saddozai pretender and the young Barakzai prince, would represent the opposing political poles of Harlan's life for the next two decades.

The chronic instability of Afghanistan had infected the surrounding regions. Harlan estimated that his 600-mile route to Peshawar led

through at least "four independent principalities, divided into many
subordinate chieftainships, some as fiefs and others as tributaries to the
above mentioned principalities." None of these were remotely predictable
and any, or all, might be hostile. The region was also infested with bandits, and Harlan had to restrain his natural inclination to wander off
alone in search of plants. The most immediate menace, however, came
from Harlan's own troops; he had not been out of Ludhiana more than
a few days before confronting the first threat to his life.

From among his Indian domestics, Harlan had appointed a quartermaster whose task was to travel ahead of the main body of troops to select that night's campground and obtain supplies. Although Harlan
chose the man he believed to be the most honest of his staff, he rapidly
came to suspect that the quartermaster was buying cheap food and retaining a profit. "More than human patience and foresight are necessary
for one to guard against the chicanery, deceit and falsehood of domestics in India," Harlan wrote in exasperation, a familiar complaint among
colonists. Once Harlan had established his guilt, the quartermaster was
promptly demoted. This should have been a routine matter, but the incident swiftly erupted into Harlan's first major crisis when the former
quartermaster appeared at Harlan's tent, "determined upon revenge"
and carrying a loaded and cocked musket. As Harlan emerged, the man
aimed the weapon at his head. Harlan reacted instinctively. "To knock
up the fellow's musket and throw myself upon him and seize him by the
throat was the act of a moment. He fell back and prostrate from the
force with which I projected myself against him. The musket changed
hands and he was now the victim with the weapon at his breast! He had
not a word to utter or a struggle of resistance." By disarming the muti-
neer, Harlan subdued a potentially wider revolt. "Had this fellow's insolence been suffered with immunity, I should have been utterly at the
mercy of my servants," he wrote. The rest of the entourage, expressing
elaborate abhorrence at such behavior, cheerfully offered to kill the
miscreant on the spot to demonstrate their fidelity. Harlan preferred
clemency and merely ordered the man to be manacled and placed under
guard. At the next village, he was handed into the custody of the local
village headman. Harlan remarked: "He was probably released immediately after I left."

The confrontation convinced Harlan that there was only one member of the party he could trust implicitly. "Amongst my followers there

was one of low degree who held an elevated position in my regard and was certainly the most faithful, disinterested and by no means the least useful of the cortege," wrote Harlan. He was referring, of course, to his dog, Dash.

Harlan was anxious to push on quickly, but the baggage animals flatly declined to be hurried. "The old camels especially cannot be made to move about one coss and a half per hour," he complained. A coss was the old unit of Indian measurement, which Harlan calculated at one mile and three quarters. Distance seemed to expand as the column trudged on through a landscape of desert fringed with jungle, and such measurements became almost meaningless, Harlan reflected. "The peasant whom you interrogate as to the distance of the next village will sometimes reply, 'As far as the twice boiling of a pot of milk' [or] 'As far as you can carry a leaf without [it] wilting.'" The population was sparse, but the local tribespeople seemed reasonably well fed, with a diet that included mutton from the fat-tailed sheep, goats' meat, beef, fowl, eggs, and butter. Harlan gorged on "the finest perch and a species of catfish peculiar to the Indus," but noticed that locals seemed to regard fish as an inferior food. Finding grain and forage for the cattle was far more problematic. As a visiting dignitary, he expected to be sustained with free supplies from the local chiefs, in accordance with the ancient traditions of hospitality. If they seemed unwilling to provide such necessities, Harlan believed he would be within his rights, according to local custom, in taking what he needed. The local chiefs had once lived under Afghan rule, but they were now unwilling subjects of the aggressively expanding Sikh empire. Each paid tribute, either directly or through a superior, to Ranjit Singh. Since Harlan was assumed to be a representative of the great British power to the east, and therefore a potential counterweight to Sikh domination, he expected a cautious welcome from the native barony. "All who were opposed to the Lahore paramount—and the tributaries generally were—showed by their alacrity of service and obsequious bearing the candidness with which they desired to recognize in every Christian traveller a representative of an antagonist power." Harlan was only too happy to be mistaken for a British officer, and if the local rulers thought that by providing him with food and forage they were currying favor with the powers in India, that was just fine with him.

Harlan's attitude toward the local inhabitants, in common with most white men in India, was paternalistic, haughty, and often dismissive, and a vein of cultural condescension runs through much of his early writing. Yet his outlook was similar to that of Thomas Jefferson himself, who maintained that the American Indians were noble savages who could be absorbed into the expanding American empire through education and religion. "I believe the Indian then to be in body and mind equal to the whiteman," wrote Jefferson in 1785. In the same way, Harlan regarded the various Indian, Sikh, and Afghan tribesmen he would encounter over the next two decades as potential equals, held back not by any inherent racial inferiority but by physical circumstance and ignorance. He would immerse himself in the local ethnology, history, and languages with all the enthusiasm that Jefferson devoted to his Indian studies. He might scorn the local customs as superstitious and barbaric, yet he observed them with fascination and described them with care. This openness of mind would develop over time, as his early distrust and disdain of native ways turned to understanding and, in many cases, admiration. The colonist would eventually be colonized, not merely comprehending Afghan culture more profoundly than any foreigner before him, but adopting it.

About seventy coss from Ludhiana, after two solid weeks of marching, Harlan's troop entered the district of Mamdot, the dominion of Qutb ud-Din Khan, one of those chiefs who "strenuously desired to rid himself" of the obligation to pay tribute to the Sikh maharaja. The troops were pitching camp, when an envoy appeared from Qutb, accompanied by a troop of horsemen, to welcome the supposed British envoy with an avalanche of compliments. "This was the first instance in which I had been received with the ostentation that marks the oriental display of festive diplomacy," Harlan observed. The envoy explained that although Qutb himself was on a hunting trip, he had sent a message for the noble *feringhee* to be delivered in person by the chief's son. This, Harlan calculated, would be an excellent moment to make an impact on the locals "with the impressive dignity of a formal reception," in the knowledge that the bush telegraph would swiftly pass on news of the arrival of a powerful foreign prince and so ensure a welcoming reception farther ahead. The etiquette for the occasion was planned with care: first the tents were pitched to form a large, covered reception area, the floor spread with the finest burlap carpet. At one end of the enclosure, on an elevated platform, Harlan placed his armchair, where he would receive the prince in seated grandeur. Amirullah, toting the mace, formed a reception committee alongside Gul Khan in the full regalia of a native officer, while the guard of regular sepoys was drawn up before the tent door to greet the chief.

At the appointed hour, Qutb's son swept into the encampment mounted on a "richly caparisoned" horse and surrounded by a small army of retainers, "armed with swords, shields and matchlocks." Gul Khan held the prince's bridle as the young man dismounted, and then ushered him into the tent. Harlan was immediately struck by the "grace and dignity" of the handsome, olive-skinned youth who now bowed before him, clad in a shimmering white robe embroidered with gold, a huge shield in one hand and a long sword tucked into his waistband. Long dark curls tumbled down to his shoulders from beneath a striped silk turban decorated with golden thread, while his slippers were similarly spangled in gold and silver. Even more remarkable than his exquisite outfit, however, was the prince's age; the prince of Mamdot, calculated the astonished Harlan, could not have been more than seven years old.

"His manner and address were no different from a man of mature condition and polite education," Harlan observed. This dignified, heavily armed child approached with a peace offering: "A beautiful green bow of Lahore and a green velvet gold embroidered quiver." After a lavish exchange of compliments, the boy-prince presented a letter, complaining of the iniquities of Sikh rule, which he asked Harlan to forward to the British lords of India. Harlan, of course, had no formal connection with the British, and was anyway heading in the other direction. Tactfully, he advised the young man "that his father should represent his case in person to the Company's resident at Delhi."

The following morning, accompanied by a small contingent from Qutb's tribe to guarantee safe passage through the bandit-infested region, Harlan crossed the frontier into Bahawalpur, the land of the formidable Nawab Bahawal Khan. Founded and named after Bahawal Khan Abbasi I in 1748, the princely state of Bahawalpur had won a large measure of independence during the civil war that dissolved the Afghan empire, but it now faced simultaneous threats from the expansionist Sikhs to the north and the looming British in the east. As Harlan wrote, "the present incumbent stood in an unenviable posture, with the prospect of 'being ground between two stones' as the Persian proverb goes." Claude Wade in Ludhiana had indicated that the territory might "be taken under the protection of the British government," and like so many other native princes, Bahawal Khan was tempted to throw in his lot with the British. But as Wade warned Harlan, the nawab remained exceedingly nervous, and might not take kindly to having a force under an unknown flag marching unannounced through his territory.

Harlan, however, was breezily confident. "The friendly relations existing between that prince and the British government precluded the possibility of hostilities against a Christian," he wrote, noting that Elphinstone had been graciously received by Bahawal Khan's father. If the nawab could be persuaded to believe Harlan was a British official, he was probably safe. Moreover, he wanted to make contact with Bahawal Khan, for it was likely that Shah Shujah would have to cross Bahawalpur with a far larger army in the event of an invasion.

Harlan had penetrated some ten miles into the nawab's territories, when "a body of soldiers armed with spears, matchlocks, swords and shields mounted upon camels and horses suddenly emerged from a cloud of dust, riding down upon our party full speed." Harlan's little army immediately prepared for battle: the sepoys took up positions among the baggage animals, with muskets leveled, while Harlan and the other mounted men rode a few yards ahead, "threatening them by the evolutions of our firearms with a reception at once repulsive and determined." The demonstration had the desired effect. "They rode down upon us in a swarm, but our display made them draw up [and] they spread out upon the plain, apparently intending to surround our party." Harlan ordered Gul Khan to shout out that unless they halted where they were, the men would open fire.

Retreating just beyond rifle range, the riders now stared at the intruders with what seemed, to Harlan, more like curiosity than hostility. They were a most fearsome-looking group. "Their filthy appearance and barbarous visages peering out from beneath long black and greasy locks of matted hair seemed to forbid the conclusion that they could be men entertained in the military service of a chief." This, however, is precisely what they proved to be. A series of shouted exchanges between Gul Khan and the leader of the other troop established that these were scouts of Bahawal Khan's army who had heard of the approach of "an army of *feringhees* accompanied by Shah Shujah" and had come to reconnoiter.

While the local warriors watched from a distance, Harlan ordered the advance, collecting the sepoys around his horse with bayonets fixed. Still looking distinctly unfriendly, the hairy horsemen and camel riders fell in some distance behind. The strange procession had gone less than a mile, however, when a smartly dressed individual, flanked by two horsemen, rode up to Harlan and presented himself as "the attaché of Nadir Shah, commander of the Nawab's forces." With a low bow, the envoy welcomed Harlan in the name of Bahawal Khan, and invited him to pitch camp at a village a little way ahead where "supplies of every kind could readily be procured." In spite of the man's polite manner, Harlan was deeply suspicious. The line moved off once more, with Bahawal Khan's man leading the way, and an hour later they pitched camp outside a small, apparently deserted village. As he had feared, Harlan was now effectively a prisoner. "Our camp was quickly surrounded by numerous irregular infantry of the Rohillah and Beloochee races, soldiers in the service of Nawab Bhawal Khan," he wrote. These had been instructed to prevent the advance of the newcomers until orders arrived from Bahawal Khan himself. Harlan was furious. "I entertained a feeling of infinite contempt as a military force for the miserable guards surrounding us," he wrote. Summoning Gul Khan to his tent, Harlan told his lieutenant that they would march the following day, and if the nawab's troops tried to stop them, they would fight their way out. The Rohillah accepted this order with visible and entirely justified apprehension. The nawab's army might look a fright, but they were numerous, heavily armed, and, if provoked, likely to prove murderous. But Harlan was not to be dissuaded. Not for the last time, he wondered quite how valiant his warlike commander would prove in a fight.

At sunrise the next morning, the bugle sounded, the camels were loaded, and the men were preparing to march when Gul Khan, who had spent the previous hour "in earnest conversation" with the leader of the native troops, approached Harlan, ashen faced, and warned that the nawab's men were "determined to prevent our baggage from leaving without orders from their chief." The surrounding troops began to close in. Harlan's solution to the impasse was simple and dramatic. "I called the captain of Bhawal Khan's men into my presence and immediately placed him under a guard of fixed bayonets, holding him as a hostage with the threat of instant death in case of any turbulent movement on the part of his troops."

Feeling exceedingly pleased with himself, Harlan now marched off with his new hostage, in chains alongside him, the troops in fine regimental order, and a mob of Bahawal Khan's soldiers trailing angrily behind. They had not marched two miles before, as Harlan put it, "the consequences of my headstrong efforts began to show themselves." On the eastern horizon, he saw "a vast cloud of dust rising in the desert." Minutes later, a troop of tribesmen mounted on camels appeared just out of range, and then vanished. They were followed by horsemen, galloping in circles, their cries carrying across the flat land, impossible to count due to "the clouds of dust that obscured their movements." Through the gritty haze, Harlan glimpsed foot soldiers stretched out across the desert, and finally, in the distance, "a train of heavy artillery drawn by oxen slowly lumbered upon carriages lazily creeping over the plain." It was now that Gul Khan belatedly passed on a rather crucial piece of information: the man he had taken hostage was none other than the brother of Nadir Shah, military commander of Bahawalpur, who had now mobilized the full force of Nawab Bahawal Khan's army to get him back.

As Harlan was wondering what to do next, a horseman appeared through the dust and respectfully invited the visitor to pitch camp at the next village where his master, Nadir Shah, "desired the honour of an interview." Harlan reluctantly complied. "We found ourselves in the same situation as we were at sunrise," he remarked. The only difference being that they were now surrounded by an entire army, "encamped a short distance from us, out of view, secluded within the vast jungle of high reed grass which grew in tufts tall enough to hide a mounted spearman [for] many miles in all directions." Any attempt to force their way out would be suicide. Releasing his hostage, Harlan now adopted a different, but equally brazen tactic: he would treat this Nadir Shah with complete contempt. "I refused to see him," wrote Harlan, "replying to his earnest solicitude with the cool and phlegmatic indifference of a superior." Whenever Nadir's *mirza*, or envoy, politely tried to arrange a meeting with Harlan, the American replied, with feigned petulance: "I'm not in the vein." Nadir Shah was a man to be reckoned with in Bahawalpur, and Harlan's lofty manner, despite being surrounded by thousands of hostile warriors, sent the envoy into a paroxysm of toadying. "With reverential respect and servile attitude, he said that his master was a great man, a very great man, no less a person than the dignified commander in chief of Nawab Bhawal Khan's invincible army, the unconquered and exalted chief of chiefs, the cream of his contemporaries and the pillar of empire etc., etc.," wrote Harlan, who resolutely declined to be impressed and sent the *mirza* back with the message that he intended to march the next day. "I gave him to understand I acknowledged no superior and that my sword was my passport."

Apparently bowing to the inevitable, Nadir Shah sent a guide, a senior member of his entourage, to show the strangers the way, but no sooner had the army set off again than it became clear the man was deliberately trying to buy time by leading Harlan on "a devious line, sometimes to the right and at others to the left, like a ship in a headwind." Once again, Harlan's riposte was to place the guide in chains and proceed "in a direct line, being governed by my pocket compass."

Gul Khan made no secret of his belief that by chaining up the locals at every turn Harlan was inviting disaster and contravening all the rules of Oriental diplomacy. "The old blear-eyed Rohillah rolled up his eyes in astonishment, exclaiming: 'May God bring good in the future.'" Nettled by his lieutenant's negativity, Harlan demanded: "Wherefore is Gool Khan afraid of these ragged mendicants?" and then immediately regretted it, for the question prompted a torrent of oratory from the one-armed soldier on the subject of his own bravery and the corresponding villainy of the local people. Exhausted by the tense march and Gul Khan's loquacity, Harlan ordered a halt near a small village. As soon as the tents were pitched, he released the guide and sent him to collect supplies, and retired to rest. "The whole camp excepting a single sentry soon fell into a deep sleep solicited by unusual fatigue," he wrote, but less than an hour later, Harlan awoke to find yet another crisis brewing. Outside his tent stood Gul Khan looking more than usually glum, "with elevated brows and protruding heavy lips, holding the stump of his arm in his hand."

"It'll be later before we get the forage, unless Your Highness is disposed to become responsible for the unoffending blood of our guide," he said gloomily.

While Harlan had been asleep, the luckless guide had requested food at the nearby fortress, where he had promptly been taken prisoner. The commander of the fort, Gul Khan explained, was not only refusing to provide food and forage but threatening to cut off the guide's head if the troops helped themselves. Harlan faced a dilemma. Seizing what he needed by force could lead to the death of an innocent man and that, he reflected, would be "ungenerous and unbecoming a man of high sentiments." A little of Shah Shujah's money would surely bring the commander round. Sure enough, after some bargaining by Gul Khan, the guide was released and supplies provided. Grateful that the unpredictable *feringhee* had seen fit to prevent him being beheaded, the guide was now as helpful as he had previously been obstructive. Instead of pushing on quickly, it was agreed that the force would proceed slowly toward Bahawalpur and await a decision by the nawab.

After three days of slow marching, a messenger from Bahawal Khan was conducted to Harlan's tent. There he ceremoniously handed over a letter, written on the finest paper, embellished with gold leaf and tucked into a bag of gold brocade with a pair of the nawab's oval seals attached, each three inches in diameter. The letter, in Persian, was addressed to: "His Highness the Saheban of exalted dignity." *Saheban* is the plural of the honorific sahib: "a term" as Harlan observed, "applied to the Christians governing India" and often used of an individual to connote respect. The nawab had concluded that Harlan was a British official, albeit a most eccentric one, and his letter "set forth in florid terms the Nawab's regard and was profuse in the profession of friendship." The chief of Bahawalpur looked forward to a meeting when Harlan reached Ahmadpur, his capital south of the Sutlej on the edge of the Cholistan desert, but in the meantime "the country, himself and his possessions were at my service." Finally the nawab's envoy handed over a gift that made Harlan's hungry eyes light up. "A large quantity of the fresh fruits of Kabul were presented, such as delicious grapes packed in boxes upon layers of cotton, apples and pears of Samercand, cantaloupes, dried apricots, raisins and watermelons of the country." Harlan adored fresh fruit, and the crops of Kabul were fabled throughout Central Asia. This was the first time Harlan had tasted them; in time, the fruits of Kabul would become an obsession.

The evidence of the nawab's friendly intentions was a relief to all, not least the guide who had so nearly been decapitated. Harlan sent him on his way with a handful of rupees, "as a reward, and to solace his feelings for the cavalier regard bestowed upon him." After days of wondering whether he and his men would be massacred on the spot, Harlan was thoroughly enjoying his new incarnation as the honored guest of the nawab, who had given orders that the newcomers should be provided with every necessity. Another march of three days brought the party to the town of Bahawalpur, which had been the province's capital before Bahawal Khan had moved his court to Ahmadpur, some thirty miles to the south. This was a substantial town "about four miles in circumference, with gardens of mangoe trees within the walls [and] houses of unburnt bricks." Here Harlan received another gold-leafed missive from the prince, even more polite than the last, "conveying his impatience to be exalted by an interview." Harlan declined to be rushed, calculating that the longer he took to get to Ahmadpur, the keener Bahawal Khan would be to pay his respects to the haughty *feringhee* chief. A terse message was sent back to the nawab, declaring that Harlan was suffering from "a *phlegmon*," a skin inflammation, and would not reach Ahmadpur for at least ten days.

While encamped at Bahawalpur, Harlan made a point of staying inside his tent, thus ensuring the cultivation of his own mystery. "A crowd assembled daily from the town to get a view of the stranger," and wild rumors about its occupant spread rapidly. It was even claimed that the tall, bearded stranger was none other than "the ex-king Shujah Ul Moolk travelling under the incognito of a Saheb from Ludhiana." The story, put about by Gul Khan, that Harlan was "merely an amateur traveller," met with blank incredulity from Bahawal Khan's envoys: "What could have attracted an amateur traveller to an insignificant, worthless, poverty-stricken country like this region of Bhawulpore that yielded nothing but sand and thorns?" they demanded. "An amateur traveller would have passed on with the rapidity of a flowing stream."

The locals seemed more curious than hostile; which was just as well, Harlan reflected, since "several hundred miles now intervened between my position and the nearest English cantonment." If relations turned nasty, there was nowhere to flee. Only one Westerner had come this way before, and left a record of the fact. "The Honourable Mount Stewart Elphinstone passed through Bhawulpore about twenty years before my transit on an embassy to the king of Cabul," Harlan recorded proudly, "but with this exception no Christian of note had been known to appear in the territory." He was therefore astonished, and a little piqued, to learn from an excited Gul Khan, just hours before leaving Bahawalpur, that he was not the only *feringhee* in the vicinity. A few weeks earlier, the locals reported, two ragged white men had staggered into Ahmadpur, claiming to be European soldiers and offering their military services to the nawab. Both were said to be stricken by chronic fever. Harlan now recalled that before he left Ludhiana, Wade had shown him a message from Calcutta warning that two deserters from the Company artillery named James Lewis and Richard Potter might be heading west and should be apprehended if possible. "I concluded these men were probably the individuals alluded to in that document," wrote Harlan.

Eager to see if his hunch was right, Harlan hastened to Ahmadpur. After a two-day march, the troop pitched camp on the outskirts of the town, where Harlan was welcomed by "a person of grave deportment" who turned out to be the nawab's vizier, Yacoob Ally Khan. The vizier explained that his master would be returning shortly from a hunting trip, and after numerous "messages of congratulations, tinged with inflated protestations of service," he handed over a large, dead antelope, which he explained had been killed by the nawab himself. It was agreed that an interview would take place in five days' time. Harlan wondered whether the nawab was really away hunting, or merely stalling. Taking advantage of the delay, he dispatched a messenger to the two sickly Europeans lodged in the town, inviting them to his camp and "offering to afford them medical relief."

The two Europeans were indeed the deserters Lewis and Potter, who had changed their names, respectively, to Charles Masson and, somewhat unimaginatively, John Brown—names by which they would be known for the rest of their lives. Masson was no ordinary soldier. An educated and cultured man, a fluent French speaker and classicist with a passion for archaeology and chronic wanderlust, over the next thirteen years, he would excavate early Buddhist sites and amass a vast collection of ancient coins in Baluchistan, the Punjab, and Afghanistan, in a solitary quest as impressive as it was eccentric. This nomadic scholar would eventually become one of the foremost antiquarians of Central Asia, but at the time he encountered Harlan he was merely a deserter, an outcast who faced the death penalty if caught by the British.

The path that had led Masson to a desert on the edge of India was as circuitous as that of Harlan himself. Indeed, their past histories and present passions were oddly similar. In 1822, at the age of twenty-one, London-born Masson, then James Lewis, had enlisted in the Company's army and sailed for Bengal, looking for adventure. But after five years' service in the artillery, when his regiment was stationed near Agra, he and a comrade, Richard Potter, decided they had had enough of soldiering. Unlike Harlan, however, they did not wait for permission to quit the ranks or purchase their discharges, but simply set off on foot, heading west. Masson may already have been fired by a desire to explore the history of the region. His biographer speculates that "as it is certain that he had already studied with some thoroughness the routes of Alexander the Great on his Persian and Indian campaigns, he may have had at the back of his mind a desire to explore Afghanistan." Brown's aspirations were less elevated, and his past hazier. He appears to have deserted with the intention of entering the service of one or another of the native princes offering better pay and the possibility of swift advancement.

The two former artillerymen were very different characters. Masson was highly intelligent and capable of enduring astonishing hardships as he trudged, often barefoot and in rags, from one corner of the region to the other. But he could also be quixotic and ill-tempered, dismissive of those he considered inferiors, overly free with his criticisms, and often petulant. He made close friendships with Afghans, Sikhs, and Persians, but some of his fellow Europeans found him priggish, cold, and impenetrable. Brown, by contrast, was steady and unimaginative, a gentle soul with neither Masson's arrogance nor his resilience. In his memoirs, written when he had acquired respectability and an official pardon, Masson makes no reference to his desertion, noting merely that "having traversed the Rajput States of Shekhawati, and the Kingdom of Bikanir, I entered the desert frontiers of the Khan of Bahwalpur." The journey, and the illnesses they picked up en route, had almost killed them both. The nawab had provided sustenance but showed no eagerness to employ these two diseased and disreputable-looking Europeans, and the deserters were facing a grim choice between pushing on into the unknown or returning to face the rough justice of British India, when Harlan came to their aid.

Two days after Harlan's arrival in Ahmadpur, a man appeared at the door of his tent, clad "in the dress of a native with his head shorn in the

Indo-Muhammadan style." Harlan studied the tattered figure before him with amused interest. "The light and straggling hair upon the upper lip in conjunction with the blue eyes at once revealed the true nativity of his caste. I addressed him without hesitation as a European deserter from the Horse Artillery at Mut'hra, of whom I had already read a description at Loodiana." Charles Masson attempted a bluff, "asserting that he belonged to Bombay and was merely travelling for amusement in this direction with the intention of proceeding home over land." The performance was undermined by Masson's demeanor, for the Englishman was visibly petrified, convinced that Harlan was a Company officer about to arrest him. "Perceiving his extremely uncomfortable position by the tremor of his voice and personal demonstrations of alarm, I quieted his terror with the assurance that I was not an Englishman and had no connection with the British government and consequently neither interest nor duty could induce me to betray him now or hereafter." A relieved Masson gave up the pretense and admitted that he and his "chum," who was too weak to walk, were indeed fugitives from the British army. "He stated that he had been some time ill of fever and ague but was now convalescent," and desperate to get away from Bahawalpur.

Recognizing a kindred spirit, Harlan made Masson an offer, even though by aiding deserters he was putting his own tenuous relationship with the British in jeopardy. "I gave him medicines appropriate to their condition and offered them saddle horses and subsistence if they chose to accompany me to Kabul." Masson accepted with alacrity and gratitude, and the following day the two Englishmen were installed as Harlan's mounted orderlies. The deserters had retained their artillery uniforms and broadswords, and Harlan remarked to himself that the addition of two officers in Western dress would add to the military panache of the outfit. Moreover, he now believed he had companions he could trust. "I reflected that I should be provided with at least two confidential retainers of interests identical with my own in case of personal danger arising from my peculiarly insulated situation."

Harlan and Masson swiftly discovered their shared interests, and the American was delighted to have some educated company after so many weeks with no one to talk to (or rather, listen to) but Gul Khan. Masson and Brown decided that a pretense of American citizenship would

offer additional protection against exposure as deserters, and they studied Harlan closely to pick up the manners of the New World. Masson
would henceforth claim to be from Kentucky, a deception so successful
that long after his death he was still being described, quite erroneously,
as an American. The two Englishmen would play important roles in
Harlan's life: one would become his friend, stand by him in bad times,
and then vanish into obscurity; the other would become his enemy,
blacken his name at every opportunity, and become more famous than
Harlan ever did.

4

THE YOUNG ALEXANDER

The long-awaited meeting with Bahawal Khan would require all the pomp and dignity Harlan could muster. In Harlan's opinion, at least, this was a considerable degree of dignity. "All my military retainers, now amounting to about one hundred armed men, were drawn up before the gateway," he wrote with pride of this "military pageant." Harlan, mounted on Flora and wearing his Company uniform, took his place at the head of the troops, flanked by Masson and Brown. "I mounted, the bugle sounded, arms were presented," and with jangling spurs and clanking muskets, and some appreciative shouting from spectators, the American and his private army set off to meet the prince. Amirullah led the way on foot, carrying the silver mace like a club, while Gul Khan followed with the rest of the troops: first the sepoys, marching in time, then the Rohillahs, with rather less discipline, and finally a score of what Harlan euphemistically called "irregulars" who did not march at all, but clattered along behind in a disorganized and enthusiastic mob.

Bahawal Khan was not going to be out-pomped and had put on his own show of military force, assembling "his elite battalion of Seapoys armed in the European fashion and dressed in red jackets." At least a thousand of these troops lined both sides of the town's main street, and as the cortege passed, each soldier saluted by putting his right hand in front of his forehead—this was a gesture which, as Harlan observed, "appears extremely awkward with shouldered arms." Behind the uniformed ranks, milled an array of "irregular cavalry and dismounted cavaliers," while the terraces of the houses on either side were packed with spectators craning for a look at the *feringhee* and his soldiers.

The nawab had set up a large pavilion about ten yards square in the middle of the town to receive his guest, but "so settled were his apprehensions of violence or sinister design" that the prince had packed it with his own guards, leaving little room for the visitors. Harlan strode confidently into the enclosure in his most grand manner and was unceremoniously mobbed. "The moment I entered, the Nawab's confidential servants, armed to the teeth with every variety of weapons—spears, matchlocks, pistols, blunderbusses, swords, daggers, shields *au bras*— pressed around me and rather bore me up to the seat near the Nawab scarcely admitting the use of my legs!"

Gul Kahn, "by valiant efforts," mange to squeeze in behind Harlan's chair, ready to act as interpreter. Harlan studied Bahawal Khan closely: "He was a young man, apparently about twenty-five years old, of middle stature and delicate form." The "unassuming deportment" and "subdued bearing" of the chief, who welcomed the visitor while "scarcely raising his eyes from the ground," masked a man who was canny, ruthless, and convinced that this tall stranger had come to depose or kill him.

Harlan beckoned Amirullah forward and presented the prince with "a pair of handsome and valuable English pistols." Bahawal Khan examined the gift with undisguised admiration, remarking on the craftsmanship. The ice broken, Harlan instructed Gul Khan to tell the prince that he had "a confidential communication for the Nawab's private ear." Reassured that he was not about to be assassinated, the nawab ordered his bodyguards to draw back, and Harlan broached the subject of his mission: "I then referred to the object of my journey towards Kabul, and demanded to know what the ex-king might expect when he passed through his jurisdiction." The nawab's reply was cautious: "his house had always been faithful to the king of Kabul's interests," he remarked, but then pointedly added that his country was a poor one. The hint was clear: if Shah Shujah wanted to be restored, then he would have to pay for it. As Harlan rose to depart, the nawab's vizier moved forward, bearing in his arms an exquisite tribal outfit, which "consisted of several pieces of fine cotton cloth including a turban of golden brocade." This was a "dress of honour," the first of many that would be presented to the American over the coming years, a formal gift that, as Harlan elegantly put it, formed part of a "system of diplomatic language throughout the east." With elaborate expressions of mutual regard, the meeting ended and Harlan rode back to his encampment, convinced that his first diplomatic foray on behalf of the exiled king had been a resounding success.

On December 10, Harlan and his troops marched out of Ahmadpur, leaving the Sutlej and heading west across country toward the Indus River. Harlan was in a pensive mood, for with every step toward Afghanistan his past life seemed to grow more distant and irretrievable. "Heretofore I had not thoroughly divested myself of the familiar feeling one cherishes for the gradually receding associations of departing relations," he wrote, in an oblique reference to Eliza Swaim. The pain of that episode was slowly ebbing, for Harlan had little time for emotional reflection. "These scenes, a strange country, an unknown people and these objects in varied and diurnal recurrence filled up the tablets of observation." Finally, he was on the trail of Alexander the Great. "My mind was now full with the contemplation of the past," he wrote. "I was about to enter the country and became familiar with objects which have been made conspicuous to the world as the arena and subject of Alexander's exploits."

In these deserts, in 325 B.C., Alexander had battled the warlike Indian tribe of the Malloi. Besieging the fortress of Multan to the north, the great Macedonian general had led the charge, receiving an Indian arrow in the chest that nearly killed him. While his troops slaughtered the inhabitants of Multan, the wounded Alexander was carried away on the shield of Achilles. An attendant quoted Homer: "The man of action is the debtor to suffering and pain." Harlan would have reason to recall the motto of Achilles.

With Masson, whose classical knowledge was equal to his own, Harlan eagerly discussed possible links between the names of the villages they passed and the places alluded to by Plutarch and Quintus Curtius. "All the evidence to confirm the fact of Alexander's invasion is to be found in numismatology and etymological inferences," observed Harlan, noting with regret that "the devastation of two thousand years have not, I believe, left a single architectural monument of the Macedonian conquests in India." The ferocious warrior tribes that had once opposed Alexander's troops were now "a population oppressed with poverty." They ran away as the troops approached, or peered out furtively from behind the walls of crumbling mud huts.

Crossing the Sutlej south of Ahmadpur, Harlan used his compass to set the march in a northwesterly direction, hoping to cross the river Jhelum, the Hydaspes of Alexander's time, about seventy miles downriver from Multan. "Our march lay through high grass and the country was overgrown with vast forests of tamarisk," wrote Harlan. The soil was covered with an "efflorescent soda, resembling snow." The Jhelum marked the westernmost frontier of Bahawal Khan's lands, and there Harlan dismissed the nawab's guide. "For the remainder of my route to Derah Ghazee Khan, I was left to my own resources, and [the] assistance of guides procured from the villages in our line of march."

The land teemed with wild game. On the eastern bank of the river the mud had been churned up, with tracks suggesting a recent fight between a tiger and a buffalo. "Wild boar, Mooltaun lions and tigers abound," Harlan recorded. The wildlife seemed more plentiful, or at least more visible, than the population. Word of the approaching troops had preceded them, and "the few miserable mud huts or wagwams of nomadic shepherds were often found deserted." The people had fled, Harlan reflected, fearing "the rough treatment which poverty usually receives at the hands of an inconsiderate soldiery, especially those constituting a foreign army." Successive armies, from Alexander on, had passed through, looting and destroying; nothing in the appearance of Harlan's troop betrayed the fact that its leader was an invader of a very different stamp.

Five days after crossing the Jhelum, Harlan caught his first glimpse of the Indus, the mighty river that flows from deep in the Himalayas to the Arabian Sea, so vast that its Sanskrit name, Sindhu, means the ocean itself. The Greeks called it Sinthus, which became Indus, from which India derives its name. Harlan was elated. The Indus Valley had seen a flourishing of early civilization: Aryans, Buddhists, Mauryans, Scythians, and Kushans. For Harlan, the waters of the Indus with their backdrop of towering hills, spoke of Alexander's empire. "To look for the first time upon the furthest stream that had borne upon its surface the world's victor two thousand years ago. To gaze upon the landscape he had viewed. To tread upon the earth where Alexander bled. To stand upon that spot where the wounded hero knelt exhausted when pierced by the arrows of the barbarians." The river marked the farthest boundary of India, the edge of the unknown. When Elphinstone got here in 1809, he had found that even the local tribes were uncertain what lay beyond. "All we could learn was, that beyond the hills was something wild, strange, and new, which we might hope one day to explore." Charles Masson was also moved by the sight of the Indus, reflecting, like Harlan, "on the people and scenes I was about to leave behind, and on the unknown lands and races the passage of the river would open."

Here a new hazard presented itself, for the river was bordered by plains of quicksand, indistinguishable from dry land, which could swallow a horse or a man in moments. Harlan ordered the troops to form a single file and follow a high narrow path snaking toward the river through the sands and high reeds. "A step upon either side would be attended with disaster," reflected Harlan, wishing he had a sure-footed elephant under him rather than the skittery and nervous Flora: "When an elephant falls into a difficulty of this nature, he instantly throws himself upon one side and lies perfectly still. His great breadth and quietness will save him from sinking. His keeper throws him boughs of trees and reeds or bundles of jungle grass. These he takes with his trunk and places them under his body by rolling over upon them, thus forming a bridge towards the solid ground." The river itself was yet more treacherous, fast flowing, infested with crocodiles, and crossed by a narrow submerged ford with more quicksand on either side. After several tense hours the men, horses, and camels had successfully reached the opposite bank, where Harlan found a large and malodorous reminder of how lucky they had been to cross without loss of life. There lay "an immense dead crockodile, about sixteen feet long and about six feet around the thickest part of its body."

Soon they were marching through a land still more savage than Bahawalpur, where even the merchant caravans seldom penetrated. "The communities bordering the shores of the Indus are nearly altogether predatory [and] semi-barbarous," wrote Harlan. Marching with the Indus to his right, he led his army upriver, finally reaching the town of Dera Ghazi Khan on Christmas Day 1827. The sight of the settlement, surrounded by date groves and gardens, lifted the spirits of the troops. That night Harlan and the two Englishmen shared a nutritious Christmas dinner composed of the fruits of Kabul.

Dera Ghazi Khan came under the ever-expanding dominion of Maharaja Ranjit Singh, but until recently it had been part of Afghanistan, ruled over by a Afghan governor, the most recent of whom was Nawab

Jubber Khan, half brother of Dost Mohammed Khan, amir of Kabul. The locals "affectionately remembered Jubber Khan, extolling his liberality and humanity." Harlan would soon come to know the nawab's liberality more intimately.

"A vast distance intervened between our position and the frontier of British India," wrote Harlan, in an expansive vein. "We were in a community far beyond the control of European influence and I felt myself fairly launched upon the sea of adventure with self reliance alone for my guide." Self-reliance and Alexander the Great. Harlan's study of "the system by which Alexander the Great conquered, civilized, and maintained possession of Persia, Scythia, Bactria and India," had led him to conclude that the key to imperial success lay in establishing a linked chain of military bases, each located in a natural defensive position. "The genius displayed by Alexander in the selection of sites for this purpose," he wrote, had made him "the unrivalled architect of empires." If Harlan were now to conquer Afghanistan, he would need to do the same, and establish a fortified outpost on the Afghan frontier on the Alexandrine model, somewhere between the Indus to the east and the mountains to the west. Ranjit Singh held sway over Dera Ghazi Khan, but in the countryside, where there was no centralized government of any sort, various petty tribal chieftains vied for supremacy among themselves in the traditional bloodthirsty manner. These clan chiefs included several secret supporters of Shah Shujah, Harlan wrote, "some from hereditary respect, some as antagonists to the aspiring and increasing power of the Siks."

West of Dera Ismail Khan, the next large town up the Indus, lay the bastion of Tak, or Takht-I-Sulaiman as it is known today. "On the skirt of the mountains, there was an ancient fortress which commanded one of the passes from the upper region of the valley of the Indus. The fortress was situated on a ridge of the rocky ledge of mountains extending some distance into the river and might have made an impregnable stronghold." Harlan had heard of the place before setting out from Ludhiana; indeed, he had blithely informed Claude Wade that "he intended to take possession of the fortress of Tak." Charles Masson was sent ahead to reconnoiter. Tak, he reported, was a formidable fort, "the most massive piece of defensive erection I have seen in these parts," with high, mudbrick walls, a deep trench, and at least a dozen pieces of artillery emplaced at the towers on each corner of the citadel. It would make an ideal outpost. There was only one problem: Tak already had a chief, by the name of Sirwa Khan, a self-made warlord with a reputation for extreme brutality and paranoia who was said to be constantly adding additional defenses, because "a faquir predicted to him that the duration of his rule and prosperity depend upon his never ceasing to build." Harlan's mind was made up. "The fortress of Tak was deemed in every respect a favourable position for our purposes." Most of Sirwa Khan's forces were not local warriors, but Rohillahs, the same tribe as Gul Khan. Harlan's lieutenant was instructed to make contact with his fellow mercenaries and find out if they would care to desert, for a consideration. Harlan felt no compunction in attempting to bribe the Rohillahs since "their profession as military adventurers left them perfectly free to choose their leader amongst the highest bidders." From among his own Rohillahs, Gul Khan produced a man who had once been part of the garrison at Tak; this "secret messenger was accordingly dispatched to the head of the Rohillah garrison of Tak, with private instructions to tamper with his late comrades if he found their leader accessible to our design."

Sirwa Khan, Harlan reasoned, held his fort only by virtue of force, and by force or bribery he might therefore be legitimately deprived of it. Alexander, after all, had not hesitated to subdue and subvert local chiefs in building his empire. "The strong fortress of Tak," he wrote, is "one of those many retreats and fastnesses which the feudal system has made an essential construction for the safeguard of fortuitous power. Its possessor portrayed in his precautions the precarious nature of authority where might governs right by tyranny."

While awaiting word from Tak, Harlan was visited by an Afghan noble, a member of the Saddozai clan and a relative of Shah Shujah. This fellow claimed to have been in service with Gul Khan and described the Rohillah as a turncoat of the worst sort, who had had his hand cut off for treason. Harlan put the story down to malice.

Meanwhile, his convoy was growing, with the addition of a group of Afghan pilgrims returning from Mecca to Peshawar, who asked if they could join his caravan on the march north. Harlan was impressed by these humble Muslims, whose resolute piety seemed reminiscent of his own Quaker faith. He did not have the heart to turn them away. "These poor people availed themselves of our protection to escape from oppression and the dangers of robbery."

With pilgrims in tow, the army made its way through "flat country densely covered with camels, grazing in great herds upon the everlasting tamarisk," guarded by a lone herdsman armed with a matchlock, sword, and shield. Harlan was fascinated by these ungainly but hardy beasts, and he began to take copious notes of their habits and peculiarities, their food, character, milk, speed, voice, and gait. The camel might be mocked as a horse designed by committee, but the committee had done its research and this peculiar animal was ideally adapted to its world. Harlan described it in his own intimate, inimitable style:

> The camel is a great eater of fresh forage, with which he swells himself out thoroughly. He browses throughout the day, resting during the noon heat, and ruminates immediately after he ceases to feed. His forage sometimes ferments upon the stomach when his eructations become disgustingly offensive. When his food is digested he has a habit of gritting his teeth. Nothing can be more vociferous than the camel in his intercourse with man; he never allows his person to be touched either to load or unload without roaring louder and not unlike a tiger. The simultaneous preparations of the camp followers when about to march with the roaring camels creates a tremendous uproar and noise that rouses all the camp however desirous one may be to indulge undisturbed in the sweet luxury of a matin slumber. The horse is an excellent carrying beast but the camel less costly, more hardy, surer, is better adapted to the poor man, and his slow methodical gait is congenial to his driver's indolent habits. His great strength and a rude diet make him an invaluable auxiliary. He is a hard working creature and when in health a faithful attendant, but he has a delicate temperament. The camel is perfectly docile in his temper and of admirable tractability. His gait is patient, moving both feet at the same time, and will go at his utmost speed one hundred miles daily in consecutive marches with proper periods of rest and food. Camel milk is nutritious and used with avidity by the tribes who have access to it. They say the matrons amongst the Arabs who are anxious for their daughters to appear attractive in the eyes of an intended husband cause the affianced bride to drink freely and profusely of it until the victim rapidly increasing in obesity becomes grossly fat. In that state, the lady is an object of admiration.

Over the years, Harlan would assemble an immense dossier on camel behavior. Afghan camels, like the fruits of Kabul, would become a fixation.

A march of three days brought the troop to Surgur, the fiefdom of one Asad Khan, who duly appeared with food and forage in abundance as the men were making camp. Asad Khan was a striking figure in full tribal regalia, a great beard reaching to his waist and a long *talwar* thrust in his belt. This was the first Afghan chief Harlan had met and he was struck that his ferocious-looking visitor made no demands in return for his generosity except "a request for medicine modestly proffered." Hitherto the army had encountered only the tribes of the Indus Valley, but now Harlan was entering the country of the Pathans, the frontier tribe ruled by an uncompromising code of personal honor that valued hospitality and revenge above all else. Winston Churchill, who encountered the Pathans in 1897 as a twenty-two-year-old soldier, wrote: "The Pathan tribes are always engaged in public or private war. Every family cultivates its vendetta; every clan its feud. The numerous tribes and combinations of tribes all have their accounts to settle with one another. Nothing is ever forgotten and very few debts are left unpaid . . . the life of the Pathan is thus full of interest." *Pukhtunwali* (or *Pashtunwali*), the way of the Pathans, was strict and uncompromising: anyone seeking asylum or hospitality, even an enemy, should be welcomed, and any offense to a Pathan's personal honor, injury or insult, should be met with retaliation. In time, Harlan would adopt much of the code as his own.

Word of Harlan's medical skill traveled ahead of him, and every morning a line of sick and injured people could now be found waiting silently outside his tent. "During my frequent halts, numbers of the people applied for medical aid, upon all of whom I conferred the benefit of my clinical experience," wrote Harlan, who never turned a patient away. Eye diseases, and particularly cataracts, were endemic. In some cases Harlan was able to restore the sight of cataract sufferers by means of a simple operation. "My fame in this particular department of surgery had been conveyed from one to another, until the miracle of curing blindness by the touch was accredited to me," he wrote, with some embarrassment. Harlan's cataract operation was crude in the extreme, requiring only "a steel lancet, a copper needle similar to a bodkin," and a steady hand. One such operation was particularly memorable:

> An elderly woman came to me who had been totally blind many years. When I alluded to the precarious nature of remedial measures and told her the painful nature of the means by which she could hope for relief, she promptly replied, with a firmness of invincible decision: "Why should I fear? Am I not an Avghaun?" The lens of the right eye was depressed, the

patient refusing to have her head restrained. She remained unmoved as the point of the lancet penetrated the eye, and in a moment the light of day again illumed the vision that had been so long extinguished. I told her to look up, which she did, and with a calm and pious fervour she ejaculated her gratitude to Heaven. I desired to apply the usual dressings, consisting of a compress and bandage lightly bound, but she resisted and explained: "Let me first look upon the face of my deliverer to whom I owe a second creation." She prostrated herself before me with expressions of devout adoration whilst I endeavoured to proceed with the bandaging.

Having given instructions for her convalescence, Harlan told the delighted woman she should now go home.

This she would by no means agree to, insisting that I would "thrust the lancet into the other eye." I found it impossible to satisfy her importunity without complying with her request as she repeated 'I am an Avghaun. Proceed. I fear nothing.' After the operation she rose up from the carpet upon which she had been seated, invoked endless blessings upon myself and posterity for seven generations, and suffered herself to be led away, repeating as she walked off with surprising self-confidence in her step and exultation in her voice: "God is great! Thanks and praise be to God, and blessing on the Christian!"

Harlan had never met people like these Pathans, proud and fierce, but also generous and tenderhearted when least expected.

After a three-day pause, the party resumed its progress up the west bank of the Indus toward Dera Ismail Khan, passing "through a country of unvaried wild uncultivated scenery" of desert scrub, jungle, and rocky outcrops. The few inhabitants seemed peaceable, but food and forage were becoming scarce. Harlan always offered to pay for what he needed, a gesture that puzzled the locals, who were more used to being pillaged than paid. "Their surprise at just treatment from one who had the power to exact submission gave proofs of the misery through which the poor here struggle against the oppressors of their race," wrote Harlan. To supplement the increasingly sparse diet, Harlan resorted to his fowling piece, providing the pot with hare, partridges, doves, and other birds. A crack shot, Harlan had caught the British passion for hunting, the *shikar*, in India, and such forays provided opportunities to study the local flora, while killing some of its fauna.

Lean as a wolf, Harlan carried the privations lightly, and like Alexander, he declined to eat when his men were hungry. "A man may fast throughout the day without much concern for his comfort," he wrote cheerfully, citing Shakespeare's *Richard II*. "He may in some measure for a limited period dull the hungry edge of appetite with bare imagination of a feast. One substantial meal in twenty-four hours taken about bedtime will supply the waste of life during that period." The men grumbled when there was not enough food to fill the *dekshies* for the evening meal, but Harlan was far more concerned that the animals should be properly fed, giving rice from his private store to the horses when there was no grain to be had.

Finally the tired troops struggled into Dera Ismail Khan, a trading post on the upper Indus, inhabited mainly by Baluchis. The town had been conquered by Baluchi chiefs in the sixteenth century and now came under the rule of Ranjit Singh. Standing out from the Baluchis and Sikhs were numerous Afghan traders from the mountains, "large, and boney men, with long, coarse hair, loose turbans, and sheep-skin cloaks: plain, and rough, but pleasing in their manners." There was another exotic species in Dera Ismail Khan that was far harder to pick out from the crowd: the "newswriter," a creature to be found throughout imperial India, who combined the roles of gossip, journalist, undercover agent, and spy. Native newswriters gathered information, usually of a political nature, and secretly sold it to whoever would pay them. Claude Wade and Ranjit Singh both deployed networks of newswriters, to tell them whose star was rising and whose was falling, who had murdered whom, about the blood feuds, plots, and dynastic marriages that formed the convoluted politics of the region. Such unofficial reports were invaluable, although often wildly inaccurate. As Harlan observed: "These people are employed to furnish the daily report of occurrences and form a numerous body in the service of chiefs and princes who require to be informed of their neighbours' designs. By means of bribery they gain access to the most direct springs of action, one or more of them being always stationed as spies upon the actions of every leader or man of note." Harlan now became aware, probably through a rival newswriter, that he was under surveillance, with his movements being reported back to Ranjit Singh in Lahore. "One of these worthies, I had good reason to believe, had followed in the rear of my march from the day I left Loodianah and was still secretly engaged in this clandestine employment." This unnamed spy was about to make Harlan's life very difficult indeed.

Ranjit Singh, the prince of the Punjab and Shah Shujah's onetime jailer, appears to have been aware of Harlan's plans to restore Shujah from the moment he left British-controlled India. Ranjit detested Dost Mohammed Khan, the ruler in Kabul, but equally he had no desire to see the exiled king return to power. He had therefore sent instructions to the various princes along Harlan's route, who held their territories as fiefdoms of the Sikh potentate, to treat the American with extreme care and to give no encouragement to any plan for the restoration of Shujah. Ranjit told his feudal underlings that the *feringhee* should not be permitted to remain "anywhere within their territories for a longer period than the ordinary necessities of an amateur traveller might suggest."

This had placed the nawab of Dera Ismail Khan in a most uncomfortable position. The nawab was a Saddozai, a cousin of Shah Shujah himself, and thus favorable to the restoration of the exiled king. Like other chiefs, he chafed under Sikh domination. But equally, he was anxious not to antagonize Ranjit Singh, who would welcome an excuse to oust him and annex Dera Ismail Khan. The nawab's messenger duly appeared before Harlan with a gift of three hundred rupees to explain, delicately, that while the visitor was most welcome, it would be altogether better if he left, quickly. Harlan tried to reassure the nawab's envoy that he would soon be traveling on to Peshawar, but at this the man looked doubtful. There were, he explained, only three ways to get past the exceptionally hostile Afghan tribes between Dera and Peshawar: bribery, violence, or stealth. "The road to Peshawar would be unpassable through the mountain tribes by any party which was too numerous for disguise," the man explained. "Whilst our force was not sufficient to effect a passage by arms." One might try to buy a way through, he added, but "the tribes inhabiting the mountains were treacherous and cruel," and likely to assume that if a traveler was rich enough to pay a bribe, then he was certainly worth robbing.

Idly, the man observed that the Rohillah garrison at Tak had mutinied for lack of pay. If Harlan had money, he might enlist these men as a guard against the mountain tribes. Harlan was astonished. "This was the first intimation I had received of the movements of my agents at

Tak," he wrote. Did the nawab know that the mutiny had been insti-
gated by Harlan himself? Was this some sort of ploy? Harlan carefully
cross-examined his informant, but concluded that he had no suspicions
as to the true cause of the mutiny.

That night, the Rohillah commander from Tak presented himself in
person. Dusty and bedraggled from the thirty-mile ride, the Rohillah
officer saluted and declared, in Harlan's words, that he and his three
hundred men were "mad with the prospect of entering my service."
Subsequent questioning, however, revealed that the mutiny was still at
the negotiating stage. If Harlan would send his sepoys, the Rohillah observed, then the fortress could be taken with ease. For the first time
Harlan began to have misgivings. How did this fellow expect a handful
of "men in military uniform to enforce a result that could not be otherwise accomplished by his 300 Rohillahs?" Even more worrying was the
demeanor of Gul Khan. Harlan summoned the scarred old fighter to a
private council of war, but found him distinctly unwarlike. Was this not
the moment to launch a full-scale assault on the fortress? Harlan asked.
Gul Khan looked at his feet. Perhaps Gul Khan might care to go to Tak
and coordinate the mutiny in person? Once more, Gul Khan demurred:
he would not be able to live with himself, he said, "if any misfortune
happened to Saheb." The Rohillahs could not be relied on, he added,
and Tak was miles away, "near the mountains which are inhabited by
spirits and demons."

Perhaps the old mercenary was right, Harlan pondered: "Caution is
creditable where desperation does not marshal our designs. Those who
have no other hope may be justly desperate: To win or lose, to sink or
swim as fortune may approve, death or victory." This was not yet the
moment for a desperate gamble. Even so, Gul Khan's spinelessness was
not encouraging. The Rohillah from Tak was handed one thousand rupees, an advance against the five thousand payable if the mutiny was
successful, and instructed to return to the fortress. While he organized
the mutiny, Harlan would slowly advance on Tak and lead, if necessary,
an assault on the fortress in support of the mutineers.

The following day, after stocking up on powder and lead shot at the
town bazaar, Harlan led his men out of Dera Ismail Khan and set out
for Tak, "still holding the Indus on my right within a convenient distance to secure a retreat in case of adverse results in the audacious en-

terprise." Harlan was not leaving Dera a moment too soon, for strange stories were circulating, and the nawab's behavior had become increasingly unfriendly. "He had been informed that I possessed a wonderful missile of violence which could be thrown into the area of a fort by the hand where its explosion would cause the death of the garrison and blow down the walls in an instant." In addition to this magical hand grenade, the *feringhee* was said to possess other weapons of mass destruction, including a rapid-assembly cannon "constructed in parts and fastened with screws so as to be put up and arranged in order of battle at a moment's notice." Even more worryingly, from the nawab's point of view, there was a rumor that Shah Shujah himself was hiding inside one of Harlan's trunks. The gossip was patently absurd, but it was enough to convince the already nervous nawab that Harlan represented a serious threat to his own security.

Fourteen miles out of Dera, Harlan made camp in the ruins of an ancient fortress known as Kafir Qila, or Fort of the Infidel, to await word on the progress of the mutiny. From the low hill, the plain stretched away to mountains, the dense jungle of dwarf tamarisk broken here and there by patches of cultivation. Herds of camels and goats browsed among the thorn trees, and small plumes of white smoke arose quietly into the still air from the fires of unseen herdsmen. In this landscape, unchanged for centuries, Harlan reflected that his tented encampment in the fort of the infidel made "an unusual and picturesque scene," an improbable tribute to American endeavor.

> Over the principal tent, a few feet above the apex, the American flag displayed its stars and stripes, flickering in the quietly drifting breeze. There were no villages in sight but the curling smoke told of many abodes, and the tinkling bells of the flocks that fed unheedingly in the waste, broke the desolation of the scene. In the midst of that wild landscape, the flag of America seemed a dreamy illusion of the imagination, but it was the harbinger of enterprise which distance, space and time had not appalled, for the undaunted sons of Columbia are second to no people in the pursuit of adventure where ever the world is trodden by man.

Waiting anxiously for news from Tak, Harlan decided to hold a dress parade of the troops. "A hundred men in a single rank dressed in the costume of Rohillahs, armed with long matchlocks sloped over their left shoulders, Hindustani swords and shields, some with the addition of pistols thrust into the waist belt and a few with blunderbusses." To the right of the line, in rather more regimental order, the uniformed sepoys were drawn up, with musket and bayonet. His officers, Harlan observed, were also a mixed bag: "Two Europeans in military habits and forage caps with English broadswords suspended from their belts attended in advance of the line, accompanied by a portly Rohillah minus the left hand."

Harlan studied Gul Khan's expression and did not like what he saw. The mercenary "gazed wistfully towards the mountains, his bleared right eye partially closed, as he stood grasping the stump of his arm in his hand." Gul Khan's anxiety seemed to have affected the troops, for "silent expectation and enquiring glances amongst the men expressed apprehension and doubt."

Dismissing the troops, Harlan summoned Gul Khan into his tent. "Gool Khan" he began. "You are an old soldier and if report speaks truly, a brave man. My confidence in you has been unbounded. To you as a native acquainted with the country and the people I submitted the direction of my will." Why, Harlan demanded, had the Rohillah turned down the opportunity to launch an assault on Tak? "Had you not discountenanced my determination to proceed in person to attack, Sirwa Khan would now have been my prisoner, the fortress in our possession, the King proclaimed and the whole country forthwith up in arms for the royal cause."

Gul Khan's self-defense was a masterpiece of "querulous loquacity," rising in a crescendo. "Death to the King's enemies and may his salt become dirt in the mouths of traitors! Tell me where death is the reward of duty, and I swear by your salt, an instant's hesitation shall not delay the execution of Your Highness's will. Now, this instant, speak but the word and the Saheb's slave is ready!"

But Harlan had by now heard enough of Gul Khan's belligerent bombast. "'Tis too late," he said, glumly. "I apprehend the scheme has failed, for good news would have reached our camp quickly if Tak has fallen. This long silence can proceed only from hesitating cowardice." Gul Khan said nothing, but "raised his arms in an attitude of respectful supplication, his right hand grasping the stump of his mutilated limb," and backed out of the tent.

Harlan's gloomy prediction proved only too accurate. The next morning, a message arrived from the Rohillah officer at Tak: he was ready to order the mutiny, but only if Harlan would send his regular soldiers and force Sirwa Khan to pay their arrears. Harlan exploded. "Traitors and cowards! I offered to enlist them! Do you see those mountains before us? Can such wretches, who are unable to seize an empty fortress, scale those heights and force the fortresses in possession of savage robbers? They have proved themselves women in the affairs of men. Such retainers I need not. I know their value." Harlan gave the order to march within the hour: he would storm Tak himself.

Still spitting with rage, Harlan had buckled on his sword and was loading his pistols when loyal Drigpal, the *jemadar* in command of the sepoys, appeared at the tent door, out of uniform and visibly distraught. The Hindu officer "touched his forehead with the back of his hand and then assuming an attitude of respect with his hands closed before his breast and downcast eyes" delivered the worst possible news. The entire force of regular soldiers had deserted.

"What? All?" demanded Harlan incredulously.

"With the exception of four men who are my friends and Your Highness's slaves."

Reeling, Harlan ordered Gul Khan to find out "the motive and extent of this desertion," and slumped into a chair, declaring: "Let everyone retire, and leave me to myself." Gul Khan returned a few moments later. The sepoys had indeed vanished, he said, defecting en masse to the nawab of Dera Ismail Khan who had secretly sent agents to recruit them. "The fears of these people were excited by the dangerous nature of our enterprise," wrote Harlan bitterly, "and they accepted the Nawab's offer of service, deserting in a cowardly and traitorous manner at the moment of active necessity."

The Rohillahs were still at their posts, but Harlan perceived that "an air of despondency prevailed amongst the remaining soldiers, who consisted now principally of lawless adventurers of the worst class." To make matters worse, Harlan suspected that his one-handed lieutenant was double-dealing. "The conduct and management of Gool Khan appeared incompetent, selfish and suspicious," particularly as he had "already refused to proceed to Tak to head the mutineers in an assault." Surrounded by heavily armed and probably mutinous mercenaries, reliant on a man whose loyalty was now seriously in doubt, hundreds of miles from British India and with the local chief conspiring against him, Harlan found his granite optimism beginning to crumble.

"My affairs," he wrote, with splendid understatement, "began to assume a dangerous and gloomy aspect, [which] induced me to contemplate a retreat." The next morning the situation became even darker, when Gul Khan reported that the Englishman Charles Masson had also vanished, "decamping surreptitiously before day." This new desertion, Harlan decided, was also the work of the nawab's agents. Certainly Masson later recorded that he had spent several weeks in Dera Ismail Khan, where he was "handsomely entertained by the chief of that district." It seems equally possible that the eccentric Englishman had merely wandered off alone. Either way, Harlan was furious and deeply hurt by what he regarded as Masson's rank treachery. The two men would meet again. Having briefly been friends, they would henceforth be the most bitter enemies.

John Brown, solid and dependable, remained at Harlan's side, but Masson's disloyalty had convinced the American that the time had come to take "measures that should allay the storm rising around me, threatening to involve in its turmoil the personal security of our party." Once more, he wondered whether to lead an attack on Tak with his remaining forces but that, he reflected, would be a huge and unnecessary gamble. "I was restrained from doing so only by the extravagance and desperation of the enterprise. My resources were numerous and my prospects sufficiently encouraging to forbid placing all my aspirations upon the result of a forlorn hope. Had I been desperate, the affair of Tak would have been a final determination, and must have decided my fortunes either to sink or swim, but there remained many other ways of accomplishing my designs more feasible, if not less dangerous." The idea of retreat was anathema. He would push on, whatever the danger. "From the latter it will appear I never shrank," he later wrote. "Indeed, incidents of that nature accrued during my intrigues at Kabul in 1828 surpassing all my previous conceptions."

5

THE DERVISH FROM CHESTER COUNTY

Harlan's first priority was to get away from Dera Ismail Khan as fast as possible. The deserters had surely by now confirmed what the nawab already suspected: that the *feringhee* was no amateur traveler. More worrying yet was the general atmosphere of insubordination emanating from his remaining troops, and from Gul Khan in particular. The once-cheery Rohillah now exuded an "air of disappointment and coldness." Plainly, Harlan decided, the man was planning some vile treachery, and perhaps already "gloating over the prospect of a golden prize in the plunder of my establishment." He must get rid of his dwindling army, before it tried to get rid of him. "Not one individual could be relied on, with the exception of the remaining European who, as he had already declined accompanying his chum, appeared to have preferred attaching himself to my fortunes."

Harlan was now working on a different plan. Instead of establishing a beachhead by force, he would head into the Afghan interior in disguise with just a handful of attendants. Every item of nonessential baggage would be abandoned. "I brought myself to the condition of primitive simplicity," wrote Harlan. "Thus conforming to the order and example of Alexander to his victorious followers after the conquest of Persia, which was to burn their baggage, inferring that new victories and extended acquisitions of empire would accumulate plunder."

Harlan handpicked twelve men to accompany him, "carefully avoiding volunteers." The five loyal sepoys were dismissed, with a gift of two months' pay and letters of recommendation to the French officers in Ranjit's service. Harlan chose his companions with care. These included

John Brown, the Englishman, Sayyid Mohammed, "a man of respectable character," and an Afghan named Bairam Khan. The latter had been involved in negotiations with the fainthearted mutineers of Tak, and though Harlan suspected him of dishonesty, Bairam Khan was an enterprising individual, too useful to be left behind. Amirullah, the Afghan mace-bearer, was also selected to join the little party. Loquacious and pompous, Amirullah was "one of the most declamatory vociferators of services promised or performed," wrote Harlan, but his command of Persian and Pushtu made him a most "useful and necessary attaché." The entire party would consist of the mace-bearer on foot, five horsemen, and six men on foot, who could ride on one of the six camels when they were tired.

As the preparations were made, restive Rohillahs became positively threatening. "Expedition on my part became every moment more urgent," wrote Harlan. Each man was paid his wages a month in advance and while the money was being doled out, Harlan summoned Gul Khan and delivered a very public speech, emphasizing that the Rohillah was now guardian of his possessions. "You have all my camp equipage, my trunks and baggage to acquire your attention, and in this position you must be vigilant." What Gul Khan did not know was that the contents of the trunks were almost worthless. "All the valuables of my establishment I had secretly packed away in ordinary loads which were ready to be placed on the camels, trusting nothing to the Rohillahs but the camp equipage and trunks of books." Henceforth Harlan would carry only what was absolutely necessary for his campaign, most importantly a fortune in silver and gold coinage stuffed into two pairs of large leather hampers. Harlan finished by telling Gul Khan he would send further instructions when he reached Peshawar. The old rascal did not disguise his disappointment and distrust, but this was nothing compared to the frustration he would suffer when he duly ransacked Harlan's baggage, to find it contained nothing but worthless books and bedding.

Fearing Gul Khan might try to prevent him from leaving, Harlan gave orders "for an immediate march" at dawn the next day. That night, in his tent, Harlan climbed into his disguise, consisting of a long flowing robe, topped off with a large, white turban: "I was now to personate the character of a Saheb Zader, returning home from a pilgrimage to

Mecca," he wrote. "A Saheb Zader is a holy man to whom is ascribed the supernatural powers and revered as instructive in religion." Dressing as a Muslim divine, or dervish, was a typical Harlan gamble, and an extraordinarily risky one. Any stranger ran the risk of being attacked, and it was marginally safer to be recognized as a foreign infidel than mistaken for a local one. Masson, for example, once "encountered a man, who drew his sword, and was about to sacrifice me as an infidel Sikh. I had barely the time to apprise him that I was a *Feringhi*, when he instantly sheathed his weapon and, placing his arm around my waist in a friendly mode, conducted me to a village near at hand, where I was hospitably entertained." An infidel masquerading as a Muslim holy man was liable to be killed at once if discovered, but Harlan was convinced that his disguise would fool any casual observer. "I looked the character with perfect effect," he declared. "My complexion so much lighter than the natives but similar to the higher order of Arabs rather confirmed than detracted from the disguise, and when I added a large rosary of beads made from olive wood which were thrown around my neck and assumed a staff of the same material, the disguise was an impenetrable safeguard and effectual passport." The only problem was that such holy persons were regarded as founts of religious wisdom and, as Harlan admitted, his "knowledge of the Persian language and Moslem usages at that time was by no means sufficient to sustain even through casual intercourse the reputation my appearance indicated." He did not relish the prospect of being grilled on the finer points of the Koran, and then murdered if he failed to answer correctly.

Amirullah put his mind at rest by promising to intervene whenever a stranger approached. If they were among Persian-speakers, the macebearer would represent Harlan as "an Arab unacquainted with the Persian tongue," and in the unlikely event they should meet someone fluent in both languages, Harlan would simply pretend to be too absorbed in religious contemplation to answer. "I could be allowed to presume much upon the holy nature of my mental occupations [and] seclude myself without cause of offence from replies and interrogations."

"Should anyone enter upon casuistical discussion," promised Amirullah, "all you have to do is look grave and count your rosary in silence."

At five o'clock the next morning, the little posse prepared to set off. Harlan was distressed to have to abandon his library, but delighted to see the back of Gul Khan and his villainous Rohillahs. As Dash scampered around Flora's hooves, Harlan reflected that he had been able to "depend more upon the instinctive attachment of true fidelity in the watchful services of my dog, secured by kindness, than on the less efficacious results of services purchased by gold and available from man!" Yet he would now be relying on money to achieve his aims: the camels grunted as their loads were secured, for "the rupees added so much to the weight as to risk revealing the nature of the contents."

Amirullah had successfully badgered Harlan into buying him a pony, insisting that a man of his dignity should be mounted, and as the party set off with the mace-bearer leading the way, a crowd of locals gathered, "who waved their hands and stroked their beards as they exclaimed *bis 'millah*, In the name of God." From a short distance away, Gul Khan watched them go with sullen resentment.

And so, wrote Harlan, "commenced a journey which forms an era in my life, in a strange country distant from civilised or friendly resources, attended by a body of men without responsible restraints, known to be in the possession of valuable property and among a lawless race of free-booters." He could not have been happier. "With a light heart full of the turbulence of newly conceived adventure, my bark floated fairly upon the sea of enterprise."

That evening they stopped at a humble mosque and after a light meal of bread and mutton followed by a shared pipe, the party settled down to sleep "as a pious man should, with our heads towards Mecca." Neither Harlan nor Dash could sleep: the dog "seemed conscious of danger," but his master's reasons for wakefulness were more prosaic. Before setting off, Harlan had had a belt made with several dozen silver coins stitched into it, as an emergency store, and it was not easy to get comfortable with a pound of solid silver sitting on one's stomach. The next morning, Harlan told Amirullah that he "felt much incommoded by the load of silver pieces in my purse belt," and suggested that the cache be entrusted to someone else. The Afghan looked appalled and clapped his hands to his own pockets: "Keep your property near yourself. The Avghauns are an infamous set of scoundrels, never to be trusted. I, your slave bought with gold, tell Your Highness, never trust an Avghaun, for they are a bad people." Harlan took the advice to heart. Each of the party had a matchlock and sword, but none was better armed than

Harlan himself, who also carried his loaded double-barreled fowling piece and a pair of pistols holstered at his waist. He made a point of demonstrating "the accurate use I could make of my weapons upon the stork and hare," just in case any member of the party should be in doubt as to his marksmanship. Before retiring for the night, Harlan carefully stacked the loaded guns within reach, with the ever-watchful Dash curled up alongside them.

Amirullah was as protective of Harlan's dignity as his money, demanding that everyone they encountered on the track show respect to the holy Sahib Zader. Harlan was delighted to be treated with such reverence. "I was gratified to observe the charm of my reputation could command obedience from the faithful," he observed, and whenever anyone sought a blessing, Harlan readily conferred one. The opportunities were few, however, for as the camels plodded slowly up the reed-covered bank of the Indus, the population grew thinner, the weather colder and the climate more harsh. When the road made a detour into the mountains, the air crackled with cold and the men drew their sheepskin cloaks tightly around them. Sometimes the party would ride for hours before coming across a lone fakir's hut, "the residence of some ascetic refugee from the crowds of life," as Harlan put it. As a refugee from conventional life himself, Harlan was intrigued by these strange holy hermits, and invariably stopped to smoke and converse with them before pressing on. "The mild vapour of Kandahar tobacco," he wrote, "administers a degree of placid refreshment which, if confirmed by a cup of tea, enables the traveller to endure renewed exertion with little inconvenience from fatigue."

At the end of the third day's march, the party made camp alongside a meager village. The sun had set and Harlan was exhausted. Giving orders that he was not to be woken under any circumstances, he rolled himself in his blanket and immediately fell into a deep sleep. "I had not enjoyed the rest but a few moments," he wrote, when something or someone gently squeezed his foot. Dash growled in the gloom, his hackles on end. "I started up and laid my hand on the sword. In the dim light of a flickering lamp, I observed the indistinct outline of a white figure, resembling a corpse, with a covered tray presented towards me." Harlan could deal with any number of human and animal foes, but the arrival of a ghoul in his tent in the middle of the night momentarily paralyzed him. "I am no believer in ghosts," he wrote later. "Yet I must admit I felt much amazed at the incident, which might indeed have disturbed the strongest nerves." He was on his feet and preparing to do battle with the phantom, when Amirullah spoke up in the darkness: "My Lord here is a disciple, with an offering for Your Highness." This was one of the disadvantages of holiness: people appearing at odd hours to demand blessings.

A bizarre pantomime ensued:

AMIRULLAH: "The chief of the village seeks your blessing and has sent this female slave with a request to accept the offering of hospitality due to your holiness."

HARLAN: (aside) "Well, what is to be done?"

AMIRULLAH: (aside) "Leave that to me." (Then, addressing the slave in a tone of grave self-importance): "Daughter, tell your master the Saheb Zader extends blessings upon himself and his house."

SLAVE GIRL: "Alas, father, my master's house is without an heir."

AMIRULLAH: "Most happily then, is your offering laid at the Saheb Zader's feet."

This was Harlan's cue: "I raised my hands, smoothed my beard with the palms and repeated a few words in English which were as good as orthodox Arabic to all the audience."

The slave girl was dismissed, with an assurance that her master would certainly produce an heir within a year. Harlan was pleased with his first impromptu performance as a holy man, and was now rather peckish. The girl had left a dish of pottage sweetened with sugar, which was "much esteemed as a delicate offering to a hungry divine." Harlan might congratulate himself on the effectiveness of his disguise, but in reality the news of the approach of an eccentric white man pretending to be a holy man was moving ahead of him with the magical speed of Afghan gossip. "Supposing my incognito had not been divulged, I fearlessly marched on," he wrote. That illusion was about to be rudely shattered.

Allah, when he made the world, had a pile of rocks left over and with these, it was said, he had created Afghanistan. As Harlan swung away from the Indus, heading north, those elemental rocks reared up into a landscape of rugged, lonely hills; every dozen miles or so, a beige mud-brick fort would rear in silhouette on the skyline, marking the territory of another tribal chief. Near one of these imposing citadels, the party encountered a heavily armed soldier, who inquired if they had "seen or heard of the Feringee who reports said was expected along shortly." Amirullah replied that they had seen no such personage. Shaken, Harlan ordered his men to quicken the pace, but the camels stolidly declined to accelerate, and by nightfall they had reached a miserable village no more than ten miles from the fort, whose inhabitants gathered at a distance, eyeing Harlan and his party suspiciously. Amirullah called out that the revered Sahib Zader needed a place to spend the night. Dash, sensing danger, began snarling furiously. Stepping forward, the leading villager declared, with calculated insolence, that there was nowhere to stay since the village was "seldom troubled with guests." Amirullah launched into a tirade. "Have we got amongst infidels that no one proffers the hospitality of a night's lodging to a holy man? Where is your mosque, oh Mussulmen? Surely there is a house of God here, although this community are more like infidels than true believers."

The villager disdainfully pointed to a square mud platform that served as the point of worship, and said that the visitors were welcome to sleep under it if they wished. Harlan pointed out that "the position was unenclosed and afforded no protection against the banditti amongst whom I began to think we had fallen," and ordered the men to take up positions inside a ruined, roofless hut on the edge of the village. All requests for sustenance met with flat refusal, so a scanty meal had to be concocted out of emergency rations. Harlan had not been treated with open hostility before. A double guard was posted with orders "to be more than usually wakeful," and Harlan settled down to try to sleep. His eyes had barely closed when the guard challenged someone in the darkness and a distinguished-looking old man entered, bowed as if entering a palace rather than a collapsing hut, and presented Harlan with a letter addressed to: "The Feringee Saheb of exalted degree and victorious arms." The man explained that he was the vizier of the chief whose fort Harlan had passed earlier in the day, and that his master, one Ahmed Khan, would like to invite the esteemed visitor to his castle. Harlan, suspecting "a villainous design," chose to bluff it out: "There is a mistake," he insisted. "I am not the person you seek. You may perceive I am a true believer and no Feringee."

The vizier, somewhat nonplussed, declared that Ahmed Khan had sent gifts: two fat sheep, flour, ghee, and an excellent camel. The arrival of the vizier had had a dramatic effect on the hostile villagers, who now fell over one another to be hospitable. "A house was instantly cleared and placed at my disposal. Cots and carpets were brought, grain, firewood and forage abundantly produced in the twinkling of an eye." Harlan kept up his denials, but the vizier, grinning broadly, was not to be put off: "As a holy man you are entitled to our duty. I therefore pray you to accept this offering due to your sanctity," he said, and vanished into the night, declaring that he would return in the morning to escort Harlan to Ahmed Khan's fort.

Harlan knew that he had been rumbled, but instead of abandoning his pretense, he set about improving on it. John Brown's "ruddy complexion and flaxen hair" were simply too Caucasian, and so, using a burned cork, Harlan transformed him from a red-faced Englishman into a fake African. When the vizier duly reappeared at dawn, he was informed that the sooty apparition alongside Harlan was an Ethiopian slave, purchased at Mecca. Brown's new camouflage was not wholly convincing, according to Harlan, for "the vizier looked astounded and seemed debating with himself whether this was effrontery or real truth." Before he could say anything, Harlan cut in: "Tell Ahmed Khan you have been disappointed, and that the Feringee is still in the rear of our march. Say moreover that I have accepted the gifts which you insisted upon presenting and give him in return the blessing due to his disinterested hospitality." And with that, Harlan mounted his horse and trotted away, leaving the gaping villagers gathered at a respectful distance, along with the astonished vizier and his camel. Harlan had accepted the gift of the sheep, but returned the dromedary: as everyone knows, there is no such thing as a free camel. Did the vizier return to Ahmed Khan, explaining that there had been a mistake, and that the traveler was really a holy man? Or did he instead tell the strange tale of the white men who pretended to be Ethiopian slaves by covering themselves in burned cork?

At the next village, Karrabagh, Harlan was tempted to abandon his disguise altogether, for there, waiting to greet him in a welcoming knot, were the Peshawar pilgrims who had attached themselves to his troop earlier in the journey. "They saluted me as an old acquaintance with cheerful faces, and of course there was an end to my incognito." Even though not a soul in Karrabagh believed him to be a real holy man, he decided to keep his cloak and staff, reflecting that, "My native habit would secure me from collision with the reckless in remote places and save me from the impudent effrontery of rustic curiosity whilst in towns." Also, although he does not quite say so and indulges in frequent self-mockery, Harlan enjoyed being treated as a holy man.

Karrabagh was a fly-blown, sandblasted place, a tiny hamlet clinging to the edge of a hillside. Its inhabitants appeared close to starvation, and the pilgrims, too, seemed hungry. Harlan therefore declared, as a visiting holy man and distributor of divine blessings, that he would throw a party in his own honor.

> The sheep given to me by Ahmed Khan's vizier was cooked into the finest pilao. Everyone was made welcome to the feast, which was served up in borrowed utensils being much too magnificent for the small appurtenances then constituting my travelling cuisine. Cakes of wheat bread two feet long and an inch thick of superb leavened flour supplied the place of dishes. A carpet was spread upon the floor, and upon it a white sheet opened out for a tablecloth. I assumed my position at the head of the room. Before me was placed a large plate of pilao and a little distance below, about the centre of the cloth, another of similar dimensions. His Holiness, according to the divine dignity of his character, ate alone but allowed the chief servants of his establishment to be present and to refresh themselves at the lower dish.

Amirullah, as mace-bearer, stood at the doorway to welcome guests, while Bairam Khan and Sayyid Mohammed flanked Harlan in their full military regalia: gold-fringed turbans, Damascus sabers in green leather sheaths, and shields of black buffalo hide sixteen inches across with bosses of engraved steel. The villagers filed in, carefully respecting the usual formalities: each fell to his knees, holding his sword curved inward across the right thigh, before crouching around the edge of the tent. Afghans could sit this way for hours, but as Harlan now knew from experience, the Afghan squat was agony for the uninitiated: "To the stiff joints of most Europeans this posture is extremely painful and if obliged to remain in that constrained situation the pain surpasses endurance."

A ewer and basin were passed around for ritual ablution, with each guest raising his hands, repeating a grace, and stroking his beard in turn. "Now all was prepared for a set to," wrote Harlan, who, as host and guest of honor, got the meal underway. "I first thrust my right hand up to the knuckles in the pilao before me." The guests followed suit, after which the servants began distributing further plates of food to the pilgrims and barefoot villagers clustered at the door of the tent. Finally, once the entire party was gorged to bursting, the village headman requested a blessing from the Sahib Zader. This Harlan "willingly bestowed, although I apprehended no one was ignorant of my real character."

Then the fake holy man, his retainers, servants, and guests together indulged in another tradition that the American found most impressive: the emitting of appreciative postprandial wind. "The strongest and indeed the only proof of a full stomach is a long drawn, loud and indubitable eructation. This is supposed to compliment the host by its volume and vastness and unconstrained exit, following by the exclamation 'Thanks and praise be to God.'" Harlan burped away happily with his guests. These were not the table manners instilled by Joshua and Sarah Harlan back in Chester County, Pennsylvania. The hookah was fired up, and the evening slowly wound to a close in a convivial fog of smoke, wind, and desultory conversation. Harlan's first Afghan dinner party had been a huge success.

The following morning, Harlan set off once more, accompanied by two local guides provided by the headman of Karrabagh. The route to Peshawar now ascended the rugged mountain range inhabited by the Bangash tribe. This was Harlan's first taste of Afghan mountains in their bleak magnificence, a brutally beautiful world far removed from the verdant landscape of the Indus Valley. "Neither water nor inhabitants were observed," he wrote, as they "threaded innumerable dells, ravines, and thin washed waterways surmounting rocky barren hills rising in succession above the river Indus." The guides were under instructions to present the travelers to the local chief, but the warlike Bangash came with a fearsome reputation, as "a faithless race of cruel robbers whom no consideration restrains from plundering unprotected travellers."

As they climbed deeper into the mountains, Harlan noticed that his followers had fallen silent, and that Bairam Khan, in particular, wore "a clouded aspect." Sure enough, the party had traveled only a few miles before Harlan heard "the rumbling of Bairam's voice, bursting out in invectives and execrations and a torrent of abusive terms." Harlan's command of Persian was not yet perfect, but he knew enough to realize that the Afghan was challenging his authority with every dirty word he could think of: "These," as Harlan remarked, "are the first a tyro learns, and I was sufficiently familiar with them to comprehend his meaning." Wheeling his horse around, Harlan rode up to Bairam and ordered him to dismount, "at the same time drawing a pistol from my holster." The Afghan's "black countenance assumed a deeper hue as he scowled an angry look."

"Down dog," Harlan barked, "or by the body of Christ I'll scatter your brains. Down, I say."

At this point Amirullah ran up and seized the bridle of Bairam's horse while Sayyid Mohammed laid his hand upon his arm. Reluctantly, Bairam got off his horse. Harlan was slow to anger, but once angry, he was exceptionally difficult to pacify. "I continued to give full vent to my rage, dashing my turban to the ground—a gesture of inveterate anger—I clapped the pistol to my own temple."

This histrionic display appeared to have the desired effect, for the fight abruptly went out of Bairam, who now bowed submissively and began attempting to embrace Harlan's feet with protestations of fidelity. Mollified, Harlan holstered his gun and silently extended his hand for Bairam to kiss. The precise cause of Bairam's outburst was never made clear, but Harlan congratulated himself that his swift overreaction had "quelled a rising squall by the boisterous and unexpected intrusion of a hurricane!"

In theory, the Bangash chief whose fort dominated the meager town of Shukre Darra held his territory in feudal tenure from the Kabul ruler. In practice, high in the mountains, he was his own master, a princely bandit who specialized in preying on passing merchants and "levying blackmail upon all who were too weak to oppose his predatory habits." On arrival in Shukre Darra, therefore, Harlan dispatched a polite message to the fort, asking if the chief would kindly spare another pair of guides for the next leg of his journey. The request met with ominous silence. The Bangash, it appears, had learned of the arrival of "a feringee of high distinction going to Peshawar on a political mission," and were even now debating whether to kill him and steal everything he possessed. "Exaggerated reports of the wealth and grandeur of Europeans and their supposed inexhaustible resource" had reached the Bangash,

wrote Harlan, and "the opportunity to enrich himself by a simple trans-
fer of property seemed to the inhospitable chief of Bangush a godsend
not to be declined."

Harlan's arrival had led to the convening of a Bangash tribal council
and a fierce debate among the elders over whether or not to slaughter
his party. The leader of the plundering faction was the chief himself,
who declared: "Let us fall upon these strangers whom God has sent to
enrich our house. Is not the Koran our law and shall not the infidel fall
before the sword of the faith?" This suggestion would doubtless have
been carried out, had not an old, white-bearded man risen to speak, citing the name of Mountstuart Elphinstone. "Years have passed, my children, since a Feringee chief once became a guest of the Bangush tribe.
Kindness conferred upon that race is redoubled to the benefactor," said
the old man. "Think not that a feringee would come amongst hungry
men with unprotected treasures. This man is bold but not imprudent.
You may imbue your hands in the blood of a guest but the reward of infamy waits upon the breach of hospitality. A hair of his beard cannot be
injured without terrific vengeance upon the offender."

Harlan claimed that Amirullah had witnessed the council in disguise. It seems more plausible that Harlan pieced events together later
and simply imagined the scene in his journal. Bangash warriors began
to circle the camp, and it rapidly became clear that unless they departed
soon, they would not be leaving at all. "A crowd collected around us
as we were about to set out, betraying in their sulky demeanour that
all was not right." Harlan gave orders to his men to load their muskets
and prepare for a fight. At that moment, two horsemen appeared and
gruffly announced they had been sent by the chief to act as guides.
"Armed with matchlocks, their matches lighted," the guides looked anything but helpful. The party departed in silence.

Heading deeper into the hills, Amirullah directed a steady stream of
insults, sotto voce, at the guides. "Curse them for dogs and robbers.
May they sink down, down to the seventh hell," muttered the mace-
bearer, spurring on his pony and erupting every few yards with exclamations of contempt. Harlan usually took the lead, but on this occasion
he took up the rear-guard position until some two hundred yards separated him from the rest of the party. Unnoticed, the two guides also fell
back, until they were directly in Harlan's path. Suddenly, wrote Harlan,

"they halted and one of them called to me, at the same time taking his matchlock from his shoulder and blowing the ashes from the match." Harlan instantly reached for his pistol. "The next moment must have been fatal to the scoundrel, when the voice of Amirullah saluted my ears." The mace-bearer charged up, followed by the rest of the group, guns cocked, as Amirullah bellowed: "Ho! Ho! Children of the devil. Dogs! Villains! What are you about?" The sheer force of his invective took the Bangash guides by surprise; they backed off, hesitated, and then galloped away.

Amirullah's moment of triumph was immediately followed by despondency. "Well, master. What madness is this? Here we are in the midst of these inhospitable mountains without guides and no road in view. Those villains are doubtless gone to some den of robbers to get assistance in their black intentions." Harlan gave orders to press on swiftly, and after a hard climb along a narrow track, they emerged at the top of a pass. "We were about to congratulate ourselves on the escape from danger, when the path we stood upon was observed to terminate abruptly at the edge of a precipice formed by a vast chasm." On a nearby peak Harlan spotted the guides, just beyond musket range, watching intently and plainly enjoying their predicament. Amirullah called to them in Persian, promising huge rewards if they would merely point out the route, but "his words were spoken upon the desert air as those suspicious freebooters coolly turned away and disappeared amongst the heights." Amirullah's gloom deepened. "My lord, you are our leader. We are ready to follow you through all hazards, but here's no road for man or beast. If Mohammad doesn't help us, we shall be lost."

But Harlan had carefully noted the direction in which the guides had ridden. Inadvertently, they had revealed the path to safety. "We will descend the mountain and follow those villain guides," he said, slapping Amirullah firmly on the back, "and if we meet with inhabitants, we'll trust in providence for the result."

As the day wore on, they slowly picked their way after the guides, down sheep tracks that threatened to tumble into the ravines, expecting to hear at any moment the crack of a long-muzzled *jezail* from behind some distant rock. Harlan was beginning to fear that they would have to camp on the freezing mountainside, at the mercy of the Bangash, when Bairam shouted that he had spotted camels grazing in the valley below. Harlan had never been happier to see a camel. As night fell, the party rode into the village of Kohat, blessing Mohammed or Providence, and "not forgetting to bestow a malediction upon the rascally thieves of Bangush from whom we had escaped."

Stopping before the largest house in the village, Harlan announced that this was where he intended to spend the night, and while the men unloaded the camels and picketed the horses, the American, in his guise as a holy man, introduced himself to the owner. This turned out to be a "respectable lady whose husband was absent" who immediately set about preparing a meal, her hospitality a marked contrast to the "detestable incivility of the Bangush tribe." Harlan was just preparing to tuck in, however, when the local mullah appeared and announced that, as the senior religious figure in Kohat, he wished to converse with the learned Sahib Zader. This was precisely the situation Harlan had feared, and with Amirullah nowhere in sight, the moment threatened to prove deeply embarrassing and possibly dangerous.

"I responded with becoming gravity," wrote Harlan. The mullah immediately launched into "a string of interrogatories in Arabic, the commencement of which—'great revered father'—was all I could understand." Harlan fiddled with his rosary and tried to appear deep in pious thought. "I looked at him calmly, and with a great gravity turned up the palms of my hands to heaven and then, sinking my chin into the collar of thoughtfulness again, I continued lost in the abstraction of adoration, impatiently wishing for the absent mace-bearer." The mullah, somewhat perplexed at this Delphic response, switched to Persian. "Of this language I could understand enough to comprehend the object of his intrusion—there were some doctrinal points of the Koran he wished to have explained. But I retained an imperturbable silence, still motionless as a statue, my chin resting on my breast, my eyes closed and the rosary in hand."

After what must have seemed like an eternity, Amirullah finally reappeared and, grasping the situation, rushed to Harlan's aid. "What audacity is this?" he roared at the hapless mullah. "The sacred retirement of our holy father is to be trifled with by madmen? By the life of the four Khuleefas! Has sacrilege become a familiar vice with the faithful that holy men are intruded upon in the moment of pious abstraction? Vanish wretch!" The poor mullah, who had come only seeking spiritual enlightenment, "sprang away from the threatening mace-bearer's upraised staff in wild astonishment," and backed out, at the double, after "begging permission to embrace the holy pilgrim's feet." Once they had stopped laughing, Harlan explained how he had maintained his devout disguise, and Amirullah observed sagely: "The secret of holiness consists more in a sanctified bearing than the active demonstration of piety."

Word of the devout, though oddly silent holy man spread swiftly. Anyone that solemn, it was assumed, must have magic powers. Sure enough, once dinner had been cleared away, a female slave girl entered holding the hand of a small boy of about six. The girl explained that the child, the son of Harlan's hostess, was showing signs of being extremely stupid, and she would be grateful if the revered Sahib Zader would cast a spell "to sharpen his wits." Harlan did not hesitate: "The dullness of his intellectual powers was removed by administering a lump of candy." Now the slave girl herself nervously asked Harlan for a love potion, to make the object of her affections more receptive. The girl was draped in the all-enveloping burka, through which only her eyes could be glimpsed. Wearing such a garment, reflected Harlan, must be like being "thrust into a bag." Unwilling to disappoint the love-struck creature, he made her a talisman consisting of "a string with seven knots tied in it" and assured her it would have the desired effect.

Harlan had issued instructions to his troop to conceal his identity, but Amirullah's vanity was such that he could not resist revealing the truth to his hostess, who begged the mace-bearer to arrange a furtive view of this miracle worker from distant India. "This he effected unknown to me from behind a screen," wrote Harlan, who plainly relished being the object of such curiosity. "I understood our hostess with her attendants amused herself in the contemplation of rarest novel sight!"

Harlan might have lingered in Kohat, surrounded by admiring would-be devotees and potentially pretty Afghan girls, but Peshawar, the great frontier city of Afghanistan, was now less than two days' ride away. The overnight theft of several muskets and a valuable shotgun added additional urgency, for the party's firepower was seriously diminished, making them vulnerable to ambush. As Harlan wrote, the road to Peshawar was said to be "infested with rebels, and we were so far disarmed that a hostile attempt could not have been successfully resisted unless at close quarters." Afghan bandits tended to avoid hand-to-hand

combat, preferring instead to harass from afar with deadly marksmanship. "In those mountains where a highwayman can select his position
and barricade himself a distance from the road, perched upon some
convenient inaccessible knoll, we could not anticipate a close conflict,"
wrote Harlan. "We were therefore obliged to rely alone upon the sanctity of my disguise."

In the freezing dawn of January 15, 1828, which would be remembered as "one of the coldest days known in the traditional lore of
Peshawar," Harlan reached a small hill overlooking the city where Central
Asia meets the subcontinent. An ancient jewel set in the midst of a fertile valley, the very word *Peshawar* means border town. Harlan never
forgot his first sight of the city, glittering in the frosty distance. "The
surrounding high mountains were covered with snow and the sun,
shining bright and clear, was reflected with a brilliant lustre from the
vast surfaces which wrapped within their bosoms a world at rest." Instead of heading toward the walled city, however, Harlan made for the
nearby hamlet of Musezai, where Amirullah obtained directions to the
home of Mea Kummer ud-Din Sahib Zader: holy man, politician, plotter,
alchemist, and soon to become Harlan's closest friend and confidant.

Harlan had adopted the role of a Muslim divine, but Mea Kummer
ud-Din was the real thing, "a holy man famous for the sanctity of his
habits and of vast celebrity." *Mea* or *Mian* was an informal religious title, but Harlan would also refer to this individual as the *Dervish*, a term
which usually indicated a religious mendicant but could also be used
generically to describe a holy personage. In reality the man shortly to
become Harlan's host and protector was much more than merely a
religious divine. His uncle had been one of the most holy figures in
Afghanistan, widely regarded as a saint, with miraculous powers that
enabled him to get to Mecca and back in half an hour. From this uncle,
Mea Kummer ud-Din had inherited the mantle of holiness and a considerable estate. He was a man to be reckoned with in Peshawar, with
followers across the country and even outside it for, as Harlan observed,
Shah Shujah himself was a devotee—which was why the American
headed straight to the holy man's home, armed with a letter of commendation from the exiled king.

Kummer ud-Din had just completed morning prayers when Amirullah banged loudly on the gate of the mea's home with his silver mace.

"Tell your master," he told the gatekeeper, "an acquaintance of his friend in India has arrived from Loodianah." Harlan was duly ushered into the walled compound. There, in the middle of his garden, sat the mea, surrounded by a small and respectful crowd of adherents.

The crowd fell back in wonder at the sudden arrival of a group of armed men led by a pale-faced giant with a great spade beard. Mea Kummer ud-Din, however, had been tipped off to expect an emissary from the king disguised as an Arab pilgrim arrived from Mecca and he now stepped forward and embraced the American with a simple greeting: "Thou art most welcome." Harlan gratefully took a seat alongside the mea and gravely handed him the king's letter, "folded in the Persian style." As the holy man read the letter, Harlan took in the extraordinary personage before him.

> His figure was tall and spare, and stooped by premature infirmity. The face was long and narrow, forehead high, nose long and curved downwards. The upper lip was long and thin and the mouth large, and lower lip thick and pendant. His moustaches were of a mixed white and black, the lip shaven under the septum of the nose. The head was also shaven and displayed long pendulous ears. His eyelids were heavy and their lashes long, giving him a downcast look. The colour of his eyes was a placid grey, beaming with beneficence. His chest was ample in breadth but depressed transversely and he was afflicted with a racking cough which aggravated his physical weakness. The voice was measured and serene, deep sonorous and guttural.

The mea was simply dressed, in a close-fitting cotton cap, loose drawers fastened with a felt waist-string, and a tunic with sleeves narrowing to a point at the wrists that "fell in gathered folds like petticoats to his ankles." The mea rose to his feet and solemnly declared that Harlan was now his honored guest for as long as he cared to remain in Peshawar.

Harlan's arrival had coincided with a period of roiling instability in the frontier city. Peshawar was currently under the tenuous rule of the five Barakzai "sirdars," or chiefs, half brothers of Dost Mohammed Khan, the amir of Kabul. Nominally, these owed allegiance to Dost Mohammed; in reality they plotted continually: against him, one another, and the neighboring Sikhs. The brothers exercised local power, but since 1819 the province had been under the effective control of

Ranjit Singh, who extracted annual tribute from the sirdars and insisted on keeping at least one of their sons a hostage in Lahore at all times. The expansionist maharaja was waiting for the right moment to annex Peshawar outright.

Since Mea Kummar ud-Din was a known partisan of the exiled Saddozai king, the Peshawar sirdars distrusted him intensely and, as it happened, wisely. But since he was also wealthy and had numerous devoted disciples, they did not dare confront him openly. "They, the chiefs, are princes of the plains," the mea would tell Harlan flippantly, "whilst we rule in the mountains." Etiquette had to be observed, and once Harlan was comfortably installed in his new quarters, word was sent to the chiefs informing them of the arrival of a distinguished guest. That night they dined on a terrace overlooking a garden of lime trees, where "tessellated pavements of diverse coloured marbles," wound among flower borders and fountains. Once the meal had been cleared away, the mea led Harlan to an inner room and got down to politics. "With cautious regard to profound secrecy, this excellent man, without circumlocution, proposed to affect the restoration of Shujah Ul Moolk" with British backing. The cost of this enterprise, he added nonchalantly, would be ten laks of rupees, or about a hundred thousand pounds sterling, to be spent on "fiscal diplomacy," or more specifically, bribery.

Embarrassed, Harlan pointed out that his commission was to enter Kabul, foment revolution, and destabilize Dost Mohammed Khan, while Shah Shujah prepared an invasion. "I promptly undeceived the good man," wrote Harlan, who explained that he was not in a position to start a revolution in Peshawar, did not represent the British, and did not have a hundred thousand pounds. The mea took this rebuff in his stride and recommended that Harlan reveal his plans to no one. "Let that be kept a secret betwixt ourselves," he advised. Harlan had never met a man quite like this Afghan sage, at once playful and profound, worldly and simple, with a "simplicity of address, evincing great strengths of mind and unparalleled self control." Here, thought Harlan, was a man he could trust.

The mea was adamant that "the season was too far advanced to admit of reaching Kabul without the prospect of danger and suffering from the deep snow then covering the mountains." Harlan and his entourage must move into the house adjoining his own, declared the holy man, and stay at least until the spring thaw. Harlan offered to pay for board and lodging. The mea would not hear of such an idea, and in accordance with *Pukhtunwali*, his hospitality was obstinate, and lavish. The mea's kitchen was famous throughout Peshawar and his "bill of fare," as Harlan called it, offered a veritable feast: "pilau of mutton or poultry, vegetables, stews, soups and ragouts of fine wheat bread in sufficiency for all of us." Thus, wrote a grateful Harlan, "my party was comfortably domiciled with the intention of passing the winter." After so many grueling weeks in the saddle, the mea's home seemed like an exotic heaven, a place of downy cushions and ornate gardens, where delicately flavored dishes cooked by an invisible harem were served by shy female slaves. Like every earthly paradise, this one had hidden perils.

6

FROM PESHAWAR TO KABUL

Harlan had so far attempted to cloak his plans in a "veil of secrecy impenetrable to the inquiring gaze." Of his immediate retainers, only Gul Khan and Amirullah had been let into his confidence, and now the mea was also party to the secret. To everyone else, Harlan did his best to appear mysterious. But he was also a realist: "It was not to be supposed I could leave Loodianah upon this expedition without my designs having been distantly divulged."

The sudden appearance of a *feringhee* had set off a frenzy of speculation and gossip among the newsmongers of Peshawar. The Barakzai chiefs were particularly keen to know whether the new arrival was an agent for either Shah Shujah or the distant but steadily approaching British Empire, or both. The notion that he might simply be traveling "in pursuit of novelty and adventure," wrote Harlan, was dismissed as ludicrous, although some pointed out that another white man, Moorcroft, had passed through two years earlier, never to be seen again, without bringing an army in his wake. It was possible that Harlan was just another suicidal but harmless Englishman.

Everybody in Peshawar knew the mea's new guest was a *feringhee*, but Harlan decided to retain "the costume of a pilgrim which had so successfully secured me a safe transit." The mea enjoyed having a fake fakir under his roof, and "facetiously bestowed upon me the cognomen of Shaikh Ul Islam or Doctor of the Faith." Harlan felt entirely at home in the holy man's dwelling, recording that "each day a part of my time was passed in the Dirvesh's society, and in that of his associates." Among these was one Mohammed Ali Khan Lesghee, a learned Persian who was the Sunni holy man's closest confidant, despite being a Shia Muslim and therefore technically a heretic in Sunni eyes. Harlan liked this eccentric character from the moment they met.

> He was a man of short stature, broad shoulders and a very large head which was shaven every day, except the lock upon the crown that marked his creed. His beard was grey, but being well dyed appeared a jet black, bushy and stiff, while the moustaches full, thick, unshorn in the middle, covered the whole upper lip [like] hog's bristles, a simile that would horrify any Mohammedan to hear. His large head and bushy beard was clipped round and sticking out in all directions like the spread tail of a turkey. The neck was secluded by the beard, which descending upon the breast, caused his body to appear much shorter than it really was, while the turban worn full and large gave his person a contour of ill balanced gravity, still more exaggerated by his features and deep-dyed beetle brow.

In fact, concluded Harlan, after drawing a cartoon of this bizarre figure in his journal, he resembled nothing so much as "a cone standing upon its apex."

Despite his unusual appearance, Mohammed Ali was a refined and intellectual man with a reputation for magic powers. He was rumored to be rich, although none could say where his wealth came from, and a superb horseman who had once galloped from Herat to Peshawar faster than anyone before. Most intriguingly, this mysterious Persian was reputed to be a master alchemist, able to create gold from lead, mercury, salt, and even sand.

Mohammed Ali could always be found at the mea's house, wearing his "scanty Persian slippers" and lost in what appeared to be the deepest scholarly thought. Harlan was intrigued: "If you asked his opinion, he had a trick of tasting with his lips and enjoining his brain with the end of his tongue, which he rolled round his mouth in the act of contemplation, the large separated lips aghast, as he seemed to be literally chewing the cud of abstraction." Harlan spent hours with this strange, hairy little intellectual, in learned conversation about the secrets of alchemy, a subject of increasing fascination to the young American adventurer.

The origins of alchemy lay in ancient Greece and Egypt, a fusion of science, art, religion, and mysticism. On one level, ancient alchemy was the precursor of modern science and medicine, an attempt to explore nature before the tools of scientific investigation were available; on another it was magic, the secret of purifying matter and the search for the philosopher's stone, the elixir of eternal life. After the fall of the Roman Empire, the focus of alchemical thought had moved to the Arab and Persian world, bringing together Pythagorean philosophy, Aristotelian and Platonic thought, hermetical science based on the four elements of earth, air, fire, and water, and Islamic numerology. Islamic alchemy flowed back to Europe, where it was associated with sorcery but also with philosophical, religious, and scientific inquiry. Alchemy, it was believed, could purify metal to make gold, but might also cleanse the soul, forging immortality. Throughout the Middle Ages alchemists sought out such mysteries, pushing forward the frontier of science and medicine: Roger Bacon, Saint Thomas Aquinas, and Isaac Newton, were all students of alchemy. By the start of the nineteenth century, European alchemy had been rendered moribund by the birth of modern chemistry and rationalism, its occult practitioners dismissed as cranks or crooks; yet in much of the Middle East and Asia it continued to thrive.

In addition to Mohammed Ali, the in-house alchemist, the mea's circle included, somewhat surprisingly, two retainers of Yar Mohammed Khan, the most senior of the Peshawar chiefs. The two officers, Sikandar and Jafar, were "gentlemen or persons of culture," in Harlan's opinion, and like many soldiers they were also passionate huntsmen, adept in the ancient aristocratic sport of falconry. One evening, during a dinner at the mea's house, they invited Harlan to join them in the next day's hunt. The following morning Sikandar and Jafar appeared, mounted on Turcoman stallions, with three casts of hawks, a pointer, three Persian greyhounds, and twelve mounted followers: four as valets, two falconers, two whippers in, and four huntsmen. As they rode into the countryside, Sikandar (whose name means Alexander in Persian) explained that the hawks had been trained to seize pheasant, waterfowl, storks, pigeons, peacocks, and partridges, but would also go for larger game, such as hare, and might even attack a mountain lion. Harlan's dog was every bit as excited as his master. "Dash accompanied the party and displayed no less spirit, energy and enthusiasm in the sport than his better trained comrades," wrote Harlan. But as always, Dash, like Harlan himself, was inclined to bite first and ask questions later. "These strange dogs were received by him with suspicious demonstrations and apparently punctilious etiquette, but the object of our movements, which he readily understood to be one of pleasure, calmed his excitement and subdued his aversion to the canine guests whom he condescended to join in the chase."

The party was eight miles out of the mea's village when they spotted an eagle following them at a great height. As in Afghan politics, the predators were themselves quarry, for while the hawks preyed on weaker birds, the falcons were liable to attack from the eagle which, Harlan noted with admiration, "has been known to descend with the rapidity of lightning and carry off hawks whilst in the act of seizing a quarry." The hunters drew their swords, and by reflecting the sun off the blades, drove the eagle away. There were also human predators around in the form of the marauding mountain tribes, so the mea sent his son to accompany the party. No one would attack or rob a relative of the revered saint.

In a small clearing the hunters stopped and pointed toward a dense patch of high, withered grass. The pointer stiffened and the falconers prepared to unleash their birds, at which point Dash did his best to wreck the entire enterprise, for his "undrilled nose had scented the birds and he dashed in amongst them with an unbecoming ardour." The covey rose with a clatter, three hawks in pursuit. "Each selected its quarry, gliding after their prey with the velocity of lightning, their bells tinkling as they flew beneath their victims," wrote Harlan. "Another moment, and the hawks turned with their beaks down and striking the game with their claws brought it beneath them as they again turned in the descent with their tallons thrust into the quivering breast." A hare broke cover and the largest of the hawks soared gracefully upward, and then plummeted: "She seized the hare by the back and bore it up a few feet above the earth, flying with it until the powerful grasp of her tallons broke the animal's back. She then alighted upon the ground and the mounted huntsman who had followed, dismounting, ended the struggle with his dagger or sword, the razor-like edge of which he drew across the hare's throat. The *baz* thrust her beak into the gurgling stream amid the death scream of her victim." Harlan had never seen a spectacle so savage, and so beautiful. As the hawks swooped, time after time, Harlan felt himself transported to medieval times. "The force of imagination carried the mind back to an heroic period, and enabled me to realise the feelings which existed amongst the elite of past ages."

Sikandar and Jafar proposed that the day's sport should end with a boar hunt in the woods. The hounds duly picked up a scent, and the entire party hurtled off in wild pursuit. After a chase of several miles, the dogs brought the great, panting beast to bay against a small cliff, and a pitched battle ensued. One hound was gored to death, and then another; the huntsmen raised their muskets, but dared not fire for fear of injuring the dogs that swarmed over the thrashing boar. "Dash was there," Harlan noted proudly, "and had seized the monster under the shoulder." Finally, one of the hunters darted forward, spear raised, and ran "this ferocious antagonist" through the heart. Dash was still clinging on when the animal finally expired. Not content with the courage he had already shown, Dash immediately celebrated by attacking one of the greyhounds, "to exhibit his amateur demonstrations over and above the professional duty required of him." The party rode back in triumph, carrying twenty brace of partridges, eleven hares, two pigeons, and a boar.

Word of the *feringhee*'s hunting expedition, and his ferocious dog, soon spread, and similar offers of hospitality and entertainment began to arrive from prominent Peshawaris keen to get a glimpse of the stranger. Although curious to see inside the walled city, Harlan politely turned down every invitation. During his visit in 1809, Mountstuart Elphinstone of the East India Company had "distributed a gift of gold and precious stuff with an undiscriminating hand," and an elaborate mythology had grown up around his largesse. It was even claimed that when the Englishman left he had ordered his entourage to drop handfuls of rupees in their wake, "so that many villagers when they sallied out after daylight were astonished to observe the ground strewn with silver coin." Harlan could not compete with such generosity, and had he tried, this might merely have served to confirm the prevailing opinion that he was a secret agent of the British government. Rather than disappoint his hosts with niggardly gifts, Harlan adopted a policy of mixing only with the mea's immediate circle.

Harlan's reasoning was sound, but his reluctance to socialize did not sit well with the sirdars of Peshawar, who sent repeated, pressing invitations. Harlan was convinced that meeting one chief would excite the envy of the others, "for each one had separate interests and a visit to either must have compromised the comfort of my host, if not my personal safety." To each chiefly invite, Harlan replied that he was merely a "humble pilgrim" unworthy of such attention.

Yar Mohammed, the primus inter pares of the chiefs, was not to be palmed off so easily. One morning a message arrived from Yar Mohammed's vizier, Murad Ali, claiming that he was unwell and seeking medical help from the *feringhee* doctor. Harlan could not refuse such a request. "Accordingly, taking along with me such medicines as were thought necessary, I rode into town attended by three of my own servants and two of the Dervish's."

This was Harlan's first foray inside the walls of Peshawar, a teeming city of a hundred thousand souls, a rich and bustling commercial center with markets and shops, its narrow streets "crowded with men of all nations and languages, in every variety of dress and appearance." Here the races and tribes seemed to intermingle in one great, clamoring cacophony: "People of the town in white turbans, some in large white and dark blue frocks, and others in sheep-skin coats; Persian and Afghauns, in brown woollen tunics, or flowing mantles, and caps of black sheep skin or coloured silk; Khyberees, with the straw sandals and the wild dress and air of their mountains; Hindoos, uniting the peculiar features and manners of their own nation to the long beard and dress of the country; and Hazaurehs, not more remarkable for their conical caps of skin, and for their broad faces and little eyes, than for their want of the beard, which is the ornament of every other face in the city." The arrival of one more bearded stranger in the commotion passed unnoticed.

At Murad Ali's house, Harlan was ushered upstairs to where the vizier lay, reclining upon cushions, but perfectly healthy. Harlan performed a perfunctory examination and prescribed a dose of Epsom salts, a preparation of magnesium sulfate used as a purgative, which he happened to have in his bag. He was about to leave when a messenger entered and whispered to the "patient," followed, a moment later, by a bearded barrel of a man, gorgeously dressed "in green cashmere cloth embroidered with gold, a scarlet *tchaga* [upper garment] of the same material, similarly decorated, with a cashmere shawl, turban and waist belt." Around him clustered a dozen-strong bodyguard, sporting "Persian daggers, with Avghaun knives and pistols in their belts, Persian swords and flintlock muskets." Yar Mohammed, the principal chief of Peshawar, was taking no chances.

Harlan, irritated at being lured out under false pretenses, decided on a show of arrogance. "I remained in a sitting posture with my legs extended, a disrespectful position. When the chief's name was announced to me I recognised him with a patronising air and enquired after his health. His manner was discomposed and restless as he viewed me with scrutinising stare." Murad handed the vial of Epsom salts to his chief, who "took up the medicine, smelt it and tasted it, enquiring what it was, with evident disgust." At this moment, the call to prayer sounded, and as the chief's entourage turned toward Mecca and knelt facedown, Harlan took the opportunity of leaving, with a perfunctory bow to the chief's raised bottom.

It had not been a happy meeting, but the sights, sounds, and smells of Peshawar had captured Harlan's imagination, as they had bewitched others before and many after him. His first glimpse of the city had left a profound impression: the elegant three-story mud-brick houses, the mingling of races and creeds, the cries of the vendors, the jingle and clatter of gaily clad, heavily armed horsemen, and the loaded camels swaying down narrow streets suffused with the tang of the hookah, spices, and roasting meat. He was itching to go back. Literally itching, because for nearly three months Harlan had not bathed properly, and the town boasted a large and well-appointed *hamman*, or Oriental bathhouse, which Harlan was eager to experience, "as much to gratify my curiosity as for the purpose of ablution." An invitation to dine at Jafar's home in town was the ideal opportunity, and Harlan duly rode one evening to the bathhouse, salivating at the prospect. His description of the delights of an Afghan sauna and massage runs for eight full pages, the breathless account of an entranced and desperately dirty man: "Visitors are received in the first room adjoining the entrance, the temperature of which is much warmer than the external air. Thence after a few moments delay they are conducted into the middle apartment, where the heat is increased to about 90 degrees of Fahrenheit. Here they disrobe and are accommodated with a loongee or long wrapper intended to be folded around the waist and allowed to hang about the person not unlike a petticoat. The floors of all the apartments are of tessellated marble, laid upon low arches communicating with each other to admit the circulation of heat." In addition to the underfloor heating, steam belched out of pipes from a vast copper-bottomed cauldron outside. The fire, Harlan later discovered, was kept going using "a strange kind of fuel": namely human excrement, or, as Harlan delicately put it, "the night soil accumulated by vagrant speculators in their suburban perambulations." (Harlan was a master of euphemism, but "suburban night soil speculator" is among his best.) With an American's sense of hygiene, Harlan swiftly pointed out that "however disgusting the mode of procuring heat," the bathers smelled nothing since the fire was exterior to the building.

With sweat pouring off him, Harlan was led into a recess in the wall to have his beard, which now reached to his midriff, dyed with pigment of wild indigo leaves. "The substance is dried and ground fine, when it is of a yellowish colour, a sufficiency of this is made into a paste with water and being rubbed thoroughly into the beard and mustache, a cloth is tied over the head and under the jaw." While Harlan's whiskers were turning a deep blue-black, the barber set to work using henna "to colour the palms and soles and nails of the hands and feet a dull yellowish red."

"The visitor is then allowed to swelter awhile in the steam pervading the room at a temperature much higher than we are accustomed to take the hottest water bath," he wrote. After a boiling lasting fifteen minutes, it was time for "the manipulator" or masseur. "This official approaches his customer with a metal pot holding about a quart of hot water and dashing the contents over him by repeated effusions commences soaping the person from head to foot. This finished, he draws upon his hand a mitten of horse hair." Harlan was about to be scrubbed and scraped clean with the nearest equivalent to wire wool. "Taking the bather's hand, he rubs the palm of his own upon the arm upwards from the wrist. At every movement large flakes of accumulated scurf will be collected in rolls, the size of coarse packed threads or larger, and until they cease to form under the mitten as it passes over the skin." The scouring process continued for about half an hour, and ended with a fresh dousing in even hotter water. Finally came the massage itself.

> The operator stands with his feet upon the bather's extended hands presented palm up and arms at length resting upon the marble floor. In this position the manipulator inclines his person and placing the heels of his palm upon the bather's thighs presses hard as he gradually slides them down towards the knees. This movement is frequently repeated, the calves of the leg and the arms are also well kneaded and the bather is turned over. The operator now places his heel at the back of the neck.

and slides downwards, first on one side and then the other of the back-bone. He stands upon the calves, the thighs and presses firmly with his feet or hands all the fleshy parts of the person. The operator concludes his manipulations by cracking the joints, beginning with the toes. Every one of these is made to respond to his efforts, the ankles, knees, fingers, wrists and elbow joints. Even the neck responds to a forcible twist and concluding with the *chef d'oeuvre*: a sudden crack of the back startles the patient with surprise!

Harlan's beard was rinsed with soap and milk before "a general effusion of hot water concluded the process." Having been boiled, soaped, scoured, scraped, trampled, pummeled, dyed, and bent for nearly two hours, Harlan sat smoking a hookah in the drying room, exhausted and exhilarated. The experience had imparted "a sense of rest and freedom from fatigue which leaves the bather in a state of inexpressible placidity and physical comfort," he reflected, "with feelings of elasticity and in-vigoration surrounding his frame." His beard blue-black, his face red, his palms yellow, his skin tingling and completely clean for perhaps the first time since leaving America, Harlan felt, and looked, extraordinary. He wobbled back onto his horse and rode unsteadily to his dinner ap-pointment, wondering whether this might be "a process too shocking for delicate persons to endure."

The dinner at Jafar's house was "of ordinary style," but its conclusion was extraordinary. "After the cloth had been removed, I was astounded by Jafar calling to his valet in the tone of a Bacchanal—'bring me the joy inspiring wine.'" Jafar then proceeded to get impressively drunk, first by quaffing wine, and when that failed to do the trick with sufficient speed, on brandy. Harlan held firm views about alcohol—a hangover, as it were, from his Quaker upbringing—and the sight of a Muslim getting drunk, in a country where alcohol was banned, shocked him. Jafar no-ticed the look on his guest's face, and the emptiness of his glass, and asked whether drinking was prohibited by Harlan's religion. There fol-lowed a bizarre exchange between an orthodox Muslim, arguing that the only point of drinking was to get drunk, and a Quaker, pointing out the medical and social benefits of drinking with restraint. "I endeav-oured to explain to him our custom of temperate indulgence at meals for dietetic purposes and the gentle exhilaration that enhanced the heart and accelerated the flow of wit and conversation, but his faculties being already clouded by his potations, my remarks were lost in the noisy revel of vociferous mirth."

The disagreement did nothing to spoil the evening, and it was not until dawn that Harlan returned to the mea's residence. His departure was noticed by a servant of Yar Mohammed, who reported the sighting back to the chief. Enraged that the *feringhee* had been carousing with his courtiers while rejecting all overtures from himself, Yar Mohammed decided to deal with this unfriendly and uninvited visitor. The mea had numerous spies at court, and word reached him that the chief was planning "the violation of his domicile by the imprisonment of his guest and the confiscation of his property." The mea swiftly dispatched messages to his court allies asking them to use their influence on the chief. At the same time, the holy man resorted to the traditional Afghan diplomatic technique of setting one brother against another. Yar Mohammed was only one of five Peshawar chiefs, and the mea now approached another of the sirdars, Sultan Mohammed Khan, who was known to be less impetuous than his older brother and "favourable to European intercourse," having acted as Moorcroft's host during the Englishman's brief visit to Peshawar. Sultan Mohammed Khan was charming, ruthlessly ambitious, and a sophisticated schemer, preferring to gain his ends by trickery rather than force. He promised to try to restrain his brother's temper.

Flora, Harlan's beloved mare, had given birth to a handsome colt the previous year. The young horse was now in the mea's stables, where Harlan liked to visit him every day. "The next morning about nine o'clock, I sat contemplating the beauties of this young companion when I was interrupted by the sudden and unceremonious entrance of a cavalry soldier, armed *cap á pied*." The Afghan soldier saluted and abruptly declared: "The Sirdar commands your attendance."

"Well," replied Harlan. "Suppose I don't choose to go?"

"Then I shall take you."

Harlan pondered this threat for a moment and, since he was unarmed, thought twice about resistance: "I shall accompany you, but remember I go under the condition of arrest."

If Yar Mohammed intended violence, Harlan was determined to be properly dressed for the occasion. "Ordering my horse to be saddled, I returned into my chamber and habited myself in the military costume I wore when a surgeon in the English service: a red coat, cockaded hat

and sword." The costume had a marked effect on Yar Mohammed's in-
solent messenger, who "started with astonishment, his air instantly
changed to the respectful bearing of a subordinate." While Harlan had
been changing into his finery, a servant alerted the mea, who immediately sent runners to his collaborators in the chief's durbar. Before leaving, Harlan summoned John Brown, gave him his pistols, and told him
not to permit anyone to meddle with the baggage in his absence. It was
a wise precaution, for two soldiers accompanying the messenger had
been instructed to seize Harlan's property the moment he left the mea's
residence. Brown "thrust the pistol under his belt, and drawing his
sword assumed the duty of a sentry in my chamber."

The mea was on hand as Harlan rode out of the compound, his face
"glowering with displeasure" and muttering "invocations of vengeance
upon the violators of his sanctuary." Harlan waved with an optimism he
did not feel, fully expecting never to see the mea again. The moment
Harlan was out of sight, the two would-be plunderers burst into his
rooms, to be met by Brown, who barred their way with a blade, a pistol, and a curse. "Of the Persian language he was ignorant, but decision
of action left no doubt of his meaning when he hurled at them an English oath and presented the point of his broad sword." Dash also
mounted a vigorous defense, growling defiance at the intruders, who
backed off swiftly and vanished.

With Amirullah walking ahead with his silver mace, Harlan rode in
stately fashion to the chief's residence, fully expecting to be murdered
on arrival. A display of the utmost dignity, he reflected, was the only
method of defense. "I was predetermined to maintain an uncompromising deportment in my intercourse with the chief," he wrote. On
arriving at Yar Mohammed's walled compound, Harlan was taken
through a large wooden gate and into a peach garden "in full bloom, the
splendid blossoms unfolded by the approach of spring." Despite the
circumstances, Harlan paused to admire the flower beds of hyacinths
"silently and sweetly perfuming the breeze." Even more eye-catching
were the members of the chief's harem, who "strolled amongst the
flower beds and plucked the pearl plant for stringing garlands to adorn
their busts and hair." Yar Mohammed was a lucky man, Harlan thought
enviously, for here he might "indulge in the rapture of spring, and the
pleasures of love amidst floral beauty."

In a corner of the garden, on a low terrace with tall cypress trees rising at each corner, the bearded Yar Mohammed sat waiting with his courtiers, among whom Harlan was relieved to recognize several friends of the mea. "I raised my chappeau, which civility the chief acknowledged by partially rising." Yar Mohammed was visibly tense and uneasy, but managed to mutter a formal greeting, to which Harlan replied with what he hoped was "calmness and gravity." At a sign from the chief, some of the courtiers joined in the conversation, including one who claimed to have traveled to India and who stated quite categorically that the high sides of the Englishmen's cocked hat could be folded down in rainy weather to stop the wearer's ears from getting wet. Harlan decided not to contradict him. The stilted conversation turned to whether horse-drawn carriages were superior to riding on camel, horse, or elephant. Yar Mohammed remarked loftily that he had been presented with such a carriage by a French officer in the service of Ranjit Singh, but did not think much of the contraption. Harlan had to suppress a smile. "I was aware a gig had been presented to the chief. Himself, with two of his brothers and a driver, squeezed themselves into it, to test the comparative pleasures of riding and driving. Their weight was too much for the animal's back [and] the beast stumbled and fell and was rendered useless. They forthwith had his throat cut and regaled themselves with a feast of horse flesh."

Referring to Harlan's medical reputation, Yar Mohammed brought up the subject of his ailing nephew, the Nawab Mohammed Zeman Khan of Jalalabad. "From his description of the disorder I understood his nephew was affected with diabetes," wrote Harlan, who prescribed "abstinence from all vegetable food and strict adherence to a flesh diet." The diagnosis was probably wrong, and the prescription worse than useless, but they seemed to satisfy Yar Mohammed. The interview was over. Bowing politely, Harlan made his exit, "with the satisfied feelings a man experiences when he steps out of danger from the brink of a precipice." Once they were out of earshot, Amirullah gave vent to his relief: "Thanks and praise God we have escaped the lion's teeth. God damn them every one." A small crowd of armed attendants had gathered in the garden, "eagerly waiting for the chief's orders to seize my person." Amirullah, convinced that the danger had passed, strode through them, swinging his mace: "Get out of the way dwarfs! Open a passage! Stand aside!"

The mea was delighted to see his friend return in one piece. He explained that his friends at court had lobbied hard on Harlan's behalf, pointing out to the chief that the mea's holy sanctuary had been violated and appealing to Sultan Mohammed Khan "as the obligated friend of Moorcroft and his race." The intervention of Yar Mohammed's brother had tipped the balance, for the younger chief had "joined his entreaties and protestations to theirs and the durbar were actually engaged in disputation upon the affair when the messenger announced my approach," Harlan learned. It was not the last time Harlan would thank Sultan Mohammed Khan for saving his life.

Yar Mohammed had been dissuaded from murder and robbery, but there was no guarantee that he would not change his mind again. With regret, Mea Kummer ud-Din urged Harlan to leave Peshawar at once, since he could no longer guarantee his safety. Besides, the frozen passes to Kabul would be starting to thaw. Harlan immediately gave orders to his followers to prepare for the march north. Mohammed Ali Khan Lesghee, the mea's confidant, shuffled into Harlan's room as he was packing, and on a whim Harlan asked if he would accompany him to Kabul. Harlan had grown fond of the mysterious and learned little man, and the mea himself pointed out that, as a Persian Shiite, Mohammed Ali "might prove a useful companion and influential agent among the Kizzilbash of Kabul," the powerful tribe of Persian mercenaries who formed the amir's praetorian guard. After an initial display of reluctance, Mohammed Ali accepted.

The route to Peshawar was swarming with thieves and Khyberee bandits, so Harlan asked to leave behind a substantial portion of the money he had brought from Ludhiana, amounting to some thirty-seven thousand rupees. It was agreed that the safest place to leave the money under the mea's care was under the mea, "buried beneath his bed in the secret recess of his domicile." A hole was dug, the silver rupees sealed inside an earthenware jug, and the money "deposited in the bank of mother earth." The mea flatly declined to accept a penny in return for his hospitality.

At the end of February 1828, the little party left Peshawar heading north, and after a ride of two days reached the province of Angoo, whose feudal chief, Suddoo Khan, was an ally of the mea's. Though spring was on the way, the land still "presented the bleak appearance of naked vegetation [and] snow still covered the elevated peaks and hills." It was clearly still too early to attempt the mountain passage; the party would remain in Suddoo Khan's comfortable hill fortress until the end of Ramadan.

Harlan observed the holy Muslim fast with interest, noting the "cadaverous faces, haggard looks and impatience of manner" of the hungry faithful, deprived of food from dawn to dusk. While his hosts and companions fasted, Harlan spent his days pleasantly, conversing with the local mullahs, perfecting his Persian, hawking, shooting, or strolling in the greening gardens. There was a limit to how far he might wander alone, since "the power of Suddoo Khan extended no further than the range of his muskets," but during his forays outside the fort, he discovered that Shah Shujah remained popular among the mountain people. Elaborate rumors about his mission, and for that matter his identity, had preceded him. One morning he was approached, as he sat alone in the fort gardens, by "an old negress" who had been a household slave of Shah Shujah. The woman stared hard at Harlan before bursting into tears and throwing herself at his feet, exclaiming: "Alas the happy days when I nursed and caressed you. Time has changed my form and you no longer recognise your old nurse."

"My good woman you mistake me for another," Harlan protested.

"Oh no, my lord and prince, I know you well. Would you conceal yourself from your old nurse who carried you in her arms? I am not to be deceived, well I know you are the heir of our good king Shah Shujah."

Handing the woman a few rupees, Harlan insisted he was not related in any way to the exiled royal family. The old woman remained adamant. "Oh very well my son. I'll keep the secret. Never fear me," and with a low bow, she vanished. When Harlan related the incident to Suddoo Khan and Mohammed Ali, they "laughed heartily at the old nurse's singular mistake." Even so, Harlan had enjoyed being taken for royalty.

By the end of March, as the air brought a hint of spring warmth, Harlan resolved to press on, but he had also reached another conclusion: the entourage that had accompanied him so far knew, or suspected, too much about his plans and would certainly give the game away if they reached Kabul. Every retainer was generously paid off and dismissed, apart from Amirullah, who was sent back to Ludhiana with a letter informing Shah Shujah of Harlan's progress and requesting further instructions. In their place Harlan recruited local servants who knew nothing of his intentions. "With the exception of Mohammed Ali Khan, my confidential friend, no other individual of the party was acquainted with my brief," he wrote. "Consequently my secret might be considered in safe keeping." John Brown, the companion who had watched Harlan's back and guarded his secrets for so long, was urged to come too, but the worthy Englishman declined, expressing "his desire to push his fortunes in the Punjab, at the court of Runjeet'h Singh." Harlan let Brown go with regret, giving him a bag of cash, a horse, pistols, and two armed servants to escort him to Lahore. As he shook hands with Brown—or Potter, to restore his original name—Harlan declared that they would meet again. He was right.

Suddoo Khan provided Harlan with a pair of local guides, having taken one of their tribe hostage with the pledge that this luckless individual would be killed instantly if anything untoward befell the *feringhee* and his party. The hostage had every reason to feel nervous for, as Harlan observed, they were entering one of "the least civilised portions of Afghanistan, the inhabitants of that alpine waste being characterised by predatory habits." On April 1, Harlan began the last stage of his journey to the realms of Dost Mohammed Khan: "I turned my face towards Kabul with impatient anticipation of the novelties and adventures the future held."

Instead of taking the Khyber Pass and exposing himself to the fierce Pathan tribe of Afridis who controlled it, Harlan planned a more roundabout route along the south side of the White Mountains, then northwest to the district of Logar, and on to Kabul via Hindki. This passage led through territories nominally held in feudal tenure under the Barakzai brothers, but in reality the mountain chiefs were independent, uniformly ferocious, and wholly unpredictable.

"The scenery is magnificent, grave and picturesque," wrote Harlan. It was also uninhabited for long stretches, save for a few bands of pastoral nomads living in tents of black hair cloth. A profusion of wildflowers spread across the rocky landscape: bright yellow eremurus, blue and white vetch, mauve campanula, and clumps of white meadowsweet. Harlan diligently noted them all: "The blossom of the pomegranate decorates the waste with a deep scarlet flower, intermixed with the red and white rose, whilst the wild poppy expands its dark scarlet cup in great profusion." Once again, the party was reliant for food on whatever the mountain people might offer or sell. Often this was very little, "provided with more generosity than taste." Mohammed Ali was particularly unimpressed by the local cuisine, and visibly shocked to be faced, for breakfast, by a bowl of mutton soup with a layer of fat on the surface half an inch thick. "Mahomed Ali, with his fastidious Persian air, demanded soft bread to absorb the fat before he could do honour to the host's favour." Even Dash turned his nose up at this disgusting fare. De-termined to feed his dog, Harlan bought a sheep at an exorbitant price, and had it roasted. "We all partook of the feast, as Mahomed Ali sarcas-tically remarked: 'We luxuriate tonight by the good fortune of a dog.'" The slaughter of the sheep gave Harlan the opportunity to witness an ancient form of Afghan medicine, when the attendants of a sick female traveler in an adjoining apartment of the mosque they occupied begged to use the sheep's skin for medicinal purposes. "They drew the warm skin, which was stripped off whole, over the naked person of the pa-tient, skin side inward. When the skin adhered to a patient's person, which it would do after being worn a few minutes, it was suddenly stripped over her head for the purpose of lacerating the patient's hide and so secure the effects of a blister. This process was said to be a re-source applied only in extreme cases."

As the party approached the fertile Khorum Valley, the population grew denser, with larger villages, each of which appeared to be at war with its neighbors. "Crossing the valley which is five or six miles broad, we were obliged to change our guides three times owing to the strife amongst the fractious chiefs of different towns." Here were cultivated fields, but the laborer, Harlan wrote, "follows his plough armed with musket, sword and shield." Reaching the walled, mud-brick village of Perwar, Harlan noted the towers at each corner, bastions where the in-habitants could retreat in case of attack, with loop holes for firing down on their assailants.

In exchange for twenty rupees, the headman of Perwar agreed to provide a guide to the Kabul frontier. "The ascent of the mountain over-hanging Perwar was accomplished with considerable fatigue," wrote Harlan, "and after a long march over high passes and through dense pine forests we found ourselves crowded into a small hut with a fire of pinewood in the centre." When they emerged in the morning, the entire party, including Dash, had been kippered black from the smoke. Twenty miles deeper into the mountains the party reached a mean cluster of huts. With extreme reluctance, the inhabitants were persuaded to vacate one of these, and the party squeezed together for another uncomfortable night.

The villagers who had seemed so unfriendly the night before were positively belligerent by morning, demanding money in exchange for the miserable accommodation. "Mahomed Ali refused compliance. They threatened to plunder the baggage. He defied them and they flew to arms. Several of the villagers now surrounded us, armed with muskets and matches lighted. I drew a pistol and called out for Mahomed Ali to advance. One of them seized my bridle for which he got a kick in the chops, and being mounted on a vicious 'cutter' I caused him to lash out with his heels." As suddenly as they had attacked, the villagers now vanished, apparently with the intention of intercepting the bulk of the baggage-laden party which had already set off. Harlan and Mohammed Ali rushed to join the rest of the group. "We hastened our steps, expecting to have a flare up with these rascals, but when we reached our baggage we saw the camels jogging slowly and quietly along, led by the servants, unconscious of danger." The attackers had simply melted into the scenery.

At nightfall they reached a tiny ruined village whose only inhabitants were two women, part of a tribe of nomadic shepherds whose men were away with the herds. The women were unable to provide anything to eat for the party. They seemed close to starvation themselves, and utterly terrified. Fearing they were about to set upon, in a desperate act of self-defense the women claimed to be lepers, which they quite obviously were not. With coarse flour, Mohammed Ali cobbled together some unleavened bread from the ashes of the fire. "I found it so execrable that I preferred fasting and threw a part of it to Dash. But he also seemed to think very much as I did myself and followed my example." The meager cakes were tossed to the two women, who devoured them on the spot. As the men stretched out to sleep on the ground, a freezing rain began to fall, forcing Harlan and Mohammed Ali to take refuge in a hut with a partially collapsed roof. The ruin, however, was not as empty as it looked, for "the fleas and other vermin soon asserted their right of preoccupation and drove my companion out." Harlan, however, was untroubled by the clouds of mosquitoes and "slept soundly and sweetly in the vile den of the predators." When Harlan emerged the next morning without a bite on him, Mohammed Ali and the servants were deeply impressed, believing that he must have some magical mosquito repellent, a charm that enabled him to sleep unmolested.

That night they arrived in Logar, at the outer frontier of the territory under the control of Kabul. The existence of at least rudimentary government became apparent, when a troop of horsemen appeared and officiously demanded "a passport or the alternative of permitting an examination of the baggage." Harlan's response was characteristic: "I objected as a breach of etiquette. They insisted, and I prepared to add resistance to protest." Mohammed Ali stepped in before Harlan started shooting, explaining that this was the revenue collector's guard, soldiers who enforced Dost Mohammed's tax collections and who would be happy with a bribe. "When they found I was not disposed to submit to their designs, a cursory survey of the baggage, consisting chiefly of books, medicines and clothing, satisfied their inquisitional duties." Harlan had been in the country only a few hours before his first confrontation with the authority of Dost Mohammed Khan.

The party pressed on through Hindki, for Kabul was now less than one day's ride away. As they neared the mountain city, the population grew more numerous, and gathered in the doorways of their mud-brick huts. The small children shouted greetings; their elders squatted and watched. In the hazy distance Harlan could see plumes of smoke rising from the ragged, honey-colored city, ringed by purple mountains capped with snow. On the outskirts they halted in the fabled gardens of Emperor Babur, descendant of Tamerlane and Genghis Khan, the great conqueror from east of Samarkand who had seized Kabul in 1504 before moving on to take Delhi and found the mighty Mogul dynasty that would rule India for two centuries. Babur was a man after Harlan's heart: poet, horticulturalist, and warrior, an admirer of the princely virtues with a passion for cataloguing every plant and creature. Babur carefully listed sixteen species of spring tulips to be found in the Kabul mountains; he highly recommended the rhubarb. Babur loved Kabul more than any other city he conquered, and the gardens he designed, and where he was buried in 1530, were of legendary beauty.

From here, beside Babur's tomb, surrounded by the floral legacy of

the mighty emperor of India, Harlan dispatched one message of greeting to Dost Mohammed Khan and another to Nawab Jubber Khan, his
brother, an old friend of Mea Kummer ud-Din who was known to be
hospitable and interested in the world outside. The nawab immediately
sent a message back, inviting Harlan to his house, but "on the advice of
Mahomed Ali, the kindness was declined with the pretext of first paying
my respects to Dost Mahomed, the paramount chief." Soon enough, a
message arrived from the amir himself, instructing Harlan to follow the
bearer to the Bala Hisar, royal palace of Babur, citadel of Dost Mohammed Khan, the home of Afghan kings and, henceforth, of Josiah
Harlan. The amir's messenger bowed low and spoke courteously; but
this was more an order than an invitation.

No American, and only a tiny handful of intrepid Europeans had set
foot in Kabul before. Four adventurous officers from Napoleon's disbanded army had passed through a few years earlier, en route from Persia to the Punjab. Moorcroft, on his last, ill-fated journey had hurried
through in 1824, when Kabul was in the grip of civil war.

Dost Mohammed Khan's servant led the little party through the
winding streets of packed mud to the eastern gate of the Bala Hisar, the
walled fortress south of the river that towered over Kabul, so old that
no one knew its age. It was now dusk, and the evening call to prayer
wailed gently over the city. The air rapidly grew cold, and the buzzards
wheeled around the fortress towers, seven thousand feet above the sea.
Beside the gate, embedded in the ancient brick wall, was a marble tablet
engraved in Roman letters, a reminder of how far, and how far back in
time, Harlan had traveled. It bore a simple legend: "Here lyes the body
of Joseph Hicks the son of Thomas and Eldith who departed this lyfe
the eleventh of October 1666." The story of this man who had wandered so deep into the wilds of Asia has been lost. Perhaps he was some
English Marco Polo, a hardy merchant who had come in search of
Eastern wares, only to perish in Kabul; or a mercenary who had taken
service under the Mogul King Aurangzeb, scion of Babur, one of whose
chiefs ruled as governor of Kabul in 1666. A grave digger once claimed
that Hicks had been "an officer of artillery who stood so high in the estimation of the governor [of Kabul] that they were buried close to each
other." The tombstone was destroyed in the upheavals that would
shortly engulf Kabul, and after 1841, it vanished.

It was oddly fitting that the first thing Harlan should see as he entered his new home was a memorial to the last white adventurer to settle in Kabul, a man who had lived and died there, bequeathing only a few words on marble, and leaving the mystery of Joseph Hicks perfectly and permanently intact.

7

KABUL, CONSPIRACY, AND CHOLERA

Kabul was named, it is said, after the founders of the Afghan race, Cakool and Habul, the sons of Noah. Beginning the Afghan tradition of sibling rivalry, Cakool and Habul could not agree on a name for the city, and so, like a pantomime horse, one took the back, the other the front: Ca-bul. Timur Shah, successor to Ahmad Shah Durrani, had moved his capital here from Kandahar only in 1776, but in the early nineteenth century, it was still Babur's city. From the Bala Hisar, he had planned out a city of placid gardens and riotous commerce, and from here he looked down on the fantastic flow of trade from Asia and India pouring through his city. "Every year seven, eight or ten thousand horses arrive in Kabul," he wrote. "From Hindustan every year fifteen, twenty thousand pieces of cloth . . . slaves, white cloths, sugar candy, refined and common sugar, drugs and spices." Below the castle, mud houses sprawled out in myriad confusion, burned-brick buildings the color of dirty sand interspersed with eighty mosques and their minarets. Paths ran through the random city like runnels from some giant pot of mud poured down the hill. The smell in the narrow streets was fantastic: spices, wood smoke, and excrement, alongside mulberry blossom and the heady scent of balsam. But up in the castle, the air was as clear and cold as mountain snow: Babur called it "the most pleasing climate in the world."

The Bala Hisar was a walled village within a city. Harlan was led through its labyrinthine streets to an elegant, two-story building in the upper part of the fortress, and ushered into an airy, two-room apartment on the top floor. The floors were covered with exquisite carpets and satin pillows, but the most striking feature was the ceiling "inlaid with octagonal mosaics of wood." At one end of the larger room was an elevated banquette, the place of honor for receiving visitors, and the other looked out over the castle wall, with sliding latticework to keep out the evening breeze. Bowing low, the amir's messenger backed out, closing the door behind him.

It was just as well that the ceiling of his new abode was so intricately beautiful, because Harlan spent the next five days staring at it, awaiting word from Dost Mohammed Khan. "I remained within doors, not thinking it expedient to ride out until I had ascertained, by the nature of my reception, the temperament of the Sirdar concerning my visit." As the days passed, with no indication that the amir intended to release him from this luxurious prison, Harlan began to suspect that his visit to Kabul "might not have been viewed by him in a friendly light." It was to his intense relief, therefore, that on the sixth day Dost Mohammed Khan's *mirza*, or personal secretary, appeared with a message to say that the sirdar would receive him at six o'clock that evening. The amir's palace was on the northern side of the fortress, and at the appointed hour Harlan appeared before the iron gates, dressed in his military costume, with plumed hat and broadsword. The *mirza* led him through a connecting series of high-ceilinged chambers. They stopped before an iron-framed portal, beyond which could be heard voices, which fell silent as the *mirza* threw open the doors. In the middle of the throne room, surrounded by his courtiers on an elevated dais, sat Dost Mohammed Khan, leader of the Barakzai clan, Pearl of the Age, the reigning prince of Kabul. This was the warlord who had driven Shah Shujah into exile. But instead of the ogre he had been expecting, Harlan found "a man of slender proportions, tall, and about 37 years of age," with a quizzical, intelligent expression on his refined face.

Harlan raised his hat. The courtiers parted, bowing and staring, as the prince motioned his guest to sit alongside him. Once Harlan was seated, the amir inquired after Harlan's health and began a conversation with all "the ease and urbanity" of an aristocrat in a Philadelphia drawing room. Dost Mohammed got straight to the point, with an interrogation about the extent and power of the Indo-British government, this encroaching force of mythical might. When Harlan replied that the British were stronger and richer than the great Moguls or Durranis had ever been, the prince looked skeptical and pointed out that they could not be such an overwhelming power since Ranjit Singh was allowed to rule as an independent force in the Punjab. Harlan chose his words with care: "I remarked the existence of an inferior power in the presence of a mighty government was evidence of that government's justice [and] showed that the rights of the weak could be respected by a great power." Dost Mohammed changed the subject. What, he wondered, was Harlan's opinion of the Afghans' capacity for military discipline? He added that, like Ranjit Singh, he wished to maintain a regular body of troops, but lacked the funds for a standing army. Harlan's suggestion was characteristically forthright: the prince should launch an armed invasion of Sind, the rich province to the south once controlled by Kabul, and replenish his coffers by conquest. Dost Mohammed was delighted with this suggestion. "He said he intended doing so next fall, and would be gratified to have me accompany him."

Rising, Dost Mohammed introduced the senior members of the Barakzai nobility who clustered around, beginning with Amir Khan, his half brother and the chief of Ghazni. Amir Khan stepped forward and bowed, which was no easy task, for he was the most obese man Harlan had ever seen. Without preamble, the huge courtier asked Harlan if he could recommend any medicine that would reduce his weight, explaining that "it exceeded the strength of any horse [and] he was obliged to move about in a palankeen born by eight men, and ride upon an elephant when traveling." Next, Dost Mohammed ushered forward his son and heir, Mohammed Akbar, "a very handsome youth about 12 years old, of intelligent aspect, fair complexion, large, black, expressive eyes and much self possession." Fourteen years later, this "fat, chubby faced boy" would murder the English envoy to Kabul, as a prelude to the slaughter of a sixteen thousand–strong British army in the passes of Afghanistan. Now a black-bearded mullah pressed forward, and demanded to know whether the Christian visitor could tell him "the locality of the Seventh Heaven," which, needless to say, Harlan could not, much to the mullah's satisfaction. Yet another member of the court, with "amateur pretensions in medical science" (which was rich coming from Harlan) launched into a learned disquisition on Hippocrates and Aristotle.

Now Dost Mohammed spoke again, and the courtiers immediately fell silent as the amir's conversation turned to Harlan's homeland, this fabled place far beyond the farthest mountains. Peppered with questions about America's culture, and "riches, the number of inhabitants, the animals and many particulars," Harlan's esteem for this intellectually curious prince rose another notch: "The Sirdar was very inquisitive about America, the New World he called it, and asked innumerable questions with sound judgement." Dost Mohammed's questions tumbled out, one after the other. Are the Americans and English the same people? "I replied they were of congenial blood but politically separate." How was America ruled? "I explained to him the nature of our government, which he pleasantly remarked resembled the Avghaun system of tribes." This comparison would not have gone down well in Washington, where politicians considered themselves above tribalism, but it was close to the mark, and still is. "He asked in conclusion what, in all my travels, had been most wonderful and worthy of commemoration." Here was an opportunity for a compliment, and Harlan's response stands as the very first exchange of diplomatic pleasantries between America and Afghanistan. He replied that he had seen many wonderful sights, but no spectacle more remarkable than the one now taking place in the Bala Hisar: "Your Highness, in friendly intercourse with a native of the New World, for in that event the antipodes have come together."

There was more to this than flattery: Harlan meant what he said. The American had come to Kabul armed with assumptions of cultural superiority, but here was a prince evidently the equal, in intelligence and sophistication, of any Western ruler. In Dost Mohammed Khan, Harlan had found a man from his own mold, and a worthy adversary. As Kipling wrote:

> Oh, East is East, and West is West, and never the twain shall meet,
> Till Earth and Sky stand presently at God's great Judgement Seat;
> But there is neither East nor West, Border, nor Breed, nor Birth,
> When two strong men stand face to face, though they come from
>   the ends of the earth!

As Harlan rose to leave, Dost Mohammed "offered with characteristic suavity the freedom of his country, telling me that his city and country, poor as they were, should be at my service, and our friendly relations synonymous with one united family." This courteous, gracious, inquiring man may have been the warlord he had come to dethrone, but Harlan left the meeting, the first of many, deeply impressed.

Harlan was now free to explore his new surroundings, beginning with the Bala Hisar itself, a teeming warren of narrow streets dominated by the palace, and an extraordinary salmagundi of races and creeds: the Qizilbash, the prince's Persian bodyguard, were the most powerful tribe within the walls of the fortress, but here too lived Afghan nobles, Hindu bankers, Jews, and even a tiny community of Armenian Christians, numbering perhaps twenty-five people. Tombstones, including the grave of a bishop, indicated that there had been a Christian population in Kabul since the sixteenth or seventeenth century. Outside the city an infidel was liable to be killed on sight, but within the fortress, in a remarkable instance of natural religious tolerance, the Muslim and Christian communities happily intermarried.

From his window, Harlan could see a wooden tower with a gilt cupola where "the Saddozai kings were accustomed to sit and enjoy the breeze wafted from the snow-capped Hindoo Kush." To the north the mountains etched a cragged and forbidding skyline, but southward lay the fertile Kabul valley, "extensive plains interrupted by short ranges, disconnected low hills and undulations," a vast shimmering carpet of green stretching to the horizon, "weeping willows intermixed with the tall poplar and graceful cypress, relieving the background of rocky hills and importing an aspect of richness and grandeur to a landscape of unrivalled perfection." Harlan saddled Flora and rode out into "one vast garden of exquisite beauty."

"The city is a jewel encircled by emerald," he wrote breathlessly, "with flowers and blossoms whose odours perfume the air with a fragrance elsewhere unknown." Shujah's magnificent gardens in Ludhiana had been, he now realized, no more than a pale imitation of this "sweet assemblage of floral beauty." Harlan's writing burst into flower as he noted down the "ornamental trees, apple orchards, patches of peach and plum trees, vast numbers of the mulberry of various species, black, white and purple, with the sycamore, the tall poplar, the sweet scented and the red and white willows, the weeping willow, green meadows, running streams and hedges of roses, red, white, yellow and variegated."

Every morning and afternoon, he would ride out among the blooms and blossoms of this fragrant oasis. He was an object of curiosity to the local populace, but never one of resentment or aggression. The people of Kabul seemed remarkably tolerant of strangers: "In most countries, few Mahomedans will eat with a Christian; to salute him, even in error, is deemed unfortunate, and he is looked upon as unclean. Here none of these difficulties or feelings exist."

Accompanied by Mohammed Ali, whose curiosity was no less than his own, Harlan would meander through the teeming streets and markets of the city, delighting in the busy scene and assiduously recording every sight, sound, and smell, a notebook in one hand, and in the other a glass of grape juice or iced sherbet, cooled by fresh snow brought by donkey from "the elevated ravines of the Caucasus" (like most of his contemporaries, Harlan refers to the Hindu Kush as the "Indian Caucusus").

Wandering through the bazaar, Harlan was transfixed by the quantity and variety of fruits flowing "into Cabul with a providential munificence, blessing the people with health, plenty and cheap living." The market stalls overflowed with cherries, apricots, plums, peaches, grapes, seedless pomegranates, soft-shelled almonds, watermelons, pears, apples, and walnuts. The grapes were vast and succulent, "and so abundant and cheap that I have had my charger fed upon them in place of grain." Like Babur before him, Harlan developed a passion for the delicate wild rhubarb that grows luxuriantly on the hills about the city, and carefully listed all the ways it could be preserved, bleached, and served. The mulberries were so plentiful, he wrote, that "the poor live upon mulberries and bread, the former of which may be procured for the trouble of gathering."

After the fruits, Harlan identified every grain, every variety of rice and corn, the different species of beans, and even a strange pea (presumably chickling vetch) that, if wrongly cooked, "will cause partial palsy of the superior extremities," but when hammered into a thin wafer "may be eaten with impunity." The smell of roasting kebabs wafted deliciously through the streets. Harlan declared the mutton of the fat-tailed sheep to be "the best of its kind," but one might also buy venison, wild sheep, and, to his disgust, horse and camel, as well as quantities of water fowl, mountain partridges, and pheasants. Sparrows, netted as they migrated across the valley at the end of winter, were brought to market in their chattering thousands, although Harlan could never bring himself to try a delicacy that involved such "a vast expense of life."

Spring in Kabul was a time of festivity, "joyously hailed by the expectant natives," with feasting, dancing, and gambling, as perfumes and music filled the air. Harlan was swept up in the carnival that greeted the new season. "Bird fanciers carry out in covered cages their larks and nightingales, and their swelling throats rend the air. Crowds gather around professional storytellers. There the merry laugh, and the excited faces of wondering listeners attest to a contented and leisure loving people. The pursuit of a Cabullee is to devise and enjoy the pleasures of life, and he explains with gusto 'Each moment's pleasure is a blessing. Live whilst we live, for tomorrow we die.'" Harlan would look back on these rosy first impressions of Kabul and concede that beneath the merrymaking, there was much misery among large parts of the population: "The demonstrations of happiness exhibited by the populace are transient gleams of sunlit cheer in a clouded sky," he wrote. Yet the memory of a joyful city celebrating a new spring was one he would carry with him throughout the years that followed.

Just as he had been drawn to Dost Mohammed Khan, Harlan felt an immediate community with these tough, cheerful people. Unlike many European contemporaries, as an American Quaker his assumptions of cultural superiority did not come with an attendant belief in some inherent racial superiority. His was a lofty attitude, but never a racist one.

Not surprisingly, he made friends quickly, moving as easily among the traders of the bazaar as among the nobles and court officials. Yet there was one section of the Kabul population that he could never get to know. The women of the city were mere wraiths, hidden behind veils and the all-enveloping chador. Occasionally, Harlan would glimpse female features at a door or window, but "should a stranger inconveniently approach they quickly draw the covering over their faces and retire." Entirely distinct from the respectable veiled ladies of the Bala Hisar, however, was another class of women, made up of "professional courtezans or female singers and dancers, libidinous creatures whose lives are passed in the immodest and secret intrigues of licentiousness." Courtesans and other professionals were an integral part of court life, and for all his disapproving tone Harlan was clearly no stranger to Kabul's demimonde.

While Harlan studied Kabul, Kabul was examining him with corresponding intensity. "Many respectable persons called to make acquaintance with me and gratify their curiosity." Dost Mohammed Khan himself was particularly keen to know whether this visitor from the New World was simply the tourist he claimed to be, or something more sinister. His spies set about discreetly pumping Harlan's servants for information, but always met the same response: "We know nothing of our master's previous movements or connections." The mere fact that Harlan had arrived with servants completely ignorant of his past was enough to arouse the prince's qualms.

Dost Mohammed had good reasons for anxiety, since there was widespread lingering support for the ousted king Shah Shujah, his grip on power was still tenuous and his court was rife with intrigue. Some lesser members of the Saddozai dynasty had remained in Kabul when Shujah fled, most of whom were now poverty-stricken and the subject of suspicion at court. Harlan was receiving visitors in his apartments one morning when two young men in threadbare garments entered and seated themselves in the place of honor. After an exchange of greetings, the elder of the two leaned over and whispered: "Two grandchildren of Ahmed Shah present their respects to you, requesting a donation from your exhaustless treasure." Harlan turned to Mohammed Ali, who whispered that these were cousins of Shah Shujah, princes reduced to paupers "in the capital which once witnessed the glory and power of their absolute sway," now looking for charity and perhaps suspecting Harlan was linked to their exiled relative. Harlan sent them away with a small cash gift, but the news that indigent members of the royal family had been spotted visiting him swiftly reached the ears of Dost Mohammed, who loudly remarked that he hoped the American was not being "annoyed by the frequent intrusion of similar vagrants." As Harlan observed, "this remark showed the strict surveillance under which I lived and the necessity of extreme circumspection to avoid confirming reports fraught with danger to my personal safety."

The most powerful focus of opposition to Dost Mohammed Khan was not the remnant of the royal family in Kabul, but his own elder brother, Nawab Jubber Khan. Dost Mohammed's eldest son was approaching maturity, and the amir was determined to secure the succession for his heirs; Jubber Khan was just as keen to see his own dynasty succeed.

So the two brothers were locked in an undeclared power struggle, in which they were consistently polite to each other while perpetually plotting. Relations between any Afghan prince and his siblings tended to be strained, to put it mildly. "Let no Christian be deceived by the fraternal appellation," wrote Harlan. "Amongst the customs of the Orientals, the term brother, in a community which springs from a system of polygamy, means a natural enemy, a domestic adversary, expectant heir of a capricious parent, contending for mastery in the disturbed area of family feuds."

The nawab and Harlan were natural allies, and the amir's brother began courting the American from the moment he set foot in Kabul, repeatedly inviting him to dinner and asking for his advice on medical matters. Harlan held back. Dost Mohammed already had his suspicions, and he had no wish to compound them by consorting with his rival.

The nawab was not the only courtier to make overtures. Some had even hinted, discreetly, at sympathy for Shah Shujah's cause. The heaviest hints came from Hajji Khan, an ambitious soldier of fortune whose service to Dost Mohammed Khan had earned him the governorship of Bamian province. Hajji was an inveterate conspirator, "ever dissatisfied with his fortune, rapacious, false and invidious." These were precisely the qualities Harlan was looking for, so when Hajji Khan invited him to a secret meeting, the American agreed. Dressed in the costume of a merchant, accompanied by a lone servant, Harlan presented himself at Hajji Khan's residence at midnight.

"My host, a man of imposing personal appearance with a conspicuous black beard, was seated in an audience chamber occupying the place of honour. He arose as I entered, advanced to the edge of the carpet to meet me, and welcomed me with an animated suavity and the familiar bearing of a soldier. Fruit was laid before us upon a lacquered wooden tray—mulberries, cherries, apricots and grapes. Iced sherbets and preserves and sugar plums, cones of white sugar and tea." Before heading to India, Amirullah had advised Harlan to beware of poisoning. The warning came back to him now. "I was careful to taste only of those refreshments he first partook."

After some desultory conversation about the weather, Hajji Khan launched into a denunciation of the amir, "filled with exaggerated statements of his unrequited services to the family of Dost Mahomed, his dissatisfaction and determination to advance his individual interests." The black-bearded rebel now unveiled a simple and brutal plan. His daughter's wedding, he explained, would take place shortly in the Bala Hisar, and Dost Mohammed had been invited as guest of honor. Once the amir was seated, Hajji proposed to seize him, cut off his head, bar the gates of the fortress, and proclaim Shujah king once more. "Nothing is easier," he declared. "One word from you and the affair is accomplished!"

Harlan, not knowing whether the proposal was made "in good faith or in the wily cunning of a designing hypocrite," sensed a trap. The wrong answer would be fatal: "I might, at that instant, have felt the sudden grasp of the headsman's iron hand." If he agreed to the plot, and Hajji Khan reported him to Dost Mohammed, he would surely be killed. If he declined, and the offer was a genuine one, then Hajji Khan would fear for his own life and kill Harlan as a precaution. "I preserved my coolness," wrote Harlan. "An evasive answer was necessary. Hadjie Khan's confidence must be secured." Harlan launched into a long disquisition, made up in equal parts of flattery and fudge. Just in case one of the amir's spies might be eavesdropping, he loudly "protested against any attempt to exalt our fortunes upon the ruin of Dost Mahomed who, as my host, I could not be induced to injure in thought or deed."

Rather than ambush the prince, he suggested, why did they not join forces for an assault on the rich and accessible lands bordering the Indus—precisely the proposal that had so appealed to Dost Mohammed during their first interview. "*There* is a principality worthy the acquisition of your adventurous spirit," Harlan added ingratiatingly. Hajji Khan "started up in ecstasy, embraced me and swore by my beard that I was an angel of salvation," and then performed his own self-inflating soliloquy. "He saw himself co-equal with Dost Mahomed, a sovereign prince," remarked Harlan, no stranger to kingly ambition himself. Leaving Hajji to "these fine dreams of the imagination," Harlan hurried home, "satisfied that Hadjie Khan would report favourably to Dost Mahomed."

Harlan's command of Persian had by now improved to the point that he was able to move freely around the city, without attendants, exploring every corner of this kingdom "secluded from the world." Harlan had lived a rough and demanding life, but Kabul brought out the poetry in his soul, and as spring gave way to summer, he observed that "truly, there is no other country so worthy the name of an earthly paradise." Often he would ride out into the mountains and sit in the sun-shine reading or writing in his journal, suffused with a calm he had never known before: "The voice of music floats upon the air, the solitary shepherd attending his flock upon the mountain skirt pipes his wild notes, startling the skylark and the nightingale to responsive melody. The heat of summer is tempered by surrounding snows, and there is a soft gladness and serene repose imparted to the feelings by the sun's rays."

Then cholera struck, transforming this earthly paradise into a char-nel house. Harlan had seen cholera cases in India, and he now watched in awe as the disease advanced relentlessly on Kabul. The epidemic of 1828 was on a scale never seen before: "Reports reached us of the prog-ress of cholera from lower India to Lahore," wrote Harlan. "Thence by gradual and fatal movement along the great commercial highways of upper India, it advanced to Peshawar. Like the withering march of a vast army the plague pursued its course, striking down myriads in appar-ently systematic devastation."

Harlan was appalled and fascinated by the sheer caprice of the dis-ease, which killed so many at random and spared others, then vanished as suddenly as it had attacked. He heard the plague before he saw it. "Alarm and wailing were the harbingers of the calamity. Weeping of children for the dead, and the vociferous grief of instinctive mourning rent the air, as corpse after corpse in rapid succession was borne through deserted streets to their graves beyond the city. Shutters and doors were taken from the shops to carry away the dead. The city soon became de-serted of its inhabitants. Silence followed the tumult." According to Afghan tradition, when any member of a family was about to die, rela-tives would make a sacrifice. "Over the lintel of innumerable doors, pieces of meat, the flesh of sheep or of cattle, might be seen hanging, in-dicating the presence of cholera within." The stench of rotting flesh rose from the city and wafted up to the castle walls, which might keep out an army, but not the waterborne cholera morbus bacteria.

The tiny Christian community within the Bala Hisar appealed for Harlan's help. "Very few revived under any form of practise," he wrote, for the medicine of the time offered no effective treatment beyond shots of brandy. Severe vomiting and diarrhea were usually followed by death, within days, and sometimes hours. Frustrated by his inability to fight the disease, Harlan was moved by the stoicism of the inhabitants. In his journal, he recorded how a certain "Sooleyman, an Armenian of exemplary bearing, resignedly exclaimed over the expiring struggles of his little child, 'The lord giveth and the lord taketh away, blessed be the name of the lord.'"

Harlan expected to be infected at any moment. Instead, the disease struck his companion Mohammed Ali. The delightfully eccentric Persian had always claimed to understand the ancient mysteries of science and magic, and as the sickness gripped him, he resorted to the oldest and least effective remedy. "He sent for a bleeder and depleted freely. I looked at him from the terrace, sitting upon a stone in the court as the blood flowed from his arm. He turned towards me his purple visage, and smiled a ghastly grin." Mohammed Ali had become a dear friend, perhaps the closest human bond Harlan had known. He had often teased the little man about his fussy manners and self-important airs, but the Persian had been a staunch ally. "I had seen much of the disease in India and therefore knew his fate," wrote Harlan, who stayed by his friend's side as he "became prostrated and unconscious," his end almost certainly hastened by loss of blood. Harlan was profoundly moved by the way Mohammed Ali greeted death and "submitted to fatality with a sigh."

Harlan buried Mohammed Ali in a grave outside the city walls; grieving for his friend, unable to listen any longer to the lamentations of the bereaved. Harlan kept riding until he reached a walled village named Shennah, five miles east of the city. There he took temporary lodging and began treating himself with brandy as a "stimulating prophylactic" against the illness. "I remained at Shennah twenty days and my health was preserved throughout the awful scourge," he wrote.

Dost Mohammed Khan had been absent from Kabul on a punitive expedition when the plague struck, and he and his court were currently encamped three miles outside the city waiting for the epidemic to subside. As usual, the amir was accompanied by Hajji Khan, and Harlan now received a message from the black-bearded plotter inviting him to discuss arrangements for their forthcoming invasion of Sind. "I thought the farce should be sustained a short time longer," wrote Harlan, who promptly set out for the prince's camp, a journey requiring a long detour around the city. Arriving at the camp shortly before nightfall, he paid a brief visit to Hajji, reassured him that their plan was on course, and set out again for Shennah. He had no wish to remain in Hajji's company a moment longer than necessary, but exhaustion soon caught up with him. "Fatigue induced me to halt at a mosque. I entered the dark chamber and groped about for a cot, but being unsuccessful in the search I threw myself at length upon the straw spread out over the floor and endeavoured to sleep. Restless from the heat of the season, I rolled over and throwing out my arm felt a companion by my side. Thinking one of my servants lay there, I called to the person. My companion remained silent and immovable. I laid my hand upon his shoulder, shook him and raised his arm to awaken him, but my effort was labour bestowed upon the dead. My companion was a corpse. The body of a cholera patient."

Death, which had stalked him for so many weeks, seemed to have followed him to bed in the darkness. Terrified and nauseated, Harlan rushed outside into the moonlight, stumbling over more corpses as he fled. "Perceiving the horrible adventure," one of his servants thrust a bottle of brandy into his trembling hand, and Harlan gulped gratefully. "I felt revived and reassured by the draught," he wrote, but nothing would have induced him to reenter the morgue-mosque. He ordered his servants to saddle up again, and turned his horse's head, not toward Shennah, but into the city itself. He had now held hands with the cholera; disease-ravaged Kabul could hold no greater horrors. Dawn was breaking as Harlan, traumatized and slightly tipsy, entered a ghost town. "No inhabitant was observable. The city shops were shut, gloom and silence prevailed, only interrupted by the sound of my horse's feet ringing through the streets, reverberations which conveyed a sense of solitude and desolation in the midst of a great city."

Harlan resumed his quarters in the Bala Hisar, and waited for the first symptoms to strike. But the disease had disappeared "after 20 sanguinary days," wrote Harlan. "Five thousand dead, about four in twenty of the population, rested in the cities of silence beyond the walls of Cabul." To his astonishment and admiration, Kabul seemed to awaken, as if from a delirium, and then erupted in celebration. "Festivals and congratulations and condolences again brought together a community humiliated by affliction, and the busy tumult of life displaced once more the agonistic revery of terrific death."

8

THE ALCHEMIST

Amirullah had been waiting for the epidemic to subside before returning to Kabul, and Harlan's trusty mace-bearer now reappeared, bringing additional cash and a letter of instruction and commendation from the ex-king. As Harlan observed, "these letters reached me unintercepted, and 'twas well they did for the discovery of a correspondence with His Majesty would have been attended by fatal results to my person." Amirullah had fulfilled his mission admirably, but it would be his last service for Harlan. The garrulous interpreter announced that he wished to leave this plague-infested city and return to India. Harlan let him go with reluctance, but reflected that he was no longer dependent on the Afghan since his Persian was now fluent, and his former disguise as a holy man unnecessary.

Mohammed Ali and Amirullah had helped to steer Harlan through the perilous waters of what he called his "diplomatick movements" in Kabul, and with both gone he was more reliant than ever on his own resources. "As I could not prudently entrust my views to the execution of subordinate agents, my personal direction of the ex-king's policy, which became a difficult and dangerous affair, was of essential importance." He had by now developed an intense distrust of Hajji Khan, whose protestations of friendship were becoming ever more passionate, and less and less credible. Nawab Jubber Khan, the undeclared leader of opposition to the amir, had recently become even more popular among the discontented elements at court by opposing Dost Mohammed's new tax regime. The time was ripe, Harlan decided, to strike an alliance. "I determined upon using him for my purposes by securing his adhercnce to the ex-king, combining a powerful element of domestic treason with the issue of the royal cause." A message was duly sent to Jubber Khan, stating that Harlan was now planning to leave Kabul and would like to meet the nawab before departing.

The next morning Harlan made his way to the nawab's house in another part of the Bala Hisar, where he was greeted like an old friend by "a man of portly figure and dignified bearing." Jubber Khan was less poised than his younger brother, thought Harlan, but plainly his equal in intelligence. "Kind, affable and urbane in his deportment, sincere and unostentatious, he expressed himself highly gratified with the pleasure of making an acquaintance he had long desired to achieve." Harlan should become his guest from this moment forth, declared the nawab, seating himself on a bank of cushions and pushing a large tray of fruit toward his delighted guest. "You have, I fear, seen but little of our most attractive charms for strangers. This is the season to enjoy Cabul. Throw aside your determination to leave, and join me in an excursion to some of my gardens." Harlan, who had no intention of leaving anyway, accepted at once.

A visit the following day from Hajji Khan's oily emissary convinced Harlan that he had found his protector just in time. "This functionary informed me that Dost Mahomed was returning towards the city and had expressed to Hadjie Khan his surprise that the 'feringee' should still be living in Cabul." As a self-professed "traveller," the prince had pointed out darkly, Harlan was doing precious little traveling. Hajji Khan was fearful for Harlan's safety, his *mirza* explained, and recommended that he leave Kabul at once, "Lest your eyes receive a wound."

This was either a warning or a threat. Either way Harlan, now secure in the backing of the second most powerful member of the ruling dynasty, felt sufficiently emboldened to rid himself of Hajji Khan's meddling. "The Mizra was coolly informed that I had become the guest of Nawaub Jabber Khan and he might tell his master if any person's eyes were to be wounded, the Hadjie had better look out for his own." The secretary was stunned, and even more so when Harlan declared that he intended to remain for at least six months to enjoy autumn in Kabul. "The old man sucked his cheeks and dropped his jaw," but then "composed his excitement with a pinch of snuff, gravely stroked his beard," and backed out obsequiously. Harlan congratulated himself on another lucky escape: "As the Nawaub's guest I was independent of the Hadjie's machinations and of the Sirdar's power."

The nawab and Harlan had much in common, quite apart from any political advantage they hoped to extract from one another. An avid horticulturalist, the nawab owned extensive landed estates and two fortresses south of Kabul, each with gardens of legendary beauty. A keen socialite and generous host, Jubber Khan liked nothing more than a truly sumptuous picnic, and Harlan had been the nawab's guest for just a few days when he was invited to a party at one of his host's rural estates. This was no mean affair, but a lavish open-ended shindig, with "feasting, promenading, carrolling and playing." The American left a vivid portrait of the alfresco banquet laid on by this early-nineteenth-century Afghan party animal.

The party set off from Kabul at sunrise: the nawab and Harlan, with half a dozen servants carrying carpets, food, and bedding, and some twenty other guests, each with servants, bringing the total to about sixty people in all. Harlan felt a little conspicuous, being dressed in European costume and the only one who was armed, but the nawab soon put him at ease. At about midday, they reached the garden and settled down to what Harlan called a "déjeuner à la fourchette," consisting of "six sheep in the form of Kabob with much bread" and an array of fresh fruits. "Of these the Avghauns ate voraciously, consuming incredible quantities without appearing to stay their stomachs for the subsequent feast of roast mutton." Again, to Harlan's surprise, wineskins were produced, the nawab declaring merrily that "wine was a glorious adjunct to the enjoyment of a Cabul autumn." The nawab's harem, meanwhile, enjoyed a separate party, hidden from sight behind walls of canvas.

Once everyone was sated with food, the entertainments began. "Several learned men of the party were full of poetry, whilst the musicians played guittar solos, sang [and] performed vocal chorus with an orchestra of violins, cymbals, triangles and small drums." As the afternoon wore on, Harlan primly noted that everyone was becoming increasingly plastered. "The chief musician got drunk and abused the Nawab in the free language of a mad Bacchanal, at all of which His Highness laughed most heartily, and a mullah being overtaken by strong brandy was stuck in the midst of his genuflections, unable to rise from his knees." With the wine flowing freely, a pistol shooting competition was suggested, which gave Harlan the opportunity to show off his marksmanship and fine pistols, which were much admired by the nawab. "I regretted the inability to replace them prevented me from presenting them to him."

The conversation turned to the recent epidemic, which all agreed had been inflicted by an evil spirit. One of the guests, who was either more imaginative or drunker than the rest, claimed he had seen a "monstrous apparition [with] cloven feet and forked tongue, with bear's claws and thunderbolt tail, [which] seemed to characterise a Satanic likeness of the cholera spirit!" Another, a nephew of the nawab and a famous fighter "said to have cut in two a horseman in chain armour," declared that the cholera had been sent as a sign by Allah to the wicked people of Kabul. The ferocious young noble claimed that he had survived the epidemic "by hard drinking and smoking intoxicating drugs." (Many years later, recorded Harlan, "in a fit of melancholy, he cut off his women's heads and threw their bodies into the river" and ended up "a drinking, smoking, imprecating wretch." Harlan was nothing if not an apostle of clean living.)

At sunset the picnic finally drew to a close, but as the party rode home in the twilight, Jubber Khan turned to Harlan and remarked bibulously: "I have an attractive garden hereabout at which we may prolong the pleasure of our excursion. What say you to a halt there and another day of extemporaneous amusement?" That night, in the nawab's fortress at Hindki, Harlan slept on the finest Persian carpets, and awoke to find, outside the window, a vista that seemed to stretch into eternity. "The castle stood upon a plain, carpeted with clover and Lucerne. The garden before it was terraced and combined the ornamental display of flowers with an orchard perspective, relieved by a low range of naked rocky hills bounding the horizon." An elaborate watering system sent streams of water tumbling over the terraces, each thirty yards broad, the first planted with blue flags, tulips, white and yellow lilies bordered with wisteria, and the next thick with pink pansies, gilly flowers, scarlet poppies, and white roses. "Fountains played upon the further end of the terrace, throwing up columns of clear water that gracefully ran down, spreading and falling over the terrace's breast, whence it flooded the third and last plateau, over an extended bed of narcissus."

Breakfast was taken in the shade of a small orchard, beneath grape vines loaded with fruit. The nawab's hospitality even extended to Harlan's dog, which was treated as an honorary *feringhee*. "Dash always accompanied me in my excursions, and was a much admired guest," wrote Harlan, noting that although the animal was regarded as unclean "the maxim of 'love me love my dog' is nowhere so literally carried out as amongst the Orientals." One day led to another, and then another, each spent lounging in the nawab's garden, picking fruit off the trees, and idly chatting. Finally the nawab reluctantly suggested that the party make a move "before our pleasures palled," and they rode slowly back to Kabul, after a picnic which had continued, uninterrupted, for almost a week.

The partying was not without purpose, however, for it had enabled Harlan to sound out the nawab's intentions with regard to Shah Shujah. A most subtle and supple politician, Jubber Khan indicated that while he would be only too happy to increase his own sway at the expense of his brother, he was no revolutionary. Rather, he foresaw "strengthening his power by [opening] a communication with the Indo-British government." Harlan recommended that the nawab send a friendly letter to Claude Wade, the British agent at Ludhiana, on the back of which Harlan would add a note, explaining the nawab's position and influence.

The deepening friendship between Jubber Khan and Josiah Harlan would be pivotal for both. In the Afghan it stoked a fascination with the mysteries of Western civilization. "From this time," wrote Harlan, "he became the advocate and hospitable friend of every Christian who subsequently visited Cabul, whether amateur travellers or political agents." In Harlan, the alliance reinforced a belief that in Afghanistan chiefs and kings might be made as easily as plucking fruit from a tree, and that with the help of Jubber Khan or Shah Shujah, or both, he too could rise to power in this volatile and lovely land. On his return to Kabul, Harlan found a message from Dost Mohammed, offering a formal post as the amir's military adviser. Emboldened by his new friendship with the nawab, Harlan responded in a manner that was brazen to the point of impertinence. "I replied with sarcasm that I should not object to participating with Dost Mahomed in a share of his government as one amongst the oligarchy, but had no design of compromising my reputation by servility." Dost Mohammed's response was understandably furious: "What arrogance is this? If the Lord of India himself should visit Cabul, I am the man to command him." It was remarkable that the amir, who had killed people for less, did not have Harlan strangled instantly for such impudence.

Perhaps the nawab intervened, for Jubber Khan was genuinely fond of Harlan. A few weeks after their picnic, Harlan suffered an attack of what he called "cholic," a crippling abdominal pain and fever that confined him to a couch. The nawab was constantly at his bedside, nursing him back to health with tender care. "His kindness and solicitude were unbounded," wrote Harlan, deeply touched by the gentle benevolence of the Afghan prince. The amir also inquired after his health, although perhaps with less generous motives, and sent numerous unidentified medicines, "all of which I very carefully avoided," wrote Harlan.

With the return of his health, Harlan's restlessness revived. He had now spent more than a year in Kabul, and his efforts to unseat Dost Mohammed had reached an impasse. Indeed, he was no longer sure that such an object was even desirable. Shah Shujah had not stirred from Ludhiana, let alone launched the promised invasion, and the Kabul ruler appeared to be strengthening his hold on power. In his discussions with Jubber Khan, Harlan had implied that the British might support a restoration of Shah Shujah. The nawab's reply was a masterpiece of noncommitment. "On the presumption that Shujah be supported by financial diplomacy of the Indian government, His Majesty will find myself an able and devoted servant, but mark: without that assistance, no domestic feud shall induce me to sacrifice my family interests to the pretensions of obsolete royalty, for he is an enemy of our race." In other words, he would not betray his brother in favor of the hated Saddozai pretender, unless Shah Shujah arrived in force, backed by British gold; in which case, he would.

Harlan relayed this message to Wade, but instead of encouraging the British to back Shujah's claim, it had a rather different effect. Harlan was supposed to be gathering intelligence with the utmost discretion; he had no authority to forge alliances in the Company's name, let alone foment revolution. Wade decided that Harlan was overreaching himself. "I suggest that no further communication be held with him," the British agent told Calcutta. "In my opinion, he is merely endeavouring to impose upon the Afghans as a British Agent, and letters from us will help him to impose on these simple people." Harlan, unaware of this development, continued to believe that Shah Shujah could be restored to the throne with British support. Ten years later the British would finally do what Harlan was suggesting, but by then the American was playing for the other side.

As he prepared for a second winter in Afghanistan, Harlan dreamed of new adventures. "The season was far advanced," he wrote in November 1828. "Fleecy, scudding clouds gathered over the country and the Caucasian alps were covered with snow. The people of Cabul wrapped themselves in sheepskin cloaks. The fading vegetation and leafless trees indicated the approximation of winter." Perhaps, he told the nawab, he might continue where Moorcroft's fatal journey had ended, and try to get to Russia through Bokhara, but the nawab insisted that the road was blocked with snow. Instead, the ever-hospitable Jubber Khan invited Harlan to accompany him to his fortress near Jalalabad, where he was accustomed to winter, returning to Kabul after the snow had melted. Harlan gave in to the nawab's entreaties, but before setting out, he paid a farewell visit to Dost Mohammed. The amir was as gracious and unreadable as ever, and no doubt thoroughly relieved to see the back of Harlan. The two men had jousted from a distance, and would clash again, but even during their brief first acquaintance, Harlan had come to admire the Afghan monarch for his polished manners and ruthless political judgment: "His perfect knowledge of the people over whom he was called to rule, and his unprincipled readiness at despotic sway, made him remarkably well adapted to govern the worse than savage tribes he had to command." The amir was an inspiration.

In late November, with winter closing in, the nawab and Harlan left Kabul in the teeth of a howling snowstorm. Yet after a forced march, the altitude dropping with every step, they seemed to enter a different land, and a different season. "The transition from winter to spring is sudden and remarkable," wrote Harlan. "We left the mountains covered with snow and, in the course of a single march, we descended into a low country where we saw the earth fresh with flowers." The fortress at Tetung, "a superior castle with very lofty walls and towers," was Nawab Jubber Khan's pride and joy: eight years earlier the place had been a grim valley covered in river stones, vast and sterile, but by sheer willpower, and slave labor, the nawab had cleared away the stone and shipped in tons of soil to form a fertile crust, eighteen inches deep and a mile square, on which now flourished an artificial park, dotted with groves of mulberry trees and "redolent of flowers and narcissuses." As they descended into the valley Harlan was lost in admiration.

Harlan would remain for four months in this extraordinary man-made oasis. On fine days, he and the nawab would ride out together to explore nearby burial mounds "said to be the graves of those great men who lived contemporaneously with the patriarchs." These included an enormous mound forty yards long and known as the grave of the prophet Lot. Harlan was tempted to excavate Lot's presumbed tomb, but thought better of it out of deference to the Muslim veneration for the dead.

The evenings were spent playing chess, writing in his journal, and conversing with the nawab and his guests. Of these, there was one whom Harlan found particularly fascinating, "a prominent individual of mysterious reputation and remarkable personal appearance known by the appellation of 'Moolvie.'" No one seemed to know what his real name was. "He was a native of Lahore, a man of short stature, slightly made, very dark complexion and piercing black eyes. He wore the top of his head shorn and dressed in the costume of his native country. His deportment was grave, secluded and suspicious, contemplative and silent, [and] humility characterised his language." The Moolvie (now usually maulvi) is a theological title, and this was the most highly educated native Harlan had ever met. "His ostensible profession was medicine," Harlan recorded, but it seemed "there was no science in which this man could not attain a distinguished reputation. He was an Arabic and Persian scholar. The medicine of the ancient Greeks he had learned [and] he affected equal familiarity with the sciences of medicine, astronomy, judicial astrology and jurisprudence." More intriguing yet, he was said to be versed in "mathematics, magic and the supernatural."

Harlan also discovered, to his astonishment, that the maulvi "was an enthusiastic Rosicrucian," a member of the secretive worldwide brotherhood claiming to possess esoteric knowledge handed down from ancient times. The Rosicrucians, venerating the cross and the rose, were supposedly founded by Christian Rosenkreuz, a fourteenth-century German traveler, who was said to have acquired occult wisdom on trips to the Middle East, which was then imparted to his German followers. Rosicrucianism was also linked to the study of alchemy. The late Mohammed Ali had dabbled in alchemy, but the maulvi was a professional who proclaimed himself an expert in the art of transforming base metals into gold.

Many members of the Afghan aristocracy were fascinated by alchemy, the ancient amalgam of science, mysticism, and fraud, offering unlimited gold, and a golden opportunity for confidence tricksters. Mohan Lal, the most astute native chronicler of the period, noted several ruses used by fraudulent practitioners to hoodwink the credulous. One was to take a quantity of mercury and apparently turn it into gold over heat, by "secretly introducing some gold inside the charcoal, and, after the quicksilver has been evaporated, the more precious metal is left to delight the wisacre, and to tempt him on to further expenses." Another method involved filling a hollow stick with gold fillings and sealing the end with wax. When a pot was stirred with the stick, the wax would melt and the filings would drain into the mixture, leaving a gold residue when the liquid boiled away. In the nawab, the maulvi had found a powerful protector, for the secret of alchemy was one that many men would kill for. "The Nawaub's weak side consisted in a devoted pursuit of the Philosopher's Stone," wrote Harlan, who mocked Jubber Khan for believing that the right alchemical potions could "renew the vigour of youth, prolong life and transfuse the pallid cheek of age with the glow and radiance of youth and health." Harlan was convinced that hunting for occult secrets could drive one to madness, for he had seen several such "magicians" (presumably Sufi ascetics) on his journey through the mountains. "Men devoted to the pursuit frequently become infatuated monomaniacs. They flee from the society of their species to the solitude and silence of mountain fastness, and wander in the glens and ravines avoiding man, with the deportment of maniacs, mountain hermits, naked with the exception of girded loins, long matted hair hanging in massive locks over the face and shoulders, bright iron chains encircling the waist and armed with clubs or spears. Many of these persons pass their lives in search of alchemical herbs." The nawab had not reached this level of infatuation, but he was obsessed with alchemy in general, and with the maulvi in particular.

Harlan was equally fascinated by this strange and scholarly little man, partly because he could not decide whether the maulvi was sincere, slightly insane, or simply a fraud. "The common sense of an European education overruled the evidence of experiments which were attributed to sleight of hand." The maulvi's favorite trick was to demand some chemical, herb, or other substance that was impossible to find. Years earlier, he had been part of the entourage of Sultan Mohammed Khan of Peshawar, the chief who had come to Harlan's rescue a year before. The maulvi had begun a grand alchemical experiment for the sultan to turn mercury into solid silver, but insisted that he needed "fish of a peculiar species all weighing exactly alike" to complete the process. "With considerable expense of time, labour and pecuniary means, the river was dragged with nets for thirty miles, day after day," until finally fish meeting the specifications had been found. Whereupon, the maulvi announced that all the fish had to be of the same sex, something he had forgotten to mention before. Since the fishing season was now over, the experiment had to be abandoned. The nawab had heard these stories, but dismissed them by saying that "if true, they merely proved the Moolvie had declined disclosing his art to his former patron, which he was justified in withholding."

The maulvi resented being interrogated about his alchemical knowledge, and had a most effective method of deflecting questions. "An inquiry, however distantly proposed, would throw him into a fit of abstraction. He then drew his cloak around his person with folded arms, sank his chin upon his breast, and closing his eyes retired within himself." If the probing persisted, he would have a brief, but alarming fit. "He would sink his head up to the ears in his cloak, bend down his form with the face towards the earth and roll about his unearthly coal black eyes as he looked out through the dark, thick scowling brow. He would mutter indistinctly the words of an Arabic incantation and recover again with an electrical start his ordinary air of composure and tranquil gravity."

Harlan suspected that this was mere playacting. "The Moolvie was an imposter," he wrote. Yet he was also a most beguiling character, and good company. "This dark practiser of blacker arts could assume a gay and cheerful air, and at times he would revel in the reckless levity of loquacious intercourse." He was a master calligrapher, a poet "sublimely eloquent upon the subject of love," and a lover of music: "A fine voice would entrance his faculties [and] as sweet harmonious strains crept over his nerves, the harshness of his features relaxed and his expression assumed a placid repose."

Harlan did not believe the maulvi could make gold, yet he was intrigued by his claims, and in particular by his knowledge of the mysterious Rosicrucian rites, hermetic philosophy, astrology, and Islamic medicine. In turn, the little alchemist was convinced that Harlan was privy to powerful magic. He was particularly curious to discover that Harlan was a Freemason, and begged him to reveal the secrets of that brotherhood. "I, in return, solicited initiation in the principles of those occult dogmas which constituted the secrets of his order," wrote Harlan. History makes strange combinations, but here was one of the oddest: a Rosicrucian sorcerer from Lahore and a Freemason from Pennsylvania haggling over their secrets like bazaar merchants, inside a fortress in the Afghan mountains. "Upon this point of mutual curiosity we were occupied many days: abstract science, the Platonic and Stoic philosophy and the Pythagorean doctrine of numbers were, with Freemasonry, subjects of the Moolvie's studies and inquiries." Their discussion lasted for weeks, and then years.

The nawab and the maulvi spent hours conducting complex experiments, while Harlan looked on, making sarcastic remarks. From time to time the alchemist would demand some special ingredient, and the nawab would dispatch couriers to find whatever was needed. It was all most enjoyable, and completely pointless. "Circumstances added me to their secret investigations, but I was an amateur who observed proceedings without being involved, experiment following experiment with the same fruitless result," wrote Harlan. The maulvi kept insisting that he was on the verge of success, before finally coming up with the hilariously implausible excuse that turning base metals into gold was not possible in a snowy climate. Harlan watched with undisguised skepticism as the little alchemist hunched over his evil-smelling potions. "Results which conflicted with my knowledge of chemical laws I regarded with suspicion, aware that incredulity was the best safeguard against imposition." In vain he pointed out that the laws of science made it impossible to forge gold out of lead, let alone create silver out of fish. "These principles I explained to him at length and systematically from a treatise on the subject then in my possession," wrote Harlan. When it became clear that the maulvi was immune to persuasion, Harlan instead offered to help him translate into Persian the pharmaceutical compounds in the *Edinburgh Dispensatory*, part of his traveling library.

So the weeks passed happily, in scientific argument, horticultural conversation, and antiquarian exploration among the local ruins; but as spring arrived and Jubber Khan prepared to return to Kabul, Harlan declared that he would now be moving on. He had not restored Shujah's crown, let alone won power for himself, and he had reached the conclusion that "Dost Mohammed Khan [was] too strongly entrenched, for the time being, to be dislodged" without British help.

Alexander the Great, after subduing Afghanistan, had turned to India for his next conquest, crossing the Indus and striking deep into the Punjab. Now Harlan, too, looked east. Ranjit Singh, the great maharaja of the Punjab, was known to employ foreigners as generals and administrators, and although the Sikh ruler had rebuffed Harlan's earlier advances, and his spies had trailed the American up the Indus, he might now be prevailed upon. Harlan resolved to seek his fortune in the glittering Sikh capital of Lahore. "One of the five French officers in Runjeet'h Singh's service died about this time," he recorded, "which left an opening that encouraged me in commencing a military life and maturing my plan for the restoration of Shujah ul-Mulk by proceeding to Lahore." With gratitude and regret he took leave of Nawab Jubber Khan, his host, that most "hospitable, sincere and frank" of Afghans, who presented him with a magnificent case of hunting hawks, and cattle to carry "the superfluous baggage which had accumulated by the addition of servants to my domestic establishment of Christian, Georgian and Armenian extraction."

The maulvi accompanied Harlan for a few miles, and as they rode together, the little alchemist handed Harlan a document "noted in cipher." This, the maulvi announced gravely, was the secret formula for purifying matter, "the unfinished process of his alchemical experience," the secret of the philosopher's stone. The maulvi noticed Harlan's dubious expression as he handed over the treasure, and "his eyes flashed with indignation, but controlling himself, he gazed on my face with a clouded brow and sunk into a fit of abstraction. In a few minutes he recovered his equanimity, but his occult lessons then ceased. They were not renewed until years subsequently." Before parting, Harlan tried to offer the maulvi a bag of gold as a token of their friendship, but for a man who had spent his life trying to manufacture the stuff, the alchemist was surprisingly indifferent to wealth, and handed the gift back. "With gold," said he, "subdue the selfish and appease the oppressor. Gold is but a glittering type of infamy. Let not the altar of friendship be polluted by an evil offering. No mercenary hope supplants the claims of love." Harlan and the maulvi would meet again and continue to explore the esoteric mysteries of alchemy, with explosive results.

The most direct route to Lahore was via the Khyber Pass, but the nawab had warned that the Khyberees were not to be trusted. Instead he advised crossing over the mountain, a route that would oblige Harlan to cross and recross the Kabul River, using frames fastened on inflated skin floats, precisely the method that Alexander the Great had used to cross the Oxus. Finally, after an eight-day journey, Harlan, once again wearing the costume of a Muslim divine, arrived in Peshawar, the city he had left nearly eighteen months earlier. "It was about sunset when I entered the outskirts of Peshawar. As we passed through the narrow streets my servants, all mounted, followed in line, some carrying hawks fluttering upon their fists and others mounted upon the baggage mules. The shopkeepers and natives gazed at the retinue with exclamations of surprise at the sudden advent of a caffila [trading caravan] which from the complexion of the persons composing it they supposed to be from Kashmir."

Mea Kummer ud-Din had been given advanced warning of his friend's return, and was overjoyed to see him. "The reception I met with justified all that I have said of his kindness and hospitality," wrote Harlan. More surprisingly, the chiefs of Peshawar, including Yar Mohammed who had treated him with such suspicion before, were now the souls of hospitality. Again, Harlan could thank the Nawab Jubber Khan, who had written to his half brother, insisting that the American be received courteously. The chief's garden seemed unchanged. "The vernal equinox of 1829 was near, the flowers and blossoms were in bloom and I found the chiefs as I had left them a year before, immersed in flowers, surrounded by musicians, dancers, singers." The pleasant life of Peshawar's multiple chiefs was about to end in the most unpleasant way, at the hands of the man Harlan now looked to for employment.

Harlan explained to the mea that he was anxious to press on to Lahore, to try his hand in Ranjit's service, and the holy man duly provided a cavalry guard of twenty disciples to escort him to the Indus. Harlan had intended to cross the river at Attock, but on arriving at the river port he found a large force of Sikhs already encamped there with the intention of overawing the Peshawar chiefs into paying their annual tribute to Ranjit. Harlan could probably have persuaded the commander of the Sikh force to let him pass, "respect for the European character [be-ing] a prominent feature of the Sik policy," but he was keen not to draw attention to himself. "I preferred retaining my incognito until about to enter Lahore," he wrote. "I had now become sufficiently familiar with the Persian language and the character of the people to impersonate exactly the reputation I assumed."

Several days elapsed during which the Sikh sentries attempted to ex-tract a bribe, a delay made more frustrating by the sudden arrival of a wild-looking fakir, apparently attached to the Sikh force, who stationed himself outside Harlan's tent and demanded money, loudly and aggres-sively. "He insisted upon having a rupee and drawing forth a razor threatened to wound himself unless I complied," wrote Harlan. A ser-vant was ordered to chase the beggar away, but as he did so, the fakir "deliberately placed the edge of the razor on the top of his naked scalp and extending his left hand towards me demanded a rupee with a threat-ening aspect. I laughed at him, and he commenced gradually drawing the razor towards his forehead. Still I supposed he did not seriously in-tend to wound himself but steadily gazing in my face he proceeded with his operation, the blood streaming down his face. The determined fakir had decidedly earned a rupee by the coolness he exhibited, and really wishing to save the fellow from more serious injury, I felt compelled to give him a rupee." As a doctor, Harlan also felt obliged to stitch up and bandage his gashed head, after which the fakir "retired with an obei-sance that had more the character of sarcasm than thankfulness."

Thoroughly bored with waiting, Harlan decided that the Sikhs might procrastinate indefinitely and so rode down to the next ferry cross-ing at Shadipur, fifty miles to the south. There, however, a Sikh officer insisted on searching the party's baggage for "drugs such as are brought from Tartary via Kabul into India" and instead "discovered the inevitable cocked hat, which at once disclosed the true character of the owner." This turned out to have a most positive effect, for the Sikh had formerly been a soldier in the British army, and he now became the soul of courtesy.

Safely across the river and into the Punjab, Harlan hastened toward Lahore. No one gave a second glance to the holy man with the long bushy beard and dusty retinue who made camp a few days later on the outskirts of the great walled capital of Ranjit Singh's realm, with its sky-line of domed mosques, Hindu temples, and Sikh gurudwaras. "Next

morning, donning the full dress of a European officer with a cocked hat
and shaded by a large scarlet silk canopy, I made my entrée into the city,"
wrote Harlan, "much to the astonishment of the court who had not
heard of the approach of a European." He had sent a message ahead to
one of the French officers serving under Ranjit Singh, and now, with
solemn pomp, Harlan's cavalcade entered the great white mansion of
General Jean-François Allard, leader of the maharaja's tiny band of
foreign mercenaries.

9

COURTIER OF LAHORE

There was no greater self-made potentate than Maharaja Ranjit Singh, the Lion of Lahore, Lord of the Five Rivers, the Sikh soldier-statesman whose guile and ruthlessness had forged the disparate Sikh clans into a powerful independent kingdom with a mighty army. The scion of one of the least important of the twelve Sikh clans, Ranjit Singh was only ten when he first went into battle. At the age of thirteen, he had revealed his mettle when he was attacked by a traitor, and in response had "impaled the assailant on his lance, cut off his head, and ridden back in triumph with the gory trophy fixed to his spear-point." At seventeen, he had begun, with force, flattery, and diplomacy, to forge the warring Sikh tribes into a unified nation, and by twenty-one he was undisputed Prince of the Punjab, the most powerful independent ruler in India.

In 1809 the young maharaja had signed a pact with the British, ensuring them of Sikh support should Napoleon, as the Company feared, attempt an invasion of India. The Treaty of Amritsar confirmed him in his domination of the lands north of the Sutlej, and it would endure as long as the maharaja himself, making the Punjab, in the words of one scholar, "one of the few really successful buffer states in history." By the time Ranjit died he had swallowed up most of the surrounding principalities, in addition to the rich provinces of Kashmir and Peshawar.

The Sikh despot was a consummate diplomat and schemer: "He cared neither for the happiness nor the lives of others," wrote one British observer, "except as either might be concerned in the obstruction or advancement of his projects." Like other empires before and after it, the Sikh dominion thrived on continual expansion, and the maharaja was a paragon self-made power. As one contemporary remarked: "He has, by his own achievements and unassisted intellect raised himself from the situation of a private individual to that of a despotic monarch over a turbulent and powerful nation. By sheer force of mind, personal energy and courage . . . he has established his throne." For anyone contemplating self-created kingship, Ranjit Singh was a role model.

To build a force second in might and discipline only to the British Indian army itself, Ranjit had employed European mercenaries to train his men in Western military tactics, most notably the use of artillery. Some of these "advisers" were deserters and other military flotsam, but the most senior were former officers in Napoleon's army who had wandered east after the disaster at Waterloo. In 1822 the maharaja recruited a French chevalier, Jean-François Allard, and an Italian, Jean-Baptiste Ventura. They were joined four years later by the ferocious Neapolitan Paolo di Avitabile and another Frenchman, Claude Auguste Court. These four, aided by a Spaniard named Oms, had turned the Sikh troops into a formidable fighting force, and in return Ranjit rewarded them with every luxury: comfortable houses, gold, and concubines. Secretly he regarded one *feringhee* as much like another: "German, French or English, all these European bastards are alike," he once observed.

Harlan had first learned of Ranjit's foreign officer corps on his arrival in Ludhiana, and he now presented himself at the sumptuous home of Allard, the doyen of the group and a man of "high character, of polished manners and of a most amiable disposition." A native of Saint Tropez, Allard had been twice wounded serving in the army of the Emperor Napoleon, who awarded him the Légion d'honneur and promoted him to captain of the Seventh Hussars. Following Waterloo, Allard had wound up in the Punjab, "in a state of extreme poverty." After some hesitation, Ranjit Singh commissioned him to raise a corps of dragoons and lancers in the European manner. Allard's were "the most noble looking troops," clad in red jackets, trousers of dark blue cloth with a red stripe, and "turbans of crimson silk ornamented in the centre with a small brass half moon from which sprang a glittering sprig about two inches in height." He was awarded the rank of general, a salary of three thousand pounds per annum, and a fine house in Lahore.

General Allard was known for his hospitality toward Europeans of all ranks, and Harlan was warmly received by the Frenchman at the gates of his mansion, "a miniature Versailles in the midst of an Oriental bazaar." The Frenchman was "attired from top to toe in crimson silk," with a mighty forked beard that came to two remarkable points halfway down his chest. "His *wings* are beautiful white hair, and his moustachios and the middle of his beard quite black," wrote a later visitor. "He looks like a piebald horse." It was a simple matter for Allard to arrange for Harlan's presentation at Ranjit Singh's durbar, but he warned that there were drawbacks to working for the maharaja. "It is very difficult to get an appointment here," he observed presciently, "but still more so to get one's dismissal, when once in office."

Harlan's first audience with the one-eyed king of the Punjab was an extraordinary experience. The Lion of Lahore usually received visitors sitting "cross-legged in a golden chair, dressed in simple white, wearing no ornaments but a single string of enormous pearls around the waist, and the celebrated Koh-i-Noor, or Mountain of Light, on his arm." Ranjit's court was a gorgeous picture of color, power, and wealth, but the maharaja himself, tiny, blind in one eye, and scarred by the smallpox, was no oil painting. The traveler Baron von Hügel thought him "the most ugly and unprepossessing man I saw throughout the Punjab. His left eye, which is quite closed, disfigures him less than the other, which is always rolling about wide open and much distorted by disease. The scars of the smallpox on his face do not run into one another, but form so many dark pits in his greyish-brown skin; his short straight nose is swollen at the tip; the skinny lips are stretched tight over the teeth, which are still good; his grizzled beard, very thin on the cheeks and upper lip, meets under the chin in matted confusion; and his head, which is sunk very much on his broad shoulders, is too large for his height, and does not seem to move easily." Emily Eden, the sister of the future governor general Lord Auckland, was more succinct: "He is exactly like an old mouse, with grey whiskers and one eye."

Ranjit was fully aware of Harlan's progress into Afghanistan, and of his attempt to take the fortress at Tak. The maharaja admired ambition, and his remaining eye appraised Harlan coolly. A few months earlier, in September 1828, the Spanish officer Señor Oms had died of cholera. Without preamble, Ranjit proposed that Harlan take his place, with command over "a complete brigade, formed of five regiments." It was a substantial offer, but the American politely declined. "Harlan replied that he was a doctor, and not desirous of permanent employment, but that his main object was to proceed to Calcutta and embark for his own

country, the USA. If, however, he wished to detain him he had no ob-
jection to remaining for a few months."

Harlan was being deliberately coy. He knew that the maharaja had
even more attractive posts in his gift, including provincial governor-
ships, and by emphasizing his medical expertise Harlan was playing on
one of Ranjit's weaknesses. Although personally courageous and physi-
cally robust, the maharaja was known to be a raging hypochondriac. As
one visitor remarked, Ranjit "invariably consults every medical man
he may meet with, and almost as invariably rejects their advice," and
courtiers were obliged to test any and every treatment, whether or not
they were ill. "The medicine is always given to some of his Sirdars who
are forced to swallow it in his presence, and are then shut up that he may
be able to judge of its effects." Ranjit had particular faith in foreign medicine, believing that *feringhee* doctors could even raise the dead.

Ranjit took no offense at the rejection of his offer. Indeed, he was intrigued by the American doctor. Lahore's newswriters swiftly sent news
of Harlan's arrival to Claude Wade in Ludhiana, who reported to Calcutta that the new arrival at court in Lahore "seemed to be well provided with funds, and did not seem at all anxious for employment."
Wade astutely surmised that, "should Mr. Harlan really be desirous of
establishing himself at Lahore, he probably considers that apparent
indifference presents the best chance of success."

Harlan "negotiated on and off with the maharaja over employment,"
and a few months later Wade reported: "Mr. Harlan is still at Lahore. I
hear the Maharaja offered to employ him on Rs 1,000 a month, but there
were other conditions attaching to the offer which prevented Mr. Harlan
from accepting it." Ranjit was a stickler for small print: foreign employees were banned from eating beef, shaving their beards, and smoking.
The French officers had agreed to the first two conditions, but balked at
the third. *Feringhees* were also expected to sign formal contracts, which
might include clauses requiring them "to marry a native of the Punjab; to
serve faithfully against all Ranjit's enemies; and never to quit his country
or his service without special leave obtained for that purpose."

While angling for a lucrative post, Harlan explored Lahore, "that
wonderful, dirty, mysterious anthill" in Kipling's words, a roiling world
suffused with the "heat and smells of oil and spices, and puffs of temple
incense, and sweat, and darkness, and dirt and lust and cruelty." Lahore

was rife with disease, and Harlan's medical expertise was in hot demand, particularly among courtiers who had been forced to act as guinea pigs and who now needed treatment to counteract the effects of the maharaja's medications. "The people about the court appear to consult him frequently, and to have considerable confidence in his medical abilities," Wade reported. "But it occurs to me that Ranjit Singh is not inclined to offer Mr. Harlan sufficient temptation to stay permanently with him." John Palmer, the Calcutta merchant who had put up money for Harlan's Afghan expedition in the hope of solving the Moorcroft mystery, wondered whether the American was using Ranjit for that purpose. "I trust that Dr. Harlan will get service in Lahore and be able to screw something out of Moorcroft's plunderers by the influence of Runjeet," Palmer wrote to Wade. "If not, there is no reason why the Doctor should not restore our remittance."

As a permanent guest of the ever-hospitable Allard, and with a growing medical practice at court, Harlan was plunged into the colorful and louche world of the Lion of Lahore. No European visitor ever failed to point out that while Ranjit Singh was a fine general and a wily diplomat, he was also a dedicated debauchee, a sensualist with a passion for beautiful women and boys, a taste for laudanum, and an addiction to alcohol in the form of his own lethal homemade cocktails. His parties were fantastic bacchanalian bouts, and his sexual stamina legendary. Victorian visitors, with a shudder of ill-disguised titillation, sent home reports detailing "every species of licentious debauchery" at the Lahore court, where Ranjit "indulged without remorse or shame in sensualities of the most revolting description." Revolting perhaps, but also rather fun, to judge by the length of time these visitors chose to stay.

At such events, Ranjit's own corps of Amazons, female warriors on horseback, "selected from the prettiest girls of Cashmere, Persia and the Punjab" would gallop around "magnificently dressed, armed with bows and arrows." Ranjit liked to tell guests, with a lewd snigger, that this was the only part of his army that he was unable to discipline. He particularly enjoyed a catfight. "He orders the attendance of all his dancing girls, whom he forces to drink his wine, and when he thinks them sufficiently excited, uses all his power to set them by the ears, the result of which is a general action in the course of which they tear one another almost to pieces."

Meanwhile everyone—dancers, singers, soldiers, guests, and above all Ranjit Singh himself—got fighting drunk on the maharaja's home-brew. Exactly what was in this drink remains a mystery, but it was believed to contain, among other things, distilled grape juice, orange seeds, and precious gems. "His wine was extracted from raisins, with a quantity of pearls ground to powder, and mixed with it, for no other reason than to add to the expense of it," wrote one suffering hangover victim. "It is made for himself alone, and as at his parties he always helps you himself, it is no easy matter to avoid excess." Ranjit Singh, Maharaja of the Five Livers, sucked the concoction down in terrifying quantities, and expected his guests to do likewise: "The only food allowed you at these drinking bouts are fat quails stuffed with all sorts of spices, and the only thing to allay your thirst is this abominable liquid fire."

Like most drunks, Ranjit found the subject of alcohol quite fascinating. Visitors to Lahore were peppered with questions about their drinking habits: "Do you drink wine? How much? Did you taste the wine which I sent you yesterday? How much of it did you drink? etc., etc." Inevitably, the boozing took a toll. Charles Masson observed, after meeting him for the first time, that the maharaja's addiction to "copious cups of the strongest spirits, with his unbounded sensuality, has brought on his premature old age with a serious burthen of infirmities." Honest doctors repeatedly told Ranjit to stop drinking; he ignored them, and consulted other practitioners, for he was convinced that his potion, so far from killing him, was keeping him alive, and he entrusted the mixing of it to one man alone: Fakir Aziz ud-Din, his personal physician and adviser.

Harlan had always been an abstemious drinker and Ranjit's drunken orgies brought out the Quaker in him; although a frequent visitor to the durbar, he made a point of staying as far away as possible when the maharaja was on a bender. Instead, he tended to socialize with the other Europeans, including John Brown, his former traveling companion who had taken service with the maharaja. A strange assortment of mercenary adventurers had washed up in this distant corner of India. Allard was a charming and mild man, displaying a "gentleness to the natives of India" that was exceptional among foreign mercenaries. Like Harlan, he had taken the trouble to master Persian and was fluent enough to compose Persian poetry. But his fellow officer, the Italian Paolo di Avitabile, was of a very different stamp: often drunk, wildly eccentric, and notoriously brutal, Avitabile was terrifying to behold, being "affected with a contraction of the muscles of the face, which, on account of his long, crooked nose, appeared the more striking." Tall and well built, this Neapolitan peasant born in 1791 was "ordinarily apparelled in a magnificently laced Horse-Artillery jacket, wide crimson Turkish trousers drawn in at the ankle, golden girdle and very handsome sabre; his large Jewish features and bronzed countenance adorned with fierce moustachios, which look like twisted bayonets, with a thick grey beard, the whole surmounted by a gold-lace forage cap, which he never takes off." Avitabile was regarded by his contemporaries as "a clever, cheerful man, and full of fun." He was certainly a skilled administrator, with a genuine interest in agriculture and judicial reform, but he was also capable of spectacular cruelty, and a firm believer in summary capital punishment, whether or not the victim was guilty. Martin Honigberger, a physician from Kronstadt who became one of Ranjit's doctors, reckoned "the pleasure he took in seeing people hung by the dozens must be attributable to the affection of his brain [and] an immoderate indulgence in champagne." The whiskery Italian had more time for chickens than for the native people he terrorized. A British visitor sketched a typical Avitabile day: "He hangs a dozen unhappy culprits, looks to the payment of his troops, inspects his domestic concerns (especially his poultry yard, in which he takes much pride), sets a-going a number of musical snuff boxes, etc., all by way of recreation before dinner." A former peddler, Avitabile had developed a lucrative trade "selling artificial jewellery, watches, musical boxes and obscene pictures." A keen pornographer, Avitabile's home was decorated in supreme bad taste, the bedroom walls "covered with pictures of dancing girls."

Jean-Baptiste Ventura was another Italian, a Jew from Finale di Modena whose original name had been Reuben Ben-Teura. Handsome and arrogant, he was said, quite erroneously, to have risen to the rank of colonel under Napoleon. In fact, Ventura's military experience was as limited as Harlan's, but as infantry commander of the Fauj-i-Khas, or model brigades, he claimed much of the credit for the Sikhs' military success. (He also designed the Gurkha uniform, subsequently adopted by the British.) Ventura married a European woman in 1825, but he had entered into the swinging life of Ranjit's court with gusto, even once accepting, and winning, a bet with the maharaja that he could not seduce Lotus, the king's favorite dancing girl. The story reflects well on both men: on Ventura for having the guts to take up the bet, and on Ranjit for resisting the temptation to have him killed on the spot when he won it. The maharaja bore no grudge against his Italian general, who was rewarded with large grants of land.

Like Harlan, these were men who embraced their own solitude as foreigners in a strange land. Another foreign general, Claude Auguste Court, named his Lahore residence "L'Ermitage," while Avitabile adopted the Cistercian motto: *Beata Solitudo, Sola Beatitudo*. Initially, at least, Harlan's "relations with the French officers were excellent." Avitabile even went to the trouble of having the foreign officers painted together in a tableau. The group portrait once hung in a private home in Peshawar and has since vanished, but according to one scholar it depicted "Allard with his Napoleonic saber, Court as a sailor, Avitabile with his rapier, which had belonged to Akbar, and Harlan, once prince of Ghor in Afghanistan."

In addition to the troops under his foreign commanders, Ranjit Singh could call on an array of feudal levies and other warriors including the Ghorcharas, some with "a shirt of mail, with helmet inlaid with gold and a kalji or heron's plume; others were gay with the many-coloured splendour of velvet and silk, with pink or yellow muslin turbans, and gold-embroidered belts carrying their sword and powder-horn." The most feared of his combat troops were the Akalis, who could be seen "riding about with sword drawn in each hand, two more in the belt, a matchlock at the back and then a pair of quoits fastened around the turban—an arm peculiar to this race of people, it is a steel ring, ranging from six to nine inches in diameter, and about an inch in breadth, very thin, and at the edges very sharp; they are said to throw it with such accuracy and force as to be able to lop off a limb at sixty or eighty yards." At Ranjit's death the army numbered twenty-nine thousand men, with 192 guns. Harlan's military experience had so far involved a brief stint in British uniform, several months marching his own ragtag army toward Afghanistan, and an abortive attempt to take a fortress by bribery: he studied this imposing military machine, fashioned along European lines, with avid interest.

While negotiating with Ranjit Singh, Harlan did not forget his previous employer, although his faith in Shah Shujah was ebbing fast. After a few months in Lahore, he traveled back to Ludhiana, to pay a visit to the court. The exiled king was pleased to see him, even though his mission had not met with success. "To attest his profound appreciation of his agent's abilities," he presented Harlan with a dress of honor and bestowed upon him two splendid titles: henceforth he was to be known by the exiled Afghan court as "The King's Nearest Friend" and "Companion of the Imperial Stirrup." Harlan would later describe this honorific as "a title of nobility, beyond which there is none more exalted in an Oriental court." In addition, Shujah decreed that Harlan would become "Nawaub of Khoorum, a rich and extensive valley in the White Mountains south of Cabul," when the king regained his crown.

Not for the first time, Harlan wondered just how much energy and treasure the exiled monarch was prepared to expend in bringing that event about. Maintained by a British pension, surrounded by flowers and servile courtiers, the king seemed content to bide his time, "consoling himself for the loss of his kingdom in a domestic circle of 600 wives, but always 'sighing his soul' towards the mountains and valleys of Afghanistan, patiently waiting the *kismet*, or fate, which was to restore him to his throne."

Harlan returned to Lahore to find a summons to the durbar, for the Lion of Lahore had an improved job offer to make, of a most memorable sort. Harlan recalled the maharaja's words thus: "I will make you Governor of Gujrat, and give you 3,000 rupees a month. If you behave well, I will increase your salary. If not, I will cut off your nose." This was no idle threat, for the maharaja's retribution was absolute, swift, and exceedingly painful. Europeans never ceased to be awed, and disgusted, by Ranjit Singh's summary justice: "He is himself accuser, judge and jury; five minutes is about the duration of the longest trial in Lahore." The sentence was carried out with similar dispatch. "His executions are very prompt and simple: one blow of an axe, and then some boiling oil to stop all effusion of blood." The doctor Honigberger described one unfortunate individual "whose nose, ears and hands had been cut off by Ranjit Singh, and whose nose had been so well restored in the mountains that we were all surprised and confessed it could not have been done better in Europe. They formed the nose out of cuticle of the forehead." Harlan had no wish to endure such rustic rhinoplasty, and realizing that this was less an offer than an order, he swiftly accepted. As one contemporary observed: "The fact of his nose being entire, proved that he had done well."

Before sending him to the prosperous province of Gujrat, however, Ranjit decided first to test Harlan's administrative abilities in the districts of Nurpur, which he had seized from its rajah in 1816, and the adjoining territory of Jasrota: in Harlan's words, "two districts then newly subjugated by the King of Lahore, located on the skirt of the Himalah mountains." As one scholar has observed "these two districts were fairly wealthy, and the appointment of Harlan most honourable for a first employment." In December 1829, Harlan took up his new post as governor of Nurpur and Jasrota, becoming, in effect, the paramount local chief with his own army and broad responsibility for collecting taxes, raising feudal levies, and administering justice. "From this period," he wrote, "in the military and civil service of Ranjit Singh, I acquired a more intimate knowledge of Asiatic life, and became familiar with oriental splendour in a seven years carnival of luxurious existence." Like other provincial governors and foreign generals, he was expected to attend the Lahore durbar at regular intervals and provide reports on his activities.

While Harlan's power was growing, the terra incognita of which he ruled a part was also becoming steadily less mysterious and more interesting to the neighboring British. That interest was registered by the arrival in Lahore of one Lieutenant Alexander Burnes, a young envoy of the East India Company and an avid player of the Great Game who would gain fame and fortune in Afghanistan, and perish at the hands of the Kabul mob at the age of thirty-eight.

The fourth son of the provost of Montrose, a Scotsman with all the energy and resilience that made his countrymen such effective agents of empire, Burnes had begun his service in British India at the age of sixteen. Gifted and ambitious, he was promoted rapidly and in 1830, aged twenty-five, he had been chosen to perform an important diplomatic task: the presentation of five heavy dray horses and a carriage to Ranjit Singh, a suitably extravagant and exotic gift from Her Britannic Majesty to the Sikh monarch. Ranjit's obsession with horses was second only to his love of women and drink, and he was a superb horseman, although a comical sight on horseback since, "being of very low stature, [he] appeared, when on the back of the animal, like an ape on an elephant."

Ostensibly, Burnes's mission was to flatter the maharaja and reinforce the Anglo-Sikh alliance; secretly, he was to assess the navigability
of the Indus in case it should one day become necessary to send British
warships up it. Some thought this barely concealed espionage beneath
British dignity—"a trick . . . unworthy of our Government," wrote one
member of the governor general's council. Burnes felt no such qualms;
if Harlan never met a superior whose instructions he did not question,
Burnes never came across an order he could not bring himself to obey.

After an eventful one-thousand-mile journey up the Indus, Burnes
arrived in Lahore on June 18, 1831, where the vast gift-horses were looked
in the mouth, hooves, and ears and admiringly declared to be "little elephants." Ranjit Singh welcomed the young envoy with a salute of sixty
guns, each fired twenty-one times, a bevy of dancing girls, and a gust of
flattery that was extreme even by Oriental standards, describing him as
a "nightingale of the garden of eloquence, that bird of the winged words
of sweet discourse"—a description that the British officer lapped up, for
among his many better qualities, Burnes was deeply vain. Inevitably, he
was made to quaff pints of Ranjit Singh's disgusting beverage, and privately declared that the maharaja would surely not long survive "a
nightly dose of spirits more ardent than the strongest brandy." The cen-
sorious tone was typical, and hypocritical, for during his time in Asia this
apparently straightlaced Scot would gain a reputation as a bon vivant and
womanizer, whose unfettered libido would contribute to his unpleasant
end. Burnes and his party were wined and dined for fully two months at
Lahore, and during that time he was undoubtedly introduced to Harlan, although neither recorded their first meeting. Six years Burnes's
senior, Harlan never disguised his opinion that the younger man was a
posturing, overpromoted amateur, and Burnes was swift to sneer at the
American. Indeed, it is hard to imagine a more ill-matched pair than the
preening, privileged Scotsman and the hard-grained Pennsylvanian.

Little is recorded of Harlan's administration in Nurpur and Jasrota,
but he must have been an effective governor, for in May 1832, Ranjit
Singh fulfilled his promise and transferred him to the larger province of
Gujrat, at a starting salary of Rs 1,200 per month. Like other foreign employees, Harlan was required to swear an oath "upon his Bible that so
long as he lived he would continue to serve the Maharaja, would do nothing foreign to his interests, and discharge all of his duties faithfully, even

to fighting against his own country." The last clause was easy enough to agree to, since the chances of America going to war with the Punjab were slim indeed. The appointment was accompanied by a splendid ceremony, during which Harlan "was invested with a sword, an elephant, and a magnificent dress of honour, in the presence of the Vizier Rajah Soocheat Singh, and General Allard (the former investing him) and despatched to Guzerat'h in command of a brigade of artillery and infantry."

"I was both civil and military governor," wrote Harlan, with the power to do what he liked so long as order was maintained and taxes collected. "The military commandment is pretty much independent, and has virtual mastery by the tankhwahs (rights) he holds on the revenues and the troops he has to enforce them," one contemporary observed, while another noted his "zeal and ability" as a governor. No less a figure than Henry Lawrence, the officer who would go on to become a famed administrator of the North-West Frontier under British rule, visited Harlan soon after his installation in Gujrat and described him as "a man of considerable ability, great courage and enterprise, and judging by appearances, well cut out for partisan work."

Harlan was not the only *feringhee* to be elevated to a governorship. Paolo di Avitabile administered the province of Wazirabad, while Jean-Baptiste Ventura had been made governor of Dera Ghazi Khan in 1831. One native observer alleged that the foreign governors were just as brutal as the local chiefs. "They chop off men's hands and feet, and hang up, with as little reason as the worst of the Sikhs," he claimed. "I have seen foreigners fall into the customs, and join hand and heart in the tyrannies and vices of the Sikhs. They have the advantage of administering districts naturally rich [and] they also have the benefit, as foreigners, of being supposed by the people to be more protected by the court, and by the court to be supposed to be cared for by the British. When you count their wealth, what they own, and what they nominally receive as pay, and then look to the style in which they live, you will see that they have quickly learnt the Sikh system of government."

There is no evidence that Harlan was either corrupt or guilty of the sort of brutality inflicted by the likes of Avitabile. Indeed, his disapproval of such behavior may be one reason why his relationship with both Avitabile and Ventura began to sour, eventually turning to outright hostility. Harlan took his responsibilities seriously and attempted to improve law and order, later claiming that his combination of firmness and reform had "greatly reduced if not put aside theft in his province," while improving the morals of those over whom he ruled. But he conceded that he had used "unflinching firmness" to bring the powerful landowners of Gujrat into line. Indeed, these "filed a suit before the Maharaja against Hallan Sahib on account of his high-handed policy" and sent him "a letter full of wrath," complaining that Harlan was not treating them with the proper respect. The maharaja, a firm believer in slapping down the local aristocracy, ignored the bleating and gave his governor free rein.

Most foreigners in Ranjit Singh's service had concubines, some were married, and a few of the grander mercenaries had entire harems. There is no reason to suppose that the governor of Gujrat behaved differently, but Harlan, as always, was discreet about his romantic and sexual life. Almost all Europeans had what they termed "amours," and often children, with native women. As Richard Burton wrote during his seven years in India, a local spouse was practically official issue: "I found every officer in the corps more or less provided with one of these helpmates . . . She keeps house for him. She keeps the servants in order. She has the infallible recipe to prevent maternity and, as it is not good for man to lie alone, she makes him a manner of home." Harlan seems to have regarded women as an encumbrance to an active life, an attitude widespread among colonial administrators in British India and noted by Rudyard Kipling in the poem "The Story of the Gadsbys":

> Down to Gehenna or up to the Throne,
> He travels the fastest, who travels alone.

Kipling himself, as a young man in India, appears to have taken a somewhat utilitarian approach to sex, remarking to a friend that "the occasional woman . . . is good for health and the softening of ferocious manners." Harlan was never a philanderer. He writes admiringly of female beauty, but never of love. Tucked among his most treasured mementoes was the poem he had once written to Elizabeth Swaim.

The same year that Harlan was appointed to Gujrat, Burnes passed through the Punjab again, this time en route for Afghanistan and Transoxiana. The intrepid Scotsman was determined to explore the lands beyond the Khyber Pass, and had successfully lobbied for permission to visit Afghanistan and continue across the Hindu Kush via Balkh, Bokhara, and Samarkand to the Caspian Sea. His was to be the first formal diplomatic contact with an Afghan ruler since Mountstuart Elphinstone's mission in 1809. By May, Burnes was in Kabul where, like Harlan before him, he met Dost Mohammed Khan and lodged with the hospitable Nawab Jubber Khan. "I do not think that I ever took leave of an Asiatic with more regret than I left this worthy man," he wrote, before heading off through the mountain passes and across the Turcoman desert to the Caspian. It was an epic journey, and Burnes's superiors were almost as pleased with him as Burnes was pleased with himself. He called himself "Sikandar," Persian for Alexander, in reference to Alexander the Great. "A magnanimous name it is," he declared.

When Burnes returned to London, he found himself the toast of the capital, summoned to meet the prime minister and then the king himself. "I have been inundated by visits," he wrote in excitement to his mother, "from authors, publishers, societies, and what not . . . All, all are kind to me. I am a perfect wild beast." The attention would have turned anyone's head, and few heads turned more easily than that of Alexander Burnes. With talk of an impending clash between Russia and Britian in Central Asia reaching a pitch, his descriptions of that mysterious region sparked a furor among London's chattering classes: hostesses vied to lure him to their soirees; he was elected to the Athenaeum Club; his travelogue was awarded a gold medal by the Geographical Society. Burnes was no longer just another Company officer but "Bokhara Burnes," the "discoverer" of Afghanistan and the lands beyond the Oxus, a man fit to parlay with monarchs and potentates.

Harlan, of course, had penetrated to Kabul long before Burnes, spoke the local languages quite as well as the pushy youngster, and believed that if anyone deserved to carry the mantle of Alexander the Great, it was he. This was not a recipe for a happy relationship.

But for the time being, at least, Harlan was content to be governor of Gujrat. For company he had Dash and, somewhat to his surprise, the maulvi, the diminutive Afghan alchemist who appeared one day, unannounced. Harlan was delighted to see his friend, expecting him to stay a few days or weeks. In the event, as Harlan remarked, "the Moolvie became my guest for a period of several years." Their discussions about science, alchemy, Rosicrucianism, and Freemasonry continued where they had left off, and Harlan allowed "this black magician" to continue his experiments in the house. Although skeptical about alchemy, Harlan was fascinated by the maulvi's learning in other areas of science and philosophy. Most Europeans dismissed Eastern thought as mere mumbo jumbo, but with the maulvi as his tutor, Harlan immersed himself in "the traditional lore of Arabia" in a way that few, if any, had done before. "The Moolvie did me the honour to say he had not heretofore found a pupil like myself," he wrote. The maulvi, in turn, became convinced that Harlan was keeping some vital knowledge from him. "My refusal to explain the craft of Freemasonry added to his conviction that in the secrecy of that forbidden region of science lay the Philosopher's Stone." The maulvi even announced that he would become a Freemason himself, and "travel to Europe for the purpose of achieving the initiatory rites of membership."

The maulvi was not the only unexpected guest to appear at the governor's residence in Gujrat. Harlan had been installed for just a few months when an extraordinary, whiskery, heavily armed, six-foot apparition rode into the courtyard and introduced himself as Alexander Gardner, "Gordana Khan" to his followers: soldier of fortune, wanderer, and, even more impossibly, another American, at least by his own account. The story Gardner had to tell was almost as remarkable as that of Harlan himself. He claimed to have been born in 1785 to a Scottish father and Anglo-Spanish mother in what is now Wisconsin, although it was later alleged that he was really an Irishman from the town of Congloose. Gardner had been trained as a gunner, possibly in the British army, but ended up as a mercenary, or more accurately a roaming brigand, in the wilds of Central Asia. In the course of his adventures he had been locked in an underground dungeon for nearly a year, captured by slave traders, and attacked by wolves. Gardner insisted that he and his little band were warriors, not bandits: "We did not slaughter except in self-defence," he wrote proudly. Bizarrely, when Harlan was residing in Kabul, Gardner had been in the mountains, fighting an unsuccessful guerrilla campaign against Dost Mohammed Khan on behalf of the Afghan rebel Habibullah Khan. Gardner's wife, herself a trophy of war, and their baby had been brutally murdered by Dost Mohammed's forces, and in the wake of that tragedy Gardner had resolved to seek more regular employment: he had descended from the hills, passed through Kabul, where he was reconciled with the amir, and was on his way to Lahore to take employment with Ranjit Singh when he appeared at Harlan's door in Gujrat. There was hardly a part of Alexander Gardner that had not been injured over the years, and a gaping wound in his throat had left him unable to drink without the aid of a metal collar contraption: whenever he raised a glass, Gardner simultaneously "clutched his neck with an iron pincer."

He had been "Gordana Khan" for so long he could barely remember his original name. "I remained a few days with Dr. Harlan," he wrote, and "on meeting my countryman, I resumed the character of a foreigner, and resumed also the name of Gardner, which I had abandoned for so long that it sounded strangely in my ears." The two men shared not only a passion for adventure, but a vigorous residual nationalism. Gardner's origins may be a little hazy, but he considered himself an American Scot to the day of his death: an extraordinary photograph in his memoirs shows the whiskered fighter at the age of eighty, dressed head to foot in striking tartan, including a tam-o'-shanter-turban with an egret's plume. Harlan and Gardner took to one another instantly. They would fight on the same side for several years, and then on opposite sides for several more, but their friendship never suffered. This could not be said for Harlan's relations with other foreign officers in the maharaja's employ. Gardner himself noted the tension, for after leaving Gujrat he moved on to Wazirabad and stayed for five days with its governor, Paolo di Avitabile. "It was unfortunate that a sore animosity existed at the time between these two governors," wrote Gardner, who traveled on to Lahore and was promptly employed by Ranjit Singh as an artillery instructor.

Harlan missed Gardner's company and fantastic stories, but within a few months an even more unlikely character turned up at his door. Of all the strange and colorful figures blowing around Central Asia at this time, perhaps none was quite so eccentric, so courageously peculiar as the Reverend Dr. Joseph Wolff, missionary, theologian, traveler, and, in strict truth, semi-lunatic. Born in Bavaria in 1795, the son of a rabbi, Wolff had converted from Judaism to Lutheranism to Roman Catholicism, before finally alighting on the Church of England as the repository of the one true creed. After studying theology at Cambridge

University, he conceived his mission to be the conversion of the ten tribes of Israel, and for this purpose he set off on a bizarre, lifelong odyssey across the Middle East, Central Asia, and the Caucasus. Almost spherical in shape, he was a "most curious looking man," wrote one female acquaintance. "His frame appears very unfit to bear the trials and hardships to which he has been exposed upon his travels. His face is very flat, deeply marked with smallpox; his complexion that of dough, and his hair flaxen. His grey eyes roll and start and fix themselves, at times most fearfully . . . His pronunciation of English is very remarkable, aided occasionally by vehement gesticulation. His voice is deep and impressive [but] at times, having given way to great and deep enthusiasm, [it] becomes a most curious treble, the effect of which is so startling, one can scarcely refrain from laughing."

If sheer energy and conviction had been the only qualities necessary for converting the ten tribes, then Wolff might have succeeded, for he was a fizzing bundle of pure polemic, not a muscular Christian, but the argumentative sort. In the course of his wanderings Wolff fixed his wild eye on persons of every religion, and harangued them, in alternate bass and treble: "He argued with Christians and Jews, with Hindus and Mahomedans, with Catholics and Protestants, with Sunnis and Shias. He argued about almost everything; about the Pope, and the Millennium, and Mahomed, and the Second Coming, and the End of the World, and what would happen to all the fishes when the sea dried up. He argued good-humouredly, tirelessly, and without any regard whatever for the consequences." Often, the consequences were fairly dire: one Kurdish chief, faced with this ranting little blob of a man, immediately put him in chains; in Khorasan, bandits tied him to the tail of a horse; he was robbed of everything and stripped naked three times, and came close to being burned alive. Irrepressibly genial throughout his trials, Wolff's was a source of inspiration to some and hilarity to many, which probably accounts for his survival. The murderous amir of Bokhara, infamous as the man who had put two English visitors in a pit before beheading them, took one look at Wolff (who had come to ascertain the fate of the murdered pair) and got such giggles he was unable to speak. The sight of Wolff, clad in full canonicals with Bible in hand, made the amir "shake with uncontrollable laughter."

Wolff had first set out for the East in 1821 and spent five years wandering from Egypt to Palestine to Persia and beyond. On a brief return to London, he met Lady Georgiana Walpole, the daughter of an earl, at a dinner party, and married her. The odd couple immediately set off traveling together and, in Alexandria, had a son, who would go on to become Sir Henry Drummond Wolff, a noted diplomat and politician. Soon after the birth of his heir, Wolff had told his wife: "Bokhara and Bulkh are very much in my mind, for I think I shall find there the Ten Tribes." And off he went.

In 1832 Wolff was on his way back to India from the lands beyond the Hindu Kush, when he stopped off at Gujrat, "a considerable town" in his words. For a European, Wolff traveled light (his luggage was once described as "Bibles in various tongues, two or three dozen silver watches, three dozen copies of *Robinson Crusoe* translated into Arabic"). After his bags were unloaded and he had been shown to his quarters, the missionary was seated in an antechamber to await the governor, naturally assuming this would be a Sikh grandee in need of conversion to Anglicanism. As he waited "to his great surprise he heard someone singing 'Yankee Doodle,' with all the American snuffle. It was His Excellency the Governor himself. He was a fine, tall gentleman, dressed in European clothing, and with an Indian hookah in his mouth."

The vision introduced itself: "I am a free citizen of the United States, from the state of Pennsylvania, city of Philadelphia. I am the son of a Quaker. My name is Josiah Harlan."

"I was most kindly received," wrote Wolff, by this "very interesting man." Harlan, in turn, was entranced by the tubby, wandering priest, and told him his life story, including the part about faithless Elizabeth Swaim back in Philadelphia who had "played him false." Wolff recorded: "He fell in love with a young lady, who promised to marry him. He sailed again to Calcutta, but hearing that his betrothed lady had married somebody else, he determined never again to return to America." Harlan was equally candid about his ambitions, and Wolff noted that the American had already "tried to make himself king of Afghanistan."

The priest penned an admiring description of his host: "He speaks and writes Persian with great fluency; he is clever and enterprising. Dr. Harlan is a high Tory in principles, and honours kingly dignity; though on the other hand he speaks with enthusiasm of Washington, Adams, and Jefferson, who wrote the Declaration of Independence." The missionary may have been deeply eccentric, but he was highly observant. Harlan's monarchical inclinations, he saw, had been reconciled with his American republicanism. That evening Wolff "preached in the house of Dr. Harlan, to some Armenians and Musselmen in the Persian tongue." The next morning he left, eventually returning to England, but not before a detour to the United States, where he addressed Congress and was awarded an honorary degree at Annapolis. No doubt the missionary told his American hosts about the huge, hookah-smoking Quaker who ruled a province deep in the Punjab. No doubt he was roundly disbelieved.

While Harlan was winning new friends, he was also making new enemies. Relations with his fellow officers steadily deteriorated to the point where Harlan felt moved to complain about the behavior of Avitabile and Ventura to Ranjit Singh himself. He remained friendly with Allard, and in October 1833, wrote to the Frenchman imploring him "not to think that his declarations to Sarkar [Ranjit Singh] were directed against him, but purely against Ventura, whose politics the doctor said he could not abide." Harlan disapproved of the Italian's administrative methods, but according to one scholar, "Ventura's jaghirs [land holdings] in the territory of Gujrat may be the reason for the dispute." The Napoleonic officers looked down on Gardner and Harlan as upstart Americans. "The French and Italian officers in Ranjit Singh's service held much aloof from those of other nationalities," wrote Gardner, "and this also must have contributed to the unfriendliness."

Harlan still retained a lingering loyalty to Shah Shujah. Wolff reported that the American "informed me that the restoration of Shoojah-ool-Moolk would be of the greatest advantage to the British government." But as an employee of Ranjit Singh, he was in a delicate political position, particularly since he also "managed to keep up communication with Ludhiana." According to Henry Lawrence's native informant, the governor of Gujrat maintained good relations with the British: "Harland [sic] was once their nokar [servant], and may be so again." In 1834, his allegiances were put to the test, when Shah Shujah finally bestirred himself to make a bid, in force, for his throne. The previous year, the exiled king had struck a deal with Lahore that allowed him to march through Sikh territory; in return he would formally cede Peshawar to Ranjit Singh if the maharaja could oust the Peshawar chiefs. Shujah had set off from Ludhiana with a sizable army, aiming to take Kandahar before besieging Kabul; meanwhile the Sikhs, under General Hari Singh Nalwa, moved on Peshawar. Shujah's approach set off a fresh flurry of plotting among the Barakzai brothers; the chiefs of Kandahar and Peshawar, including Sultan Mohammed Khan, tried to persuade Dost Mohammed to come to their aid, while secretly planning to take Kabul themselves. Faithless Hajji Khan defected to the Peshawar sirdars. Dost Mohammed, however, out-flanked them all: he first reinforced his strength by taking Jalalabad, and then, at Kandahar in July 1834, narrowly defeated Shah Shujah, who quit the field while the fighting was still in progress and fled back to Ludhiana. Regardless of Shujah's flight, the Sikhs went ahead with their side of the bargain, seizing Peshawar and ousting the sirdars. Sultan Mohammed Khan fled to the mountains, as did many other prominent Peshawaris, including Mea Kummer ud-Din, Harlan's friend. The mea, already ailing, would die in the hills.

Dost Mohammed Khan had strengthened his own position by defeating Shah Shujah and out-scheming his brothers, but the great city of Peshawar, for so long a part of Afghanistan, was now under hated Sikh rule. Dost Mohammed's loathing of Ranjit Singh, and his determination to regain Peshawar, would become an obsession.

Harlan had remained aloof from these new convulsions. It was later claimed, without evidence, that he had reneged on a deal with Shah Shujah, under which he was to raise a battalion and "join him with 500 men and a lakh of rupees." More likely, as governor of Gurjat, Harlan was simply not in a position to aid Shujah, even if he had wanted to. Ranjit Singh was not about to let one of his own governors fight on behalf of the Afghan pretender and, as yet, Harlan had no cause for discontent with his employer. The rewards for serving the Sikh maharaja were great, but so were the perils, and any hint of disloyalty was likely to be met with summary punishment. (Harlan's successor in the governorship of Gujrat, an Anglo-Indian mercenary named Holmes who had "risen from bandmaster to colonel," would discover this in the most unpleasant way. Holmes, suspected of treason against the durbar, was shot and beheaded by his own men.)

Moreover, Harlan had become disillusioned with Shah Shujah. No longer did he see him as a "legitimate monarch, the victim of treasonable practices" but as "a wayward tyrant, inflexible in moods, vindictive in his enmities, faithless in his attachments, unnatural in his affections. He remembered his misfortunes only to avenge them." After the lack of gumption Shujah had displayed at Kandahar, Harlan regarded him as "vile and incapable." Harlan would play a central role in the next round of Afghan upheaval, but no longer as the King's Nearest Friend.

As the year 1834 ended, Harlan was wealthy and secure in his position. He could congratulate himself on avoiding further entanglement with Shah Shujah, whom he now considered a broken reed. Yet he was also bored, eager for a new challenge, and isolated in his fortress at Gujrat. That autumn Dash died, and Harlan was bereft. "Let his name be commemorated with the affection due to a generous nature and may the remains of my dog Dash rest in peace," he wrote, recalling the hound that had accompanied him "with unabated zeal throughout the dangers and trials of those eventful years." Harlan buried his dog within the ramparts of Amritsar, the religious capital of the Punjab. Indulged, resolute, touchy, and utterly self-confident, Dash had always considered himself to be far superior to the common canine pack, and the equal of any two-legged beast. If Harlan was the Man Who Would Be King, then Dash was the Dog Who Would Be Man.

10

THE MAHARAJA'S AMBASSADOR

Dost Mohammed Khan demanded the return of the rich and fertile province of Peshawar, and sent an elegantly aggressive warning to Ranjit Singh: "If out of haughtiness the Maharaja does not pay heed to my request, I will gird up my loins for battle and become a thorn in the courtyard of your rose garden. I will muster an army of crusaders who know nothing except fighting unto death. I will create tumult on all sides and a scene of chaos everywhere." Ranjit Singh's reply was blunt: "We have broken the heads of refractory chiefs and put our foes in irons. If the Dost, out of avarice and greed, desires to give battle with the small force he has, let him come."

The Afghan forces were indeed weak compared to the mighty Sikh army, but the amir had a powerful weapon in his armory: the fanatical religious antipathy felt by many Afghans toward the infidel Sikhs. This he now set about harnessing. Dost Mohammed had hitherto eschewed grand titles. When supporters had suggested he take the title of "shah," like his Durrani predecessors, he had replied: "I am too poor to support my dignity as a Sirdar; it would be absurd for me to call myself King." But he now assumed an even more emotive title: Amir-ul-Momineen, "Commander of the Faithful," no longer merely one prince among several, but the Sword of Islam. Dost Mohammed was personally tolerant of other faiths, a "fanatic in profession, but not a bigot in practice" in Harlan's words. By manipulating Islamic extremism among his people, however, he could unleash a holy war against the unbelievers to win back what the Sikhs had seized.

To retake Peshawar, Amir Dost Mohammed Khan needed gold, and this he began to collect by wholesale extortion. Those who refused to pay up were threatened and persecuted. When one particularly rich and unlucky merchant died under torture, the amir observed bleakly that he "wanted his money and not his death." The winter of 1834–35 was spent raising money and stirring up religious fervor in the countryside, and by spring he was ready to march his army of zealots through the Khyber Pass and down on Peshawar. There it would be supplemented by reinforcements from Bajaur under Sultan Mohammed Khan, his un-trustworthy but still powerful half brother, the recently ousted chief of Peshawar. Sultan Mohammed was just as anxious to regain Peshawar, although for his own purposes.

Ranjit Singh prepared to defend his new-won territory. More than pride was at stake, for to lose Peshawar would undoubtedly encourage other refractory elements within his domains, and possibly spark a ma-jor rebellion against Sikh rule. On the other hand, if the hated Afghans could be decisively thrashed, he might extend his dominions beyond Peshawar to Jalalabad, and perhaps even to Kabul itself. The full force of the Sikh army was assembled. Allard, Ventura, Avitabile, and Court would command the twenty-thousand-strong Fauj-i-Khas, or French division, while Ranjit Singh planned to march in person at the head of the main body of troops. Force would be met with force, but also with diplo-macy and intrigue. For this Ranjit needed someone who knew the court of Kabul, who could manipulate the intrigues among the Barakzai brothers, and who might be considered sufficiently independent to gain the respect, if not the trust, of both sides. In short, he needed Josiah Harlan. The American was summoned from Gujrat to join the ma-haraja's war party.

Dost Mohammed's army of the faithful swelled as it marched from Kabul to Jalalabad and down through the pass. "From Kohistan, from the hills beyond, from the regions of the Hindu Kush, from the remote fast-ness of Turkistan, multitudes of various tribes and denominations came flocking to the Amir's standard. Ghilzyes and Kohistanis, sleek Kuzzil-bashes and rugged Oozbegs, horsemen and footmen came pouring." Har-lan estimated that Dost Mohammed's army consisted of "50,000 musketeers, comprising a large portion of the undisciplined but able bod-ied populace of his principality," as well as numerous Ghazis, fanatical ir-regulars from the mountains. Sultan Mohammed Khan, still nominally loyal to Dost Mohammed, assembled some ten thousand Bajaur milita and waited in the wings.

Immediately after arriving at the Sikh military encampment outside Peshawar, Harlan rode out to take a look through his telescope at the motley Afghan host now swarming into the lush valley. It was a terrifying sight: "Fifty thousand belligerent candidates for martyrdom and immortality. Savages from the remotest recesses of the mountainous districts, many of them giants in form and strength, promiscuously armed with sword and shield, bows and arrows, matchlocks, rifles, spears and blunderbusses, concentrated themselves around the standard of religion, and were prepared to slay, plunder and destroy, for the sake of God and the Prophet, the unenlightened infidels of the Punjab."

The Sikhs prepared for battle. Thirty-five battalions of regular infantry and cavalry were arranged in the shape of a horseshoe around the city, the *Fauj-i-Khas*, under the foreign generals, moved up on the Afghan flank and the main Sikh force, perhaps eighty thousand strong, poised to attack Dost Mohammed's center. There Ranjit Singh paused. The Sikhs could probably have routed the undisciplined Afghans, but Ranjit, for all his belligerence, preferred to win by guile if possible, and by bloodshed only when necessary.

Harlan was summoned to the maharaja's presence and appointed an emissary of the Lahore court, Ranjit's personal ambassador to the amir of Kabul. His orders were to find out Dost Mohammed's intentions, establish terms on which he might be prepared to withdraw, and buy time for the Sikh forces to consolidate, while fomenting dissension among the Kabul chiefs and between the amir and his brothers. Harlan was to be accompanied in this mission by Fakir Aziz ud-Din, Ranjit's personal physician, barber, bartender, and confidential adviser. The fakir was a powerful presence in the Lahore court, "a fine-looking man, of about five and forty, not over clean in his person, but with a pleasant and good-humoured, though crafty-looking countenance [and] manners so kind and unassuming that it is impossible not to like him." In addition to providing counsel and medical advice, the fakir performed another vital role which, as Alexander Gardner observed, made him indispensable to the maharaja: "He alone could prepare the mysterious compounded cordial which gave the monarch fictitious strength."

Skirmishing between advance parties of the two armies had already begun when Josiah Harlan and Aziz ud-Din departed Ranjit's camp, mounted on elephants and accompanied by a small armed guard. The no-man's-land between the armies was roamed by raiding parties from both sides: the ferocious Afghan Ghazis and the equally fearsome Sikh Akalis. Gardner, who was commanding an artillery battalion, observed that "the Sikhs sadly lost many lives at the merciless hands of the Ghazis, who, each with his little green Moslem flag, boldly pressed on, freely and fairly courting death and martyrdom." The Akalis took just as many Afghan lives, with their sharpened steel quoits. Having left the Sikh lines the diplomatic party turned, not toward the teeming camp of Dost Mohammed Khan, but in the direction of the Bajaur encampment commanded by the amir's half brother.

Harlan had reason to be grateful to Sultan Mohammed Khan for interceding on his behalf during his first visit to Peshawar, but he also knew that the sultan was an inveterate schemer, determined to regain possession of Peshawar for himself. He had betrayed his half brother before, and might, Harlan calculated, be induced to do so again. For personal reasons, the sultan appears to have been more disposed to treachery than usual, for "not long before, the Amir had seized and married by force a beautiful princess upon whom the Sultan Mohammed Khan had turned a quickened and acquisitive eye. Indeed, when Dost Mohammed Khan seized the lady she was already en route to join and marry the Sultan."

News that Harlan had arrived at the sultan's camp swiftly reached Dost Mohammed, who assumed quite correctly that perfidy was afoot and his brother was preparing to defect to the Sikhs. Shortly, however, a letter arrived from Sultan Mohammed Khan "stating the fact of Mr. Harlan's arrival, and that he had been put to death, while his elephants and property had been made booty." Harlan had become a feared, almost mythical figure among the Afghans, and the news created a sensation in their camp. Amid scenes of rejoicing it was declared that "now the brothers had become one, and had wiped away their enmities in Feringhi blood."

Harlan, of course, could not have been in better health. Far from being murdered, he had been heartily welcomed by Sultan Mohammed, a fact that soon filtered back to the main Afghan camp. "A day or two disclosed that Mr. Harlan's reception had been most flattering," one ob-

Josiah Harlan in his Afghan robes. This is the only known photograph of the adventurer.

View of Kabul from the East, showing the great ramparts of the Bala Hisar, royal palace of the Afghan kings

Harlan's sketch of Shah Shujah al-Moolk. Harlan was struck by "the grace and dignity" of the exiled Afghan king, and only later came to see the truth—that he was a man of "unparalleled debauchery."

Harlan's sketch of Dost Mohammed Khan. "The outline of his face is Roman. The nose is aquiline, high and rather long, and finished with beautiful delicacy; the brow open, arched and pencilled; the eyes are hazel-grey, not large, and of an elephantine expression."

Maharaja Ranjit Singh, the Lion of Lahore, Lord of the Five Rivers, and the ultimate self-made potentate

Fakir Aziz ud-Din, Ranjit's personal physician, barber, bartender, and confidential adviser

General Jean-François Allard, the most senior of Ranjit's foreign officers, a veteran of Napoleon's army whose rigorous training helped to transform the maharaja's troops into a formidable force

General Paolo di Avitabile, the cheerful, clever Neapolitan sadist whose brutal methods finally brought rebellious Peshawar to heel

Dr. Joseph Wolff, missionary, theologian, and traveler. "He argued with Christians and Jews, with Hindus and Mahomedans, with Catholics and Protestants, with Sunnis and Shias . . . He argued good-humouredly, tirelessly, and without any regard whatever for the consequences."

Allard's Cuirassier, Lahore, 1837–1843. "The most noble looking troops," with scarlet jackets, dark blue trousers, and "turbans of crimson silk"

Three Akalis, Sikh fundamentalists who fought as the maharaja's most ferocious combat troops

Alexander Gardner. The whiskery soldier of fortune is pictured here in retirement at the age of eighty, still dressed from head to toe in tartan.

Sir Alexander Burnes in the costume of Bokhara, the most famous, flamboyant, and tragic player of the Great Game

Sir William Hay Macnaghten. The British envoy was a "self-conceited gentleman," in Harlan's opinion, who "marched into Avghanistaun with the air of a Bombastes Furioso."

The Afghan irregulars might be "a miscellaneous collection of semi-independent ruffians," in the words of one Englishman, but they were deadly shots with their long-barreled *jezail* muskets.

The Bolan Pass. The Army of Indus—including some 20,000 soldiers, 38,000 camp followers, 30,000 camels, and a pack of fox hounds—marched through the mighty defile leading to Afghanistan in 1839.

The storming of Ghazni. The "impregnable" Afghan fortress fell after Lieutenant Henry Durand blew open the Kabul gate with nine hundred pounds of gunpowder, leaving the road to Kabul open.

Afghan marksmen "traditionally employed," according to the contemporary caption. As the British fled through the winter passes, the Afghan muskets were employed to murderous effect.

(*above*) Dr. William Brydon, the only person to complete the retreat from Kabul, staggering toward the gates of Jalalabad on January 13, 1842, in Lady Elizabeth Butler's painting *The Remnants of an Army*

Dost Mohammed Khan in March 1841, shortly before the massacre. Years later he remained perplexed that "the rulers of so great an empire should have gone across the Indus to deprive me of my poor and barren country."

server reported, and it was never known "whether the letter was really sent by Sultan Mohamed Khan, or fabricated." Meanwhile Harlan set to work on the duplicitous sultan, pointing out that Dost Mohammed Khan was motivated by pure self-interest and intended to keep Peshawar, if he could wrest it from the Sikhs, for himself. Sultan Mohammed Khan should go over at once to Ranjit Singh's side, Harlan urged, promising that the maharaja "would receive him munificently, and satisfy him in all his hopes." The bait was swallowed.

Harlan's next démarche was even more brazen. Accompanied by Sultan Mohammed Khan himself and a contingent of Bajaur tribesmen, the American envoy rode into Dost Mohammed's camp, which only a few days earlier had been celebrating news of his death. The visitors were installed in a large and comfortable tent, and the following morning they were summoned to the amir's presence. The sultan insisted on bringing his Bajaur bodyguard along, although if an assassination was intended, this would prove a meager defense against the entire Afghan army.

Dost Mohammed entered, cautiously welcomed his brother and the Sikh envoys, and an exceptionally tense meeting got underway. While Sultan Mohammed Khan and Fakir Aziz ud-Din held back, the American and the amir, with an aggressive display of military plumage, circled one another like fighting cocks.

"He boasted to me that he was followed by 100,000 armed men at the moment I entered his camp," wrote Harlan. With what he hoped was sangfroid, Harlan replied: "If the Prince of the Punjab chose to assemble the militia of his dominions, he could bring ten times that number into the field, but you will have regular troops to fight, and your *sans culottes* militia will vanish like mist before the sun."

Dost Mohammed Khan was not used to being addressed this way by anyone, let alone by an infidel who had recently enjoyed his hospitality, but Harlan pressed on, speaking "in an exalted strain" of the might of the Sikh army and Ranjit's fabulous wealth, in a way precisely calculated to irritate Dost Mohammed. "He lost his temper, which he readily did, and became enraged, and then his eyes glared upon me as he replied with a characteristic shake of the head, and elevated brows." The amir's reply was a bald threat, but one couched in terms of a classical allusion that he knew Harlan, of all people, would understand. "Your appearance in the midst of my camp at this moment of general excitement may be attended by personal danger," he warned. "When Secunder [Alexander the Great] visited this country, he sent a confidential agent to the Prince hereabout, and the mountaineers murdered Secunder's ambassador!"

Harlan refused to be cowed. "Feeling myself strong in the friendship of his brothers, and the intimacy of his most influential chiefs, I answered roughly without hesitating: 'I am not accredited to you but to your brother, who is now a guest amongst you, as I am myself.' "

"My brother!" Dost Mohammed Khan exploded. "Who is the brother independent of my will? Is not the policy of my court controlled by myself, that the enemy sends an ambassador to another in the midst of my camp? Know that I am all in all!"

At this moment, despite the amir's rising fury, servants arrived with food, in accordance with diplomatic etiquette. "Civility required that food should be placed before the Ameer's brother," wrote Harlan. "Preserves, and bread, and cheese were proferred, which Sultan Mahomed declined with acknowledgments of the hospitality." The amir, however, was pressing, insisting that since the day was exceedingly hot his brother should at least take a drink of *doug*, a concoction made from fermented milk. The sultan was now convinced that the amir intended to poison him, and so began a potentially lethal gastronomic-diplomatic exchange between the brothers, under the guise of good Afghan table manners. The sultan "hesitatingly declined the proposed kindness; but the Ameer importuned him, and forthwith ordered a servant who was in waiting to produce the beverage." As the servant approached with the bowl of frothing liquid, the sultan motioned that the amir should drink first. "The Ameer excused himself, saying, 'I have breakfasted Lalla [brother]; help yourself.' " Harlan found the situation excruciatingly amusing, even though his own life depended on the outcome. "Then commenced a scene of protestation and importunity which lasted several moments." At length Sultan Mohammed insisted: "Impossible brother; it is not possible for me to take it until you have first refreshed yourself."

The bowl was placed before the amir. No one spoke. If he still refused to drink, it would be a tacit admission that the *doug* was poisoned. This was the situation Dost Mohammed Khan had hoped to engineer. To the astonishment of all, he picked up the bowl, drank deeply and then handed it to his guest. The amir had not only outmaneuvered his brother in protocol, he had also ascertained that the sultan believed his life was in danger, a clear indication of guilt.

"I drank from the same bowl and of the identical contents with which the princes refreshed themselves," Harlan wrote, adding wryly: "Sour milk surpasses any other beverage to quench thirst in a sultry climate on a hot day." As he put down the bowl, Dost Mohammed rounded on him, accusing him of interfering in matters that did not concern him, and of promoting dissension between him and his brother. Sensing that to goad Dost Mohammed further would be counterproductive, and possibly suicidal, Harlan took a concilatory tack, hinting that Ranjit might be induced to relinquish Peshawar.

The meeting ended with the correct formalities and barely concealed mutual mistrust. As Harlan and the sultan left the tent, Mirza Sami Khan, one of the amir's trusted advisers, "remarked that Mr. Harlan had used many sweet words, but that he was aware that Feringhis were like trees, full of leaves, but bearing no fruit." Sultan Mohammed Khan rode back to his camp, and Harlan prepared to return to the safety of the Sikh lines. Realizing that his position was perilous, Harlan made Dost Mohammed a peace offering of a copy of the Koran.

The amir was far from mollified, and the next day, in a last act of saber rattling, Harlan was summoned to inspect the Afghan troops so he might inform his master Ranjit Singh of the army he faced. "After witnessing a review of the army," Harlan was finally allowed to leave, but his departure was preceded by a hilarious scene. The Afghan prince had intended to ride away dramatically, having dismissed Harlan from his presence. However, to Harlan's amusement, he "put the wrong foot in the stirrup, which would have placed his face towards the animal's tail." The incident showed how thoroughly Dost Mohammed had been discomfited, according to Harlan, who managed not to laugh out loud.

For days, Harlan and the fakir shuttled between the camps, playing one party off against another and attempting to sow treachery with "Sikh gold, judiciously distributed." Alexander Gardner observed the envoys moving "day and night, backward and forward, parleying direct between Ranjit Singh and Dost Muhammad. They certainly performed this duty at great personal risk, as serious and heavy cannonading and skirmishing took place every day from morning till night between the two armies." During one visit to the Afghan camp, Harlan was reunited with Nawab Jubber Khan, who had joined his brother on the battlefield and was now actively involved in the negotiations. The amir had dispatched the nawab "to frustrate the designs of the Sikh mission, and to induce the Sultan Mohammed Khan to join his camp with the Bajaur militia." Harlan and Jubber Khan found themselves vying for the sultan's support, with no adverse affect on their friendship. As always, it was impossible to tell whose side the nawab was really on, and Harlan implied that Jubber Khan was ready to defect from Dost Mohammed: "I divided his brothers against him, exciting their jealousy of his growing power, and exasperating the family feuds, with which from my previous acquaintance I was familiar, and stirred up the feudal lords of his durbar with the prospect of pecuniary advantages."

The confrontation was at crisis point; the restless Afghan Ghazis were hungry for plunder, and the Sikh forces were ready for battle. Harlan and Aziz ud-Din paid a final visit to the amir's camp, with an ultimatum either to retire or to fight. While the envoys were awaiting the amir's response, a messenger arrived with news that "the Sikh army had already surrounded the Afghans with a heavy park of artillery." Dost Mohammed Khan summoned his counselors: some urged immediate attack, but others argued that the fight was already lost. Nawab Jubber Khan, possibly prompted by Harlan, "proposed to retire without the hazard of battle." Reluctantly, the amir agreed. There was a danger, however, that retreat might become a rout, forcing the amir to leave behind "guns, munitions, stores, and equipage, when he would be reduced to the level of any other of his relatives." Given the nature of the amir's relatives, this would certainly mean renewed civil war.

After another council of war, Dost Mohammed Khan came up with a radical solution: he would kidnap Harlan and Aziz ud-Din and hold them as hostages. Ranjit Singh plainly put great faith in his envoys, and it was known that "the old Sikh chief could scarcely exist without the faquir, who officiated as his physician, prepared his drams and was absolutely necessary to him." With the envoys in his power, he might transform the situation, compelling the maharaja either to give up Peshawar, or to pay a large sum for their ransom.

Even by the treacherous standards of Afghan diplomacy, imprisoning official ambassadors was frowned upon. The amir therefore decided to kill two birds with one stone: instead of kidnapping the American and the fakir himself, he would persuade his treacherous brother to do the deed. "It was agreed to incriminate Sultan Mahomed Khan. That Sirdar was accordingly sent for, and the amir, exchanging oaths on the Koran, informed him of what was mediated, and expressed his wishes that, as the [envoys had] come to the camp in his company, so he should carry them off." The sultan, realizing that he was being used as a fall guy, gave every appearance of enthusiasm, "promised entire compliance and took all the oaths on the Koran required of him, considering them, made under such circumstances, as invalid."

The amir summoned Harlan and Aziz ud-Din to his tent, where he "coarsely reproached and reviled them—foul language with Afghans being the preliminary step when more violent measures are contemplated." As the Afghan bodyguards moved in, both men remonstrated that they were accredited ambassadors with traditional diplomatic immunity. Dost Mohammed replied simply that "infidels and their agents were beyond the pale of diplomatic convention." Harlan and the fakir, still protesting vigorously, were handed over to Sultan Mohammed Khan's guard and marched away.

The amir still had to make his own escape before the Sikhs discovered what had happened, and that evening, as night fell, he led his army back into the mountains. It was dark by the time they reached the safety of the Khyber Pass, according to an eyewitness. "There his ears were assailed by the reports of the Sikh salvos, discharged in triumph at his flight. He turned around, and looking towards Peshawar, uttered an obscene oath: 'Ah! You kafirs [infidels], I have taken you in!' referring to the capture of the faquir and Mr. Harlan, who, as he supposed, were in the custody of Sultan Mahomed Khan in the rear."

What Dost Mohammed did not know was that Sultan Mohammed Khan had switched sides, and both Harlan and Aziz ud-Din were already safe in the Sikh camp. Harlan claimed the credit for this successful sleight of hand: "I induced Sooltan Mahomed Khan, the lately deposed chief of Peshawar, with 10,000 retainers, to withdraw suddenly from his camp around nightfall. The chief accompanied me towards the Seik camp, whilst his followers fled to their mountain fastness." The sultan escorted the two emissaries to safety, and then rejoined his troops in the mountains. As day broke, Harlan marveled at the way the Afghan army had evaporated "without the beat of drum or sound of bugle or the trumpet's blast, in the quiet stillness of midnight." The plain was deserted. "No vestige of the Afghan camp was seen, where six hours before 50,000 men and 10,000 horses, with all the host of attendants, were rife with the tumult of wild emotion."

The amir swiftly learned that his plan had failed utterly. A few hours into the retreat, he demanded to know where Sultan Mohammed Khan was holding Harlan and Aziz ud-Din. "No one could find him or them in the camp." As this information was sinking in, a messenger arrived with a letter from the sultan—"a tissue of violent abuse" accusing the amir of perfidy and violating the rules of diplomacy. "This appalling news wounded the feelings of the Amir most bitterly. There were no bounds to the sweat of shame and folly which flowed over his face, and there was no limit to the laughter of the people at his being deceived and ridiculed." With what remained of his disintegrating army, "chagrined and mortified," Dost Mohammed continued back up the Khyber Pass and finally reached Kabul with his forces in a state of near-mutiny. Having regained the Bala Hisar, according to Harlan, the amir locked himself away and, "in bitterness of spirit, plunged himself into the study of the Koran."

Harlan rejoiced: the sultan had won the game by "changing position on the board, and castling with the King of Lahore." He could be forgiven for congratulating himself. All involved had been double-dealing, but he had played the winning hand, and as a result of his maneuvering the Sikhs had seen off the Afghans with little loss to themselves. "By this one month's sparring, coquetting and skirmishing with Dost Muhammad, Ranjit Singh gained his long-wished for object, the undisputed occupation and mastership of the Peshawar valley."

The Afghans, including Dost Mohammed himself, expressed admiration for the way Harlan had worsted them. Not so Ranjit Singh. "The prey had escaped him, the dream of conquering Jalalabad and Cabul had failed to materialise," and instead of congratulating his envoys, he was dismissive: "When such sure people commit such maladroit actions, what can you expect from the others?" The ingratitude stung painfully, and the moment marked the start of a steady corrosion in relations between Harlan and Ranjit Singh.

Harlan believed he deserved to be made governor of Peshawar in recognition of his service, and according to one source had made "a vain attempt at acquiring as a grant the ta'aluqa [governorship] of Peshawar from Ranjit Singh." Instead, the plum job went to Hari Singh Nalwa, the Sikh general. Harlan loved Peshawar. Here he had enjoyed the hospitality of Mea Kummer ud-Din, strolled in the gardens of the Barakzai chiefs, hunted with hawks in the hills, and luxuriated for the first time in an Afghan steam bath. The mea was no more, but Harlan retained a deep fondness for the people of Peshawar. Hari Singh, the new governor, felt no such affection for the Pathans, and now set about curbing "the insurrectionist tendency of the wild tribesmen by the simple expedient of extermination."

Disappointed to have been passed over, Harlan returned to Gujrat. For a time life continued as it had before, with the American combining the duties of a provincial governor with the "somewhat anomalous position of Physician and Captain at the court of Lahore." He sent regular bulletins to Claude Wade about "the state of affairs at the court of Lahore, whether paid for it or not," as well as "reports concerning Ranjit Singh's health." The British were anxious to know how long the hard-living maharaja might survive. Ranjit had a steel constitution, but he had been worn down by "the excesses and fatigues of war and pleasure, excessive hard work, and constant physical exposure to the rigour of endless campaigns"—not to mention opium, alcohol, and other "highly potent but harmful medications to sustain him in his debaucheries." To his already extreme hypochondria was added the fear of impotence, a condition so terrifying to the old satyr that he could not bring himself to mention it when examined by a visiting French doctor: "Modesty made him complain of his stomach only, but I and everyone else knew what he meant by that."

On August 19, 1835, Ranjit Singh suffered a stroke, which left him partially paralyzed and stammering. "He became hesitant of speech, his eye became listless as if the sight was quite gone, and he could hardly mount a horse." In fact, the maharaja would cling to life for several more years but he and everyone else assumed that he was dying, and the jackals began to circle. Harlan and the Europeans had long been viewed with jealousy by their Sikh rivals at court, which would make their position precarious in the event of Ranjit Singh's death. Casting around for new medical opinions he could reject, Ranjit summoned Harlan to conduct an examination and cure his stutter. Aware of the maharaja's superstitious nature, Harlan gravely looked in his mouth and then "constructed a talisman to open the tongue . . . a gold chain around a pig representing the talisman of life." Needless to say, this trinket had no medical effect whatever, and may have caused the first serious disagreement between Harlan and his employer. In May 1836, Wade wrote to Ranjit Singh, apparently trying to patch up a quarrel between them, in which he observed that "Hallen Sahib [sic] was a very wise and intelligent person and that the Talisman prepared by him was quite accurate and exact."

Harlan's next suggestion, while more soundly based in the medicine of the time, damaged relations further, for the ingenious American now proposed that the best cure for this half-crippled, drink-raddled old king was to run a large jolt of electricity through him. There are conflicting accounts about what happened next. According to one source, "once the Maharaja fell ill and his tongue began to stammer, Harlan was called, as he was known to have learned the art of medicine. After feeling the pulse of the Maharaja he declared that he could cure him on the condition that he might be granted one lakh of rupees." Another account states that the use of electricity "had been recommended by Dr. H. [and] his plan of galvanising the Maharaja met with a ready consent on the part of the latter." However a bitter argument then erupted over "the exorbitant sum which the doctor demanded for constructing a galvanic battery (£5,000 sterling)." In a display of impudence remarkable even for Harlan, the American allegedly demanded payment in advance "as he did not trust the Maharaja." Ranjit Singh flew into a fantastic rage. Harlan was pushing his luck, but perhaps the price he asked was not unreasonable given the risks associated with electrifying an elderly, violent, and irascible absolute monarch who had already threatened to cut off his nose. This was an operation that Ranjit Singh was unlikely to enjoy, and that might easily kill him. Plans for the procedure went ahead anyway, and "acting on Harlan's suggestion, Ranjit Singh expressed a wish to the British government that the services of a British doctor competent in the application of galvanism to his emaciated body should be placed at his disposal." Dr. William McGregor, duly dispatched to Lahore with the necessary equipment, gave an account of the operation:

After some delay, a day was appointed for electrifying the Maharaja, but a difficulty arose on the part of his Highness's attendants, who were afraid that the shock might be attended by fatal consequences. At length the Maharaja begged them to be quiet, and said he would take the Biglee (electricity). We purposely put a small charge in the Leyden phial, and the Maharaja received it without evincing any particular emotion. Once witnessing the slight effect on their master, all the courtiers entreated that we should give them a shock; and this time we resolved to give them its full effect! The Minister Dhyan Singh joined hands with Jemandeer Khooshyal Singh, and he with others, until a chain was formed of the whole party present in the durbar. The jar now being charged to the full extent, they received a powerful shock, which made them all jump. Not making allowance for the difference in the charge, the Maharaja naturally received the credit of possessing a stouter heart and stronger nerves than any of his suite; this first trial was satisfactory for all parties.

While electrifying the Sikh court, in every sense, Dr. McGregor attempted to interest Ranjit in other practical applications of this new technology. "We endeavored to explain the wonderful rapidity of electricity, and in what way the Maharaja might communicate through it, in an instant of time, with the most distant parts of the kingdom, but Runjeet Singh, though curious on the subject, was rather sceptical on the latter point."

The electrification does not seem to have done much harm to the maharaja, but the episode had seriously damaged his rapport with Harlan, whose enemies at court were actively conspiring to turn opinion against him. Realizing the extreme danger he was in, Harlan took refuge with Allard. A dispute over a horse further damaged the relationship between the king and his American courtier. Flora's colt Mugnaan, "sired by an important English horse, Peverill of the Bute arms stud," had grown into a magnificent stallion, a rival to the finest horse in the maharaja's stables. Ranjit seems to have coveted the animal, but Harlan declined to surrender it. Mugnaan, he wrote darkly, was "the cause of important events affecting some of the chief incidents that marked the concluding scenes of my intercourse with Runjeet'h Singh, prince of the Punjab."

The final confrontation, however, erupted not over court politics, equine envy, medicine, or money, but over alchemy. Dr. Martin Honigberger reported a conversation with the maharaja that took place at around this time: "Runjeet Sing related to me that Dr. Allen [sic], (an American and governor of Gujrat) used secretly to employ his time in his fortress in the practice of alchemy and transmutation of metals." Honigberger was dismissive: "I could not forebear laughing at the idea of his expecting to convert common metals into gold, as the conversion of quicksilver into silver was found to be quite impossible." The maharaja's spies, however, had made further inquiries and duly reported that a diminutive person known as "The Moolvie" was living in Harlan's Gujrat home and conducting peculiar experiments. As Harlan knew, "to become notorious as a successful alchemist, without the protection of an influential patron, is to incur the certain consequences of torture and probable death." To have acquired a knowledge of alchemy was dangerous enough in Ranjit's mind; refusing to share that knowledge was tantamount to treason. Even more damaging allegations followed, when it was reported that Harlan was not only making gold, but manufacturing false coin with it. Counterfeiting was not merely a crime, it was a direct challenge to Ranjit's authority, since "the privilege of coining is the monopoly of royalty in the east" and "the very first thing which a king does on ascending the throne is to institute a coinage." As a mark of the highest honor, Ranjit had granted Hari Singh the right to strike his own coins in Peshawar, but Harlan had been awarded no such privilege in Gujrat. If the allegations were true, Harlan was getting rich through magic, appropriating a royal prerogative, and making a mint.

Harlan never admitted counterfeiting, but he was undoubtedly aware of the process involved. Nawab Jubber Khan had dabbled in forgery as well as alchemy, and he had shown Harlan how to strike coins "by a rolling process which enabled him to imitate the original, debasing the metal with an alloy of copper." Did Harlan mint his own coinage? Honigberger is adamant: "Harlan was making false money."

The animosity that had been slowly fermenting between Harlan and his employer exploded early in 1836, when they met for the last time in Lahore and a blistering argument ensued. Sacking his governor on the spot, Ranjit berated the American "in no very flattering terms." Harlan appears to have responded with equal asperity. Between two such volatile men, reconciliation was impossible: "Any regard between them was converted into hate." According to one source, Ranjit Singh was "beside himself with rage, and gave orders that Harlan should be stripped and put across the Sutlej." Another version states that the maharaja "threatened to wreak his vengeance on Dr. H. if he did not speedily leave his dominions [and] Dr. H., well knowing the character of the man he had to deal with, lost no time in making his escape." Harlan scooped up his journals, mounted Mugnaan, and fled to Ludhiana.

"After seven years residence in the enjoyment of wealth and luxury of the most sumptuous court in Asia," Harlan found himself back in British India, possibly barefoot, certainly penniless, and utterly livid. His sense of grievance, after he had served the maharaja so loyally and effectively, was incandescent, and lasted the rest of his life. Quick to anger and slow to forgive, raging with "contempt and disgust for Runjeeth's duplicity," he swore vengeance against the king of the Punjab.

"Monarch as he was, absolute and voluptuous in the possession of treasured wealth and military power, I resolved to avenge myself and cause him to tremble in the midst of his magnificence."

11

THE KING'S NEAREST FRIEND

Back in Ludhiana, Harlan told anyone who would listen that he intended to take his revenge on Ranjit Singh, but he was enough of a realist to know that he could not do this alone. Shah Shujah was living comfortably off his British pension, and was the last man to come to Harlan's aid in a personal vendetta against Ranjit. The British, anxious to retain good relations with the Lion of Lahore were even less likely to countenance a move against him. There was only one person with the military power to take on Ranjit Singh, and whose hatred for the one-eyed Sikh monarch matched that of Harlan: Dost Mohammed Khan, amir of Kabul. Nearly ten years after his first foray into Afghanistan, Harlan prepared to set out on the same route again, this time with the intention of forging an alliance with the prince he had recently worsted in diplomacy and once sought to depose.

Harlan made no secret of his plans, and Ranjit's newswriters inevitably got wind of them. The maharaja appears to have had second thoughts about his treatment of the hot-tempered American, for in May 1836, he sent "a conciliatory message for Harlan, assuring him of royal favour." But it was too late. Harlan ignored the overture, and in late summer he set off, retracing his steps back to Afghanistan. The British watched him go with detached interest: "Mr. Harlan, who was for many years in Sikh service, quitted it a short time ago and came to Ludhiana. After remaining some time he set out for Bahawalpore, with the intention of joining Dost Mahomed at Kabul," wrote the political assistant at Ludhiana in October 1836. "His declared intention is to bring down an army to avenge himself on his former master for the injuries he had received (he says) at his hands. He is an eccentric, and undoubtedly an enterprising man; but that he has a talent to gain such an ascendancy over the ruler at Kabul as will enable him to carry out his threat, is, in my opinion, more than doubtful."

Harlan had received word from Dost Mohammed Khan that he would be delighted to welcome him back to Kabul. Just months earlier, the amir had kidnapped Harlan and threatened to kill him, but Dost Mohammed was too supple to allow past history to affect present possibilities. Harlan was just the man he needed to knock his army into shape. The American, as always, reached for a classical allusion to describe what he considered his triumphal return to Kabul: "I was received by Dost Mahomed Khan with much the same feeling of exultation that the King of Persia is known to have indulged in when his Court was visited by Themistocles"—a reference to the Athenian general who led the Greeks to victory over the Persians, but then fell from favor and defected to Persia where the king made him governor of Magnesia.

Making allowances for Harlan's tendency to exaggerate, his reception by his old enemy does appear to have been singularly warm; the amir had plainly decided to forgive and forget—as much as anything was ever forgiven or forgotten in Afghanistan. According to one account, "Dost Mohamed received General Harlan as a brother, ever addressed him by that title, seated him in the Durbar at his side, and gave him command of his regular troops with the title of Sir-I-Lushkcr (Sirraskier), or General-in-chief, and Mus-a-hib, or Aid-de-camp." Some British sources have questioned whether Harlan commanded the amir's entire army, but the official Indian archive documents clearly describe him as being "at the head of the Afghan troops"; and the *Calcutta Journal*, the official gazette of British India, noted that he had been appointed following the dismissal of the "commander in chief of the Kabul foot troops." Harlan glossed over his part in the defection of the amir's brother during the conflict with the Sikhs, asserting that "he did not deceive Sultan Mahomed Khan, but allowed him to deceive himself." The amir unceremoniously evicted the occupant of a large property in the Bala Hisar and moved Harlan in.

The humiliating retreat from Peshawar had convinced the amir of the need to improve his army, which was little more than "a miscellaneous collection of semi-independent ruffians, quite untrained, and heterogeneously armed." Every tribe followed its own leader, and all preferred the ancient methods of warfare: "Desultory sniping, followed by a swift and confused rush." The Afghans had been fighting this way forever. One British officer dismissively observed that "in all the records of Afghan battles, there is no evidence of attack or defence, and to speak of officer or staff in connection with such a rabble is utterly ridiculous." But the Afghans were courageous fighters, and turning this horde into an effective army was neither ridiculous nor impossible. The amir, noted another source, had "about three thousand splendid cavalry, Affghans [sic], and the pick of them, mounted on his own horses." In addition to his household cavalry and the Qizilbash guard, in 1838 it was estimated that the amir had "a park of 45 guns," a standing army of twenty-five hundred infantry, and perhaps twelve thousand cavalry. With the aid of two deserters from the British army, Harlan now set about trying to do for the amir what the French officers had done for Ranjit Singh.

Harlan was delighted to be back in Kabul with his Afghan friends, but rather less pleased to encounter another former associate, Charles Masson, the ex-soldier who had abandoned Harlan during his first journey to Afghanistan. In the intervening years, Masson had wandered more widely between the Indus and the Persian Gulf than any traveler before him. In an astonishing solitary odyssey, he had tramped across the desert to Shikarpur, Ghazni, Kandahar, and then back to Lahore; he had sailed from Karachi to Muscat and then walked to Baghdad; he had started a collection of ancient coins, catalogued various Buddhist sites, and begun to send his researches to Company officials in Bombay, all the time maintaining that he was Charles Masson, American traveler and antiquarian, rather than James Lewis, deserter and fugitive.

In the summer of 1832, Masson's restless wandering had led him to Kabul and there, for the next six years, he made his home. Like Harlan before him, he had been adopted by both Nawab Jubber Khan and Hajji Khan, accompanying the latter on a tribute-extracting expedition to Bamian in the Hindu Kush. In 1834, under his assumed name, Masson had published an account of his discoveries in the *Journal of the Asiatic Society of Bengal*. It was through his writings that Masson caught the attention of the indefatigable Claude Wade in Ludhiana, who told his superiors that he "believed him to be a deserter from our artillery." Harlan had promised to report any interesting developments to Wade, and it was almost certainly he who informed the British agent of Masson's true identity, possibly as early as 1828 during his first residence in Kabul. It is hard to blame Harlan for passing on this tidbit, although some subsequently did. Harlan had not forgiven the Englishman who had vanished "so unceremoniously," at Dera Ismail Khan, leaving him in the lurch at a critical moment and, Harlan believed, encouraging others to do the same.

Alerted to Masson's secret, Wade did not seek to expose him, but rather to make use of him at a time when pressure was growing from London to expand British influence into Afghanistan. "The information which he has collected on the government and resources of a country which is of daily increasing interest to the British government, cannot be an object of indifference," wrote Wade, who began sending Masson small amounts of money while angling to obtain a pardon for him. This was duly granted in February 1835, but even before then, Wade informed Masson that he had been appointed "Agent in Kabul for communicating intelligence on the state of affairs in that quarter," with a salary of 250 rupees a month. Masson was relieved to see his name cleared, but rather less to have the task of spy "imposed" on him, as he put it. From now until he finally left Kabul, he would be Britain's eyes and ears in Afghanistan.

The meeting between Harlan and Masson was painfully frosty. Masson almost certainly knew that Harlan had informed Wade of his identity. Both men could be prickly, and both nursed their grudges: had they been less alike, perhaps they might have liked one another more. On reacquaintance their rivalry swiftly blossomed into a deep mutual loathing, and within months of Harlan's return to Kabul, Masson was writing poisonous letters to his spymasters, denouncing the American as "an adventurer here in the Amir's service" and "a violent and unprincipled man." The enmity would grow more acute over time, but for the moment Harlan had more important vendettas on his mind.

He would later claim that Dost Mohammed Khan's renewed assault on the Sikhs was at his instigation, but the amir, smarting from the last debacle, needed little prompting to resume hostilities with Ranjit Singh. Since the last confrontation, the Sikhs had garrisoned forts along the frontier and Hari Singh Nalwa had established an iron rule over Peshawar. The Sikh general was elegant, clever, and ruthless: "A man of ex-

tremist views, he was diabolical in his hatred of the Afghans, and overtly
aired his determination of carrying Sikh arms to the heart of Kabul and
annexing the Kingdom of Afghanistan." Such an attack seemed imminent early in 1837, when Hari Singh seized the fort at Jamrud, at the
mouth of the Khyber, in what appeared from Kabul to be a prelude to
full-scale Sikh invasion. It was judged necessary to make a display of force.

In March 1837, the maharaja recalled many of his best troops to Lahore in order to impress a British delegation there to celebrate his son's
wedding. Dost Mohammed Khan chose that moment to strike, but this
time he would not command the troops in person. The amir had recently
survived an assassination attempt, and "so closely was he beset that he
never moved abroad but in daylight." Instead Mirza Sami Khan, his confidential secretary, was appointed to superintend operations, while Mohammed Akbar Khan, the amir's heir, was placed in overall command.
Nawab Jubber Khan, that veteran campaigner, was also dispatched to
provide the advice of an elder statesman. Masson later sought to deny
Harlan any credit in the ensuing battle, writing to Wade: "An opinion
has prevailed that the Afghans were aided in their late operations near Peshawar by the presence of Mr. Harlan. It is a popular error. Neither he,
nor any of the Europeans with the Amir was present with his troops."
This was untrue. Even Harlan's most vigorous critics concede that "like
all the Europeans, he was present with the Afghans" and in the peculiar
position of waging war against his former comrades in arms.

The Afghan army poured down the Khyber pass once more, "a force
8,000–10,000 strong with 50 cannon, fierce Afghan tribesmen fired by
religious fanaticism swelled that number to 20,000 horse and foot."
Many local Pathans joined the ranks, as the Afghans laid siege to Jamrud and began "devastating the plains of Peshawar up to the very walls
of the city." Deprived of his elite troops, Hari Singh "could make no
head against them," reported Alexander Gardner, in the thick of the fray
as ever. On April 30, 1837, the Sikh commander marched out in person
to relieve besieged Jamrud, and the two armies clashed in a pitched battle. Hari Singh's artillery tore gaping holes in the Afghan ranks, but a ferocious counterattack drove the Sikhs back. In the ensuing melee, Hari
Singh himself was mortally injured. "That gallant chief expired, and was
burnt the evening of the action," wrote Masson. An estimated two
thousand Sikhs were killed, and one thousand Afghans. Mirza Sami

Khan, the Afghan commander, had run away during the battle to hide in a cave where, "in despair, he sobbed, beat his breast, tore his beard and knocked his head upon the ground." Once the fighting was over, however, he emerged, declaring that the triumph was the direct result of his prayers. "Mahomed Akbar Khan plumed himself on a transcendent victory," but no one on the Afghan side was more delighted than Harlan, who regarded the outcome as a personal vindication. He imagined Ranjit Singh squirming with fury: "The proud King of Lahore quailed upon his threatened throne, as he exclaimed with terror and approaching despair, 'Harlan has avenged himself, this is all his work.'"

A British officer happened to be with the old king when news of the battle arrived. Ranjit Singh "seemed to bear the reverse with great equanimity . . . and said that a trifling defeat now and then was useful, as it taught both men and officers caution." In truth, the maharaja was devastated by the death of Hari Singh, a childhood friend and the "flower of Sikh chivalry," whose death "cast a gloom over Lahore." Harlan, with wishful thinking, even claimed that "the old Prince's infirmities were so much aggravated by the disgrace of defeat, that from the date of this misfortune he declined more rapidly and never again rallied to the former energies of his ambitious and vigorous spirit."

The Battle of Jamrud was actually rather less decisive than the Afghans claimed and Ranjit feared. The Afghan commanders violently disagreed over whether to press on and besiege Peshawar itself, and Sikh reinforcements were swiftly dispatched under General Allard. On May 9, 1837, the Afghans retreated into the foothills, and then went home. Far from losing Peshawar, Ranjit Singh had confirmed his hold on the province. He was determined to avoid any repetition of the Pathan uprising that had accompanied the Afghan attack, so Paolo di Avitabile was appointed civilian commander of Peshawar. The Neapolitan set about cowing the local population with "remorseless cruelty, shameless rapacity, and signal skill and success." Even Hari Singh seemed gentle by comparison. Avitabile gloried in his brutality:

> When I marched into Peshawar, I sent on in advance a number of wooden posts which my men erected around the walls of the city. The men scoffed at them and laughed at the madness of the feringhee, and harder still when my men came in and laid coils of rope at the foot of the posts . . . However, when my preparations were completed and they

found one fine morning dangling from these posts, fifty of the worst characters in Peshawar, they thought different. And I repeated the exhibition every day till I had made a scarcity of brigands and murderers. Then I had to deal with the liars and tale bearers. My method with them was to cut out their tongues. When a surgeon appeared and professed to be able to restore their speech, I sent for him and cut out his tongue also. After that there was peace.

Harlan was not alone in his horror at such methods. "He acts as a savage among savage men," observed Alexander Gardner. "Under his rule small pains are taken to distinguish between innocence and guilt, and many a man, ignorant of the alleged crime, pays for it with his blood." Even so, the Afghans considered that they had given Ranjit Singh a bloody nose, and the army returned to Kabul in high spirits. Harlan's stock soared. The amir had never doubted his talents, but he had always distrusted him, and with good reason. Now, to Harlan's delight, he was admitted to the inner circle of his court. "As the Ameer's aid-de-camp and general of his regular troops, I possessed the rank of a chief Sirdar. My place in durbar was alongside of the Ameer, on the left." This was a signal honor, for physical proximity to the amir was a measure of social standing, and only four people were permitted to share the same rug as the prince: Nawab Jubber Khan, the heir apparent Akbar Khan, Akbar's father-in-law, and Harlan. In addition to his military command, the American was appointed to oversee the Kabul mint, a position of great responsibility. "I was instructed by the prince to cause an issue of sequins along with the gold and silver coin of the country. But the bankers being averse to receive them, I represented the impolicy of the measure which was subsequently countermanded." Ironically, in view of the reasons for Harlan's expulsion from the Punjab, he was soon approached by a professional forger "offering to coin ducats and teach me his science. He was permitted to disclose his art and then seized with his apparatus and taken before the prince. Dost Mahomed merely cautioned the artist not to debase the coin." The incident suggests that, whatever the allegations, Harlan was no counterfeiter. In a final demonstration of gratitude, the amir presented Harlan with "a gold-mounted Damascus blade," a fabulous curved sword elaborately embossed in solid gold.

As the amir's left-hand man, the American now had a unique vantage point from which to study the hitherto hidden world of the Kabul court, and an opportunity to observe the feline enigma that was Dost Mohammed Khan: proud and haughty, occasionally brutal, but the most assiduous and accessible of monarchs, a study in kingship. The amir would rise at dawn to pray, read the Koran in Persian, and then get down to the business of running a large and extremely unruly kingdom. The same routine was followed every day except Thursday, the day of the weekly royal bath. First the senior chiefs made their entry to the durbar, bowing to the amir and "touching the forehead as they leaned forward with the inner surface of the four fingers of the right hand." They were seated, according to seniority, by a master of ceremonies carrying "a long official wand of olive wood, turned and lacquered yellow." The first part of the morning was spent in a discussion of domestic affairs, followed by a slap-up breakfast. "About 11 o'clock, a.m., the people and officials, suitors and attendants, were dismissed, with the exception of those who usually ate in company with his highness: his brother, one of two of his chief counsellors, and myself," wrote Harlan. This select group shared one plate, while other dishes were ranged down the room to be devoured according to a strict pecking order, the quality of food deteriorating with distance from the prince. "Fiddlers huddled together over the lowest dish, which was cooked, in reference to its debased position, with very little ghee (melted butter) and probably without the viand."

Harlan considered himself a connoisseur of Afghan cuisine, and judged the creations of the prince's kitchen to be as good as anything found in a Parisian restaurant. "The standing dish is pilau made of rice and meat, usually mutton, sometimes fowl. There were ragouts of fowl and partridge; soup, boiled pot-herbs, pickles and preserves: a large bowl of sherbet occupied the middle of the feast. Our bread was leavened, and formed into a flat, round cake, a foot in diameter, grooved at intervals with ridges about two fingers broad and served as a plate; it was excellent, and highly creditable to the Kabul bakers, as the whole feast was the *cuisine* of the 'artiste' who manipulated the comestibles. The cooks are natives of Cashmere, and their service and concoction of delicious preparations, [is] not surpassed by those superb Frenchmen who have thought themselves unrivalled in the science of Potology."

After breakfast, the amir continued royal business, and then, at midday, retired to the harem for a two-hour siesta. When he reemerged, the prince would mount his horse and set out on his daily ride around Kabul. A crowd of petitioners was always waiting at the gates of the fortress, and justice was dispensed on the hoof, the amir's rulings being noted down by the accompanying *mirza*. "I have frequently seen him with his hand over the saddle, and one foot in the stirrup, listening patiently to some ragged person, with a degree of equanimity I never yet witnessed in any European functionary." The ad hoc dispensation of justice continued day and night. On one occasion Harlan was sitting in conversation with Dost Mohammed in the early hours of the morning, when the *cauzee*, the senior judicial official of Kabul, presented two prisoners, a man and a woman, who had been surprised in the midst of a "nocturnal orgie." The rest of the party had bolted, but the captured pair had been "too drunk to escape and fell into the charley's hands." Dost Mohammed "listened to the charge of licentiousness and immorality [and] executed summary judgement, by ordering the fellow's beard to be singed off and commanding the police officer to slip the woman into a bag and punish her with 40 lashes." When Harlan asked why it was necessary to bag up the woman before punishing her, the amir simply replied: "To avoid the indecency of exposure."

Only once did Harlan try to influence the judicial process, after his neighbor, an officer of the guard, had strangled one of his wives, "a young Cashmerian girl." Seeking justice on behalf of the dead woman's family, Harlan appealed to the amir, but without success. "My proceeding was considered gratuitous and malapropos. The criminal readily proved by his family and a servant that an indigestible supper brought on an attack of cholera, of which the woman suddenly died." Disgusted by the miscarriage of justice, Harlan observed that "a man may sell his wife [like] selling a cow with a halter around her neck."

Harlan often accompanied the amir on his mounted excursions: "In the summer and fall he luxuriated in the picturesque scenery around the city from a favourite prospective point; seated himself, with a few friends, on the bank of a running stream and enjoyed a cup of tea; or visited some of the magnificent, ornamental gardens near the suburbs of Cabul, accompanied by a train of musicians." In the late afternoon, the prince would visit his stud and sit on an elevated wooden terrace covered with carpets, as his splendid horses were paraded before him. The amir lived amid a permanent throng of courtiers, made up of senior

chiefs, advisers, and various mullahs, who "passed their time in smoking the cullioon [Persian water pipe or hookah], desultory conversation, and admiration of the promising brood of young colts, which
were the delight of His Highness."

Court favorites were expected to remain with the amir until he retired, which was usually well after midnight. Harlan "repeatedly sat up
with him until three a.m.," smoking, storytelling, or playing board games,
which the amir invariably won: "When His Highness was engaged at
chess the conversation ceased, and the interlocutors gathered to observe
the game and applaud the sagacity he displayed. I never knew him [to]
lose a game." The amir's favorite opponent was the *cauzee*, Kabul's senior judge, who was so good at chess he managed to lose repeatedly
without making it obvious. The games were really part of court etiquette, a ritual, predictable victory by the invincible ruler, but "occasionally someone, more privileged than the rest, had been heard to
taunt the Ameer, by hinting that the Cauzee played bad intentionally,
and lost to flatter him. He took this rallying always in good part." The
amir loved to listen to stories told from memory, and was himself a fine
raconteur with a taste for dirty jokes, usually in reference to his own
amorous conquests. Harlan was slightly shocked at the amir's ribaldry.
"He was much addicted to telling stories of his personal adventures
[and] his anecdotes were not infrequently gross and sensual." Dost
Mohammed Khan teased the prudish American and, for that matter,
everyone else, including himself. "Ridicule was a weapon that he flourished with considerable effect, and he could good-humouredly make
himself the subject of ludicrous wit."

As the water pipe was passed around, the courtiers would boast of
the places they had been, the enemies they had killed, and the maidens
they had wooed, for bragging, as Harlan observed, was "one of the essential elements of Asiatic bravery." He joined in with gusto, entertain-
ing the court with stories of the war in Burma and the distant land of
America. The amir never tired of hearing tales of this New World, of
"the manners and customs of the people, the character of the prince, the
government, religion, and particularly geography and topography, for
which sciences he seemed to have a strong inclination."

Harlan found himself drawn to this extraordinary man, delicate and
judicious in his rulings but astonishingly avaricious; at once refined,

playful, and affectionate, but capable of great cruelty: "In conversation
he is boisterous and energetic, extremely susceptible to flattery, beyond
measure vain, and fond of pleasantry," wrote Harlan, whose physical
description of Amir Dost Mohammed Khan, drawn from life, is unique
in its detail and perception.

> The Ameer is in vigorous health. When he stands erect his height is six
> feet, but there is a slight stoop in the neck arising from a rounded con-
> tour of the shoulders, characteristic of his family. He had large features
> and muscular frame; a heavy tread in his walk, placing the sole of his
> foot all at once flat upon the ground, which indicates that the instep is
> not well arched. The outline of his face is Roman. Having a curved jaw,
> a low retreating forehead, hair of the head shaven, and the turban worn
> far back, gives an appearance of elevation to the frontal region. The an-
> gle is scarcely less acute than in some of the higher orders of simiae. The
> nose is aquiline, high and rather long, and finished with beautiful deli-
> cacy; the brow open, arched and pencilled; the eyes are hazel-grey, not
> large, and of an elephantine expression; the mouth large and vulgar and
> full of bad teeth; the lips moderately thick; ears large. The shape of the
> face is oval, rather broad across the cheeks, and the chin covered with
> a full, strong beard, originally black, now mixed with grey hairs.

When the amir wasn't looking, Harlan made a sketch of him in his
notebook, portraying a dapper, intense-featured man, rather more elegant than the Roman monkey with flat feet described above.

"Loud and vociferous on most occasions," the amir was also liable to
fits of the deepest gloom. "When the Ameer gave way to a desponding
tone of mind, which was frequently the case, his perfidious principles
caused him to mistrust everybody, and he is consequently without a
friend." Like Shakespeare's Henry V, the young Dost Mohammed had
been a libertine, but like Prince Hal he had reformed himself, "by breaking through the foul and ugly mists of vapours that did seem to strangle
him." Tales of the amir's early drinking brought out the puritan in Harlan, and his description of Dost Mohammed's youthful binges was
probably based on Ranjit Singh's spectacular orgies. "The Ameer, in
early life and until the age of thirty, was addicted to drunkenness. During his fits of intoxication, many ruthless acts of indiscriminate barbarity were the result of these depraved hallucinations. Surrounded by a
crowd of drunken revellers, maddened by the manic draught of the

frantic bowl, friend and colleague, master, man, and slave, all indiscriminate and promiscuous actors in the wild, voluptuous, licentious scene of shameless bacchanals, they caroused and drank with prostitutes, and singers, and fiddlers, day and night, in one long, interminable cycle, the libertine's eternity of sensual excitement and continuous debauchery." Power had changed Dost Mohammed, and the "acquisition of sovereignty presented the prince in the character of a sincere reformer, in which effort of morals he was imitated by his court."

Yet in politics he was entirely amoral, a pure disciple, though he could not know it, of Machiavelli. "He is no believer in human principle, but a self-convicted and unchanging doubter of every motive but self-interest. He has no honesty in any sense, no morals, no piety; a liar in the completest sense of the word; subtle, cunning, timorous, and governed in all things, sacred and profane, political and civil, moral and physical, by interest, social, sensual and avaricious." His lust for money was obsessive, and he would kill for gold without remorse. "His eyes had a feline glare when he looked full in the face of any one, and they assumed an awakened stare of attention when the accumulation of gold was the subject of his thoughts." The American was particularly repelled by the way Dost Mohammed hypocritically held forth on the iniquities of slavery, "while a large number of the personal attendants then present were slaves, many born of free parents." The amir's household slaves were principally of the Hazara tribe from the central highlands of Afghanistan. "Hundreds of these Hazarrahs are annually disposed of in his city of Cabul," wrote Harlan.

Whatever Harlan might see as his moral failings, Dost Mohammed Khan was the only man capable of uniting the warring Afghan tribes. By 1837, he had so far consolidated his grip on power that even his brothers were quiescent. Nawab Jubber Khan, who had once schemed against him, was now reconciled to his brother's rule and, like Harlan, played a pivotal role in his administration. But if the internal threat to the amir had receded, outside pressures were mounting steadily. Afghanistan was about to become a bloody pawn in the Great Game being played for supremacy in Central Asia between the empires of Russia and Great Britain. Officials in London and Calcutta were convinced that Russia was steadily encroaching on Britain's sphere of influence, with designs on India itself. Anti-Russian feeling was raging. "From the frontiers of

Hungary to the heart of Burmah and Nepaul," declared *The Times*, "the Russian fiend has been haunting and troubling the human race, and diligently perpetrating his malignant frauds to the vexation of this industrious and essentially pacific empire." From London, it appeared that the expansion of Russian power into Central Asia made conflict inevitable. Czarist influence had been steadily growing in Tehran, and in 1837, at Russia's urging, the shah's troops marched on Herat, the city in west Afghanistan long claimed by Persia and ruled over by Kamran Shah, Shah Shujah's nephew. In an echo of Harlan's journey, a young English officer named Eldred Pottinger had disguised himself as a Muslim holy man and slipped into Herat shortly before the Persians, aided by Russian military advisers, laid siege to the city. Pottinger would play a key role in the ten-month siege of Herat, helping to prevent the Russians from gaining a foothold in western Afghanistan. But while Russia and Britain were fighting by proxy over Herat, another undeclared battle was underway in Kabul where the amir soon found himself, in Harlan's phrase, "ground between two stones."

Dost Mohammed had not given up hope of retrieving Peshawar from Ranjit Singh's maw. When Lord Auckland was appointed governor general in March 1836, the amir sent him a letter, the purple language of which suggests that Harlan may have been the author: "The field of my hopes, which had before been chilled by the cold blast of wintry times, has by the happy tidings of your Lordship's arrival become the envy of the Garden of Paradise." The flattery was followed by a request for British help in forcing "the reckless and misguided Sikhs" to surrender Peshawar. Auckland's reply was friendly, but stern: "My friend, you are aware that it is not the practice of the British government to interfere with the affairs of other independent states." That assertion would ring distinctly hollow when, less than three years later, Dost Mohammed was ousted by an invading British army. In the meantime, as a precaution, the amir cautiously put out feelers to the Russians.

The Company's directors, increasingly alarmed by the encroaching Czarist bear, had instructed Auckland to "watch more closely the progress of events in Afghanistan and to counteract the progress of Russian influence in that quarter." The time had come, it was secretly declared, "to interfere decidedly in the affairs of Afghanistan." Masson was already sending back regular reports, but Auckland wanted his own man on the spot, a political agent who could act for Britain under the guise of arranging a commercial treaty with Afghanistan. There was one obvious candidate for the job.

On September 20, 1837, Alexander "Bokhara" Burnes, the toast of London, returned to Kabul in triumph. "We were received with great pomp and splendour by a fine body of Afghan cavalry, led by the Amir's son, Akhbar Khan. He did me the honour to place me on the same elephant as the one upon which he himself rode." From his howdah, Burnes may have heard a premonition of his own fate. "As we passed through the city some of the people cried out: 'Take care of Cabool. Do not destroy Cabool.'" He and his entourage were installed in a large mansion inside the Bala Hisar.

It may be imagined what Harlan thought of this red-carpet treatment for a man he considered "remarkable for his obstinacy and stupidity." When the American had first arrived there, Kabul was virtually unknown to the outside world. Now no fewer than three foreigners were in residence—Harlan, Burnes, and Masson—living cheek by jowl, united only in rivalry and mutual antipathy. Masson took particular exception to Burnes's opinion that "the Afghans were to be treated as children," and he unfairly blamed the Scotsman for all that subsequently ensued. Harlan was even more damning: "The utter and deplorable incapacity of the English agent originated a line of bewildering policy, commenced in the feebleness of a narrow mind, and finished with a deluge of misery and blood."

The morning after his spectacular entry into Kabul, Burnes was received at court and warmly welcomed by Dost Mohammed Khan, with Harlan at his side. Remembering Elphinstone's extravagance three decades earlier, Calcutta had given strict orders that any presents for the Afghan prince and his harem "ought not to be of a costly nature, but should be chosen particularly with a view to exhibit the superiority of British manufacture." Burnes had followed his instructions, thus committing what was, in Harlan's view, "a breach of etiquette most inexcusable in any one pretending to a knowledge of Oriental customs." Instead of the valuable gifts the Afghan courtiers had expected, Burnes produced trinkets, "adapted only to the frivolous tastes of savages, or the wretched fancies of rude infatuated Africans," wrote Harlan. "They consisted of pins, needles, scissors, penknives, silk handkerchiefs, toys, watches, musical snuff boxes &c., all of which were received with inexpressible surprise, followed by a sense of strong disgust, intermingled with mortification and disappointment."

The gifts for the amir himself were little better. Harlan was scathing: "His Highness was honoured with a pair of pistols and a spyglass, as though the Governor-General would have suggested to the Ameer an allegory of the conservative and offensive symbols of good government!" The prince managed to hide his dismay, but once Burnes was out of earshot, he was disdainful. "Dost Mahomed observed with a 'pish!' as he threw them down before him and averted his face. 'Behold! I have feasted and honoured this Feringhee to the extent of six thousand rupees, and have now a lot of pins and needles and sundry petty toys to show for my folly.'" Burnes's mission could not have started more inauspiciously. Dost Mohammed's wives and concubines had been expecting a windfall and the disappointment, in Harlan's words, "almost caused an insurrection amongst the inmates of the haram."

After swallowing his irritation, Dost Mohammed carefully explained his position to the envoy: he desired nothing more than a treaty with the British, but he also wanted help expelling the Sikhs from Peshawar, and some cash. "To the English he held out two stipulations, which he made the *sine qua non* of a treaty offensive and defensive," wrote Harlan, who was in the thick of the discussions. "Viz: a payment of twenty lacs of rupees, (two hundred thousand pounds) and that Runjeet'h Singh should be obliged to relinquish his pretensions to the natural territories of Avghanistaun west of the Indus."

Alexander Burnes firmly believed that the amir could prove a stalwart ally against the Russians. "Dost Mohammed is our man," he wrote to his superiors. "Now is the time to bind him to our side." But the view from Calcutta was different. Sir William Hay Macnaghten, the influential secretary in the Secret and Political Department, insisted that nothing should be done to upset Ranjit Singh, who was probably immovable from Peshawar anyway. "Our first feeling must be that of regard for the honour and just wishes of our old and firm ally," Macnaghten instructed Burnes, while pointing out that if Dost Mohammed proved recalcitrant, there was always Shah Shujah, with his long record of loyalty to Britain, waiting patiently in the wings to repossess his crown.

Negotiations between Burnes and the amir, with Harlan "taking part in his capacity as chief military officer of the Afghan army," would drag on for six months. Harlan bitterly criticized Burnes in later years for failing to agree to a treaty, but the envoy's freedom of movement was seriously restricted. Burnes tried to suggest a compromise by which the amir should be secretly promised Peshawar after the death of Ranjit, which could not be far off. Auckland flatly rejected the idea. Meanwhile, Dost Mohammed and Harlan tried to put pressure on the envoy, using flattery, persuasion, and even threats: "Every subterfuge that duplicity could devise, and every pretext that cunning could suggest, were used to work upon the English agent. The imaginary terrors of a Russian invasion were prominently displayed to him, and menaces of his personal safety were not spared to prevail upon him to accede to the Ameer's designs." Dost Mohammed fed Burnes a steady diet of disinformation, through "a strict system of espionage which falsified and corrupted all the channels of information through which the English agent endeavoured to accumulate facts." Other, more seductive methods were also employed: Masson reported that Burnes and his companions were cavorting nightly with Afghan women, laid on by order of the prince. One of the amir's secretaries even asked Masson if he would like to avail himself to the same service, and fill his home with "black eyed damsels." Masson was scandalized: "I asked where the damsels were to come from; and he replied I might select any I pleased, and he would take care I should have them." The Englishman demurred, pointing out that his house was "hardly large enough" to accommodate a troupe of dancing girls.

Dost Mohammed repeatedly hinted that if Britain would not support him with a treaty, then he would turn to the Russians. As if to reinforce that threat, on Christmas Eve there appeared in Kabul the dashing and enigmatic figure of Captain Yan Vitkevitch, emissary from the czar, the first official envoy from Russia. He "represented himself as a Russian courier," recorded Harlan, and "came with a complimentary letter addressed to Dost Mahomed."

Vitkevitch was a Lithuanian aristocrat by birth who had been punished for taking part in anti-Russian student demonstrations by being sent to Siberia as a military conscript. In exile, he had studied the languages and customs of Central Asia, and steadily rose through the ranks, noted for his intelligence and daring. When Dost Mohammed hinted he might welcome an envoy from the czar, it was decided that Captain Vitkevitch should mount a secret solo mission to Kabul.

With the arrival of Vitkevitch, the plot thickened considerably. Burnes was intrigued, and deeply alarmed, by the sudden appearance of this mysterious, charming, and multilingual rival: "He was a gentlemanly and agreeable man, of about thirty years of age, spoke French, Turkish and Persian fluently, and wore the uniform of an officer of Cossacks." In the grand tradition of Victorian diplomatic etiquette, Burnes invited the Russian envoy to Christmas dinner and found him intelligent and well informed. Vitkevitch's presence was proof that the Great Game had been joined in earnest in Afghanistan. "We are in a mess here," Burnes wrote to a friend. "I could not believe my eyes or ears; but Captain Vickovich [sic] arrived here with a blazing letter, three feet long, and sent immediately to pay his respects to me . . . I sent an express at once to my Lord A. telling him that after this I knew not what might happen, and it was now a neck-and-neck race between Russia and us." Masson believed that the appearance of Vitkevitch had completely unmanned Burnes, who "abandoned himself to despair, bound his head with wet towels and handkerchiefs and took to the smelling bottle."

Dost Mohammed was careful to demonstrate that he still favored a British alliance, and Vitkevitch was initially cold-shouldered. But the Afghan prince wanted a commitment from Burnes, and his frustration was mounting. Privately he told Harlan the parable of the fox and the fat-tailed sheep, in which the starving fox sees the pendulous tail of the sheep and waits in vain for it to fall off. "'This is just my position,' said His Highness with a vociferous laugh. 'I shall be looking after this European agent in expectation of something falling from him, and eventually turn away like the miserable fox, to feed on the hard fare which has always been the lot of us mountaineers.'" Burnes tried once more to persuade Calcutta that settling the Peshawar problem in the amir's favor would be "an immediate remedy against further intrigue, and a means of showing the Afghans that the British government does sympathise with them." But Auckland was adamant, and on January 20, 1838, the governor general wrote a sharp personal letter to Dost Mohammed: "You must desist from all correspondence with Russia," he commanded. "You must never receive agents from them, or have aught to do with [them] without our sanction; you must dismiss Captain Vitkevitch with courtesy; you must surrender all claims to Peshawar." Burnes, close to despair himself, was obliged to spell out the implications of this haughty missive: if Dost Mohammed dared to treat with the Russians, in defiance of British interests, he would be ousted. The tone of the letter was "so dictatorial and supercilious as to indicate the writer's intention that it should give offence." Which it did.

Harlan was with the amir when the letter arrived. "Dost Mahomed was mortified, but not terrified," he recorded. "When the didactic and imperative ultimatum of Lord Auckland was handed to the Ameer, in which he saw the frustration of his hopes, for he was decidedly in favour of an English alliance, a general council was called." Solemnly, the prince asked his senior chiefs for their views on how to deal with this threatening missive. "The document was handed to me," wrote Harlan. "I satisfied myself, by the Governor General's signature, of its authenticity, surveying the contents with extreme surprise and disappointment. The Governor General's ultimatum was handed round, and an embarrassing silence ensued." Once it had been read by all, the debate began: some chiefs urged further pacific overtures to Britain, others sided with the Russians, and a few suggested that Burnes should be summarily dealt with, to show that an Afghan prince could not be treated with contempt. Finally, a senior Barakzai chief rose to his feet and addressed the amir: "There is no other resource for you but to introduce Mr. Harlan in the negotiations with Mr. Burnes and he, through his own facilities and wisdom, will arrange a treaty, according to the European usage, for the pacific and advantageous settlement of your affairs." Harlan was duly delegated to negotiate with Burnes à deux.

Burnes was painfully aware that Auckland's offensive letter had left him with nothing to negotiate over, and he stalled. "An official note was immediately despatched to Burnes's secretary," wrote Harlan. "But by return of the messenger, an official response was received *indirectly declining* the proposition by deferring the measure to a more convenient opportunity of time." Harlan sent another, more urgent message, "referring to the Ameer's previous official communication investing me with powers to treat, containing a proposal to negotiate upon his own terms." Burnes again declined to see him. This "refusal to recommence negotiations," wrote Harlan, was the most ominous development yet, an inversion of diplomatic protocol. "The reply I received was personally friendly, but I was much astounded that it evinced a deficiency of knowledge of first principles concerning the rights of independent powers in political negotiations. I could not have believed that a gentleman of liberal education, and ordinary talent for observation, was so totally ignorant of equity and the laws of nations." The amir had been willing to strike a deal, but instead he had been rebuffed. Infuriated, Dost Mohammed summoned Vitkevitch, the Russian envoy, and "paraded him in triumph through the streets of Kabul."

At the same time it was made abundantly clear to Burnes that the days of black-eyed damsels on tap were definitively over, and he was no longer welcome. Harlan would later wonder if the amir had been a little too brusque in telling the British envoy to get out of town. "The English agent was dismissed with immediate, and somewhat indecorous, haste, though respectfully, and with presents of pacific propitiation, consisting of three or four horses, tolerably fair in value." On April 26, Burnes and his party quit Kabul in a departure as ignominious as their arrival had been grand. "Their fears were not unfounded," remarked Harlan. "For the Avgauns were indignant at the result of the negotiations." Realizing that his own position was now undermined, Masson joined Burnes in retreat.

The Afghans placed responsibility for the debacle firmly on the shoulders of Burnes himself, and Harlan likewise blamed the British envoy for failing to arrange a treaty "which should certainly have secured the friendship of the Avgauns." Masson was equally scathing, noting that the British government "had furnished no instructions, apparently confiding in the discretion of a man who had none." Angriest of all was Dost Mohammed, now hopelessly entangled in the larger imperial struggle between Britain and Russia. "Fool that I was! God had given me a competency. And, dissatisfied with enough, I have ruined my affairs by making myself the pivot of foreign diplomacy." The amir told Harlan that he should have dealt with Burnes in the traditional Afghan manner: "The greatest error of my life lay in this, that I allowed the English deceiver to escape with his head."

Alexander Burnes would soon be back, but this time at the head of an invading British army.

12

THE PRINCE OF GHOR

Harlan had spent more than a year training the Afghan troops (to the extent this was possible) and he was keen to test them in action. Dost Mohammed Khan had a target in mind, and in the summer of 1838 the amir appointed Harlan to lead a division of the Kabul army on a punitive expedition to the wilds of Tartary.

Dost Mohammed had successfully reinforced his rule over Kabul and its neighboring territories, but beyond the Hindu Kush, in Balkh, Mazar, and Kunduz, which had once formed part of the Afghan empire, his influence ranged from limited to nonexistent. North of the mountains, wrote Harlan, "all the petty chiefs of the province, sustaining a partially independent position, remained in possession of their estates, with separate interests, nominally subject to but seldom controlled by a paramount." There was one chieftain of particular concern to the amir: Murad Beg, Khan of Kunduz, the infamous Uzbek warlord and slave trader.

Murad Beg was a spectacular tyrant, toward his neighbors, his own people, and most especially toward any outsiders unlucky or unwise enough to cross his path. He had effectively held William Moorcroft for ransom in 1824, and was suspected of arranging the English adventurer's death. Burnes had narrowly escaped his clutches on his way to Bokhara. The chief of Kunduz maintained control by force, but his power was based on the slave trade. "This robber annually carries off men, women and children, cattle and produce" Harlan observed, while countless others were "driven into exile by the frequent hostile visits of the Kundooz chief."

In some ways Murad was a "fortunate adventurer," not unlike Harlan himself, a self-made prince who had risen to power largely through his own efforts. But there any similarity ended, for "this princely robber," as Harlan termed him, was a man of imaginative cruelty, who did not think twice about capturing entire villages and shipping the inhabitants to the slave markets of Turkistan. The slave-trading marauder looked the part. "A great bear of a man with harsh Tartar features. His eyes were small and hard as bullets, while his broad forehead was creased in a perpetual frown. He wore no beard and was no more richly dressed than his followers, except that his long knife was richly chased, as was the smaller dagger with which he toyed while talking." By browbeating neighboring chiefs and fomenting feuds among his rivals, the Uzbek had established himself as paramount chief of the region, with a formidable cavalry army. So lucrative were his slaving raids among the Hazara tribes of the central highlands, that his forces had begun to scavenge farther south, to the alarm of Dost Mohammed. Murad now threatened Bamian, at the northern frontier of the amir's territory, and had begun demanding transit dues from the few merchants he did not plunder, levies that Dost Mohammed considered his by right.

The idea of punishing a notorious slave dealer appealed to Harlan's sense of moral justice, but there was another compelling reason why he leaped at the chance to do battle with Murad Beg. In 329 B.C., Alexander the Great had crossed the Hindu Kush in pursuit of the rebel satrap Bessus, seizing Bactria and crossing the Oxus. Bessus had been one of the murderers of the Persian King Darius, and had proclaimed himself the new king of Asia in direct defiance of Alexander. Dragging siege equipment and stone-throwers through the freezing passes, living on roots and the flesh of slaughtered pack animals, and battling the fierce nomadic tribes as they went, Alexander's army had finally reached the plain on the other side of the mountains. Bessus was captured, deprived of ears and nose, and executed, but Alexander had pressed on, reaching Samarkand and finally founding Alexandria Eschate, Alexandria-at-the-end-of-the-world, traditionally identified with Khojand in Tajikistan.

Here was an opportunity for Harlan to pursue Alexander's trail still deeper into the interior, and to punish Murad Beg as Alexander had once trounced the refractory Bessus. The task was not one for the faint-hearted. "The Indian Caucasus between Bulkh and Cabul is three hundred miles broad," Harlan observed. "The country is filled up with great mountain ranges, the routes are through narrow defiles, ravines and upland valleys, and over passes rising to the gelid altitudes of perennial snow." He now faced the prospect of leading an army over this daunting barrier, where Alexander's invasion force had gone before. The very scale of the undertaking offered another rationale for the expedition. Many military tacticians of the day regarded the Hindu Kush as an insurmountable obstacle, a frozen barrier across which no modern army could cross, let alone one dragging artillery. If Harlan could prove otherwise, he would redraw the geopolitical map, by demonstrating that a Russian army could feasibly descend from the north, threatening British India itself.

The authorities in Calcutta would be most interested in the outcome of this dangerous military experiment; those in Saint Petersburg, even more so; and Dost Mohammed, given his delicate diplomatic position pinned between the two powers, most of all. The expedition was one more throw of the dice in the Great Game, an opportunity to establish what Russophobes in London most feared and Russian imperialists, in their wilder fantasies, dreamed of.

To cow Murad Beg, Harlan would need a substantial force, and over the late summer and early autumn, he assembled his army: 1,400 cavalry, 1,100 infantry, 2,000 horses, and 400 camels. Cooks, servants, grooms, and other camp followers brought the total to nearly 4,000 men. Like Alexander before him, Harlan planned to recruit additional native forces en route. Artillery was of paramount importance, both to test whether a modern army could make the passage and to demolish the walls of Kunduz if necessary; one hundred artillerymen were detailed to man the train of cannon, consisting of four six-pounders and two battering guns. The baggage would be carried by tough crossbred camels, part Bactrian, part dromedary, and *yaboos*, hardy little ponies capable of covering 30 miles a day with a load of 300 pounds. Harlan was a great admirer of the *yaboo*, "a strong, enduring, and sure-footed animal, frequently piebald and fantastically spotted, with a rough and shaggy coat, fetlocks sweeping the ground, and heavy tail and mane."

As a final majestic addition to his expedition, Harlan recruited a large bull elephant. "His services were useful in assisting the artillery," he wrote. But here, once again, was an echo of Alexander the Great, for the elephant was the mighty mascot of the Macedonian conqueror: Egyptian coins show him dressed in a cap of elephant skin; the great pachyderms guarded his tent and adorned his funeral chariot. Other classical conquerors followed suit: Caesar took an elephant to Britain; Pompey harnessed two to his chariot; and Hannibal, most memorably, took his over the Alps, mere hillocks compared to the range now facing Harlan. An elephant was de rigueur for the epic-minded invader.

As nominal commander in chief of the expedition, Dost Mohammed Khan appointed one of his younger sons, Akram Khan, "a lad of about 18 years of age" in Harlan's words. The young prince would grow into an impressive military leader, but in Harlan's opinion he had also inherited his father's less attractive traits, being "an avaricious and parsimonious young man." As general of the prince's staff, and "councilor and aide-de-camp to the young chief," there was little doubt who was in overall control of the expedition. "The young man commanded the expedition into Tartary," wrote Harlan, but "under my tutelage." Ever one for formalities, Harlan also brought along one of the amir's secretaries, to carry the prince's seal and underline the official nature of the enterprise.

By September Harlan was ready to march, blithely unaware that the British were also assembling an army with the intention of ousting Dost Mohammed and restoring Shah Shujah, at long last, as a British puppet on the Afghan throne. Claude Wade and William Macnaghten, the chief secretary, had successfully argued that the best way to resist Russian encroachment was to reinstate Shujah. Burnes had tried to defend Dost Mohammed. "If half you must do for others were done for him, he would abandon Russia . . . tomorrow," he wrote, adding that he had "no very high opinion" of Shah Shujah. It was too late for such arguments. Macnaghten was a cultured and clever man, but he was also an avid Russophobe, utterly convinced of the rectitude of his own opinions. He had made up his mind, and that of Lord Auckland. The British juggernaut was rolling and, despite his misgivings, Alexander Burnes would dutifully climb aboard.

Macnaghten was dispatched to the court of Ranjit Singh to negotiate a tripartite alliance with Shah Shujah against Dost Mohammed Khan. The maharaja was now "an old man in an advanced state of decrepitude, clothed in faded crimson, his head wrapped up in folds of the same colour." His strength was ebbing, but his memory was not, and the prospect of inflicting a final defeat on his old Afghan enemy, not to mention Harlan, seemed to give him renewed strength. Burnes was present during negotiations, and at one point Ranjit turned to him and asked for news of Harlan. Burnes took the opportunity to blacken the American's name, observing that he and anyone else who had dared to quit the maharaja's service "were not expected to gain anything by their faithlessness and were sure to be punished for their bad deeds." Macnaghten was received even more enthusiastically in Ludhiana by Shah Shujah, who was now presented with the longed-for opportunity to regain his throne at British expense. Afghanistan was primed to explode, he declared. "It merely requires the lighted torch to be applied." Shujah agreed to march his own army on Kandahar, while the Sikhs advanced through the Khyber Pass. In the end, however, it was British bayonets that would bring Shah Shujah back to Afghanistan.

On October 1, 1838, Lord Auckland published the Simla Manifesto, the formal, cynical justification for a full-scale invasion of Afghanistan, the necessity for which was laid entirely at the door of Dost Mohammed Khan: "He avowed schemes of aggrandisement and ambition injurious to the peace and of the frontiers of India; he openly threatened, in furtherance of those schemes, to call in every foreign aid which he could command . . . So long as Caubul remained under his government, we could never hope that the tranquillity of our neighbourhood would be secured, or that the interests of our Indian empire would be preserved inviolate." This aggressive amir was the same one who, just a few months earlier, had been pleading for a British alliance. The treaty concluded with ill-judged optimism: "His Majesty Shah Soojah-oll-Moolk will enter Afghanistan surrounded by his own troops, and will be supported against foreign interference and factious opposition by the British army. The Governor General confidently hopes that the Shah will be speedily replaced on his throne by his own subjects and adherents; and when once he shall be secured in power, and the independence and integrity of Afghanistan restored, the British army shall be withdrawn." The most prescient voice was that of old Mountstuart Elphinstone, the retired Company official whose writing had so inspired Harlan decades earlier. Elphinstone told the warmongers: "The Afghans were neutral and would have received your aid against invaders with gratitude. They will now be disaffected and glad to join any invader to drive you out." Amid the loud preparations for war, his wise warning went unheard.

Harlan, on top of his elephant deep in the mountains, was much too far away to hear the approaching rumble. His departure from Kabul in September at the head of his troops had been a grand ceremonial affair. The idea that Afghan forces were being withdrawn at the precise moment a vast army was mobilizing across the border never occurred to anyone, least of all Amir Dost Mohammed Khan. As Harlan later observed: "His Highness never conceived that the English would project the invasion of Cabul."

Harlan's army headed northeast toward the white-capped peaks of the Hindu Kush, through a glowing autumnal landscape. "Beautiful orchards, wild flowers and plants in profuse abundance grew along the margins of the innumerable brooks which intersect the valleys. Every hill with a southern aspect had a vineyard on it, and raisins were spread out on the ground, and imparted a purple tinge to the hills." Here the soldiers could scoop up food by the handful, but Harlan knew well that once they reached the mountains, with winter approaching, the privations would begin.

The army was following the age-old pilgrim and merchant trail between Kabul, Bamian, Balkh, and Bokhara, "the route of Alexander the Great to the province of Bulkh, the Bactria of ancient times," in Harlan's words. For any student of Alexander, the place where the Macedonian supposedly took the native princess Roxanne as his wife held mythical resonance. "Bulkh is called the Mother of all Cities," wrote Harlan. "Traditions assert its antiquity beyond all other cities of the world." Once more he felt himself marching into history, and once again he imagined himself as a latter-day Alexander, preparing to conquer a fabled wilderness where "the savage Bactrians submitted to his sway and received the civilization of Greece."

Before leaving Kabul, Harlan had been given a tiny piece of ancient Greek jewelry, possibly by Dost Mohammed himself, an engraved ruby in the form of a signet that had been discovered at Bagram, near the site of the ancient Hellenic city Alexandria ad Caucasum. The jewel was a minute work of art, "about the thickness of a playing card, highly polished [and] no larger than a central section of a split pea," with a carving depicting the goddess Athena "the tutelary deity of Athens, in threefold character: the patroness of navigation, of war, and of letters." The exquisite little gem seems to have symbolized Harlan's sense of his own civilizing mission, the American bringing righteous progress to a benighted land by force of arms, just as the Macedonian had once done. "The bold and scientific execution of the engraving, the polish of the gem, the voluminous design, indicate the arts, the sciences, the commerce, war, and letters predominant twenty-two centuries ago in the heart of Asia, implanted there by a European philanthropist." Here was Harlan's code, carved in miniature: exploration, conquest, and knowledge. The ancient Bactrians, however, had not seen Alexander in quite such a rosy light, any more than their descendants would celebrate the arrival of his self-styled successor.

The route to Bamian led across a mighty mountain range, the Koh-i-Baba, or Father of Mountains, the southernmost extension of the Hindu Kush, which rises 16,244 feet above sea level. As the army began to climb, Harlan gazed in awe at "the ruggedness of its outline, interrupted by vast elevated peaks." Alexander had crossed the mountains in May 329 B.C. by way of the Khaiwak Pass north of Kabul, before dropping into Bactria. Harlan now headed for the more westerly and even higher Kharzar Pass (or Hajigak Pass), which slices through the mountains at 15,900 feet. The mountain paths, wrote Harlan, "would foil an expert topographer in their tortuous delineations," while the looming skyline ahead was "broken by steep, rugged peaks, naked rocks and abrupt hills." From the mountain track, Harlan peered down over "wild and broken precipices" to where "huge fragments rent asunder from the cliffs" had crashed into the valleys below. There was little plant life up here, and no human life, save a few hardy bandits. But the soldiers were not the only creatures toiling over the mountains: with the air too thin for flight, "large storks could be seen labouring up the steep passes on foot."

At night, Harlan and his men slept in *khirgahs*, native tents that were, he cheerily declared, the ideal "winter residence, far superior to a single-roomed house." At night, huddled around dung fires, they listened to the wild animals in the ravines. "The yelling of the jackal is a frightful noise," wrote Harlan, "and when heard in the dark, still night, creates a feeling of terror in the listener." Still worse were the marauding packs of wolves circling the tents. Mountain-bred mastiffs were posted to protect the livestock, to little avail. "I have known wolves to enter our camp and carry off five or six sheep in the course of a single night," Harlan observed.

The army was still several days' march from the pass when the weather closed in with brutal ferocity. Harlan tied strips of wool from ankle to knee, declaring that such leggings "support the muscles of the legs and enable the wearer to persevere in his efforts with less fatigue." On his head he clamped "a closely fitting chintz padded cap or one of sheep skin and the turban of Khorassan." Wrapped up in his fox-fur cloak and his thoughts of Alexander, he spurred his horse on through the drifts. As tough as aged saddle leather, he seldom mentioned the cold in his writings, but others in the party suffered bitterly, notably the poor elephant, which was showing signs of exhaustion and frostbite. As the landscape and climate grew ever harsher, Harlan was moved to lyricism:

> We ascended passes through regions where glaciers and silent dells, and frowning rocks, blackened by ages of weatherbeaten fame, preserved the quiet domain of remotest time, shrouded in perennial snow. We struggled on amid the heights of those Alpine ranges—until now supposed inaccessible to the labour of man—infantry and cavalry, artillery, camp followers and beasts of burden—surmounting difficulties by obdurate endurance, defying the pitiless pelting of the snow and rain, as these phenomena alternately and capriciously coquetted with our everchanging climate. We pressed onward, scaling those stony girdles of the earth, dim shades, as children of the mists far above the nether world, toiling amidst the clouds like restless spirits of another sphere.

Finally, they reached the summit and an exultant Harlan ordered a full military review, and one of the oddest American flag–raising ceremonies ever staged. "I surmounted the Indian Caucasus, and there upon the mountain heights, unfurled my country's banner to the breeze, under a salute of twenty-six guns. On the highest pass of the frosty Caucasus, that of Kharzar, the star-spangled banner gracefully waved amidst the icy peaks and soilless rugged rocks of a sterile region, seemingly sacred to the solitude of an undisturbed eternity."

Harlan did not linger on the mountaintop, but hurried down into the Bamian Valley, where the altitude was a more livable eight thousand feet. Here two great statues of Buddha, the largest 180 feet high, had been carved out of the sandstone cliff, and a warren of caves had once been home to more than a thousand Buddhist monks. The town was teeming with people, camels, and horses, for Harlan's arrival had coincided with that of a merchant convoy also heading north toward Mazar, with "cashmere shawls, indigo, white and printed piece goods" intended for the markets of Turkistan, Persia, and Russia. Harlan counted "sixteen hundred camels and six hundred pack horses, accompanied by about two thousand people, men, women and children." The country beyond Bamian was notorious for banditry, and when the leader of the merchants requested that the caravan might attach itself to his army and enjoy the protection of the invading force, Harlan agreed.

Ahead lay the unmapped territory of the Hazaras, Persian-speaking Shia Muslims with flat features and narrow eyes said to be the descendants of the thirteenth-century Mongol hordes of Genghis Khan. The region, Harlan recorded, went by many names. The Roman historian Quintus Curtius had called it "the plain of Pamezan," while "Mahomedan historians of a later date treat of that mountain district under the denomination of Ghoree." Harlan himself uses the Greek name for the Hindu Kush, the Paropamisus, derived from the Persian word *uparisena*, meaning "peak over which the eagle cannot fly." To the people who lived there, however, this was the "Hazarajat," the land of a thousand tribes and, inevitably, a thousand feuds.

The great convoy lumbered out of Bamian in the last week of October, the original four thousand-strong force reinforced by the armed men accompanying the civilian *karrovan*. But the army had also suffered its first major casualty. The elephant, having carried Harlan up the highest mountain in the Hindu Kush and down the other side, could take no more of the climate. With regret, Harlan sent the suffering beast "back to Cabul from Bameean, in consequence of the cold, from which he suffered much." It was some consolation that Alexander the Great had also been forced to leave his elephants behind in "the elephant parks to the west of Kandahar [where] they could wallow in swamps of warm mud, happy in the winter comforts which they needed."

As his army marched north, Harlan studied the local Hazara people with fascination. Regarded as heretics by Sunnis, they were quite different in appearance from other Afghans, "a strong, hardy, athletic race, remarkable for *en bon point* and blunt features," with angled eyes and flatter noses. "They have large ears, thick lips, broad faces and high cheekbones," he wrote. "The hair is black and glossy, beards sparse." As the column advanced, small groups of mounted Hazara warriors armed with swords, shields, and spears attached themselves to the swelling army. Harlan ordered the newcomers brought to his tent, and was impressed by their manners and appearance: "They are a merry, unsophisticated race, fickle, passionate and capricious."

The Hazaras were supposed to pay an annual tribute to Kabul, and Harlan's expedition was, in part, a show of force to ensure they continued doing so. While many Hazara chiefs resented the domination of Kabul, they were delighted to see punishment meted out to Murad Beg and his tribe, of whose depredations they lived in constant fear. The new recruits brought horrific tales of Murad's slave raids and the cruelties he visited not just on the Hazaras, but on his own people. Harlan was righteously appalled. "That prince seizes every opportunity of selling his subjects into slavery of whom thousands, and frequently village communities en masse, are removed from their homes, parents torn from their children, the bonds of natural affection severed between members of the same family and their sisters and daughters and brothers abandoned to the vile depravity of beastly sensualists."

No one, it seemed, was safe from the Uzbeks. "All unprotected strangers travelling in this part of Tatary would be liable to seizure and condemnation to slavery and no question asked," Harlan recorded. The Uzbek tended to strike at night, "lying in wait and rushing out from an ambush and falling upon his destined prey with frightful and unearthly yells. He attacks with his long spear, to the end of which he has fastened a composition of wild fire, lighted into a blaze." Harlan described the "diabolical contrivance" with which the Uzbek raiders literally sewed the captives to their saddles. "To oblige the prisoner to keep up a strand of horse hair is passed by means of a long crooked needle, under and around the collar bone, a few inches from its junction at the sternum; with the hair, a loop is formed to which they attach a rope that may be fastened to the saddle. The captive is constrained to keep near the retreating horsemen, and with hands tied behind his person, is altogether helpless."

Slavery would soon provoke civil war in America, and Harlan's views on the subject were progressive and passionate, for he regarded the ownership of one man by another not merely as evil, but socially toxic: "The corrupt and baneful morals resulting from the institution of slavery seem to have poisoned or permanently closed up the natural benevolence of humanity, which is found in all primitive and unsophisticated communities." The Kunduz chief's role in the slave industry added a moral dimension to Harlan's small crusade: "Muraad Beg is the great wholesale dealer in this unholy merchandise," he declared. "The traffic in Toorkistaun is no less destructive of human rights than that in the interior of Africa."

Fear of the slave raiders was reflected in the very architecture of the countryside. As Harlan penetrated deeper into the Hazarajat, the dwellings seemed to shrink fearfully into the landscape, with the houses "half sunk into slopes of hills" beneath "a bastion constructed of sun-dried mud, where the people of the village resort in case of danger from the sudden forays of the Tatar robbers." The population grew sparse, but the wildlife became more plentiful. "Wolves, foxes and hares infest the hills and ravines," wrote Harlan, who was particularly impressed by the wild sheep roaming the highest crags. "A noble animal, his horns frequently attain the thickness of a man's thigh; he is bold and agile and exceedingly ferocious in his amatory combats." The wild sheep had a reputation for devouring snakes, and its gallbladder was used as a treatment for snakebite. Dr. Harlan offered the prescription in his journal: "The gallstone is used by first dividing it in two parts through its diameter. The flat surfaces are then applied to the snake bite. The substance being porous, draws out the poison by absorption, adhering to the wound until it becomes replete with moisture."

Peeping out from the rocks was another creature Harlan had never seen before: "It has the fur of a rabbit and much the appearance of one half grown, except the ears. In shape it more nearly resembles a guinea pig. Teeth and claws of a rat, broad, flat forehead, and a hare lip." This was a marmot, a sort of hard-bitten hamster that plays an intriguing role in Greek mythology. Herodotus had written about the "gold-digging ants" of the Himalayas that "as they burrow underground, throw up sand in heaps, which have a rich content of gold." Alexander's men had tried to find these natural gold diggers, but what Herodotus described as an "ant" was probably a marmot, mistranslated from the ancient Persian term for the animal, which was "mountain ant." Harlan gave orders for one to be brought to him, and immediately adopted it as a successor to the late Dash. "It is a sociable animal," he noted, "becoming familiar immediately after being captured."

The route north led near to the fortress at Saighan, stronghold of Mohammed Ali Beg, an ethnic Tajik chieftain who was also notorious for his slave-raiding activities against the Hazaras. Subduing Ali Beg would be an excellent dress rehearsal for the hostilities to come, and since his fortress was considered impregnable, a successful siege would demonstrate the effectiveness of Harlan's battering guns and awe the Hazara chiefs. Ali Beg appears, quite sensibly, to have taken flight before the Afghans' arrival, but even with only a handful of defenders Saighan was an impressive sight. "The position is a natural fortress," wrote Harlan, "supposed to have been in existence at the period of Alexander's invasion of India." As always, Harlan reached for a classical parallel: "The appearance of this stronghold reminds one forcibly of the rock of Aornus as described by Q. Curtius." Harlan provided no details of the attack on Saighan, other than to note that "a practical demonstration of artillery service was displayed" in its capture. Mud walls were no defense against battering guns. The news that Saighan was now in Afghan hands was sent by messenger to the most important Hazara chiefs, along with "letters of a most friendly tenure" inviting them to a meeting with the invading forces.

The fall of Saighan particularly impressed one Mohammed Reffee Beg, prince of Ghoree (or Ghor), paramount chief of the Day Zangi Hazaras. "The Ghorian princes sprang from a race of hardy mountaineers who inhabited the highest arable altitudes of the Paropamisus," wrote Harlan. Some ten years before Harlan's arrival, Mohammed Reffee Beg had made a secret trip to Kunduz, where he was inspired by Murad Beg's subjugation of his neighbors. "Undisguisedly ambitious of concentrating a similar power in his own country" he had set about dominating his fellow chiefs "by matrimonial alliances, a conciliatory policy and treaties offensive and defensive," and by 1838 had succeeded in establishing himself as the paramount chief of the region, the most powerful of all the mountain warlords. The news that an Afghan army had seized Saighan made a strong impression on Mohammed Reffee: weapons that could reduce a fort to rubble might prove exceedingly useful in expanding his own domain.

Leaving a garrison at Saighan, the Afghan army marched on to the Valley of Khamerd, which marked the border between Hazara country and Turkistan, to await the arrival of the Hazara chiefs, "who had been invited, in token of submission and friendly alliance, to be present when the army seized this, their frontier." That evening Mohammed Reffee Beg trotted into the camp, accompanied by his brothers, the chiefs of several allied clans, and "three hundred cavalry selected for their fidelity and fine appearance, the elite of his followers." The Hazara horsemen made a vivid spectacle, "clad in elegant Cashmere turbans" and brightly colored Uzbek cloaks, each man carrying a variety of weaponry. "Their arms are a sword and shield, with a long spear or matchlock, embellished and mounted with gold and silver ornamentation. Their saddles are mounted with gold and silver and their housings are made of scarlet broad cloth embroidered with gold and the brocade of Benares." Even the grooms carried "Persian daggers, Tatar knives, and pistols stuck in their waist belts like small arms around the masts of a privateer. Every man was a frigate freighted with portentous belligerent impulses."

Mohammed Reffee and his brothers, "all men of athletic forms and noble bearing," presented themselves to the leaders of the war party and bowed before Akram Khan, the amir's son. After an exchange of courtly pleasantries, a feast was laid on for the Hazaras, who then withdrew and set up a separate encampment. In accordance with Afghan tradition Mohammed Reffee expected to be treated as an honored guest. Akram Khan, however, displayed his natural parsimony, rudely informing the Hazaras that since his own army was short of food they would have to fend for themselves. Embarrassed by such discourtesy, Harlan believed "the Prince of Cabul should have provided for them at the sacrifice of his own comfort," particularly since the Hazara visitors were "three marches away from home."

Mohammed Reffee Beg never traveled without his holy man, or *pir*, Sayyid Najaf, who also acted as his vizier. This man now approached Harlan and explained that unless some food could be procured, a regrettable and potentially violent diplomatic incident might ensue. Harlan had been discreetly stockpiling supplies for just such a contingency. "I readily shared with Mahommed Reffee, and the chiefs accompanying him, the flour, rice, *roghum*, barley and sheep, I had accumulated and treasured up," he wrote. "The chief and his principal attaches became the writer's guests during the ten days of their sojourn at Kamerd."

Harlan now had an opportunity to observe Mohammed Reffee at closer quarters. He liked what he saw. "In person he is a tall, portly man, about forty years of age, with flattened nose and Negro expression. He is fond of display and encourages a similar taste in his followers." He was also astute, and as thrusting as Harlan himself. "A man of vigorous mind, said to be sometimes cruel in the execution of his will, crafty, and temperate. His life has been actively passed in military service and he is familiar with the habits and practices of a predatory soldier. He is bold in action, but cautious, and courageous, far surpassing in those qualities any of his competitors. His deportment is silent, modest and reserved [but] his insatiable passion is an ambition to achieve political power."

The American and the Hazara chief had much in common. "He is anxious to sustain his position by the introduction of foreign influence," wrote Harlan, "and he would willingly attempt the permanent subjugation of his subordinate allies in conjunction with a foreign ally." Such a talented, unscrupulous, and forceful personality could forge a mighty kingdom, the American mused. Indeed, "the resources that might be made subject to his control would, in the hands of an intelligent agent, establish the foundation of an empire." Great empires of the past had started small, he reflected, including Babur's Mogul dynasty that, "from an origin still more insignificant, ultimately swept over the surface of Asia as a hurricane over the deep." Might not this chief, with his ferocious followers and passion for power, be the man to help carve out the kingdom Harlan imagined?

First, however, Mohammed Reffee would need to be given a demonstration of what a modern army, under Harlan's command, could do. "This Hazarrah prince, greatly to his astonishment and admiration, was entertained with a review of the brigade . . . The organisation and discipline of the corps appeared to the chief an inconceivable achievement, and the rapid evolutions of the field battery surpassed the credibility of belief." His brothers "acquainted only with the primitive and circumscribed experience acquired amongst their crags and dells" were equally impressed.

Suitably awestruck, the prince asked Harlan whether his Hazaras could be made into soldiers. Harlan was blunt. Reffee's followers, he pointed out, were merely "promiscuous bodies of badly-mounted men, armed with long, heavy spears, without order or method in their move-

ments, incapable of combined attack, and inefficient for any other purpose of war than the wild, savage foray."

"I speak of them as they are," Harlan declared, "but discipline would
no doubt work a wonderful change in their present habits, and it is possible they might be moulded into a useful arm of aggression." The Hazaras were superb marksmen with their long-handled muskets or *jezails*,
capable of firing an ounce ball as far as "a six pound field piece" and even
shooting from the saddle, Harlan noted, they "seldom miss their mark
when at full speed." The long-distance ambush was a Hazara speciality.
"Each one lies down with his head towards the enemy, before which he
places a large stone. He rolls upon his back to reload, selects his mark,
and kills at an incredible distance with little personal risk." As Harlan
had anticipated, Mohammed Reffee's eyes lit up when the artillery was
fired, but then the Hazara chief grew pensive. "Silent and thoughtful,
he evolved in his mind the immense power a regular military system
would secure to him in the execution of his plans. The result was soon
evidenced by the proposals he subsequently submitted to the writer."

After ten days of eating Harlan's food and studying his army, the
Hazaras prepared to return home. Pointing out that his fortress was but
a short distance away, Mohammed Reffee urged Harlan to accompany
him and promised to provide a force of Hazaras to accompany him back
to the main army in a few days. "These Hazarrah princes, the principal
and most influential of whom were present, invited me collectively and
individually to visit them in their mountain homes," wrote Harlan, flat-
tered but hesitant, for the Hazaras had a fearsome reputation. "I suggested that the residence of a stranger might become a cause of offence
to his people and excite a disposition to insubordination. He replied,
with a savage pride, 'I am the master of the lives of my people and if I
chose to sell them all to the Uzbecks not one would dare oppose my
will! They are all my slaves!'"

Three days later, Harlan found himself in Reffee Beg's mountain
fortress, where the chief laid on a lavish display of Hazara hospitality. It
was now Harlan's turn to be impressed, as the prince summoned his retinue to attend the distinguished foreigner, the first *feringhee* most had
laid eyes on. Harlan compared Reffee's entourage to feudal knights, an
aristocratic warrior caste who, like their European counterparts of the
Middle Ages, were "proud of their arms and martial decorations" and

extravagant in their costume. "The pantaloons are wide but they draw on long closely fitting stockings, and should they have the Uzbeck fancy, wear the high-heeled boot of that people [while] those who have been lucky in foray wear Cashmere shawls plundered from karrovans. A taste for the elegant may be said to appear in their fanciful decorations of military display. This principle is exhibited in their admiration of gay and brilliant colours."

Reffee Beg ruled like a medieval prince. "The government is patriarchal, feudal and absolute," wrote Harlan. But the system seemed to work surprisingly well: "The occurrence of serious crimes is exceedingly rare. Murder and theft are unknown and capital punishment is never inflicted. Slavery is the extreme punishment."

The Hazaras generally existed in "a rude condition of life, owing to their insulated position," but the longer Harlan spent among them, the more he admired their fierce manners and code of honor. "They are by no means to be classed as savages. A distinction must be made between the rude primeval simplicity of nature and the rudeness of licentiousness and depravity of morals arising from the corruptions of vice. The first is the foundation of a pure system of morals [for] rudeness, frugality and despotic military government are evidences of simplicity and natural purity favourable to the existence of moral virtue." Rousseau would have recognized his noble savage in Harlan's description of his new friends. These Hazaras, Harlan decided, must be descendants of the Scythians who fought Alexander. "They are the 'Spirits of the waste' who inhabit the wild and sterile deserts of the Caucasian mountains. They have been transiently subdued, but never enslaved or permanently conquered and held in subjugation. The experience of history, derived from the period of Alexander, prove[s] the unconquerable nature of these semi-civilized communities inhabiting the vast range of mountains." To Harlan the Hazaras recalled an ancient way of life, which disdained commerce in favor of martial virtue. "The mountains are known to have wealth in unwrought ores and valuable metals," he wrote, yet "coined money is unknown among them." At night, around the prince's fire, they would swap tales of military valor and listen to music, played on "a gourd and three strings, which is accompanied by the voice, a reed, resembling the flageolet; a small drum; and cymbals." They celebrated without the benefit of drink, always an issue close to Harlan's Quaker heart: "Intoxicating liquors or habits of intemperance are not among the vices of the inhabitants," he observed with approval. Harlan spent only a short time among the Hazaras, but he idealized them, devoting page after page to their manners and customs, their rituals and habits. The American believed he had found a savage mountain paradise, an ancient kingdom of tough, teetotal warriors, boasting untapped wealth and noble customs; the kernel, perhaps, of an empire.

There was one aspect of Hazara culture that seems to have impressed Harlan more than any other: elsewhere in his writings he seldom refers to the opposite sex, but the liberated women of the Hazarjat had a most powerful effect upon him. Instead of being hidden away behind walls or veils, the women lived, worked, hunted, and even went into battle alongside their husbands: "The men display remarkable deference for the opinions of their wives. The wife and husband amongst the Hazarrahs are inseparable. She sits with her husband in the divan, dressed like him and booted, ready for the chase and even the military foray," in which the women were quite as ferocious as the men. "The men address their wives with the respectful and significant title of *Aga*, which means mistress. They associate with them as equal companions, consult with them on all occasions, and in weighty matters, when they are not present, defer a conclusion until the opinions of their women can be heard." Harlan had spent most of his adult life in societies where women were regarded with "indifference and contempt," but here, high in the mountains, he had found an unlikely bastion of sexual equality. During the hunt, the Hazara women unleashed their swift smooth-haired black greyhounds on the wild deer, and then hurtled in pursuit, shooting and shouting, galloping "unshod horses over the precipitous deer path, regardless of danger, and bring down the game at full speed." The women were not only proud and fearless, but strikingly attractive: "Hazarrah ladies have the beautiful tint of a healthy, florid English complexion," wrote Harlan, breathlessly.

Twenty-two centuries earlier, at the age of twenty-nine, Alexander the Great had taken as his bride the princess Roxanne, "little star," the daughter of a Sogdian baron and by myth the most beautiful woman in all Asia. The marriage was celebrated with a great banquet, and the Greek painter Aetion depicted Roxanne on her wedding night: "Smiling cupids were in attendance; one stood behind and pulled back the veil from her face; another removed her shoe, while a third was tugging Alexander towards her by the cloak." Alexander was in love, the legend writers insisted, but the marriage was also a sound political gesture, symbolizing alliance with and domination of the local tribes.

Did Harlan too find love high in the mountains of the Hazarajat? Did Reffee Beg, like the Sogdian baron Oxyartes, present the invader with a wife or lover, his own Roxanne? Harlan described in detail the wedding of the Hazara chief's daughter, including the "horses, slaves, felts, carpets and clothing" given in dowry, and the "marriage celebrated at the house of the bride's father, with feasting, horse racing, target shooting and the interchange of presents among the guests." Perhaps his visit just happened to coincide with a princely wedding, or perhaps he was part of it. Harlan is not explicit, but he romanticized the Hazara women in a way that suggests his heart had been touched. A strange, oblique passage in his journals gives the clearest hint that some sort of emotional catharsis took place in the Hazarajat. As always when writing of emotion, his imagery is intensely floral. "In the remotest mountain glens and vales of the frosty Caucasus, devoted to the fairy conceptions of imaginative romance, there the soul of love sighed not, but luxuriated in the delicious exuberance of ideality, and associated in fellowship with the nightingale, whose only dream was of carnation roses, and Cupid gambolling in a bed of pansies, and who sang so sweetly in her vesper song of never dying happiness in love's uninvaded bower." Years before, he had written a similar love poem, in flowers, to the fickle Eliza Swaim. He still kept a copy in his saddlebag, but the pain it contained was ebbing.

The days passed in hunting and riding, the nights in feasting and plotting. "Men of ambitious views may be always found or created in divided communities," remarked Harlan, and none were more ambitious than Mohammed Reffee Beg, who had convinced himself, and his brothers, that with Harlan's military knowledge they could create a "regular military system by means of which they [might] subdue to their purposes the inferior, refractory parties." Harlan hinted that the British, or more likely the Russians, might be willing to underwrite such a project, laying before Mohammed Reffee's acquisitive gaze "a splendid perspective of conquest, dominion and glory."

Harlan's price for promising to help the Hazaras was a high one. But finally, the night before he was due to leave, an agreement was reached.

A treaty was written out in elegant Persian script, sealed with Mohammed Reffee's signet, witnessed by the holy man, and signed on the
Koran. Its terms were simple and extraordinary: high on a desolate
mountain, surrounded by Afghan tribesmen, the American was made
king. In Harlan's words, the Hazara prince "transferred his principality
to me in feudal service, binding himself and his tribe to pay tribute for
ever, stipulating that he should be made Vizier. The absolute and complete possession of his government was legally conveyed according to
official form, by a treaty which I have still preserved. There was an article in the treaty by which I was bound to raise, organize, discipline and
command, a regular corps of infantry and artillery, for the pay and
maintenance of which the revenues of the country were an adequate ap-
propriation." These terms, Harlan declared, were binding in perpetuity:
"The Prince of Ghoree, now Yengoreah, pledged the fidelity of himself,
his heirs and tribe, in feudal tenure, to serve, obey and pay tribute for
ever . . . The sovereignty was secured to me and my heirs, and the
Vizarat to himself and his heirs."

To formalize the agreement, Sayyid Najaf, Mohammed Reffee's
holy man, penned a formal legal guarantee in Persian, an elaborate act
of submission to the American adventurer. The document, which has
survived, was stamped with the chief's personal seal.

> I, who am the highly stationed slave of the Court Muhammed Reffee
> Begim Yanghur, at this time have made a valid, correct, legal acknowl-
> edgement. Since at this time I have instituted between myself and the
> highly stationed one, equipped with ardour and might, chief of the
> mighty Khans, paragon of the magnificent grandees, companion of
> the King, intimate Sovereignty, Harlan Sahib Bahadur friendship, devo-
> tion, service and obedience in making arrangements for the affairs of the
> Yanghur governors, whenever the kindly and benevolent Sahib comes to
> the lands of Surkhjuy, I shall not deviate by a hair's breadth from obedi-
> ence to the orders of the said Sahib. In whatever is required by way of
> service and devotion I shall not spare myself in any respect, but rather,
> morning and evening, and constantly, in serving the benevolent Sahib,
> year upon year and for countless centuries, by all my children and broth-
> ers, shall not spare myself in the matter of obedience to His command,
> or, slave of the Court that I am, by all the Yanghur forebears, hold back
> in any way. These few words were penned by way of a compact so that
> they may subsequently serve as documentation. On the date of the 7th of
> the exalted month of Shaban in the year 1255 [October 16, 1839].

Mohammed Reffee Beg's promises may not have been worth the paper they were written on. The treaty articles specifying that Harlan would raise a trained corps are still missing, and perhaps the promise to serve Harlan for all eternity was mere flattery. But Harlan himself was in deadly earnest: with Mohammed Reffee as his vizier, he would build a new kingdom using Hazara warriors, modern military tactics, and outside help if necessary. "Our views contemplated the centralization of political power," he declared. "A firm footing may be established in the most inaccessible part of the Hazarrahjaut'h and the whole of eastern Khorassan, from the Indus to Meshed, be brought under foreign influence by any power possessing stability and permanency of purpose." Taking leave of Mohammed Reffee, Harlan promised that he would soon return with his own troops to fulfill his side of the bargain, and rode back to rejoin the rest of the army, with a piece of paper in his pocket proclaiming him prince, accompanied by his retinue of one thousand mounted Hazara auxiliaries.

Harlan had long imagined himself as a civilizing conqueror, a self-made potentate combining the virtues of American wisdom with the might of modern empire. Contemporaries believed his goal had always been to rule in Afghanistan. He had parlayed with princes, ruled swathes of the Punjab under Ranjit Singh, and marched an army across the Hindu Kush. But now he had achieved his ambition to become "a sovereign prince, the crown of Ghor having been secured to him and his heirs by a voluntary act." In the violent Hazarajat, paramount chiefs seldom stayed that way for long. Harlan's "rule" would be exceptional in its brevity. The newly made American prince of Ghor would never see his principality again.

13

PROMETHEUS FROM PENNSYLVANIA

Back at Khamerd, Harlan was greeted by "a tall, robust and corpulent person, with a ruddy complexion," who introduced himself as the Meer i Wullee, Uzbek prince of Kholum and chief of Tash Khoorghaun, the territory lying between Balkh and Kunduz. The meer was a bitter rival of Murad Beg, having lost most of his heredity possessions to that warlord. He announced that he wanted to join forces with the invading army to attack Murad, and had brought with him one thousand Uzbek horsemen for the purpose.

Harlan, who now regarded himself as an honorary Hazara, was predisposed against the slave-trading Uzbeks, but he immediately took to Meer i Wullee, a most appealing and hideous barbarian: "His eyes are dark and penetrating, one of them being remarkable for a slight leprous cast. His mouth is large, the lips protuberant, a round face and high full cheeks. In manners he is stately and urbane; and in social intercourse fastidious, formal and dignified. He is intelligent, enterprising, bold and ambitious." Leprosy, and an addiction to snuff, had left the Uzbek with a most memorable nose. This was "originally well-shaped and somewhat trousée, but the effect of disease has depressed the ridge of it and elevated the tip so as to expose a view into the nostrils. He takes a great deal of snuff and constant intrusion of the fingers, which he screws into his nostrils together with a handkerchief, has increased their capacity to an unusual size." Harlan tried a pinch of Uzbek snuff and declared it "finely levigated, resembling the Scotch preparation [and] kept in gourds about the size of a goose egg, ornamented with exquisite carving of floral designs."

After a halt of twenty-two days in Khamerd, the army finally set off again, now supplemented by two thousand Uzbeks and Hazaras. "These subsisted upon the resources of the country," observed Harlan — a euphemism for pillage. As they marched north, the apricot groves of Khamerd Valley gave way to a harsher landscape, with little worth stealing. The route to Mazar and ancient Balkh led across the Kara Kotul, or Black Pass, and the footing on the narrow path to the summit, with a sheer drop on either side, grew ever more precarious. Suddenly "one of the horse artillery guns plunged over the precipice, rolled over several times, striking the bottom with a surge that broke the iron axle." In places Harlan estimated the path sloped upwards at thirty-five degrees, "perilous even for single horsemen," to say nothing of heavily burdened pack animals. The elephant would never have completed the climb. Finally, the army struggled over the summit, into open hill country for a few miles, and then "through a stony valley in many places barely wide enough for the passage of a gun carriage." The occasional pile of stones marked the grave of a nomad, the only sign of humanity in this inhospitable wasteland until they reached the tiny settlement of Doab. From here, the road grew ever more daunting and restricted, blocked by huge boulders "over which it was necessary in three instances to lift the guns by manual force" and sometimes so narrow that the carriages had to be dismantled and the gun barrels dragged through on ropes.

At last, looming through the mist, appeared the fort of Derra i Esoff, stronghold of the Uzbek chief Soofey Beg, another notorious slaver. After a consultation with Meer i Wullee, it was decided to lay siege to the castle, partly to demonstrate once more the efficacy of the Afghan guns, but also to satisfy Harlan's sense of justice, for his righteous wrath had again been fired by tales of slavery. "Soofey Beg," he wrote, "has been known to exchange his guests for horses with Uzbeck slave dealers." Indeed, some three hundred Hazara families had recently placed themselves under his protection, only to be kidnapped en masse. "Many of them were disposed of like a flock of stray sheep, and were carried away by the slave traders," but some were still being held inside the fort. Harlan, the new Hazara prince, could not resist the opportunity to set his people free.

Within minutes his guns had battered a hole in the mud walls, and the troops rushed in with the Hazaras, to Harlan's intense satisfaction, leading the charge. "In the storming of Derrah i Esoff these men were amongst the first to mount the breach, along with the regimental colours. Their firmness and bravery, and, more especially, their fidelity to their officers, were creditably displayed on many occasions." Two hundred fifty Hazaras had been incorporated into the regular regiment, a unit Harlan now regarded as his own royal troops and "the best soldiers in the corps: frugal, provident, steady, submissive, and intelligent, they possessed more physical strength and would toil through more labour than their comrades. Indefatigable and persevering on two pounds of barley bread, they dragged the artillery over those almost impassable barriers, through rivers in the middle of winter, surmounting all obstacles with unparalleled fortitude and determination, without grumbling." Inside the fortress, Harlan found two hundred captive Hazaras, who were immediately "released from a loathsome confinement in the dry wells and dungeons of the castle and sent home to their friends." The army struck north once more, following the course of the Derra i Esoff River. Its banks were covered with a dense jungle of reeds and coarse grass, but the marching was easier. Forage and fuel were plentiful, noted Harlan, and within a few days they had reached the settlement of Ish Kale Beg, in a broad vale that ended in a range of low hills, the last barrier before the Oxus valley. The exhausted army crawled slowly toward the ridge, but Harlan cantered ahead, and then stood alone, gazing down in the direction of Alexander's city: "Surmounting this elevation the plain of the Oxus breaks upon the eye. This vast plateau or steppe gently declines towards the ancient city of Bulkh."

After a march of three months, two sieges, and one contractual coronation, Harlan walked through what was once a Hellenic city, now little more than a shell, with mounds that were formerly Greek buildings. Genghis Khan had destroyed ancient Balkh so thoroughly in the thirteenth century that a Chinese visitor who arrived after the Mongols reported finding only dogs in the ravaged city. The destruction had continued steadily thereafter, most recently by Murad Beg, whose depredations, Harlan insisted angrily, had "converted what remained of this once smiling paradise into a sterile desert waste."

"Every remnant of antiquity has disappeared," he wrote, but that did not prevent Harlan from imagining the past, and possibly future, glory of Balkh. From here Alexander had set out across the Hindu Kush to complete "the subjugation of the known world by the conquest of India." Among these ruins, surrounded by malarial marsh, Harlan imagined a new empire. "Bulkh is the capital of central Asia, morally and politically; and the power holding possession of this far-famed city, would be enabled to exercise supremacy over the superstitious natives." Local myth told how a great force would one day dominate the world, its advent presaged by the rebuilding of Balkh. Harlan had now proved that a modern army could be brought across the mountains, and if the Russians, say, would make their base at Balkh and look south, a new chapter in history might be written. "Possession of the city," he wrote, "confers the nominal title of empire and if the pretensions of an adventurer be sustained by force, his right to assert his claims could not be impugned without violating tradition and privilege." Once he had established his rule in the Hazarajat, Balkh might be the capital of his own empire.

One reason for the region's strategic importance was first discovered by Alexander the Great's army in 328 B.C., when a strange unknown substance was spotted bubbling out of the earth, "no different in smell or taste or brightness from olive oil." This observation puts Greek salad in a new light, for Alexander was the first Westerner to strike petroleum in Central Asia. The age of oil had not yet dawned, but Harlan, remarkably enough, could see it coming: "Coal and wood will be superseded by the use of inflammable substances of concentrate force, and electric fluid or other means now unimagined [will] become familiar sources of locomotion." As he imagined the past, Harlan was standing near a reservoir of a substance that would shape the world's future.

William Moorcroft and his party had perished near Balkh, and Harlan was convinced that the chief of nearby Mazar (now Mazar i Sharif), "a bad man of mysterious motives and of hidden resolves, of cruel, cold and heartless principles," had been responsible. For all its glorious associations, Balkh was a grim spot, and not a place to linger. From Mazar the army marched east, and after two days arrived at Meer i Wullee's fortress. "The place is well-fortified," noted Harlan. "The citadel of Tash Khoorghaun crowns a height south of the town within a spacious enclosure surrounded by a high wall." It was also the ideal vantage point from which to intimidate, and if necessary attack, Murad Beg at Kunduz, just fifty miles to the east.

The Uzbek warlord, however, was in no mood for a fight. News had reached him of the fall of Saighan and Derra i Esoff, and of the host of Afghans, Hazaras and enemy Uzbeks heading his way under the command of a powerful *feringhee* prince armed with mighty guns. As Harlan grew closer, Murad Beg began to panic. "The Uzbecks are not acquainted with the management of cannon in the field," wrote Harlan, and the Khan of Kunduz had only a few old pieces of which his troops were terrified, fearing that they would be more dangerous to themselves than to an enemy. Murad Beg did, however, have one gun of monstrous size, a cannon left behind by Nadir Shah, the Persian conqueror who had subjugated Afghanistan almost a century earlier. This was a fantastic-looking weapon, but quite useless since there was no ammunition to fit it. Yet the approach of Harlan and his men required desperate measures. The ancient iron gun was duly stuck together and dragged to the causeway leading into Kunduz in the hope of frightening the invaders.

Harlan, meanwhile, settled down to enjoy a rest as the guest of Meer i Wullee. He had grown fond of the leprous prince with the grotesque nostrils, but as a self-appointed Hazara he made it his business to look down on the Uzbeks in general. "They are all obsequious to their superiors and generally overbearing to their inferiors, and they are great venerators of wealth and power," he wrote, based on the most brief acquaintance with the tribe. "Timorous, crafty, ignorant and bigoted, neither seeking nor appreciating knowledge, selfishness is a prominent and undisguised feature of their character and they have a self-applauding contempt for all foreigners." He was particularly incensed by the Uzbek preference for trading slaves over growing flowers. "Little attention is bestowed upon the elegant in horticulture," he sniffed. "Their flowers are, consequently, few and not of a pleasing variety."

In one respect, however, the Uzbeks won Harlan's unqualified admiration, and that was in the growing of melons. He had been told that the finest cantaloupes were produced in Uzbek country, and he wanted to try one. "A melon of this description was brought to me from Kundooz in the month of February, which had been artificially preserved, that weighed about eight pounds! When fresh it must have been something heavier." Believing that the marshy atmosphere was the cause of malaria among the local population, Harlan also quaffed pints of fresh pomegranate juice, declaring "there is nothing so refreshing or more conducive to the health of an invalid from fever than the juice of the pomegranate."

While Harlan munched prize melons and Murad ran around desperately brandishing his elderly cannon, discreet diplomatic feelers were extended by both sides, for the American was aware that the Uzbek would probably rather talk than fight. "The Uzbecks have a great horror of bloodshed, and think that prudence is the better part of valour," he observed. Uzbek battles tended to follow a pattern. When the opposing armies meet, wrote Harlan, "a few individual sallies of vaunting cavaliers are made in advance, the parties uttering unearthly yells of defiance, and assuming threatening attitudes. A parley ensues, an interview between the leaders follows, and the affair terminates with the harmless festivities of a tournament."

True to form, after several weeks of belligerent posturing and rising anxiety, Murad Beg capitulated without firing a shot, let alone his cannon, which would probably have flattened a large part of Kunduz. Under the terms of the treaty he now signed, Murad agreed that the frontier of Turkistan, hitherto marked by the fortress at Saighan, would henceforth be the Kara Kotul Pass, while the Hindu Kush range would form "the barrier of political jurisdiction between the two countries, beyond which he was not to carry his predatory excursions." He also agreed to return the land he had seized from Meer i Wullee, and "relinquished the transit dues upon karrovans passing between northern Asia and India." As Harlan pointed out, since "a duty of two and one half percent is collected on the transit trade from Moslem merchants and five percent from non-professors of that religion," this represented a substantial addition to the Kabul treasury. In the language of the treaty, Murad acknowledged himself "the younger brother of the Ameer" and stated that Dost Mohammed would exercise "control in the politics of the province of the Bulkh." Harlan was convinced that Murad's days were now numbered. "His power was much reduced," he declared, and "he has in great measure lost his tribe's respect." Meer i Wullee, Harlan predicted, would eventually take over as chief of Kunduz. At the signing of the treaty, Harlan noticed that bullet-eyed Murad, formerly so terrifying, appeared to have had the stuffing knocked out of him. Sure enough, once the Afghans withdrew, "he fell sick and became melancholy, family feuds arose and his son and nephew marshalled their parties for a struggle."

Harlan was entirely satisfied with the results of the expedition: Murad Beg had been brought to heel, two forts had been seized, important alliances had been struck with both Hazaras and Uzbeks, he had successfully crossed the mountains with a large army, and he had eaten the largest melon he had ever seen. Most important, he had ascended the Hindu Kush as an American general and descended it as an Afghan prince.

"The punishment of the recalcitrant prince of Kundooz attended to," in March 1839, Harlan prepared to return to Kabul, anticipating a hero's welcome. He was eager to boast of his exploits to Dost Mohammed Khan, renew contact with the Russians, and set in train plans to rebuild Alexander's empire outward from Balkh and the Hazarajat. "By my expedition into Tatary from Cabul to Bulkh in 1838–39 an enterprise of great magnitude was accomplished," he declared, in his most grandiloquent style. "Commanding a division of the Cabul army, and accompanied by a train of artillery, that stupendous range of mountains the Indian Caucasus was crossed through the Paropamisus. The military topography and resources of the country were practically tested. Impediments which were supposed to present insurmountable obstacles to the passage of an army proved to be readily vanquished by labour and perseverance, and the practicability of invading India from the north, no longer doubtful, has become a feasible and demonstrable operation."

Instead of returning over the Kharzar Pass, which was now closed by snow, Harlan proposed to take what he called "the direct route" via the more easterly Shibar, or Sibber, Pass into the Ghorband valley and on to Kabul. His haste to return before the spring would prove to be a serious tactical error. The mountains were still in the grip of winter, and the army was now retracing its steps through lands already stripped of anything resembling food. After a few days hunger began to stalk his force in earnest, and for the first time Harlan started to feel serious apprehensions.

> Upon the whole route there was deficiency of forage and grain, as we had consumed almost everything in the nature of supplies on the advance journey. For forage the withered grass of the preceding year, now

buried in the snow, was got at by much labour, but it proved inadequate for the meagre subsistence of our horses and cattle. A great many horses, camels and bullocks died from fatigue and starvation. The men of my force seldom had more than a single daily meal: they not infrequently fasted every other day when the accidental supply of flesh from the animals which died failed them.

As the force neared Bamian, forage became ever more scarce. The local people had buried what little grain they had and hidden their hay in high ravines, knowing that without it their animals would surely starve. The soldiers did what armies always do, and what Alexander's men had done two millennia earlier: they took what they needed by force. Harlan was appalled at the "revolting cruelties" used by the Hazaras and Uzbeks to force the local population, already facing famine, to surrender what little they had. "The cry was 'thou shalt want ere I want' and the maxim was cried out with robber-like ferocity," he observed. He was careful to stress, however, that "these remarks refer entirely to the irregular troops of our force. The men under my immediate charge were better provided for by the scanty supply of flour and grain our carriage cattle, overburdened as they were, could convey."

In their freezing tents, the men huddled around the *sendillee*, a chafing dish filled with smouldering *chelma*, dried animal manure. Over the embers, suspended on a post, a quilt of sheepskins was thrown; the inmates of the tent would gather with feet and arms under the covering, and a *posteen*, or sheepskin cloak, over their backs to keep out the extreme cold. This ingenious if malodorous form of central heating staved off frostbite, but even manure was in desperately short supply, for the local people depended on the substance not only for fuel, but the walls of their miserable huts were usually constructed with dung. Dried and powdered *chelma* was even used as a disgusting substitute for tobacco. "A more drastic substance cannot be conceived," wrote Harlan, who was addicted to his pipe but drew the line at smoking powdered animal excrement. "This is drawn into their lungs by deep inspirations. To one unaccustomed to this horrid dose, the effect is to bewilder, and if incautiously used, would cause epilepsy."

Bamian, which had been teeming with life and supplies the previous autumn, was now stripped bare. The army trudged on toward the Sibber Pass. "The ascent is steep and passes through a narrow defile bounded on each side by lofty mountains of naked rocks. It is obstructed by ledges of rocks and winds abruptly over a rugged path flanked by deep craggy precipices," Harlan wrote gloomily. "This is a most difficult place for a train of artillery." On March 27, 1839, the vanguard reached the pass. Below, deep in snow, lay the Sheikh Ali valley. Just below the summit a blizzard engulfed them. "We crossed the pass in the midst of a violent storm of snow. It fell without intermission in dense flakes, two nights and three days [and] those who had halted at the upper end of Sheikh Ali had their tents nearly covered by the snow." To Harlan's intense pride, the army toiled on. "During the height of the storm the guns were dragged over the pass by the soldiers of the regiment and they performed the labour suffering from hunger and fatigue, without fuel and without other food than a scanty supply of dry flour and a few grains of wheat and barley."

The cold was devastating. "Three men, two Hindoos and one Moslem, natives of Cabul, were frozen to death upon the pass," wrote Harlan, glumly reflecting that Hindu Kush "literally means Hindoo Murderer, and may allude to the extreme cold, so fatal to Hindoos, that prevails among the regions of perpetual snow." The blizzard showed no sign of letting up. "Snowdrifts of an inconceivable depth filled up the ravines. A horse which had slipped from the beaten track, plunged into a ravine and disappeared, leaving a mussed spot upon the surface that marked the place of his descent." Like the officers of Alexander's army, the mounted men wrapped their horses' feet in leather to get a better purchase on the snow, but even so "in many places the declivity was so great as to oblige the dismounted horses led by their owners to slide a distance of two hundred feet."

Harlan had bought a pair of green leather boots "from a Jew in Bulkh for ten rupees" and he now had reason to bless the extravagance. "I kept my footing by means of the high iron shod heels of my Uzbeck boots, thrusting them into the beaten snow at every step. My horse placed his forefeet together and slid along, ploughing up the snow and the mud of a loose soil." Everyone was now suffering acute snow blindness. "Our eyes were all inflamed by the reflection from the snow to a painful degree," wrote Harlan, who developed a simple cure. "Opium moistened with water and dropped between the lids relieved the eyes from pain in one hour." Horses and camels were perishing at an alarming rate, but Harlan noticed the ingenious way the native soldiers used the still-warm skins of the dead animals as protection against the weather by fashioning primitive galoshes, known as *sooklies*: "The feet are wrapped in the skin with the hair outside and tightly sewed on, reaching a trifle above the ankle. With this protection the feet will never become frost bitten."

Crossing the ten-thousand-foot Sibber Pass took three agonizing days. The situation was little better on the other side, for the inhabitants had "fled to their strongholds in the mountains, carrying off their flocks and burying their grain, refusing all pacific overtures for supplies." Alexander's men had suffered in the same way, tormented by snow blindness and freezing, half-starved because "the natives had stored their supplies in underground pits." The Greeks and Macedonians had survived on roots, herbs, and horseflesh "seasoned with the juice of silphium and eaten raw." Harlan's army was reduced to similar fare: "Our only remedy was to run the gauntlet by starvation and snow storms. The men subsisted upon green clover and by stealing a handful of barley from the nosebags of the horses, who, indeed, could ill afford to spare it." The *yaboo* ponies, which "instinctively dig up the roots below the snow for food," helped the soldiers fend off starvation.

Typically, despite the imminent danger of death through hunger and exposure, Harlan paused to admire an enormous cavern penetrating deep into the mountainside, and speculated that this must be the "Cave of Prometheus, famous in Greek myth." According to the legend, as a punishment for stealing fire from the Gods and giving it to man, Prometheus was chained to a peak of the Caucasus where his liver was daily devoured by an eagle. Alexander's men also believed they had found the cavern of Prometheus, "along with the nest of the mythical eagle and the marks of his chains." Since Alexander's route is a matter of conjecture, we cannot know whether Harlan saw the same cave, but as one biographer observes, "to Alexander's officers, geography was only accurate if it first fitted myth." The same was true for Harlan. But as he trudged on through the pelting snow, with his soldiers and animals dying around him, he must have wondered whether he, like Prometheus, was paying the price for defying the Gods.

The route through Ghorband Valley was no more than a rocky track, crossing and recrossing a river swollen by melted snow. At the ford beside the town of Ghorband, the local guides sucked their cheeks and shook their heads, pointing out that even at its lowest point the water was up to the horses' saddle girths. The smaller guns were dismantled and loaded on camels, which were painfully dragged and kicked across the icy torrent. The first of the heavy guns was successfully manhandled to the other side using ropes, but then came calamity. Harlan looked on in horror as "one hundred men attempting to drag one of the pieces across the river were all swept away by the rushing current and three only escaped drowning." It was by far the worst loss of life so far, but with nothing left to eat, there was no choice but to push on. Finally, the remaining guns were hauled over the river "after five days of hard labour and the loss of many lives."

One final obstacle lay between Harlan and Kabul: the fearsome pass at Charikar. Though somewhat lower than the Sibber, at around nine thousand feet, Harlan considered this "the worst of all the passes I have seen between Cabul and Bulkh," a narrow break in the ice-bound mountains approached by a steep scree of slippery rock. "Eight or ten horses died in their efforts to surmount it; debilitated as they were by a winter in the course of which they fasted as often as they fed," but in one last, heroic push, the army crawled over the pass and at last looked down through the clouds on Kabul Valley.

On April 5, 1839, the army staggered back into the city, half-starved, snowblind, and frostbitten, their feet wrapped in the skins of their dead horses. But Harlan was determined to arrive in style for this, his moment of triumph. At the head of the ragged column he rode, his horse splendidly caparisoned in the Hazara style, "with gold, silver or plated buckles and studs of feroze stones set in silver, saddle blanket made of worsted silk and gold brocade, and velvet, green, yellow and scarlet, decorated with gold embroidery." Over a "long frock made of camel hair and pantaloons of the same material," he wore a thick sheepskin robe. On his feet were the bright green Uzbek riding boots, and on his head, as befits a prince, he wore "a white cat's skin foraging cap with a glittering gold band." The people of Kabul stood gaping from their doorways at the fantastical figure who trotted proudly toward the gates of the Bala Hisar, his military panache only slightly undermined by the pet marmot peeping out of one pocket.

Harlan was ushered into the throne room, where he was greeted by a solemn Dost Mohammed Khan. The amir was deeply relieved to see the return of the army and his *feringhee* general, but not for the reasons Harlan had anticipated. Indeed, Harlan never got an opportunity to brag of his adventures, of his great trek across the mountains and his feat in humbling the Uzbek prince. Dost Mohammed was no longer remotely concerned about Murad Beg, for in Harlan's absence an altogether more potent enemy had appeared on the horizon: even now a mighty British army was marching on Kabul, with the avowed intention of bringing down the amir and, it could safely be assumed, the self-created prince of Ghor.

14

❧

A GRAND PROMENADE

While Harlan was scrambling down the icy passes of the Hindu Kush, the Army of the Indus had begun to rumble toward Afghanistan: 9,500 soldiers of the Bengal army, a 3,000-strong column from Bombay, a contingent of 6,000 under Shah Shujah, 38,000 camp followers, and 30,000 camels. The army was, in effect, a heavily fortified, lavishly equipped mobile city, for the British were determined to ensure that the removal of Dost Mohammed Khan and his replacement with Shah Shujah should be achieved in style and comfort. One brigadier required sixty camels simply to tote his personal baggage, and even junior officers brought scores of servants, preserved food, eau de cologne, clean linen, polo mallets, mistresses, and anything else that might make life more pleasant during what was expected to be a brief and glorious campaign, nothing more than "a grand military promenade." Two camels were needed to carry the officers' cigars. One Afghan observed the cavalcade as it left British India and remarked darkly to an English officer: "You are an army of tents and camels, *our* army is one of men and horses."

William Macnaghten had been chosen as the lead political officer of the operation, somewhat to the annoyance of Alexander Burnes who, despite his misgivings about deposing Dost Mohammed, had hoped to be chosen as envoy and minister of the government of India himself. Instead, Burnes was knighted, promoted, and sent ahead to prepare the way for the advancing army: at thirty-three years old, he was now Lieutenant Colonel Sir Alexander Burnes, and in the glow of self-satisfaction he managed to suppress any lingering doubts about the operation.

The route to Afghanistan chosen by the British military planners led from the rendezvous point at Ferozepur, down through Sind, then northwest across the Indus, through the mighty Bolan Pass, and on to Kandahar, Ghazni, and Kabul. The campaign got off to a bad start: the camels, dromedaries from the Indian plains quite unused to the harsh conditions, died in droves; the soldiers suffered horribly in the desert sun, and stragglers were picked off by bandits. But through a combination of bribery and threats, the army successfully cowed the amirs of Sind, crossed the Indus on pontoons, and on March 10 arrived at the Bolan Pass, controlled by Mehrab Khan of Kelat. The Baluchi prince happily accepted a large bribe, but as the British army slowly moved through the great defile, Mehrab Khan offered a warning, which Burnes duly reported back to Macnaghten: "The Khan declared that the Chief of Caubul, Dost Mahomed, was a man of ability and resource, and though we could easily put him down . . . we could never win over the Afghan nation by it." Macnaghten dismissed anyone who questioned his decisions as "a croaker," and pressed on for Kandahar, where Dost Mohammed's brothers, the Kandahar sirdars, were in an advanced state of fully justified terror.

Thanks to a traditional combination of bribery and treachery, Kandahar fell without a shot; the sirdars fled, and on April 25, just two weeks after Harlan had marched his tattered army into Kabul, his old employer, Shah Shujah, paraded through the gates of Kandahar. Macnaghten claimed the Saddozai king was greeted with "feelings very nearly mounting to adoration." In reality, the attitude of the Kandaharis ranged from apathy to extreme hostility. A ceremonial review was held outside the city, Shah Shujah was enthroned in gorgeous style, a salvo of 101 guns was fired, and the troops marched past in full regalia. But fewer than a hundred Afghans turned up for the show, a display of "mortifying indifference" that did not escape the more astute observers but worried Macnaghten and Shujah not one jot. The Army of the Indus would remain in Kandahar for two months, accumulating supplies and preparing for the next stage of the campaign, an assault on the fortified city of Ghazni, the main obstacle on the road to Dost Mohammed's capital.

In Kabul, feverish military preparations were underway to meet the approaching threat. Harlan later asserted that Dost Mohammed appointed him "generalissimo of his forces, and himself assumed a subor-

dinate station in the contemplated arrangements for meeting, and opposing, Shujah ul Moolk and the English." Certainly Harlan appears to
have played a key role in defensive measures, and remained at Dost Mohammed's side throughout the tumultuous events that followed. The
extended halt by the British at Kandahar appears to have given Dost
Mohammed false hope, and "he concluded that the British must be
planning a move towards Herat, and that the Army of the Indus would
branch off to the west, deferring operations against Kabul until the following year." Making a vital strategic error, he dispatched some of his
best troops, under Akram Khan, to confront the Sikh forces approaching from the east.

Ranjit Singh would be denied the final act of vengeance in his long-
running feud with Dost Mohammed and Josiah Harlan. The previous
December, during a grand summit meeting between the Sikh monarch
and Lord Auckland, the British had noted that the old king was sinking
fast, and drinking faster. "Runjit insisted that his lordship should take
his part in drinking, requesting each time that he should drain the fiery
liquid he presented to the dregs. The excess committed by the Maharaja
on this occasion produced a severe fit of apoplexy, and when Lord
Auckland took leave of him, he was lying on a couch, scarcely able to ar-
ticulate." Ranjit had suffered another stroke, but he remained alert to
the end. It was "a curious and interesting sight," wrote one British observer, "to behold the fast decaying monarch, his mind still alive, still
receiving reports, and assisted by the faithful Uzeez-ud-deen." The maharaja, though barely able to speak, was keen to know how the campaign
against Dost Mohammed was progressing. "By a slight turn of his hand
to the south, he would inquire news of the British frontier; by a similar
turn to the west, he would demand tidings from the invading army; and
most anxious he was for intelligence from Afghanistan." But on June 27,
as the British moved toward Ghazni and Sikh troops prepared to storm
the Khyber Pass, Ranjit Singh expired: once a friend to Harlan, then his
mortal enemy, he was always a role model, a one-eyed rascal of genius
who had invented himself as the greatest autocrat of his age, as tough
and dazzling as the diamond he wore on his arm.

In late July, after a broiling four-week march, the Army of the Indus
came in sight of the clifflike ramparts of Ghazni, now reinforced by
three thousand Afghans under the command of another of Dost Mo-

hammed's sons, Hyder Khan, and bristling with artillery, including a forty-eight-pound brass cannon with a range of two thousand yards. Dost Mohammed Khan was convinced that Ghazni was impregnable, and even Sir John Keane, the British commander, doubted his artillery could breach a castle rendered so strong "both by nature and by art." They were both wrong.

On the night of July 22, Lieutenant Henry Durand of the Bengal Engineers crept up to the walls of the fort with a small group of sappers, and stacked nine hundred pounds of gunpowder against the Kabul gate. At three in the morning, a diversionary attack was mounted at the opposite side of the fort and after a nerve-grating few moments when the fuse failed to light, the gate was torn apart by a huge explosion. The light infantry fixed bayonets and charged through the hold. Though some had also been bribed to run away, many Afghans fought ferociously, and they were killed by the hundreds. By nightfall the British flag fluttered over the walls, with the loss of just seventeen British soldiers.

The capture of Ghazni, ninety miles south of Kabul, was a devastating blow to Afghan confidence, and in Harlan's words it "produced a moral impression which could not be withstood by the resources and military array" of Dost Mohammed. Even among Harlan's trained and hardened troops, morale was ebbing fast.

The Nawab Jubber Khan, Harlan's old friend, was sent to negotiate. Under a flag of truce, he told the British that his brother was prepared to submit to the rule of Shah Shujah, as long as he retained the title of vizier, the same arrangement Harlan had made with the king many years before, and with Mohammed Reffee Beg just a few months earlier. In reply Shah Shujah flatly insisted that Dost Mohammed Khan must leave Afghanistan and live in exile in India, as he himself had done for so many years. Jubber Khan "indignantly rejected the offer and declared that he and his brother would fight to the last," then stiffly remounted and rode back to Kabul. He had once plotted against his brother; now, like Harlan, he would stand by him.

Something close to panic, however, was spreading through the Afghan ranks. To make matters worse, spies working for the British had infiltrated Kabul and were actively bribing senior courtiers to defect. To Harlan's fury, one by one, the chiefs began to slip away into the mountains, their saddlebags filled with the coin of British spies. "In their audacity they offered to purchase Dost Mahomed himself, by tendering that prince a bribe to relinquish his sovereignty."

For Harlan, the allure of gold meant little. He had once been Shah Shujah's "Nearest Friend" and "Companion of the Imperial Stirrup," but now he stood alongside the amir as an Afghan prince in his own right. Once he had acted on the British side in the Great Game; now he would stake his life defending an independent prince against British aggression. As he had once waited for the steadily advancing cholera to strike Kabul, he now prepared for the British onslaught.

Dost Mohammed was also prepared to fight to the last, but for that he needed soldiers. Even his Praetorian guard of Qizilbash mercenaries was melting away. The Afghan army had been drawn up in bivouacs outside the city walls, and the amir summoned his commanders to make a final appeal. "You have eaten my salt these thirteen years," he declared. "Grant me but one favour in requital for that long period of maintenance and kindness—enable me to die with honour. Stand by the brother of Futeh Khan while he executes one last charge against the cavalry of these Feringhee dogs; in that onset he will fall; then go and make your own terms with Shah Soojah."

Dost Mohammed Khan's plea was met with silence. "He resumed his serenity of demeanour, and, addressing himself to the Kuzzilbashes, formally gave them their discharge." Then, with magnificent insouciance, he retired to his tent, declaring that he intended to take the royal nap. Harlan accompanied him.

The muezzin was calling the evening prayer when a servant of the Qizilbash commander appeared with a bleak message: "I can no longer be responsible for your personal safety." The remaining soldiers, he warned, were in open mutiny and preparing to murder the prince in his tent. He must flee immediately. The events that followed are vividly told in Harlan's words.

> With a countenance full of fire, he called for his attendant. But a fallen prince has not even a faithful slave: a stranger handed the vessel for his highness's ablution, and he mournfully performed, for the last time within his tent, the ceremonials of his religion. His prayers finished, he commenced putting up his turban, his horse ready caparisoned at the tent door. A crowd of noisy, disorganised troops insolently pressed close to the royal pavilion. The guards had disappeared. The groom holding

the prince's horse was unceremoniously pushed to and fro. A servant audaciously pulled away the pillow which sustained the prince's arm. Another commenced cutting a piece of the splendid Persian carpet. The beautiful praying rug of the prince was seized on by a third.

"Hold," said his Highness. "Will ye not give me time to tie on my head-dress?" A dark scowl of desperation met his eye from those who were wont to fawn upon his kindness and flatter the once potent chief. As the prince sailed from his tent, "Take all," said he "that you find within, together with the tent." In an instant the unruly crowd rushed upon the pavilion, swords gleamed in the air and descended on the tent, the canvass, the ropes, the carpets, pillows, screens &c., were seized and dispensed among the plunderers.

The Prince placed his foot in the stirrup. Quick glances were exchanged betwixt his followers, formerly the nearest friends to a prosperous prince, and now the rifest enemies of a fallen friend. These signals escaped not the penetrating glance of Dost Mahomed. Suddenly he sprang into the saddle. As the turbulent host pressed upon the fugitive Prince, and whilst they were engaged with each other for a division of the spoil, the first report of an explosion concentrated the attention of the disorganized army, which was dividing into immense swarms and hordes, each suspiciously regarding the other with inquiring looks. Another and another explosion followed: the magazine had been fired. Not a breath of air disturbed the clear atmosphere; a dense cloud of white smoke ascended by jets far into the upper space, in a circumscribed pillar, as each concussion of ignited powder drove up a herald to announce in other worlds the crash of empires on the earth beneath. An immense column rose into the still, clear air, like a genie conjured up by the magic of war. The Prince turned his horse towards that dense cloud, which seemed like a shadow, enshrining his glory—plunged into the screening veil that obscured his fallen fortunes and protected him from pursuit, as he lost himself from the view of those who wistfully contemplated his Highness's person.

Accompanied by a handful of followers, including his son Akbar and the Nawab Jubber Khan, the amir "turned his horse's head towards the regions of the Hindu Kush" and galloped away from the smoking city. "I am like a wooden spoon," he is said to have remarked grimly as he rode north. "You may throw me hither and thither, but I shall not be hurt." Among those who watched him go was Josiah Harlan. He would later declare that the amir had abandoned hope too soon, and "retreated precipitately." Over the preceding fifteen years Harlan had fought many battles, and he was not going to run away now. Besides, he had developed a profound attachment to this, his adopted home. He had a treaty in his possession declaring him king. He was not going anywhere.

On August 7, Shah Shujah made his royal entry into Kabul, flanked by Burnes and Macnaghten in full diplomatic attire of cocked hats and gold lace. The restored king, mounted on a white charger, "dazzling in a coronet, jewelled girdle and bracelet," immediately reoccupied the palace in the Bala Hisar, with his retinue of wives, concubines and mutilated servants. The inhabitants of Kabul, however, observed Shujah's return with "the most complete indifference"; the restored king had an equally low opinion of his subjects, considering them "a pack of dogs, one and all." Some of the British sneered. "The city is beastly dirty and so are the people," wrote one Captain James Douglas. "They are cunning, avaricious, proud and filthy, notwithstanding the romantic descriptions of Burnes & Co." But he was observant enough to notice the effect, or lack of it, that the restored king was having on his countrymen: "It must be admitted that Shah Soojah has not from the first met with that degree of personal attachment and active support which our government anticipated. Many say 'Who is Shah Soojah, that we should love him?'"

Richard Kennedy, a young British officer who would write a gripping memoir of the Afghan campaign, was taking in the strange new sights of the old city when he found himself face to face with an astonishing apparition, a white man with a vast beard whose outfit was so exotic as to make the newly reinstalled king and his British allies seem almost dowdy. "A tall, manly figure with a large head and gaunt face over it, dressed in a light, shining, pea-green satin jacket, maroon-coloured silk small clothes, buff boots, a silver-lace girdle fastened with a large, square buckle bigger than a soldier's breastplate, on his head a white cat's skin foraging cap with a glittering gold band and tassels." This was Harlan, calmly having breakfast in the morning sunshine, as the British moved in. He introduced himself to the astonished Kennedy as "a free and enlightened citizen of the greatest and most glorious country in the world." Kennedy was understandably intrigued to find an American in the middle of Kabul, let alone one clad in what appeared to be fancy dress.

To the Englishman's mounting astonishment, Harlan explained that he was a doctor and soldier, most recently commander in chief of the armed forces of Dost Mohammed Khan. "This gentleman was no fool, though he dressed like a mountebank," observed Kennedy, who confessed he was "astonished to find a wonderful degree of local knowledge and great shrewdness" in a figure who "would have been the pride and joy of a Tyrolese Pandean-pipes band at Vauxhall." Harlan explained that he had remained loyal to Dost Mohammed until the army mutinied and was now, for the first time in many years, at something of a loose end. "It will not be creditable to our Government if he be not provided for," wrote Kennedy. "There was no law that could have made it penal for him to have served Dost Mahomed against us, and the President and Congress would have required an answer at our hands had we made it so. He has a claim on our justice."

Harlan did not want justice or anything else from the British, or indeed, from Shah Shujah, his former patron. "I made no effort to achieve a position at court after the British entry," he wrote, for he now felt nothing but distaste for the restored monarch. Shujah had been installed for only a few days when Harlan heard a proclamation "addressed alike to the king's English friends and native subjects," read out by the royal herald from the ramparts of the Bala Hisar: "Everyone is commanded not to ascend the heights in the vicinity of the Royal harem under pain of being embowelled alive. May the king live for ever." For Harlan, it was a stark reminder of Shah Shujah's "harsh barbarity."

He did, however, make contact with the British authorities, with an offer to act as go-between with the former regime. A meeting was arranged with William Macnaghten, the queen's official envoy. Harlan took an immediate and profound dislike to this strutting little "self-conceited gentleman." Nonetheless, he stated that he was prepared to use his contacts with the ancien régime to try to prevent further bloodshed. Harlan explained that while most of Dost Mohammed's family had fled beyond the Hindu Kush, one senior member of the ousted regime, Nawab Zeman Khan, Dost Mohammed's nephew, the feudal lord of Jalalabad, had merely gone into hiding. This was the Barakzai noble "of sedate deportment inclined to obesity" whom Harlan had once diagnosed as a diabetic. Over the years, he had given him dietary advice, and the two had remained friends.

Since the British invasion, the nawab had contacted Harlan with an offer: if the British would guarantee his safety he would use his influence as chief of Jalalabad to prevent an uprising by the rebellious Ghilzai, a ferocious and fanatical tribe violently opposed to Shujah's restoration. Initially, at least, Macnaghten seemed happy to make use of Harlan's expertise, and a gentleman's agreement was struck. Shujah "issued a conciliatory Dust Khut [proclamation] with a guarantee under the resident's broad seal," stating that Zeman Khan would be well treated. In return, wrote Harlan, "the Nawaub, at my request, restrained the extensive and powerful Ghiljie tribe from violence or even the threats of disturbing the government, so called, of Shoojah." But instead of welcoming the nawab as an honored ally, the British, according to Harlan, immediately reneged on the agreement. "On his arrival at Cabul, he was allowed to re-enter his premises without a reception, and the guarantees were violated by making His Excellency a nominal prisoner at large." Harlan was furious—"trusting to English faith, I found myself compromised"—and he blamed Alexander Burnes, his old rival, "an unscrupulous personal enemy, well acquainted with and jealous of my influence." Harlan had given due warning that the Ghilzai tribes, which controlled the passes back into India, posed a serious threat to the new regime; his advice had been ignored, and instead of cultivating the men who might control them, Harlan and Nawab Zeman Khan had been humiliated. It was a decision both Macnaghten and Burnes would live to regret, shortly before dying.

As a student of Dost Mohammed Khan's rule, Harlan firmly believed there was only one way to ensure peace in Afghanistan: co-option and bribery, using the existing system of chieftainships. "The government of the Avghauns by their own institutions would have been facile," he declared. "If the English had conciliated the heads of tribes [and] arranged them around the king as sustainers of the government, which privilege they had a right to expect, they would have become willing hostages for the good conduct of their tribes." Instead, Shah Shujah was bent on vengeance. With the sanction of the British, he "imprisoned many who represented themselves for employment and honours [and] deputed the offices of state to a swarm of hungry expectants, who attended him during his 30 years' exile." The invaders might easily have purchased acquiescence: "The English, who know well the value of gold, could have controlled the Avghauns by fiscal diplomacy, without incurring the odium of invading and subjugating an unoffending people."

The British had other ideas, and Harlan's knowledge went unused. Instead, with mounting astonishment and dread, he observed the empire being transplanted, piece by piece, to Kabul. For years Harlan had immersed himself in Afghan customs; most of the British, by contrast, could not have cared less for the local culture, and either abused, displaced, or ignored it. They played polo and cricket, held tea parties, and staged amateur theatricals. Some brought their wives, the formidable British memsahibs, the better to pretend that Afghanistan was really part of India. The worst discomfort of the early days, soon remedied, was a shortage of wine and cigars. The invaders now awarded themselves medals and titles in recognition of the successful campaign: Auckland received an earldom, Macnaghten a baronetcy, and Claude Wade a knighthood. "Honours of knighthoods, ribands, and brevets were showered upon the *conquerors* of the miserable Avghauns with unsparing liberality," remarked Harlan sourly, Her Majesty's rewards for "the extinction of a free nation."

Burnes, an inveterate lecher, was well acquainted with the dancing girls of Kabul, and he and many other officers enjoyed themselves to the full with the more accommodating local ladies. The British whored their way around the city, but the official historian of the campaign naturally blamed any sexual license on the loose Afghan women: "The temptations which are most difficult to withstand were not withstood by our English officers. The attractions of the women of Caubul they did not know how to resist." They did not try very hard.

Undetected by the British, a deep undercurrent of hatred was building against these infidel invaders, who treated them with such disdain and dishonored their women. Shujah's popularity, never very high, sank by the day. "Bad ministers are in every government solid grounds for unpopularity, and I doubt if ever a king had a worse set than Shah Soojah," Burnes observed. Chief among these, and first in spite and incompetence, was Mullah Shakur, the earless vizier who had introduced Harlan to the exiled king so many years before, whose natural spite had been compounded by advancing senility: "He oppressed the people. The people complained to the British. The British remonstrated with the Mullah; and the Mullah then punished the people for having complained to the British."

Harlan shared the growing anger, bitterly recalling a time when the city had been free and independent. "Cabul, the city of a thousand gardens, in those days was a paradise," he wrote. Now the happiness was being trampled out of the Afghans. "I have seen this country, sacred to the harmony of hallowed solitude, desecrated by the rude intrusion of senseless stranger boors, vile in habits, infamous in vulgar tastes, the prompt and apathetic instruments of master minds, callous leaders in the sanguinary march of heedless conquests, who crushed the feeble heart and hushed the merry voice of mirth, hilarity and joy."

Harlan's experience in the mountains had changed him, but the transformation had begun many years earlier. He had arrived in Afghanistan as a *feringhee*, utterly convinced of his cultural and moral superiority, but slowly, first as a visitor and a spy, then as a courtier to Dost Mohammed, now as a prince, he had absorbed, and been absorbed by, the civilization he once disdained. At least one half of Harlan was now Afghan. He wore Afghan clothes, spoke their languages, and understood their traditions. Yet he was still a Westerner. A century later, T. E. Lawrence (of Arabia) described this sense of being immersed in a different way of life while held down by his own, the double life of the cultural adoptee: "I could not sincerely take on the Arab skin. It was affectation only . . . sometimes the selves would converse in the void, and then madness was very near, as I believe it would be near the man who could see things through the veils at once of two customs, two educations, two environments." Rudyard Kipling also described the experience of being caught between cultures in his poem "The Two-Sided Man":

> Something I owe to the soil that grew—
> More to the life that fed—
> But most to Allah Who gave me two
> Separate sides to my head.

Kipling brilliantly evoked the tensions of imperialism, the knowledge that the "white man's burden" and assumptions of supremacy came with his duty of cultural respect toward subject peoples. Harlan had always had two sides to his thinking: the Jeffersonian republican and the would-be monarch, the crusader for Western civilization who yet admired and adopted the native ways. He saw the British occupation through the eyes of an Afghan, but his response was that of an American, outraged at the offense to liberty.

Harlan sensed what was coming, but his warnings about the folly of attempting to hold a hostile population in subjection went unheard by the British. "They had not been a year in the country before the name of a European, previous to the invasion so popular, began to smell in the nostrils of the people, and they became a hateful and hated race."

In Britain there were similar voices of warning. Mountstuart Elphinstone observed that Shah Shujah's grip on power seemed exceedingly fragile. "Maintaining him in a poor, cold, strong and remote country among a turbulent people like the Afghans, I own it seems to me hopeless." But if the aged sage of Afghanistan was ignored, what hope was there of anyone heeding an eccentric American adventurer? The British, blithely unconcerned, were convinced that all was going swimmingly. "I lead a very pleasant life," Burnes reported, and indeed he did. His weekly dinner party was the high point of the Kabul social calendar, and in one letter home he boasted: "I can place before my friends . . . champagne, hock, Madeira, sherry, port, claret, sauterne, not forgetting a glass of curaçao and maraschino, and the hermetically sealed salmon and hotch potch—veritable hotch potch, all the way frae Aberdeen, for deuced good it is, the peas as big as if they had been soaked for bristling."

While the political agent settled down to a life of chilled champagne and hot Afghan women in his new home, a large mansion with a courtyard and garden in the old city, Harlan suddenly found someone else had moved into his house. For the last two years he had been living in the Bala Hisar property given to him by Dost Mohammed. One afternoon, he returned to find the place occupied by one of Shah Shujah's many court toadies. To add insult to injury, a surgeon of the British army, Dr. James Atkinson, was calmly riding away on one of Harlan's best horses.

"I repossessed myself of the animal by a summary process," wrote Harlan, a euphemism for throwing Dr. Atkinson off the horse. He then stormed back into his house and tossed the interloper into the street. Atkinson and the ejected courtier immediately complained to the British authorities and within hours a pompous letter arrived from one G. H. McGregor, the superintendent of police, informing Harlan that "the horse with everything else in the fort became the property of the British army by right of conquest." Harlan was incensed, and immediately penned an enraged letter to the British authorities: "I am," he declared, "an alien and temporary resident, unconnected with the British and the authorities or native government . . . I confess myself unable to recognise the right of the prize agents of the British army to the property of an American citizen." He then launched into a long-winded legal rant, citing Napoleon and the norms of international law: "To compare small things to great, the spoliations of the Emperor Napoleon upon the commerce of the United States of America have been recovered from his present majesty Louis Philippe and this question of the horse and the house, however trivial, does as I have observed, involve a principle [of] the international law of civilised nations. Upon whatever principle you choose to settle the matter, I am surely entitled to one or the other." Harlan's letter—in effect a letter of resignation, although he had nothing to resign from—ended with a furious flourish. The British should do whatever they wanted with the house, and could "consider the horse entirely at your disposal and should award it to Dr. Atkinson should you think it proper." Harlan no longer cared. Haughtily, he informed the English official that he intended to leave Kabul the following day.

Harlan was so angry he did not even bother to pack. Instead he left behind most of his worldly possessions, including his beloved library consisting of "102 books, 77 bound and 25 unbound" as well as "5 knives and a hammer, pillows, bolsters and a blanket, numerous coats, pantaloons, hats and four corsets, underdrawers, handkerchiefs, gloves, shirts and stockings." These goods were handed over for safekeeping to a friend, Yusuf Khan, for Harlan had no doubt that he would soon return to take up his rightful princely title. The plans he had laid with Mohammed Reffee Beg had merely been "for the time postponed by the British conquest of Cabul," a strictly temporary inconvenience. "This irruption, so barbarous in its progress and disastrous in its results, left to me the title of 'Prince of Ghoree' with the prospect of a reversion," he would later insist.

There may be another reason for Harlan's haste, and fury, in leaving Kabul. He always maintained that he had left of his own free will, but it is also possible that he was thrown out. The most hostile British account of his departure claims that "Harlan was sent back to India . . . After a short detention in Ludhiana, he was deported to Calcutta and from thence provided with a free passage to America at the expense of the country he never lost an opportunity of vilifying." This is plainly an exaggeration, propaganda to make it appear that the British had marched the American adventurer out of the country. Documents, including letters of introduction, clearly show that Harlan made his own way home, and there is no evidence that he was ever detained by the British. But it is entirely possible that he was encouraged to leave with a detachment of troops returning to India. The British authorities may have come to regard him as a threat to their rule, and not without reason, for Harlan himself hints at a plot to restore Dost Mohammed: "Plans were concocted, intrigues commenced with the 'outs,'" he wrote.

On October 19, 1839, Harlan rode out of Kabul, with Dost Mohammed's golden sword at his side, his old cocked hat on his head, and a curse on his lips. As he quit the country he had come to love, he was already scribbling what would later become an excoriation of the British in Afghanistan, and British imperialism in general. Over the years, he had come to believe it was possible "to conquer a dominion by controlling the political parties of a state": that is what Ranjit Singh and Dost Mohammed had achieved, and what he himself had hoped to do in the Hazarajat. But what the British had imposed was mere tyranny, with a complete disregard for local custom and politics. Alexander the Great himself had adopted Persian dress during his civilizing conquests. The Army of the Indus had simply crushed opposition, "and no condition of submission short of absolute servility, and the abolition of their national identity, could satisfy the English in their projected conquest of Avghanistaun." The result would be a disaster on a scale the British Empire had never witnessed before. Harlan wrote: "To subdue and crush the masses of a nation by military force, when all are unanimous in the determination to be free, is to attempt the imprisonment of a whole people: all such projects must be temporary and transient, and terminate in a catastrophe that force has ever to dread from the vigorous, ardent, concentrated vengeance of a nation outraged, oppressed, and insulted, and desperate with the blind fury of a determined and unanimous will."

The British did not look up from their pleasures to see the American depart. "Vainglorious and arrogant, the invaders plunged headlong toward destruction," wrote Harlan. He had been a titular monarch for exactly one year.

15

CAMEL CONNOISSEUR AND GRAPE AGENT

Harlan had once vowed never to set foot in the United States again, but in the intervening years his bitterness had faded. The gold he had accumulated during fifteen years' service with Shah Shujah, Ranjit Singh, and Dost Mohammed had been converted into letters of credit in British India, and sent back to his sister Mary in Philadelphia, where a substantial fortune awaited him. It was time to revisit the land of his birth, before returning again to Afghanistan.

As he rode back to British India along the invasion route taken by the Army of the Indus, Harlan "found the line of march literally strewn with bleaching bones," the remains of thirty thousand camels and further evidence, in his mind, of British incompetence. Had they used hardy crossbred camels "what wastage of life might have been prevented," he reflected. Finally, he found himself back in Ludhiana, the frontier town where his odyssey had begun, but he felt no urgency to get home, particularly after he received word from his siblings that Joshua Harlan, the father he had not seen for fifteen years, had died. Contrary to later British claims, he did not return through Calcutta, but opted for a more circuitous route westward, a voyage that would take him through Europe and Russia, and would last almost two years.

Harlan never wrote about this journey—he was too busy working up a book about his adventures—but it can be pieced together from his surviving documents. A letter of introduction he obtained from a British official in Ludhiana, dated March 1840 stated that "Mr. H. proposes returning to his native country via Kandahar and thence to Persia etc." He appears to have visited several missionaries in Persia, where he introduced himself as "Col. J. Harlan of Philadelphia," and by September 6, 1840, he was in Cairo, where he obtained a U.S. passport for Europe from the American consulate and, apparently, a promotion: the document is made out to "General Josiah Harlan." Long years in the Afghan sun had left him with a yellowish complexion, and the passport officer noted "sallow skin" as his distinguishing feature. Sailing from Cairo, he reached Naples in October, Rome the following month, and finally Paris in December. By June 1841 he was in Britain, for, despite his views on British colonialism, he had many English friends. In his writing he was careful to make the distinction: "In referring to English policy, I trust my English friends will distinctly draw the line of separation betwixt the system and the country at large, and allow me the privilege of admiring those whose friendship I claim."

Instead of crossing the Atlantic, however, Harlan turned his sights eastward again, toward Russia. His motives for visiting Saint Petersburg remain mysterious. Perhaps he was still driven by wanderlust, but he was plainly anxious to make contact with the Russian court. He had demonstrated that it was possible, albeit difficult, to cross the Hindu Kush with a modern army, information that might be of considerable interest to the Russians. He may even have been seeking employment from the czar. Harlan had started out on the British side in the Great Game, then performed a pivotal role playing one power off against the other; it seems entirely possible that, having witnessed British imperialism firsthand, he now contemplated playing the game for the other side.

In Britain, through the British Quaker community, he made contact with one Sarah Biller, a woman of aristocratic Russian birth who had married an English Quaker, becoming an active missionary and temperance campaigner. Harlan does not appear to have told her that he had been thrown out of the Quaker church if, indeed, he was aware of the fact, and his new friend was happy to write to her Russian contacts on Harlan's behalf, stating that he would be able to render valuable service to the czar. Harlan appears to have given Sarah Biller a distinctly colorful account of his life, boasting that as governor of Gujrat and a feudal chief in Afghanistan he had vastly improved the education and morals of the people, a process he intended to continue after his European sojourn.

In a letter to the Princess Mestchersky, Sarah Biller described Harlan as "an intelligent and well-informed American, of a most respectable

family who has passed twenty years of life in various parts of the East Indies and is now looking into our northern empire ere he turns his steps
homeward." In another, to a Madam Vasiltchikoff, she observed: "You
are so interested in the improvements of your peasantry and in raising
their moral character that I think you will enjoy conversation with General H., who has had much experience in the art of governing and has
during his administration succeeded in casting down great and national
evil propensities . . . This gentleman has greatly reduced if not put aside
theft in his province."

Harlan was a hit with the aristocratic ladies of Moscow, and played
up the image of himself as a sort of reforming Russian *boyar*, Afghan-
style. "Your peasants will regret your absence and the poor babies must
continue the victims of the apathy of their parents for one or two years
to come," one fan wrote to him. "However, what you have been able to
effect among the peasantry must be a source of much heartfelt joy . . .
May your own life long be spared to accomplish all your heart's desire
among the interesting class over whom you rule."

If Harlan did make contact with the Russian government, there is
no official record of a meeting, and the one czarist official he knew personally had met a most puzzling end. Yan Vitkevitch, the dashing young
Lithuanian who turned up in Kabul at the same time as Alexander
Burnes in 1838, had returned to Saint Petersburg expecting to be fêted
for his diplomatic efforts. When he applied to see the foreign minister,
however, he received the reply that Count Nesselrode "knew of no Captain Vikevitch [sic], except an adventurer of that name who, it was reported, had been lately engaged in some unauthorised intrigues in
Caubul." The British government, it seems, had complained about Russian meddling in Afghanistan and Saint Petersburg had opted to appease London. Vitkevitch was disowned. He returned to his hotel
room, burned all his papers, and then blew out his brains. It was a grim
lesson, had Harlan been in the mood for instruction, in the way today's
important player in the Great Game could become tomorrow's repudi-
ated adventurer.

In early summer, Harlan made his way in leisurely fashion back
across Europe and finally embarked for the United States. Word of his
return preceded him, and his arrival in Philadelphia on August 24,
1841, was greeted by an exceedingly flattering fanfare of publicity.

"Our distinguished fellow-citizen is, in fact, the 'Prince of Ghoree,'" announced the *U.S. Gazette*, which described in detail Harlan's trek into Tatary in 1839:

> We view this expedition as altogether unique since the period of Alexander's conquests. With this prominent exception, no Christian chief of European descent ever penetrated so far into the interior of Central Asia under circumstances so peculiar as characterise General Harlan's enterprise, and we relinquish the palm of antecedent honour to the Macedonian hero alone. Retracing the steps of Alexander, General Harlan has performed a feat that ranks with the passage of the Simplon. For the enterprise, the energy and military genius displayed by our distinguished compatriot, we claim an association with the names of other heroes who have attained celebrity by scaling mountains. This expedition may be viewed as a pioneering effort to prove the existence of a practicable military passage between Cabul and Bulkh, the ancient Bactra.

In a virtuoso exhibition of false modesty and genuine patriotism, Harlan pretended to play down his royal title, and it was duly reported that he "looks upon kingdoms and principalities as of frivolous import, when set in opposition to the honourable and estimable title of American citizen." He would prefer, he said, to be addressed as "General Harlan," and the American press was happy to oblige, without ever inquiring how he had gotten the rank. "Our worthy compatriot retains the military title in social intercourse, in consideration of his republican relations, and as we have heard him observe 'not to impeach my natural right of citizenship, which I value above all sovereignty.'" Nothing could have been better calculated to make the journalists swoon over King Josiah.

Adapting quickly to the demands of self-publicity, Harlan announced that he had almost completed a book about his experiences: "General Harlan is preparing a narrative of his residence and travels in Asia," it was reported. "A sojourn of eighteen years amongst the Pagan and Mahomedan communities of the East has afforded the General unequalled opportunities of becoming intimately acquainted with the religion, laws, manners and customs of the Orientals, and we are enabled to state with the fullest confidence in our compatriot's versatile talents, his abilities for observation, and his investigating tact, that the projected volume will be profoundly interesting and instructive, no less to the philosophical inquirer than to the general reader." Harlan had been accused of many things in his time, but this was the first (and last) time anyone described him as tactful. He reveled in the attention. Reunited with his siblings in Newlin, Chester County, the wanderer took up residence with his unmarried sister Mary, and dedicated every waking hour to his memoir, which was about to become more topical than he could ever have predicted.

In the months that Harlan spent traveling slowly back to the United States, events in Afghanistan had been moving swiftly toward a horrific denouement. Dost Mohammed Khan had taken refuge with Meer i Wullee, Harlan's old Uzbek ally, but after several attempts to regain his throne, the amir had finally laid down his arms and surrendered to the British. He was allowed to go into honorable exile in India, just as Shah Shujah had done before, but his son, Akbar Khan, remained in full rebellion against the British-backed puppet. Afghan resentment of the British invaders steadily smoldered, and then ignited when the British envoy William Macnaghten decided, in a cost-cutting measure, to halve the subsidy paid to the Ghilzai tribe. Harlan had warned that the Ghilzais were not to be trifled with and sure enough, in the summer of 1841, enraged at what they saw as a broken promise, tribal warriors blocked the narrow defiles of the Khyber Pass. Macnaghten, who was preparing to leave Kabul for his new post as governor of Bombay, was as insouciant and deluded as ever. "The country is perfectly quiet," he declared, as he prepared to depart. "With the exception of the Ghilzyes between this and Jalalabad, and I hope to settle their hash on the road down, if not before."

By the autumn, Kabul itself was ready to explode: the bazaar fizzed with rumors that Akbar Khan was preparing to raise his standard at Bamian, while another senior chief, whose mistress was said to have been seduced by Alexander Burnes, was stirring rebellion in the capital itself. Efforts to crush the Ghilzai revolt had failed utterly. Burnes, as ambitious as ever, was waiting to hear whether he would take over as British envoy. On October 31, 1841, his last diary entry read: "What will this day bring forth? It will make or mar me, I suppose. Before the sun sets I shall know whether I go to Europe or succeed Macnaghten."

Two days later, an angry crowd gathered outside Burnes's house and spilled into his garden, calling "Sikandar! Sikandar!" the name he had once gloried in. Burnes, who had declined to move to safer quarters

despite swirling rumors of a plot, tried to calm the rabble by addressing
them from his balcony, but the mood was ugly. A sudden gunshot killed
the secretary alongside him. The mob demanded that Burnes come into
the garden to speak to them, but instead he tried to bargain, offering
ever-larger sums of money if he and his brother, visiting from England,
were released unharmed. The pack screamed louder and the stables
were already ablaze when a mysterious figure, said to be a Kashmiri, appeared on the balcony and offered to lead the two men to safety in native dress. Alexander and Charles Burnes gratefully seized the offered
disguises. The deliverer led them downstairs, but no sooner had they
stepped into the garden than the man cried out: "See Friends! This is
Sekunder Burnes." The brothers were hacked to pieces in moments,
along with the sepoy guard of twenty-nine men. That night the remains
of Alexander Burnes, a brave and remarkable man despite his faults,
were collected in a sack by a faithful Afghan friend, and secretly buried.

Kabul erupted in rebellion. The city was saturated with weapons, in
Harlan's words "fiercely bristling with the artillery of war. Each resident
has a rifle, always ready for use." They used them now. Any British or Indian soldier caught in the open was killed, as were many Afghans perceived to be on the side of the enemy. Shah Shujah was safe enough,
barricaded behind the thick walls of the Bala Hisar, but the five thousand British troops and their families, along with some ten thousand
camp followers, were outnumbered and surrounded, besieged inside an
ill-designed cantonment defended by a low wall and a ditch. Major
General William Elphinstone, a relative of Mountstuart Elphinstone,
was the military commander of the Kabul garrison, a kindly, gouty old
gentleman, a veteran of Waterloo now incapable of command or, indeed, any sort of coherent decision. Harlan considered him "an old invalid of high character and imbecile mind." Without an effective leader,
the British officers fell to arguing among themselves. Some advocated a
dash to the safety of the Bala Hisar, but they were ignored. The insur-
gents, encouraged by the lack of an effective riposte, cut off the British
from their supplies in the commissariat fort, and picked off anyone who
tried to break out with their long-range *jezails*.

In late November, Akbar Khan, the son of Dost Mohammed, arrived in Kabul with a contingent of Uzbeks. Reluctantly, William Macnaghten decided that he had no choice but to parlay with the Afghan

prince. Never had Harlan's expertise in Afghan diplomacy been more urgently needed, but by now the American was back in Pennsylvania, quite unaware of what was happening in Kabul. Shortly before Christmas, the envoy left the cantonment with a handful of officers to meet Akbar Khan at a prearranged spot beside the Kabul River. Macnaghten brought with him an ornate pistol as a peace offering. After an exchange of greetings, the two men began to discuss a secret compact, the terms of which were familiar: Shujah could remain on the throne, as long as Akbar Khan was installed as his vizier. Macnaghten agreed to the arrangement. This, it seems, was the signal for Akbar's men to seize him and the other British officers. Macnaghten protested in fluent Persian: *Az barae Khodda!*, "For the love of God." And then he was killed, probably with the very gun he had just given to Akbar. The British envoy's body was dismembered, his head paraded through the streets of Kabul, and the remains of his corpse hung on a meat hook in the great Blue Bazaar of Ali Mardan Khan.

The news of Macnaghten's grisly murder plunged the British into deeper disarray. A few days later Elphinstone made an agreement with Akbar that was closer to capitulation, and a death warrant: the British would be allowed to withdraw from Kabul to Jalalabad, eighty miles to the east, escorted by Akbar and his men, having handed over the treasury, most of the artillery, and more than one hundred hostages to the Afghan prince. "We are to depart without a guard, without money, without provisions, without wood," one British wife told her diary bitterly, as the long, bedraggled procession of fifteen thousand soldiers, women, and children set out into the snowy passes on January 6, 1842. The column came under heavy fire from the moment it left the cantonments. On the third day of the retreat, the weather closed in and so did the Ghilzais, sniping down from the mountaintops with deadly accuracy. "A universal panic swiftly prevailed," wrote a British officer. Baggage, tents, and ammunition were abandoned in the chaos. Those who survived the Afghan guns by daylight faced death by exposure in the freezing mountain darkness. Akbar was either unable, or unwilling, to stop the slaughter, claiming that the wild Ghilzais were their own masters. His promised escort never materialized. The wounded and frostbitten had to be abandoned in the snow, where they were handily murdered and stripped of their valuables by the pursuing swarm. The

Ghilzais showed no mercy, and those left behind expected none. As Rudyard Kipling would write:

> When you're wounded and left on Afghanistan's plains
> And the women come out to cut up what remains
> Just roll to your rifle and blow out your brains
> And go to your God like a soldier.

The Afghans had erected stone and wood barricades across the passes, which the desperate survivors tried to dismantle with their bare hands, as they were killed, one after the other, by Ghilzai sharpshooters on the heights. A handful of soldiers fought their way to Gandamak, where they were surrounded. They formed a square, and fought on with just twenty muskets, and two bullets each, until all were dead.

On January 13, 1842, a lone and bloody figure was spotted by the sentries at Jalalabad, weaving toward the fort on a limping horse. His name was Dr. William Brydon, an assistant army surgeon, as Harlan once had been. Brydon's escape was miraculous: with a pony pressed on him by a dying Indian cavalryman he had managed to get through the carnage, climbing over bodies, his head bleeding profusely where an Afghan sword had removed part of his skull, alive only because the blow had been deflected by a magazine stuffed in his cap for warmth. The Jalalabad garrison lit fires on the ramparts to bring in other stragglers. But none appeared. Of the fifteen thousand who set out, Dr. Brydon was the only person to complete the retreat from Kabul, the sole remnant of the once-invincible British army.

The disaster was greeted in Britain with disbelief, dismay, and then a storm of recrimination. The catastrophe appeared complete two months later when Shah Shujah, accused by some of instigating the massacre, cautiously emerged from the Bala Hisar to review the troops arrayed outside his fortress, and was shot through the head as he sat in his chair of state. The assassin was his own godson, who rode up to the corpse, stripped off its jewels, and kicked the dead king into a ditch. "Our worst fears regarding the Afghan expedition have been justified," *The Times* declared with penetrating hindsight. Some held Alexander Burnes responsible for the disaster; others criticized Macnaghten and Auckland. Everyone condemned Akbar Khan and many blamed Shah Shujah. Questions were asked in Parliament, inquiries were launched, and an army of retribution was formed under General Pollock, Harlan's commander during the Burma war, to reassert British authority.

In the midst of this emotive mix of condemnation, humiliation, and national anger, Harlan plunged into print. May 1842 saw the publication in Philadelphia of *A Memoir of India and Avghanistaun—With observations upon the present critical state and future prospects of those Countries* by Josiah Harlan, "Late Counsellor of State; Aide-de-Camp, and General of the Staff of Dost Mahomed Khan, Ameer of Cabul." The book could not have been more timely, or more incendiary. Far from being a memoir, it was a diatribe, a furious denunciation of British imperialism in general, and the failed Afghan policy in particular.

Astringent, sometimes pompous, and relentlessly critical, Harlan's book is not his most attractive writing. In one breath he expresses "profound regret" at the loss of life in Afghanistan, but in the next he argues that the bloodshed was moral recompense, "the retributive justice of an avenging Deity." True, the British had made some terrible mistakes, and the invasion of Afghanistan was misguided from the outset, but to describe the massacre of fifteen thousand people as divine vengeance was brutally insensitive. Harlan's sympathies were entirely with the Afghans. "A king has been dethroned, and another restored; a kingdom won, and lost, and won again," he wrote. "The Avghaun people have been kept in commotion by continual domestic strife and civil wars; treasures exhausted; torrents of blood shed, and the whole affair terminated by the massacre of the invaders." The British had managed to bring about what no Afghan ruler had ever achieved, uniting "a nation whose principle of existence lies in the disunion and separate interests of its constituent tribes into one unanimous community, goaded to madness by the systematic and consecutive tyranny of the invaders."

None of the principal players escaped Harlan's wrath, as he settled old scores with gusto. "Sir William Macnaghten marched into Avghanistaun with the air of a Bombastes Furioso, advocating a policy which has wrought the reward that cruelty, false faith and criminal duplicity will ever receive." As for Alexander Burnes, "the utter and deplorable incapacity of the English agent originated a line of bewildering policy, commenced in the feebleness of a narrow mind, and finished with a deluge of misery and blood"; through "frivolity, stupidity and turpitude" Burnes had brought about "the massacre of a British army and the destruction of many a noble soldier." Lord Auckland, he declared, should be "impeached, degraded, and despoiled of his hereditary honours."

The British Empire he depicted as a vast, corrupt behemoth that had brought nothing but misery to the "oppressed and plundered millions." "Have the arts and civilization of Europe munificently blessed the communities of Asia? The sciences and *beaux arts* diffused among them?" Not at all. Instead, the "British executive government, has riveted the shackles of slavery upon the whole agricultural population of British India." Where Alexander the Great had brought civilization, the British had inflicted "famines, discontent, disaffection, rebellion, financial distress, fall of prices, reduced revenues, crime abounding . . . might against rights, cultivation declining, total absence of internal improvement, no public works, no roads, no canals, no dissemination of knowledge or improvements in education. We see here the consequences of a military despotism; a government imposed upon millions, and sustained by the sword, without a philanthropic motive; originating in cupidity, nourished and developed by tyrannous force, sealed in blood."

This vituperative attack was insulting enough to British ears, but the conclusion Harlan drew from events in Afghanistan was even more offensive. "The clouds have gathered in the Indian Caucasus, and scathed with their lightning the British army," he wrote, heralding "the destruction of every Englishman throughout the whole of India." Once the native people rise, he predicted, "British power in India expires instantly, without a struggle, except the death throes of their officers as the native army strangle them in their beds." In a final swipe, Harlan predicted that with the fall of the British Empire, czarist Russia would be hailed by the East as "a saviour and protector, the restorer of their political rights [and] the dignity of their kings." All Russia needed to do was to march an army south across the mountains into India, following the route he himself had traveled: "Should a Russian army ever take up a position in Bulkh, there will be an end to the empire of opinion in India; and there is not a stone or stick in all the country that would not become a deadly weapon in the hands of outraged millions, to drive out the pitiful handful of European oppressors." What Harlan did not mention, however, was the possibility that a Russian invasion might be the opportunity for him to regain his own kingly dignity. He not only predicted, but positively advocated the demolition of the British Empire. His trenchant criticisms of empire would be echoed in the age of decolonization, and some of his remarks were extraordinarily prescient, for the great Indian Mutiny would erupt in in 1857, shaking the Empire to its foundations. The tone and thrust of Harlan's polemic seemed intended to provoke maximum anxiety and anger in London by raising the Russian specter at a moment in the Great Game when Britain seemed most vulnerable; this was precisely its effect.

In America, the book was received politely enough. *New Books of the Month* observed that "it is pervaded by an air of truthfulness," while noting its "spirit of strong hostility to the British dominion in India." Complimentary copies were sent to Her Imperial Highness the Grand Duchess Helene in Saint Petersburg, Baron Myendorff, the Russian ambassador to Berlin, the Whig Society of Princeton, and the President of the United States. In Britain, by contrast, it was panned, described by one critic as an "extraordinary concoction of bombastic romance, deliberate perversions, false statements and virulent abuse." Sir William Kaye, whose definitive history of the Afghan campaign was in preparation, described Harlan as "clever and unscrupulous" and tried to undermine his credibility. That an American—and one who, moreover, had served under the British flag—should dare to criticize the Empire at such an emotional moment was more than English reviewers could stomach. Harlan's animus was put down to "anglophobia," yet his book made salutary reading for British officials: "His *Memoir* was officially discredited, but secretly read, under the table, by historians and British strategists."

The rage provoked by the *Memoir* stopped Harlan's literary career in its tracks. The book was intended merely to be a foretaste of his main work, a vast three-volume autobiographical narrative, based on his journals and entitled *Oriental Sketches*. Much of this had been penned on the journey home, and by 1841 it stretched to 968 handwritten pages. Harlan's notes indicate that he had also written something called "The Fall of Kipchak or Scenes in Tartary—a melodrama in four acts." Not one word of this torrent would see the printed page in Harlan's lifetime, for the "Empire of Opinion" he had rebuked so harshly, now turned on him. The British historian Charles Grey, who wrote a furious attack on Harlan in the 1920s, claimed that "the deliberate lies which appeared in the published book, were duly exposed in the English press, and created such a distrust of the Doctor, that it killed the chances of his future book, which perished still-born."

Harlan offered the manuscript of *Oriental Sketches* to several publishers, none of whom, after the storm surrounding the *Memoir*, were prepared to touch it. The British establishment closed ranks; according to one authority "everything was done to turn readers away from the *Memoir*; without readers, Harlan could not publish his narrative." Harlan's book had caused alarm in high places, and "the English officers who ran the political service feared its publication would provide detailed revelations on the activities of Burnes, Macnaghten and other political agents employed in Afghanistan." Harlan had expected the *Memoir* to make him controversial, certainly, but also rich and famous. It had precisely the opposite effect; indeed, Harlan's anonymity today is largely due to the enraged response to this, his first and only book. For American publishers appeared equally unwilling to take a second chance on so incendiary a writer. Taking their cue from 1841, almost every subsequent historian accepted the British view of Harlan as seditious, unreliable, and possibly unhinged. He never published another book.

Harlan not only found himself a publishing pariah, but rather "poorer than he anticipated." Over the years, he had sent installments of cash back to his sister Mary, with instructions that it should be invested. Mary, however, had no head for accounts, or much of anything else. "I had money sent to me from the East Indies," she said vaguely. "I could not tell what amount as he sent it at different times in different sums. He would sometimes send $500 sometimes less, and then $10,000 in one sum. He sent it as a loan to the family. I can now recollect it was sent to us to invest. You must ask Josiah why it was sent to us to invest. He sent it in a draft with a letter accompanying it by some gentleman in Calcutta directed to me." The money had been unwisely invested, and most of it had evaporated.

Harlan's fortune might have been modest, but his expectations remained extravagant, and with his remaining funds he purchased 210 acres of land near Cochransville, in Chester County. Glennville, Harlan's new home, was no mere rural homestead like the one he had grown up on, but "a great manorial estate, with a manor house, tenant houses and a mill" built in 1800 and said to be the first place in America to produce calico. In India, Harlan had seen the natives use "a device for using the same water repeatedly by raising it in spirals," and he set about constructing just such an Archimedean screw for his cotton mill. "People came long distances to see this ancient device in operation," but while Glennville might have been a local tourist attraction, as a business it was a hopeless failure, for Harlan was almost as financially inept as his siblings, spending an enormous amount of his own and borrowed money with little hope of repaying it. The first of many legal disputes over unpaid debts erupted in September 1842. For the rest of his life, Harlan would be permanently in hock, and frequently in litigation.

The irrepressible Harlan simply ignored his mounting debts, telling a friend how happy he was to be back in his homeland, at least for the time being.

> I propose to myself the indulgence of a calm and soothing solitude, a contemplative and abstract existence, such quietude as the mariner covets after weathering a thousand storms. The world may trundle on unheeded whilst I enjoy the experience of the past in the pursuits of a philosophical retirement, in the occupation of literary tastes and in the chastened contentment of undisturbed reminiscence . . . The purely intellectual may seek the cloister, the inexperienced neophyte would dive for the pearls of life beneath the surface of troublous seas. I am neither a monastic recluse nor a juvenile aspirant of fame and shall avoid both those extremes in rural retirement.

Harlan had always enjoyed solitude but, as he admitted, he was no monk. He needed a wife and, on the morning of May 1, 1849, he obtained one. Almost nothing is known about Elizabeth Baker, save that she was thirty-six, fourteen years Harlan's junior, the daughter of a local farmer, and a fellow Quaker. Harlan's ejection from the Society of Friends for violating the rules on pacifism had been rescinded, and the Quaker marriage ceremony took place at 8 a.m. in Chester County, attended by Harlan's surviving siblings and the Baker clan. "Somewhat to the disgust of the Baker relatives, the General, as he was leaving after the ceremony, said to his bride: 'Well, how does it feel to Mrs. General Harlan?'" Harlan had once been a king, and he never let himself, or anyone else, forget it. A daughter, Sarah Victoria, was born in 1852. Harlan doted on the child, but of his wife, Elizabeth, there is no mention in his writings. If the relationship was a close one, no evidence of that affection has survived; among his private documents, Harlan still kept the poem he had written to Eliza Swaim so many years before.

Harlan's true love was still Afghanistan, and though he made close friendships, he remained, as one astute observer put it, "a stranger among his own people." The same was true of many an old Eastern hand. Charles Masson, the pioneering antiquarian and Harlan's former sparring partner, had returned to England in 1842; like Harlan he strongly criticized the ineptitude of the British in Afghanistan, and suffered the wrath of the establishment. Accused of being "unreliable, mendacious and spiteful," he died in 1853, sour and unfulfilled, leaving behind a superb collection of Afghan coins and relics. Even Joseph Wolff, the fabulously eccentric "Christian Dervish," had gone into retirement. Wolff had carried out one final mission in 1844, to try to obtain the release of two British officers held in Bokhara, only to discover that they had already been beheaded. Narrowly escaping with his own life, he made his way back to England and declared: "My natural inclinations are all in favour of comfort and ease, for I dislike uncivilised life and uncivilised habits," an amazing statement given his wild and wandering life. Wolff became the vicar of a quiet Somerset parish, never left the country again, and died in his bed in 1862.

Dost Mohammed Khan ruled once more in Kabul. As Harlan had observed, no other man could control Afghanistan. With Shah Shujah dead, the amir was brought out of exile and reinstated by the British, the very people who had ousted him at such expense in blood and treasure. He remained forever baffled that "the rulers of so great an empire should have gone across the Indus to deprive me of my poor and barren country." The remains of Shujah's family returned to exile in Ludhiana. "Everything," observed a British officer, "is reverting to the old state of things—as it was before we entered the country."

Harlan followed this strange turn of the wheel in Afghanistan with avid interest. Dost Mohammed had regained his throne, and now he might do the same. Was he not the legally constituted prince of Ghor? With the amir back in power, his plan to rule in the Hazarajat by training a modern army "may still be realised," he wrote, "with or without Mahomed Reffee's individual influence, as men of his ambitious views are never wanting in a community so divided as the Hazarrahs." Rudyard Kipling expressed precisely the same idea in "The Man Who Would Be King": "In any place where they fight, a man who knows how to drill can always be a king," declares the fictional Daniel Dravot. "We shall go to those parts and say to any king we find—'D'you want to vanquish your foes?' and we will show him how to drill men."

Harlan's friends were in no doubt that he hankered to return. Among them was a certain Mordecai Rickets, a retired British army officer. When Harlan failed to reply to one of his letters, Rickets wrote that he had assumed he "had again taken flight and sought service among your old friends in Afghanistan." In the same letter, Rickets noted that "Mr. Dost Mahomed appears now all powerful" and echoed Harlan's own thoughts, pointing out that "had you remained in command of his army that unfortunate old imbecile Sooja might not have risen again and caused the bloodshed which ensued." As Shah Shujah had once waited in Ludhiana, dreaming of his lost crown, so Harlan now found himself "'sighing his soul' towards the mountains and valleys of Afghanistan, and patiently waiting the *kismet* or fate which was to restore him to his throne."

Far from allowing the world to trundle by unheeded, Harlan was keen for action again; but he was no longer a young man, and to plunge back into the wilds of Central Asia he needed backing and money. "Other travellers in Afghanistan had the aid of their governments at least as a lurking possibility." Harlan decided that he would return as an official U.S. representative; and he would get there as he had traveled to so many other places in the past, by camel.

In the 1850s, American politicians and entrepreneurs had begun to explore the possibility of importing camels to use as military beasts of burden in the Western deserts. No American had more experience with these animals than Harlan, and he duly became camel consultant to the U.S. government. The result was a voluminous document entitled *Importation of Camels*, the most thorough investigation of the subject ever undertaken.

"The introduction of the camel," it began, "has long been viewed as a matter of much national importance, particularly since the establishment of the overland routes, requiring mingled mountain and desert service, between the Atlantic States and California or Oregon." Harlan's camel credentials were laid out: during his 360-mile trek to Balkh, he had been "compelled to cross the highest range of the Indian Caucasus [and] enjoyed the most ample opportunity for becoming practically familiar with the capacities of the northern Bactrian camel, as he had been previously with those of the dromedary."

The camel, Harlan argued, was more efficient than a train, for "unlike the 'iron camel' of America, it is provided with a peculiar apparatus for retaining water in its stomach, so that it can march from well to well without great inconvenience while its steam-breathed rival refuses to labour without a half hour's draught." Indeed, he declared, "the demand for camels would be increased rather than diminished by the construction of any possible railroad to the Pacific." It would be hard to find a more inaccurate prediction about the future of American transport.

Harlan went on to extol the homely but reliable qualities of the camel. "Patient under his duties, he kneels at the command of his driver, and rises cheerfully with his load. He requires no whip or spur during his monotonous march, but when fatigued his driver sings him some cheerful snatch of his Arabian melodies." The paean to this unassuming king among animals rose in a crescendo: "As sure footed as the horse . . . As omnivorous as the goat . . . A fleece probably quite equal to that of four sheep, surpassing in silky smoothness and fineness the most delicate flannel." The camel's sole drawback, in Harlan's view, was a tendency to flatulence and overeating, which "renders his breath exceedingly offensive."

Finally came the job pitch. The "great national project" of introducing the camel to America would fail "unless government is able to secure the advice and assistance of someone thoroughly acquainted with the climes of northern India and of the United States, and also with the varieties, the mode of breeding, and the physical management of camels and dromedaries. Whoever may be employed to carry out the design, he will find his exertions of little avail, unless he is thoroughly acquainted not only with the habits and qualities of the several varieties, but also with the language and social conditions of the people and modes of dealing in those semi-savage regions." The report concluded that the job of implanting "the camel tribe in the United States" should be immediately entrusted "to some highly intelligent person, already fully acquainted with their habits, wants, and treatment, to accomplish the object with certainty and despatch." Only one person fitted this description.

Matters now moved quickly. Jefferson Davis, secretary of war under President Franklin Pierce, became an avid camel enthusiast, and on April 5, 1854, the American Camel Company was chartered "for the purpose of importing camels from Asia and Africa into the United States, so as to make that animal applicable to the purpose of burden, transportation and fabrics." Frustratingly, however, the government decided that camels might be more cheaply imported from North Africa and Asia Minor, without the expense of sending General Harlan to get them from Afghanistan. Instead, a Turkish immigrant from Smyrna was hired as trainer of the U.S. Army Camel Corps. His name was Hajji Ali, which the cowboys immediately changed to the more easily pronounceable Hi Jolly.

Nonetheless, it was in large part due to Harlan's "valuable paper" that the first camels arrived in America in 1856. Western cowboys might, conceivably, have become camelboys, had Harlan not overlooked a few key factors. The stout ponies of Central Asia had been reared alongside camels, but American horses had never seen these foul-breathed, sexually aggressive creatures before, and did not like the experience one bit: "The American horses and mules firmly declined to recognise the camels as colleagues and insisted on running away upon each encounter with the odoriferous and ungainly foreigners." Cattle tended to stampede at the sight of them, which made roundups tricky, and the soldiers got seasick from their swaying gait. The Camel Corps was disbanded in 1863. Hajji Ali, that most implausible of Wild West figures, became an army scout and then a prospector. When he died in 1902, the Turk was awarded his own monument in Quartzsite, Arizona, topped with a metal camel. The Hi Jolly Highway is a lasting testament to his transitory fame. A few camels ended up in circuses, some were put to work in the Western mines, but many were simply turned loose, "where they wandered, multiplied, and gave rise to many an incredulous tale."

Harlan did not care, because he had had another brilliant idea. Instead of importing camels, the government should send him to Afghanistan to bring back fruit, specifically grapevines. "I by no means intend to deprecate the experimental venture of importing the camel," he wrote, without a blush. "But is not the naturalisation of the wine grape of vastly more importance than the naturalization of a beast of

burden not absolutely *necessary* for our population?" The grapes of
Kabul would make his fortune, Harlan believed—a matter of some urgency, since Glennville was now mired in debt. Harlan had begun to sell
off the property, bit by bit, until all that remained was the house and
mill. Harlan purchased an interest in the Norris Iron Works at Norris-
town, Pennsylvania, but his mind was not on iron or cotton; he was
consumed by grapes.

Harlan spent nearly two years preparing another paper: *On the
Fruits of Cabul and Vicinity, With a View to the Introduction of the Grape-
Vine of that Region into the Central Climate of the United States*. Like his
treatise on camels, it remains the definitive (indeed the only) work on
the subject. Harlan's survey recalled the beauties of Afghanistan: "Numberless productive valleys, rich with the treasures of a fertile soil and
gratifying the senses with the songs of birds, the bright hues of a thousand blossoms, and an odor-loaded air, unrivalled by any other spot in
any land." He wrote passionately of the wild rhubarb, the radishes "of
mammoth size," the sweet mulberries, "cherries, apricots, plums, and
peaches in vast profusion," the "seedless pomegranates from Djillal-
abad; soft-shelled almonds from Ghorebund; the watermelons, cantaloupes, Samarcand pears, apples from the gardens of Istalif," the
elegant espaliers entwined with the roses of Kabul.

But his most effusive prose was reserved for the peerless Afghan
grape; just as he had once imagined camels riding the prairies, he now
saw great vineyards of hardy Kabul grapes spreading through the Mid-
west. The resulting trade would add "millions to the wealth of our population [and] serve to pay off our debt to other nations." The gold rush
had started in California in 1848; Harlan now predicted a grape rush:
"Another discovery equivalent to California would not surpass, if it
equalled, the inconceivable national advantages of a naturalized grape
culture." He saw his name in lights: Josiah Harlan, Grape King. "The
acclimation of a perfect wine grape would command the lasting gratitude of future generations, and place high upon the pedestal of fame the
name associated with the successful attempt to accomplish this enterprise of national concern."

Harlan was determined to lead the grape-collecting expedition in
person. "I propose myself to perform the duties of a special agent for
this occasion," he wrote, for which he would need "a saddle horse, two

ponies, equipments for caravan marching [and] some specimens of improved firearms as a present for the ruling prince, Dost Mahomed." The cost of the expedition, including his own salary and expenses, would, he estimated, amount to less than ten thousand dollars. After the camel debacle, Harlan was not about to see another Hi Jolly take his place.

> Great personal danger must be risked by Christians attempting to travel in Afghanistan. Since the destruction of the British army which essayed the conquest of their country, the jealousy of the natives has been greatly increased, and the difficulties and dangers, at all times serious and almost insurmountable, can only be avoided by the direct authority and protection of the prince. My long residence in the country and familiar social intercourse with the ruling family are incidents which secure me uninterrupted friendly relations; and in the event of any adventitious difficulties, my familiar knowledge of their language and of their manners and customs would favor the security of a successful disguise.

At the age of twenty-five, Harlan had smuggled himself into Kabul, disguised as a holy man, the agent of the exiled king; now, at the age of sixty-two, he proposed to return once more, again in disguise, but this time in an official capacity, as America's special grape agent and envoy for fruit. *On the Fruits of Cabul* was intended to be Harlan's passport back to Afghanistan. But history had other plans for him. By the time the treatise was finally presented to Congress in the spring of 1862, America was fighting the Civil War, and so was Harlan.

16

HARLAN'S LAST STAND

When war broke out between North and South, the old soldier and enemy of slavery did not hesitate. Harlan immediately dispatched a letter to the secretary of state offering the services of General Josiah Harlan, former commander of the Afghan army, to the Union cause. What Harlan had in mind was considerably grander than merely a place in the ranks: instead, he offered to raise his own regiment. The man who had trained the Afghan army and humbled the slaving warlord Murad Beg saw no reason why he should not go into battle, once more, with a private army. Bizarrely, nor did the authorities in Washington, and permission was duly granted for the formation of "Harlan's Light Cavalry." Harlan had no formal rank, no experience of the American army, and no knowledge of modern warfare. He was also sixty-two years old, but gave his age as fifty-six.

During the months of August and September 1861, Harlan set about recruiting. According to war records, "most of the men were from Philadelphia, but companies were also raised in Iowa, New York, New Jersey and Ohio," and by October Harlan's Light Cavalry was complete: 41 officers and 1,089 enlisted men. Harlan was appointed colonel, which, since he had never held any American rank before, was a remarkably swift promotion. His second in command was an ambitious young officer named Lieutenant Colonel Samuel P. Spear, while Harlan's nephew George, the son of Richard, signed on as regimental surgeon.

Harlan's Light Cavalry left Philadelphia in October and marched to Washington, where orders were received to report to Camp Palmer in Virginia for instruction and drill. The weather was dreadful, and the regiment, Harlan frankly admitted, was in a pitiful state. "The cold and rain at night, and the cloudy days of October and November, added to the inefficiency of the corps, and the starving condition of the horses threatened entire destruction to these animals." The harsh conditions "also caused many of our men to fall sick, rapidly filling the hospitals. Many of the men were without uniforms, and many also were without pantaloons, standing guard in ragged drawers." Harlan requested extra uniforms and blankets, but "no requisitions or importunities on my part could procure from the authorities a supply of necessaries [and] for these reasons the drill was relaxed, to relieve man and horse, while many were excused from nightly guard in consequence of their nakedness."

Harlan's age began to tell on him almost immediately, and he swiftly came down with what appears to have been pneumonia. "I was convalescent from extreme illness and although sufficiently well to attend the most essential of my duties, I was not in a condition to risk a relapse by living under canvass and from exposure to the chills of night." He did his best to hide his infirmity. "I did not report myself sick, but by perseverance and a desire to discharge my duties I continued such active measures as were necessary to maintain the discipline and drill of the regiment."

The officers, however, began to grumble that their commander was a rare presence in camp. While he was on his sickbed, a rumor went around that Colonel Harlan was not expected to recover, and the more ambitious wondered whether there might soon be a vacancy at the top, and promotion for all. Meanwhile they whined that "he had never attended a dress parade, that he had been at only one regimental inspection, had never instructed any of his officers or men in any aspect of military science or tactics." There was a simple reason why Harlan had not drilled his men in modern military tactics: he didn't know any. He was entirely proficient at blasting ancient mud fortresses with cannon and persuading wild Afghan tribesman into battle with matchlocks and cutlasses, but on the finer points of Western warfare he was entirely ignorant.

As Harlan's health improved, he became increasingly dictatorial, no doubt sensing the rising discontent among some of his officers. He had never had much time for the niceties of military regulation. "What in hell do you report to me for?" he bellowed at one officer who, in accordance with the rules, had reported for orders as field officer of the day. "What is your American way of doing business in camp? I know all about the English service, but nothing about your American way of camp service." When the officers complained, he sent them packing with another deafening volley of insults. "All of you are damned fools. Am I to be annoyed to death?" Harlan treated his officers as an Oriental prince would treat his underlings. This was, perhaps, unsurprising, given that he was, at least in his own estimation, an Oriental prince. He railed at them, calling them liars and fools, and periodically threatened to string them up. Then, entirely without warning, he would behave as if they were old friends and invite them into his tent for a chat. This technique had served him well during his time in the East—a combination of vigorous abuse and violent threats, combined with moments of informality, was the accepted method of maintaining discipline under the likes of Ranjit Singh and Dost Mohammed. But what had worked in the medieval wilds of Afghanistan and the Punjab did not go down well with Americans of the officer class in the second half of the nineteenth century.

On November 17, the regiment marched to Annapolis, and then moved on by transports to Fort Monroe, Virginia. "Stables and Quarters were built, and during a period of six months a thorough course of instruction and drill was followed, and some experience acquired in scouting and picket duty." To Harlan's intense annoyance, the military authorities now remembered that Congress had authorized the raising of regiments by states, not by individuals, and "consequently the formation of Harlan's Light Cavalry as an independent regiment was irregular." Changing the name of his force to the more pedestrian Eleventh Cavalry, 108th Regiment, Pennsylvania Volunteers, added considerably to Harlan's ill temper.

A week after the regiment arrived at Fort Monroe, some horses bolted from the lines and trampled a tent. Harlan summoned the officer responsible and gave him a ferocious dressing down, in what the recipient considered a "harsh and ungentlemanly" tirade, ending with the threat: "If any more of your horses get loose, sir, you had better have a rope around your neck." The grumbling grew markedly louder, to a level where it became plainly audible to Harlan himself, and on December 13, he informed a senior officer that "a sedition existed amongst many of the officers." Even so, Harlan believed that relations had improved when, shortly before Christmas, he was invited to dinner by Lieutenant James Mahan, an officer whom Harlan had previously offended by declaring that "he is the damned fool that can't pronounce his own name, 'tis Mahone, not Mahan." Harlan eagerly grasped what looked like an olive branch.

In fact, the invitation was the prelude to open rebellion, for the officers, led by Lieutenant Colonel Spear, had hatched a plot against their commanding officer that is unique in the annals of the Civil War. Harlan suddenly faced open mutiny. His offenses were many, the officers claimed, but boiled down to one: he had been very rude to them, collectively, individually, and consistently. Collectively, therefore, they now presented Harlan with a letter, baldly threatening to bring charges against him for "habitual neglect of duty" unless he stood down immediately. Signed by the lieutenant colonel, two majors, nine captains, and sixteen lieutenants, the letter stated:

> Charges and specifications of a most serious character are about to be preferred against you by the officers of the regiment. Although we have no doubt as to the result of a court martial, we are satisfied it would have the desired effect, viz: your removal. But Sir, as it is not our desire to heap upon you further disgrace than is necessary to the accomplishment of our purpose, we hereby afford you the opportunity of tendering your resignation, and we hereby apprise you, that your conduct towards us and towards the men has been such, as to force us to leave no stone unturned to remove you from the Regiment. With the expression of the hope that our reasonable request will be speedily acceded to, we subscribe ourselves below, etc. etc.

Harlan's abrasive manner had turned most of his officers against him in just five months without a shot being fired, but the whiners were an ignoble crew. Harlan could certainly be truculent, but he was also patriotic, energetic, and entirely immune to fear. The enlisted men, unlike their officers, relished serving under the whiskery old warhorse with the sharp tongue. Ambition plainly lay behind the allegations, for even before receiving a reply, the plaintiffs convened "a mass meeting in which the officers held nominations for the posts to be filled when the colonel departed and the officers would have a chance to move up the promotions ladder." To hear the complaints about Harlan's "gruff" manner one would think the officers were about to enter ballet school rather than fight the bloodiest war of the century. Harlan may have been a demanding and unconventional commander, but while his detractors were complaining about his failure to keep the regimental letter book up to date, he was raring to fight. The first battle of Harlan's war would be against his own men. Unfortunately, his response to the threatening letter is unrecorded, but we can assume it was unprintable.

The officers carried out their threat, and on January 27, 1862, at 11:30 a.m., Harlan was summoned to the Library at Fort Monroe, to appear before a court-martial panel headed by Colonel J. B. Carr. The charges were read out. In addition to neglecting his duty and "conduct unbecoming an officer and a gentleman," Harlan was accused of encouraging a subordinate to fiddle his expenses, and jeopardizing security by revealing the secret watchword to "six different persons not entitled to receive it, said persons being officers, servants, citizens and Negroes." It was also claimed that on several occasions he had been too drunk to perform his duty. Harlan pleaded not guilty to all charges, and announced that he would be conducting his own defense.

The prosecution set out its case, alleging that Colonel Harlan never spent more than fifteen minutes on parade, if he turned up at all, and addressed his officers "in a very abrupt manner," swearing and berating them in an "unofficerlike and ungentlemanly" way. The charge of drunkenness was based on ludicrously flimsy evidence: one officer claimed to have seen Harlan exhibiting "unusual cheerfulness"; another claimed to have seen the colonel "steady himself by his tent pole, and his desk" when moving across his tent. Lieutenant Colonel Spear blithely testified: "I judged from his manner that he was labouring under the effects of intoxication."

Harlan tore into the prosecution witnesses, "these promulgators of sedition," insisting: "During the whole time of my command I have never ceased to exercise an arduous, active, energetic and commanding influence of a proper military discipline." Clerical duties, such as maintaining the letter book, were the responsibility of Lieutenant Colonel Spear; if Harlan had uttered a password in public, this had been a harmless mistake, hardly deserving of a court-martial. As for the suggestion that he had clung drunkenly to his own tent pole, he pointed out: "The space in my tent [is] so much contracted as to make it difficult to move about without coming in contact with the furniture." He was, he angrily declared, a lifelong abstainer from strong drink, the innocent victim of a plot, organized by his officers, to get him drunk. When the regimental farrier or blacksmith was called to the stand, Harlan spotted an opportunity to attack the credibility of Lieutenant Mahan, and the cross-examination veered into farce.

QUESTION: Did you think I was drunk at any time during the march?
ANSWER: No.
Q: Do you think you could have known if I was drunk?
A: I think I could.
Q: Are you acquainted with Lieutenant James D. Mahan of your company?
A: I am.
Q: Since you have been in the company together, do you know of anything against his character?
A: He told me one day that he had a yellow girl with him during the night.
Q: Has Mr. Mahan ever talked with you about inviting me to dinner?
A: He told me that he had made a dinner and had invited Colonel Harlan there to make him drunk, to show the officers he would get drunk, so that they could prefer charges against him.
Q [BY THE COURT]: How came you to be engaged in this conversation with Lieutenant Mahan?
A: I went to his tent and he told me he was afraid he was burned and asked me what would be a remedy.
Q [BY COLONEL HARLAN]: Are you the farrier or the horse doctor?
A: The farrier.
Q [BY THE COURT]: What did you understand Lieutenant Mahan to mean when he said "he was afraid he had been burned"?
A: I understood him to mean he was afraid he had contracted a venereal disease.
Q: Does your practise as a farrier include that of venereal diseases?
A: No, it does not.

Having painted one of his principal accusers as a whoring, pox-ridden plotter, Harlan summed up his defense with all the oratorical passion he could muster. It was a fantastic performance.

"My reputation, which is dearer to me than life, has become a shuttlecock between malice and envy," he roared. "Is my condemnation prejudged? And is this honorable court supposed to be a compliant instrument to confirm the designs and machinations of a selfish, foul, and merciless conspiracy, whose action would give, by a blasted reputation, a drunken husband to a wife, a drunken father to an artless child, to whom that father's name must for *her* future be a malignant influence?"

The accusation of drunkenness brought Harlan to a peak of righteous indignation. "I have patiently listened to this nefarious, mendacious, and wicked assault upon the character of a gentleman whose reputation for honor and integrity of deportment is as well established as any gentleman in the community. All who know me are aware that the *whole tenor of my life* places the *seal* of falsehood upon this atrocious charge. My reputation will stand unscathed by such vile assaults! Still, like the sacred Brahmin of the East, who feels himself polluted by the *shadow* of an outcast, I am conscious that the breath of calumny may sully the purity of truth."

His accusers, he said, were nothing more than mutineers, a disgrace to the military profession, ambitious schemers undermining military discipline and "fighting not against the rebel traitors of the land, but against the great principle of our defence." The very future of the Union was at stake: "If in this volunteer army insubordination shall be countenanced in the officers, can the discipline essential to combat our enemies be established?" If calumny and sedition were allowed to triumph over truth and honor, he warned, then American democracy was doomed: "The greatest and most noble army of volunteer patriots the world has ever seen [will] become the political engine of some traitor tyrant, who from a mass of anarchised material will ultimately subject an exhausted and willing population to arbitrary domination!!" Harlan concluded with a passionate biblical blast:

> Gentlemen, you who are colonels and commanding officers, make the case your own, reflect upon your liability to suffer a similar outrage from insubordinate and seditious men, reckless of the reputation you have won by years of faithful and fastidious devotion to the service of your country and the duties of social ties; of men who would assault the most cherished principles of your existence by a satanic perversion of misplaced ambition, that sin by which the angels fell, and sacrifice all that is dear to you, to achieve for themselves a position.

On February 10, after eleven full days of hearings and 157 pages of testimony, the court gave its decision; it was a mixed verdict. The charge of expense fiddling was dropped, and Harlan was acquitted of drunkenness. The other charges, however, were upheld: Colonel Harlan was found guilty of conduct prejudicial to "good order and military discipline" and using "disrespectful and ungentlemanly language." Pending confirmation of the sentence by Major General John E. Wool, adjutant general of the army and the commanding officer of Fort Monroe, the court ordered that he be "suspended from Command, Pay and Emoluments for the period of six months." Harlan was devastated. He had fought for many things over the years: for the British Empire, for kingdoms and princes, and now for the Union, but throughout he had defended his honor. Not since his dismissal by Ranjit Singh had he felt such humiliation and hurt. Believing he had been brought down "by invisible enemies protected by their high position," Harlan retired to his tent, outraged and mortified.

The plotters were jubilant, but their relish at Harlan's disgrace was short-lived. Major General Wool took one look at the evidence and on February 26, reversed the verdict with a thundering rebuke to the court. Colonel Harlan, he declared, had fallen victim to a disgraceful mutiny. "A combination was formed, consisting of twenty-eight Officers of the Regiment, including the Lieut. Colonel, two Majors and nine Captains, with a determination and persistency seldom, if ever witnessed in the Army of the United States, to remove their Colonel from his regiment." The proof lay in the officers' threatening letter.

> It is indeed surprising that with this letter, the evidence of a meeting of a large majority of the signers when nominations were made to fill the vacancies that would occur by the removal of their Colonel, and the dinner given to him by Lieut. Mahan, one of the principal witnesses against him, to get him intoxicated, in order that charges might be preferred against him for intemperateness, that so respectable a court, no matter if all the charges against him had been fully proved, should have countenanced by its sentence a combination of Officers, whose conduct was no less insubordinate than dangerous to the discipline of the Army, and if sanctioned or overlooked would not fail to subvert every rule and principle that should govern the Officer, or the man of honour. Therefore the sentence of the Court is disproved and remitted. Colonel Harlan is released from arrest and will re-assume command of his regiment.

Under the Seventh Article of War the punishment for mutiny was death; the conspirators were lucky to escape with their lives. Harlan was vindicated. Having come so close to losing his regiment, he was back in command once more. The very next day a touching ceremony took place outside his tent, proof that while Harlan's officers detested him, the troops remained staunchly loyal. To his astonishment, Harlan was presented with a fine saber. The leader of the delegation informed him that the gift had been purchased with donations from the men, "as a token of respect towards you as commanding officer, in whom we place all trust as leader and guardian, and a native of the old Keystone state. We wish to express our sentiments by this small token of love, which we honestly owe to our leader."

Harlan was profoundly moved. "To receive from you this magnificent sabre—soon I hope to be unsheathed in common with your own weapons in defence of our beloved union—is a compliment highly flattering to me, and most honorable to yourselves. I receive it with grateful appreciation of the patriotic and personal considerations that moved you to testify, by this significant emblem of justice and government, your confidence and your regard and respect for your commanding officer." He then launched into an emotional battlefield peroration.

> We have left our happy hearths, endeared to us by the peace and comfort of honorable toil, to repel the approach of a pestilent host of Rebels—the enemies of law and order—striving vainly to destroy the best government the world has ever seen. Let us defend the Star Spangled Banner to wave over the land of the free, or be buried in our graves. 600,000 patriots are our companions in the holy cause. Our brilliant and decisive victories pursue these traitors in defeat and despair. Let us hope, my fellow soldiers, that the sheen our of sabres may be seen in the strife! Strike home to the dastards for law and for life!

Harlan had lost none of his fighting gusto, but the strain of being tried, convicted, dismissed, and then reinstated had been shattering for a man already suffering from the privations of life under canvas. The trial was the straw that broke the camel expert's back. In the wake of the court-martial, Harlan's health steadily deteriorated. At the beginning of June, he received orders to join the army of the Potomac under Major General George B. McClellan. Although suffering from acute gastric problems, Harlan summoned up the strength to lead the regiment to Suffolk, Virginia, where it was destined to take part in the peninsular campaign. The regiment was immediately "engaged in picketing scout-ing and patrol duty . . . and frequent skirmishes and engagements with the enemy took place." Harlan's claims about the training of his men were amply borne out, for they acquitted themselves bravely. "A sabre charge by an advance guard of the Eleventh never failed promptly to clear the roads of the enemy's pickets."

Harlan, however, was denied the opportunity of seeing the sheen of his own saber in battle. Indeed, he was by now too weak to lift it. On July 15, 1862, he collapsed from a combination of dysentery, dehydra-tion, and fever, and was ordered to surrender command of the regi-ment. For another month he refused to step down, insisting that he was on the mend, but finally, for the first time in his life, he admitted defeat. On August 19, he was mustered out of service, with a surgeon's certifi-cate stating that he had become "debilitated from diarrhea" [sic].

Back in Chester County, Harlan's strength slowly returned, but his war was over. He watched from the sidelines, following the regiment's progress through the letters of his nephew George. Bored and frus-trated, he was also uncomfortably poor, for the rebellion had cut off the supply of cotton from the South and the mill at Glennville was aban-doned, swiftly falling into disrepair. The Afghan grape project looked hopeless, since "the country's funds were needed to continue the war." To pass the time, in the hope of belated literary recognition, Harlan be-gan writing a vast history of North America, but his prose style was now as stiff as his joints: he reached the year 1682, after 690 impenetrable pages, and gave up.

In 1865, the bloody war finally ground to a close. Harlan, his health more or less restored, began wandering once more. His daughter was now enrolled at the Quaker Westtown School, so his wife, Elizabeth Harlan, did not accompany him. Indeed, the couple seems to have spent little time together in the postwar years.

Veteran campaigners like Harlan, the white men who had carved out such exotic careers for themselves in the wilds of Central Asia, re-sponded to old age in different ways. The ferocious Paolo di Avitabile held on as the Sikh empire gradually disintegrated, and then retired to Naples, where he built himself a large house with the wealth he had ac-crued over the years. But his retirement was not an easy one. "The man who had bullied the Pathans of Peshwar was cuckolded by a village wench [and] died soon after his marriage in circumstances which caused considerable speculation in the Italian countryside." His once-vast fortune found its way into the pockets of lawyers and people claiming to be relatives, with so many "soi-disant relations asserting their claims to a share of the General's goods as to make 'Avitabile's Cousin' a byword in Italy."

Harlan's old friend Alexander Gardner, that most resilient of mercenaries, survived the mayhem that followed the death of Ranjit Singh and finally retired to Kashmir, where he lived on happily to the age of ninety-two, firing off letters to newspapers and speaking an "English that was quaint, graphic and wonderfully good considering his 50 years among the Asiatics." The fiery gent upholstered in tartan became a tourist attraction, and "visitors to the vale of Kashmir lost no opportunity of calling on the old adventurer" with the metal throat and the fund of terrifying tales.

But Harlan could not settle down. He purchased land in Kentucky, which he then sold. In 1867 he stayed briefly in Alabama, before moving on to Nashville, Tennessee. He obtained permission to visit the Cherokee Nation, and seems to have toyed with the idea of settling out West. "Everything in the west is 'super super,'" wrote an encouraging friend in 1867. Quite what Harlan was doing during his peregrinations remains a mystery, perhaps even to himself. He was now approaching seventy; there was little prospect of returning to Afghanistan, via camels or fruit collection or any other way; the people he had known were gone, and Afghanistan, once sealed from the world, was changing rapidly. Dost Mohammed Khan finally died in 1863, leaving behind sixteen wives, twenty-seven sons, twenty-five daughters, and the foundations of a modern state, though never a peaceful one.

The first transcontinental railway was completed in 1869, and Harlan was among its first passengers, traveling to California on the "iron horse" he considered so inferior to the camel. Before leaving, in a flicker of his old pride, he amended his entry in the Philadelphia City Directory from "Harlan, Josiah, gentleman" to "Harlan, Gen., USA," a title "which put his name in front of all the other Harlans." It was to be his final self-promotion. His wife and daughter remained in Pennsylvania, as did most of his personal archive, his notes, journals, letters, and manuscripts. Elizabeth Harlan stuffed the papers into an old milk churn. It was later alleged that Mrs. Harlan, indifferent to her husband's literary legacy, "had used it to start fires."

Arriving in San Francisco, Harlan once more proclaimed himself a doctor, resuming the title he had first assumed as a young surgeon in the East India Company. He still had no qualifications, but was able to resume his old trade thanks to "the lack of regulations in the California of that day." The San Francisco Directory of 1871 lists "Harlan, J., physician, dwelling at 1091 Market Street."

On October 21, 1871, an elderly, upright man with a gaunt face and the long white beard of an ancient prophet might have been spotted walking slowly through downtown San Francisco. On West Avenue, near Twenty-second Street, the old man paused, coughed, and collapsed. The postmortem gave the cause of death as "phthisis," or tuberculosis. He was buried the next day, after a funeral without mourners.

Josiah Harlan, hereditary prince of Ghor, died without family or fanfare. In his time he had been Hallan Sahib Bahadur, friend of kings, warrior, alchemist, and poet, player of the Great Game. He had known fame, power, and wealth, but when he came to die, he did so in utter obscurity, in a place he did not know, and where none knew him. Once he had followed in the footsteps of Alexander the Great, and a sort of greatness had been his, although only he had preserved its fading emblems. Among the few possessions found in the doctor's rooms in Market Street, and returned to his widow in Pennsylvania, were a fine golden sword and an ancient ruby engraved with the image of Athena. Alongside these lay a sheaf of yellowing papers, covered in tumbling Persian script, written decades earlier by a holy man in the Hindu Kush: the royal warrants of a dead Afghan prince.

I stood on the ramparts of the once-great Bala Hisar and watched a stray dog picking among the wrecked tanks that litter the hilltop ruins. The British destroyed the fortress at the end of the nineteenth century in retribution for the second Anglo-Afghan war, but you could still trace the twisting streets where Harlan once walked with his own dog, Dash, back in 1825. The Soviets used the Bala Hisar as a command post after the invasion of Afghanistan; during the civil war the Mujahideen deployed artillery here, flailing their rivals across the valley; and the Taliban, in turn, parked tanks on the hill to cow the inhabitants of the city below.

The ancient walled palace was occupied by a succession of men who sought to control Afghanistan, but the kings and would-be kings, foreign and home-produced, seldom lasted long. Of the five royal descendants of Dost Mohammed Khan's tribe to rule Afghanistan in the twentieth century, three were assassinated and two were forced into exile. I had known some of the more recent men who would be king, such as Gulbuddin Hekmatyar, the fundamentalist Mujahideen warlord I met in the Khyber mountains on my first visit to Afghanistan. In 1990, shortly after the Soviet withdrawal, I had interviewed Mohammed Najibullah, the Communist president left clinging to power as the American-backed guerrillas closed in. The man known as the "Ox of Kabul" had taken sanctuary in the U.N. compound when the Mujahideen captured the city, but five years later the victorious Taliban hauled the former president out of hiding. Najibullah was castrated, his body dragged around the city behind a pickup and then hoisted in the Kabul bazaar, just as the mutilated corpse of William Macnaghten had once been displayed for the satisfaction of the mob.

Harlan had been right: the Afghans fought tirelessly among themselves, but when a foreign invader threatened, they united to drive him out. Even Alexander's hold had been fleeting. Macedonian, Mogul, Persian, Russian, British, and Soviet armies had all tried, and failed, to control the Afghan tribes. Harlan's words echoed down the centuries: "To subdue and crush the masses of a nation by military force, when all are unanimous in the determination to be free, is to attempt the imprisonment of a whole people: all such projects must be temporary and transient, and terminate in a catastrophe."

Like others, the Taliban had attempted to rule with fear and oppression, banning kites, music, unveiled women, pleasure, and hope. The Hazaras, as Shia heretics, suffered horribly under the Islamic fundamentalists, who despised the independent, unveiled Hazara women that Harlan had found so alluring. Thousands of Hazaras were murdered in a systemic campaign of persecution. But now the Taliban, too, was gone, swept away by American and British bombs.

From the Bala Hisar, I drove to the modern presidential palace where I had interviewed Najibullah years before. It was a year to the day after the liberation of Kabul. In the south, special forces were still combing the land for Osama bin Laden, and in Washington and London, the invasion of Iraq was being planned. The presidential compound was guarded by hard-eyed American bodyguards armed with machine guns, deployed to protect the newly installed Afghan president and the man I had come to see, Zahir Shah, king of Afghanistan, fifth-generation successor to Dost Mohammed Khan. In 1933, at the age of eighteen, the Western-educated Prince Zahir Shah had seen his father assassinated. Thrust onto the throne, he ruled for forty years, at first as a distant absolute monarch, later as an enlightened reformer, introducing freedom of speech, voting rights for women, and an experimental farm to cultivate the fruits of Kabul, with seventy-six varieties of grapes. But in 1973, while on holiday in Italy, he was ousted in a coup led by his cousin. For the next thirty years he lived in exile, as Afghanistan was invaded by the Soviets, torn apart by civil war, and then brutalized by the Taliban. In the garden of his Italian villa, the old king could be seen playing chess, just as Shah Shujah, in another age, had whiled away his exile. With the fall of the Taliban, Zahir Shah had returned as "Father of the Nation," a symbolic figurehead to help maintain a fragile peace. Many looked back on his reign as a halcyon age, which it had been only in contrast to the horror that followed. His enemies vowed to kill him.

A courtly, frail old man with a gray mustache, the king received me in a room surrounded by trophies of wild sheep horns and gold-handled flintlock muskets in glass cases. At eighty-eight years old, with a ventilation machine powering his ailing lungs, the monarch had come home to die. "I will do whatever I must do," he said simply. "This is my country." He spoke an elegant, antique French. Outside his window a shattered city was slowly rebuilding itself. I could hear the American voices of the king's bodyguard in the corridor, huddled around a single-bar heater. As we talked, it grew dark outside. The death of Zahir Shah would mark the end of the Durrani dynasty, and he knew it. Yet his whispering voice grew animated as he spoke of the past, and of a young ruler who would ride into the mountains hunting wild sheep, antelope, and wolf, surrounded by his court. "I will go back one day," said the last king of Afghanistan. We both knew this was fantasy, the valedictory of an old and dying man, a king in name and memory.

"I was a King once." The words are from "The Man Who Would Be King." Back in my hotel room I read, yet again, Rudyard Kipling's tale of the eccentric, spade-bearded adventurer who became an Afghan prince. "I'll make an Empire," Daniel Dravot declares. "I am the son of Alexander." According to David Gilmour, Kipling's biographer, the story was "inspired by the author's meeting with an unknown Freemason" when he was working as a young journalist in India—which suggests that Harlan's adventures, or a version of them, had been absorbed into Masonic folklore on the North-West Frontier. Kipling would certainly have been familiar with Harlan's history, just as he would have known of the even earlier exploits of George Thomas, the eighteenth-century Irish mercenary. In 1885, Kipling had traveled to Peshawar on assignment for the *Civil and Military Gazette* and claimed to have been shot at by a Pathan in the Khyber Pass. Although he never penetrated into the Afghan interior, the glimpse of life in the savage mountains gave him the basis for his descriptions in "The Man Who Would Be King."

In Kipling's short story, two swashbuckling adventurers, Daniel

Dravot and his helpmate, Peachy Carnehan, set off to forge a realm in the farthest corner of Afghanistan, forswearing liquor and women until they are kings of Kafiristan. The narrator, a journalist like Kipling, tells them: "You'll be turned back at the Frontier or cut up the minute you set foot in Afghanistan." But Dravot and Carnehan, disguised as a Muslim holy man and his servant, struggle over the frozen mountains to find a savage, pagan people, and a kingdom for the taking. The adventurers train a local army, carving out a realm and a new religion using the rites of Freemasonry. The Masonic symbol is found carved into a rock (a legacy, we are to assume, of Alexander the Great's passage) and Daniel is hailed as the reincarnation of Sikandar himself. "Dravot he was the King," says Peachy. "And a handsome man he looked with the gold crown on his head." But then, drunk on power, Dravot departs from his own rules. Like Alexander, he insists on taking a beautiful Afghan wife, his own Roxanne. It is the final act of hubris, for the spell is broken, and he is seen to be a mere mortal, an impostor. His fate echoes that of Alexander Burnes, another prideful man who called himself Sikandar, who shattered his own mystique with a taste for Afghan maidens, and was destroyed. The natives turn on their king: Dravot is forced onto a rope bridge, which is cut, and he plummets to his death, an imperial Icarus. "He took half an hour to fall till he struck the water, and I could see his body caught on a rock with the gold crown beside it," relates Peachy, who is horribly tortured but staggers out of Afghanistan, to reappear, dying, at the Lahore newspaper office of the narrator. From a bag he produces his friend's head and declares: "You behold now the Emperor in his habit as he lived—the King of Kafiristan with his crown upon his head. Poor old Daniel that was a monarch once."

"The Man Who Would Be King" is Kipling's most impressive early work, a crafted morality tale about imperial temptation, the tense and troubled relationship between the colonizer and the colonized, the self-invented man, and the price of overweening ambition. John Huston's movie, based on the story, is faithful to the spirit of Kipling's tale, and remains a period masterpiece, at once a celebration of imperial adventure and a warning. Huston had originally wanted Clark Gable and Humphrey Bogart to play the lead roles, but in Michael Caine (as Peachy) and Sean Connery (as Daniel), he found the ideal partnership. Shot in Morocco in 1975, Huston's film offers a vision of the rogue as hero and a sophisticated, darkly ironic perspective on colonialism, both rousing and troubling, an enduring reflection of American ambivalence toward kingly power. Dravot's manipulation of the local tribes, his lust for gold, and his growing sense of obligation to "his" subject people offer an allegory of imperialism and its rewards, obligations, temptations, and dangers. Like Harlan, Kipling was an imperialist, but within limits, acutely aware of the decadence of empire. Dravot's fate, writes Gilmour, "may be seen as a warning that empires can be overthrown when the customs of subject people's are too greatly violated." A great empire may conquer and liberate, change regimes and build nations, but without cultural deference and humility, it will only destroy and perish.

The road to Kabul airport took me past the new American embassy, encased in slabs of bomb-proof concrete with machine-gun posts at each corner. The Stars and Stripes flew over the compound, descendant of the flag that Harlan first raised here. At the barbed wire gate to the airport, a grinning Afghan guard stood exchanging jokes and cigarettes with an American serviceman: allies, albeit briefly, from different worlds.

> Oh, East is East, and West is West, and never the twain shall meet,
> Till Earth and Sky stand presently at God's great Judgement Seat;
> But there is neither East nor West, Border, nor Breed, nor Birth,
> When two strong men stand face to face, though they come from
>   the ends of the earth!

Twenty-four hours later, in the words of Kipling's narrator, I had "returned to an office where there were no Kings and no incidents outside the daily manufacture of a newspaper," and began to write the story of the man who would be king.

NOTES

A NOTE ON SOURCES AND STYLE

Josiah Harlan's writing falls into three categories: the works published in his lifetime (one book and two pamphlets); the incomplete material collected by Frank E. Ross and published as *Central Asia—Personal Narrative of General Josiah Harlan, 1823–1841*, in 1939; and the unpublished material in the Chester County Archives. A handwritten contents page attached to the latter indicates that Harlan's original memoir ran to three volumes and 968 pages: volume 1, covering the years 1824 to 1827; volume 2 entitled *Oriental Sketches*, covering the years 1827 to 1840; volume 3 entitled *Manners and Customs of the Paropamisus and Bulkh or Bactra, 1838–39*. Ross evidently found parts of volume 3, and based his edited *Narrative* on them, but the original manuscript he used has not been found. Volume 1 is also missing. All but the final section of volume 2, by far the largest part of Harlan's book and running to 390 pages, was discovered in 2002. Part autobiography and part narrative, *Oriental Sketches* appears to be a first draft. Some of it was clearly reproduced directly from Harlan's journals, and may be read as a diary written contemporaneously with the events described; other parts were obviously written with hindsight. A note, in Harlan's hand, on the bottom of the contents page reads "A.D. 1841."

A rebel in his writing style as in his life, Harlan had little use for grammar or punctuation of any sort; his sentences are fabulously long and complex, and he is content to spell the same word several different ways within a single, enormous sentence. He is particularly cavalier in the transliteration of words from local languages. In the interests of clarity, therefore, when quoting Harlan I have standardized his spelling, inserted punctuation, elided some sentences, avoided ellipses, and pared down his more elaborate circumlocutions while retaining, I hope, the flavor of his prose. Harlan's *Oriental Sketches* was never edited. I have taken the liberty of doing so.

The spelling of proper nouns was also partly a matter of selection. Kabul, for example, was variously rendered in the past as Kaubul, Cabul, Caubul, Cabool, and, in Harlan's case, most of the above at different times. I have tended to use modern spellings in the text, while leaving the period variations as they appear in quotations.

vii "If I want a crown": Rudyard Kipling, "The Man who would be King," in *Selected Stories*, p. 111.

PREFACE

xiv "I unfurled my": Josiah Harlan, *The U.S. Gazette* (Philadelphia), Jan. 20, 1842.

PROLOGUE

5 "as a dervish": Josiah Harlan, *Central Asia: Personal Narrative of General Josiah Harlan, 1823–1841*, edited by Frank Ross, p. 10.
5 "Josiah Harlan, an adventurer": U.S. State Department Web site (www.state.gov).
6 "clever and unscrupulous": W. J. Kaye, *History of the War in Afghanistan*, vol. 1, p. 135.
7 "He transferred his": *U.S. Gazette.*
7 "The absolute and complete": Ibid.

1: A COMPANY WALLAH

10 "amused himself with": J. Wolff, *Researches and Missionary Labours among the Jews, Mohammedans and other Sects*, p. 259.
11 "in the which": Ibid., p. 259.
11 "In seven years": Josiah Harlan, *A Memoir of India and Avghanistaun*, p. 64.
11 "Stripped for the": Henry Adams, *History of the United States of America During the Administrations of Thomas Jefferson*, p. 109.
11 "My ties and ballasts": Walt Whitman, quoted in Tom Chaffin, *Pathfinder: John Charles Frémont and the course of American Empire*, p. xxx.
12 "made a voyage": J. Thomas Scharf and Thompson Westcott, *History of Philadelphia 1609–1884*, vol. 2, p. 1619.
12 "supercargo": Richard Hartley Kennedy, *Narrative of the Campaign of the Army of the Indus, in Sind and Kaubool, in 1838–9*, p. 118.
12 "appreciated Freemasonry": David Gilmour, *The Long Recessional: The Imperial Life of Rudyard Kipling*, p. 17, fn.
12 "tremble at the word": George Fox, *The Journals of George Fox*, edited by Rufus H. Jones, New York, 1963, p. 59.
12 "Therefore we cannot": "A Declaration from the Harmless and Innocent people of God, called Quakers," 21st day, 11th month, 1660, to Charles II King of England. Cited in ibid, p. 225.
13 "Each quickening pulse": "Acrostick in explanation of the lines addressed to Miss Eliza S. on presenting a bouquet," handwritten poem in Chester County Archives, Pennsylvania.

14 "played him false": Wolff, *Researches*, p. 259.

14 "He fell in love": Ibid.

14 "He sailed again": Ibid.

14 "How sweet that rose": untitled handwritten poem in Chester County Archives, Pennsylvania.

15 "Gazing through": Josiah Harlan, *Oriental Sketches*, handwritten document in Chester County Archives, Pennsylvania, p. 32A.

15 what would have: Ibid., p. 33.

15 "It is from amongst": Ibid., p. 33.

15 "Grandest Society": John Keay, *The Honourable Company: A History of the English East India Company*, p. xix.

16 "the strangest of all": Lord Macaulay cited in ibid., p. 419.

16 "had in his early": Wolff, *Researches*, p. 259.

16 "taken a few of his": Harlan, *Narrative*, p. 9.

16 "presented himself": Charles Grey, *European Adventurers of Northern India 1785 to 1849*, p. 252.

16 "He was transferred": Wolff, *Researches*, p. 259.

17 "The Hindu *valet de chambre*": Harlan, *Sketches*, p. 62.

17 "rendered invaluable": Ibid., p. 49.

18 "Dash never maintained": Ibid., p. 129.

18 "Dash had always": Ibid.

18 "We thought at first": Mountstuart Elphinstone, cited in Patrick Macrory, *Kabul Catastrophe: The Invasion and Retreat of 1839–1842*, p. 32.

19 "a principle of diffusion": Ibid.

19 "How much he had": Ibid., p. 33.

19 "princely address": Ibid.

19 "about nine inches": Ibid, p. 34.

19 "Their vices are revenge": Mountstuart Elphinstone, cited in Christina Lamb, *The Sewing Circles of Herat*, p. 37.

19 "well arranged and minutely": Harlan, *Narrative*, p. 26.

19 "Harlan does not": Kaye, *History*, vol. 1, p. 230.

20 "A sharp sword": Harlan, *Memoir*, p. 53.

20 "Audacious ambition": Ibid.

20 "Under English domination": Ibid.

20 "the undaunted": Ibid., p. 33.

20 "an empire for liberty": Cited in Chaffin, *Pathfinder*, p. 11.

21 "the heady optimism": Ibid., p. 18.

21 "high Tory in principles": Wolff, *Researches*, p. 260.

21 "kingly dignity": Ibid.

21 "His power was": Harlan, *Memoir*, p. 67.

21–2 "neither British subjects": Harlan, *Sketches*, p. 31A.

22 "terra incognita": Ibid., 8-page insert at p. 42A.

22 "I enjoyed the amenities": Ibid., p. 39.

23 "with the characteristic liberality": Ibid.

23 "respectful and obedient": Ibid., p. 40.
23 "Nobody cares a": Kipling, "The Man Who Would Be King," p. 113.
23 "a master of finesse": Harlan, *Sketches*, p. 40.
23 "Dr. Harlan's principal": Punjab Records, book no. 95, letter no. 127, cited in Grey, *European Adventurers*, p. 253.
23 "the resort of foreigners": Harlan, *Sketches*, p. 35A.
24 "Very little": Ibid.

2: THE QUAKER KING-MAKER

25 "His Majesty might": Harlan, *Sketches*, 8-page insert at p. 42A.
25 "The forms and etiquette": Ibid.
26 "Sentinels were placed": Shah Shujah al-Moolk, cited in Macrory, *Kabul Catastrophe*, p. 29.
26 "Seven ranges": Ibid.
26 "Our cares and fatigues": Ibid.
27 "He wanted vigour": Kaye, *History*, vol. 1, p. 198.
27 "His Majesty strenuously": Harlan, *Sketches*, 8-page insert at p. 42A.
27 "Money would readily": Ibid., p. 38.
27 "We conversed together": Ibid., p. 40.
27 "I had determined": Ibid., 8-page insert at p. 42A.
28 "Every man": Ibid.
28 "a general proposition": Ibid.
28 "I assumed the": Ibid., p. 37.
28 "The Indian sentries": Ibid.
28 "The priest was": Ibid.
29 "flowing locks": Ibid.
29 "earless assemblage": Ibid., p. 37A.
29 "The executioner": Ibid., p. 38A.
29 "shaved the head": Ibid.
29 "Having assured": Ibid.
29 "His Majesty's tastes": Ibid., p. 36A.
30 "in the long twilight": Ibid.
30 "cool spray, scintillating": Ibid., p. 39.
30 "I replied in bad": Ibid.
30 "the grace and dignity": Ibid.
30 "Years of disappointment": Ibid., p. 36A.
31 "ascertain and organise": Ibid., pp. 39–39A.
31 "I engaged to join": Ibid., p. 39A.
31 "far preponderated": Ibid.
31 "he would instantly": Ibid.
32 "broke into a": Ibid.
32 "Kabul is called": Ibid.

32 "The dead silence": Ibid.

32 "Should success attend": Ibid.

32 "My feelings warmed": Ibid., p. 40.

32 "I saw him [as] an": Ibid., insert at p. 42A.

32 "disclosed few": Ibid.

32 "In his true colours": Ibid.

33 "he to revalue": Ibid.

33 "He started from Ludhiana": W. L. McGregor, *The History of the Sikhs*, p. 274.

33 "hoisted the American": Ibid.

33 "to make himself": Wolff, *Researches*, p. 259

33 "the powers of a": Harlan, *Narrative*, pp. 2–3.

33 "Dr. Harlan proposed": Grey, *European Adventurers*, p. 253.

35 "a wretch who": George Trebeck, cited in Karl Meyer and Shareen Brysac, *Tournament of Shadows: The Great Game and the Race for Empire in Asia*, p. 46.

35 "confusion, oppression": William Moorcroft, cited in ibid., p. 50.

35 "After burying his": Alexander Burnes, cited in James Lunt, *Bokhara Burnes*, p. 114.

36 "the sum to": Jean-Marie Lafont, *La présence française dans la royaume Sikh du Penjab, 1822–1849*, fn p. 219. See also [Public Records Office (U.K.) 64/95, no. 127, October 15, 1827.]

36 "a faithful hindoo": Harlan, *Sketches*, p. 96A.

36 "The time for my": Ibid., p. 42.

36 "another private conference": Ibid.

37 "A shadow": Ibid.

37 "Harlan enjoyed": Harlan, *Narrative*, p. 7.

37 "I had just stepped": Harlan, *Sketches*, p. 32.

38 "I have served": Ibid., p. 42.

38 "blear-eyed Avghaun": Ibid.

38 "Here I am in": Ibid., p. 42A.

38 "He had wandered": Ibid.

39 "thoroughly acquainted with": Ibid.

39 "The versatility of service": Ibid., p. 86.

39 "sustained upon": Ibid., p. 42A.

39 "He seemed averse": Ibid.

39 "I afterwards heard": Ibid.

39 "I had then": Ibid.

39 "This was an enterprise": Ibid., 2-page insert at p. 42A.

40 "The dilatory proceedings": Ibid.

40 "the Hysudrus": Ibid.

40 "the interior of Asia": Ibid., p. 44.

41 "a half-English": Ibid.

41 "a valued friend": Ibid.

41 "supplies of all kinds": Ibid., p. 64.

41 "more certain to hamper": Ibid.

41 "Long experience": Ibid.

41 "Josiah Harlan, who": Records of the Chester Country Society of Friends, Swarthmore College, reference: MR-PH 386, 2, 1835.

42 "an embossed silver": Harlan, *Sketches*, p. 49.

42 "The movements of": Ibid., p. 46.

42 "large single": Ibid.

42 "Connaughts or extensive walls": Ibid., p. 49.

42 "the display of dignity": Ibid., p. 45.

43 "A covered box": Ibid., 46.

43 "The interior being": Martin Honigberger, *Thirty-Five Years in the East*, p. 63.

43 "The comfortable seclusion": Harlan, *Sketches*, p. 45.

43 "a few days' experience": Ibid.

3: MY SWORD IS MY PASSPORT

45 "During the rule": Harlan, *Sketches*, p. 178.

46 "an operation similar": Ibid.

47 "Sovereignty was an": Ibid.

47 "Prince after prince": Ibid., 8-page insert at p. 42A.

47 "In the course of": Ibid., p. 178A.

48 "four independent principalities": Ibid., p. 51.

48 "More than human": Ibid., p. 43A.

48 "determined upon revenge": Ibid.

48 "To knock up the": Ibid.

48 "Had this fellow's": Ibid.

48 "He was probably": Ibid., p. 44.

48 "Amongst my followers": Ibid., p. 49.

49 "The old camels": Ibid.

49 "The peasant whom": Ibid., p. 50.

49 "the finest perch": Ibid., insert at p. 63A.

49 "All who were opposed": Ibid., p. 51A.

50 "I believe the": Stephen E. Ambrose, *Undaunted Courage: Meriwether Lewis, Thomas Jefferson, and the Opening of the American West*, p. 55.

50 "with the impressive dignity": Ibid., p. 54.

51 "richly caparisoned": Ibid.

51 "armed with swords": Ibid.

51 "His manner and address": Ibid.

51 "A beautiful green": Ibid.

51 "that his father should": Ibid.

51 "the present incumbent": Ibid., p. 69A.

52 "be taken under": Ibid., pp. 67–68.

52 "The friendly": Ibid., p. 58.

52 "a body of soldiers": Ibid.

52 "threatening them": Ibid.
52 "Their filthy appearance": Ibid.
52 "an army of": Ibid., p. 56.
53 "the attaché of Nadir": Ibid.
53 "supplies of every": Ibid., p. 56A.
53 "Our camp was quickly": Ibid., p. 57.
53 "I entertained a feeling": Ibid.
53 "in earnest conversation": Ibid., p. 57A.
53 "determined to prevent": Ibid.
53 "I called the captain": Ibid.
54 "the consequences of my": Ibid.
54 "a vast cloud": Ibid.
54 "the clouds of dust": Ibid.
54 "desired the honour": Ibid.
54 "We found ourselves": Ibid., p. 58.
54 "encamped a short": Ibid., p 58A.
54 "I refused to see": Ibid., p. 58.
54 "I'm not in the vein": Ibid.
54 "With reverential respect": Ibid.
55 "I gave him to": Ibid.
55 "a devious line": Ibid., p. 59.
55 "in a direct": Ibid.
55 "The old blear-eyed": Ibid.
55 "Wherefore is Gool": Ibid.
55 "The whole camp": Ibid., p. 60.
55 "with elevated brows": Ibid.
55 "It'll be later": Ibid.
56 "ungenerous and unbecoming": Ibid.
56 "His Highness the": Ibid., p. 65.
56 "a term applied": Ibid.
56 "set forth in florid": Ibid., p. 66.
56 "the country, himself": Ibid.
56 "A large quantity": Ibid., p. 66A.
56 "as a reward": Ibid., p. 65.
57 "about four miles": Mountstuart Elphinstone, *An Account of the Kingdom of Caubul*, p. 20.
57 "conveying his impatience": Harlan, *Sketches*, p. 67.
57 "a *phlegmon*": Ibid., p. 66A.
57 "A crowd assembled": Ibid., p. 67A.
57 "the ex-king": Ibid.
57 "merely an amateur": Ibid.
57 "What could have": Ibid.
57 "several hundred": Ibid., p. 68.
57 "The Honourable": Ibid., p. 69A.

58 "I concluded these": Ibid., p. 70.

58 "a person of grave": Ibid., p. 70A.

58 "messages of congratulations": Ibid.

58 "offering to afford": Ibid.

59 "as it is certain": Gordon Whitteridge, *Charles Masson of Afghanistan: Explorer, Archaeologist, Numismatist and Intelligence Agent*, p. 4.

59 "having traversed the": Charles Masson, *Narrative of Various Journeys in Balochistan, Afghanistan and the Panjab*, vol. 1, p. xi.

59 "in the dress": Harlan, *Sketches*, p. 76.

60 "The light and straggling": Ibid.

60 "asserting that": Ibid.

60 "Perceiving his extremely": Ibid.

60 "I gave him medicines": Ibid.

60 "I reflected that": Ibid., pp. 78–79.

4: THE YOUNG ALEXANDER

63 "All my military retainers": Harlan, *Sketches*, p. 71A.

63 "military pageant": Ibid.

63 "I mounted, the bugle sounded": Ibid., p. 72.

63 "his elite battalion": Ibid.

63 "appears extremely awkward": Ibid.

63 "irregular cavalry": Ibid.

64 "so settled were": Ibid.

64 "The moment I entered": Ibid., p. 73.

64 "by valiant efforts": Ibid.

64 "He was a young": Ibid., p. 74.

64 "unassuming deportment": Ibid.

64 "subdued bearing": Ibid.

64 "scarcely raising": Ibid.

64 "a pair of handsome": Ibid., p. 73.

64 "a confidential communication": Ibid.

64 "I then referred": Ibid.

64 "his house had": Ibid.

64 "consisted of several": Ibid., p. 73A.

64 "dress of honour": Ibid., p. 75A.

64 "system of diplomatic": Ibid.

65 "Heretofore I had not": Ibid., p. 78.

65 "My mind was now": Ibid.

65 "The man of action": Cited in Robin Lane Fox, *Alexander the Great*, p. 382.

65 "All the evidence": Harlan, *Sketches*, p. 78.

65 "a population": Ibid.

66 "Our march lay": Ibid., p. 79.

66 "efflorescent soda": Ibid.

66 "For the remainder": Ibid.

66 "Wild boar": Ibid., p. 79A.

66 "the few miserable": Ibid.

66 "the rough treatment": Ibid.

66 "To look for the": Harlan, *Sketches*, p. 78.

67 "All we could": Elphinstone, *Kingdom of Caubul*, p. 26.

67 "on the people": Masson, *Narrative of Various Journeys*, vol. 1, p. 31.

67 "A step upon": Harlan, *Sketches*, p. 81.

67 "When an elephant": Ibid.

67 "an immense dead": Ibid., p. 79A.

67 "The communities": Ibid., p. 82.

68 "affectionately remembered": Whitteridge, *Charles Masson*, p. 30.

68 "A vast distance": Harlan, *Sketches*, p. 85.

68 "We were in a": Ibid.

68 "the system by": Ibid., p. 48.

68 "The genius displayed": Ibid.

68 "some from hereditary": Ibid., p. 85.

68 "On the skirt of": Ibid., p. 86.

68 "he intended to take": Grey, *European Adventurers*, p. 253.

68 "the most massive": Masson, *Narrative of Various Journeys*, vol. 1, p. 49.

69 "a faquir predicted": Ibid.

69 "The fortress of Tak": Harlan, *Sketches*, p. 68A.

69 "their profession": Ibid.

69 "secret messenger": Ibid.

69 "The strong fortress": Ibid., p. 23.

69 "These poor people": Ibid., p. 88.

70 "flat country densely": Ibid.

70 "The camel is": Ibid., pp. 89–91.

71 "a request for": Ibid., p. 92.

71 "The Pathan tribes": Winston Churchill, cited in Steve Sailer, "The Afghan Insights of The Man Who Would Be King," The American Enterprise Online, March 12, 2002.

71 "During my frequent": Harlan, *Sketches*, p. 91.

71 "My fame in this": Ibid.

71 "a steel lancet": Ibid., p. 92A.

71 "An elderly woman": Ibid.

72 "through a country": Ibid., p. 93.

72 "Their surprise": Ibid., p. 93A.

73 "A man may fast": Ibid., p. 50.

73 "large, and boney": Elphinstone, *Kingdom of Caubul*, p. 29.

73 "These people": Harlan, *Sketches*, p. 94.

73 "One of these": Ibid.

74 "anywhere within": Ibid.

74 "The road to": Ibid., p. 94A.

74 "Whilst our force": Ibid., p. 95.
74 "the tribes inhabiting": Ibid.
74 "This was the first": Ibid.
75 "mad with the prospect": Ibid.
75 "men in military": Ibid.
75 "if any misfortune": Ibid.
75 "near the mountains": Ibid., p. 24A.
75 "Caution is creditable": Ibid.
75 "still holding the": Ibid., p. 95A.
76 "He had been": Ibid., p. 96.
76 "constructed in": Ibid.
76 "an unusual": Ibid., p. 23.
76 "Over the principal": Ibid.
76 "A hundred men": Ibid., p. 23A.
77 "Two Europeans": Ibid.
77 "gazed wistfully": Ibid.
77 "silent expectation": Ibid.
77 "Gool Khan": Ibid.
77 "You are an old soldier": Ibid.
77 "Had you not": Ibid.
77 "querulous loquacity": Ibid., p. 24.
77 "'Tis too late": Ibid.
77 "raised his arms": Ibid.
78 "Traitors and cowards!": Ibid., p. 29.
78 "touched his": Ibid.
78 "What? All?": Ibid.
78 "Let everyone": Ibid.
78 "The fears of": Ibid., p. 98.
78 "an air of despondency": Ibid., 96A.
78 "The conduct": Ibid.
78 "already refused": Ibid.
79 "My affairs": Ibid., p. 97.
79 "decamping surreptitiously": Ibid., p. 98.
79 "handsomely entertained": Whitteridge, *Charles Masson*, p. 30.
79 "measures that": Harlan, *Sketches*, p. 98.
79 "I was restrained": Ibid.
79 "From the latter": Ibid., p. 97.
79 "Indeed, incidents": Ibid.

5: THE DERVISH FROM CHESTER COUNTY

81 "air of disappointment": Harlan, *Sketches*, p. 98A.
81 "gloating over": Ibid.

81 "Not one individual": Ibid., p. 99.

81 "I brought myself": Ibid.

81 "Thus conforming": Ibid., p. 64.

81 "carefully avoiding": Ibid., p. 99.

82 "a man of respectable": Ibid., p. 100.

82 "one of the most": Ibid.

82 "useful and necessary": Ibid.

82 "Expedition on my": Ibid., p. 100A.

82 "You have": Ibid., p. 99A.

82 "All the valuables": Ibid., p. 100.

82 "for an immediate": Ibid.

82 "I was now to": Ibid., p. 103A.

83 "a Saheb Zader": Ibid., p. 100A.

83 "encountered a man": Whitteridge, *Charles Masson*, p. 26.

83 "I looked the character": Harlan, *Sketches*, p. 100A.

83 "My complexion": Ibid., p. 101.

83 "knowledge of the": Ibid.

83 "an Arab unacquainted": Ibid.

83 "I could": Ibid.

83 "Should anyone": Ibid.

84 "depend more upon": Ibid.

84 "the rupees added": Ibid., p. 100.

84 "who waved their": Ibid., p. 102A.

84 "commenced a journey": Ibid.

84 "With a light heart": Ibid.

84 "as a pious": Ibid.

84 "seemed conscious of": Ibid., p. 103.

84 "felt much": Ibid., p. 103A.

84 "Keep your property": Ibid., p. 104.

85 "the accurate use": Ibid.

85 "I was gratified": Ibid., p. 105.

85 "the residence": Ibid., p. 105.

85 "The mild vapour": Ibid., p. 106.

85 "I had not": Ibid.

86 "I am no believer": Ibid.

86 "The chief": Ibid.

86 "I raised my hands": Ibid.

86 "much esteemed": Ibid.

86 "Supposing my incognito": Ibid.

87 "seen or heard": Ibid., p. 107.

87 "seldom troubled": Ibid.

87 "Have we got": Ibid.

87 "the position was": Ibid.

87 "to be more": Ibid., p. 108.
87 "The Feringee Saheb": Ibid.
87 "There is a mistake": Ibid.
88 "A house was": Ibid., p. 108A.
88 "As a holy man": Ibid.
88 "ruddy complexion": Ibid.
88 "the vizier looked": Ibid., p. 108.
88 "Tell Ahmed Khan": Ibid.
88 "They saluted me": Ibid., p. 109A.
89 "My native habit": Ibid., p. 110.
89 "The sheep given": Ibid.
89 "To the stiff joints": Ibid., p. 112A.
89 "Now all was": Ibid.
90 "I first thrust": Ibid.
90 "willingly bestowed": Ibid.
90 "The strongest": Ibid.
90 "This is supposed": Ibid., p. 63A.
90 "Neither water nor": Ibid., p. 114.
90 "a faithless race": Ibid., p. 23.
90 "a clouded": Ibid., p. 113.
90 "the rumbling": Ibid.
91 "These are the": Ibid.
91 "at the same time": Ibid.
91 "black countenance": Ibid.
91 "Down dog": Ibid., p. 114.
91 "I continued": Ibid.
91 "quelled a rising": Ibid., p. 114.
91 "levying blackmail": Ibid.
91 "a feringee of high": Ibid., p. 114A.
91 "Exaggerated reports": Ibid.
92 "Let us fall": Ibid.
92 "Years have passed": Ibid., p. 116.
92 "A crowd collected": Ibid.
92 "Armed with matchlocks": Ibid.
92 "Curse them for": Ibid., p. 116A.
93 "they halted and one": Ibid.
93 "The next moment": Ibid.
93 "Ho! Ho!": Ibid., p. 117.
93 "Well, master": Ibid.
93 "We were about": Ibid.
93 "his words were spoken": Ibid.
93 "My lord": Ibid., 117A.
93 "We will descend": Ibid.

94   "not forgetting": Ibid., p. 118.
94   "a respectable lady": Ibid.
94   "detestable incivility": Ibid., p. 118A.
94   "I responded": Ibid.
94   "a string of": Ibid.
94   "I looked at him": Ibid.
94   "Of this language": Ibid.
94   "What audacity": Ibid., p. 119A.
94   "The sacred retirement": Ibid.
95   "sprang away": Ibid.
95   "begging permission": Ibid.
95   "The secret of": Ibid.
95   "to sharpen his wits": Ibid., p. 120.
95   "The dullness": Ibid.
95   "thrust into a bag": Ibid.
95   "a string with": Ibid.
95   "This he effected": Ibid., p. 120A.
95   "infested with rebels": Ibid., p. 121.
96   "In those mountains": Ibid.
96   "one of the coldest": Ibid., p. 20.
96   "The surrounding high": Ibid.
96   "a holy man famous": Ibid., p. 1.
97   "Tell your master": Ibid., p. 20.
97   "Thou art": Ibid.
97   "folded in the Persian": Ibid.
97   "His figure was": Ibid., pp. 5–7.
97   "fell in gathered": Ibid., p. 7.
98   "They, the chiefs": Ibid.
98   "tessellated pavements": Ibid., p. 8.
98   "With cautious": Ibid., p. 132A.
98   "fiscal diplomacy": Ibid., p. 123A.
98   "I promptly undeceived": Ibid.
98   "Let that be": Ibid., p. 132.
98   "simplicity of address": Ibid., p. 5.
98   "the season was": Ibid.
99   "bill of fare": Ibid.
99   "pilau of mutton": Ibid., p. 125A.
99   "my party was": Ibid., p. 121.

6: FROM PESHAWAR TO KABUL

101   "veil of secrecy": Harlan, *Sketches*, p. 124.
101   "It was not to": Ibid.

101 "in pursuit of": Ibid.
101 "the costume of": Ibid., p. 126.
101 "facetiously bestowed": Ibid., p. 125A.
101 "each day a part": Ibid., p. 15.
102 "He was a man": Ibid.
102 "a cone standing": Ibid.
102 "scanty Persian slippers": Ibid., p. 15A.
102 "If you asked": Ibid.
103 "gentlemen or persons": Ibid., p. 126.
103 "Dash accompanied": Ibid., p. 129.
103–4 "These strange": Ibid.
104 "has been known": Ibid.
104 "undrilled nose": Ibid., p. 129A.
104 "Each selected its quarry": Ibid., p. 130.
104 "Another moment": Ibid.
104 "She seized the hare": Ibid., pp. 130A–131.
104 "The force of": Ibid., p. 131.
105 "Dash was there": Ibid.
105 "this ferocious antagonist": Ibid.
105 "to exhibit his": Ibid.
105 "distributed a gift of": Ibid., p. 132.
105 "so that many": Ibid.
105 "for each one": Ibid., p. 130.
106 "humble pilgrim": Ibid., p. 133.
106 "Accordingly, taking": Ibid.
106 "crowded with men": Elphinstone, *An Account of the Kingdom of Caubul*, cited in Charles Allen, *Soldier Sahibs: The Men Who Made the North-West Frontier*, p. 15.
106 "People of the town": Ibid., p. 16.
106 "in green cashmere": Harlan, *Sketches*, p. 134A.
106 "Persian daggers": Ibid.
107 "I remained in": Ibid.
107 "took up the medicine": Ibid.
107 "as much to gratify": Ibid., p. 135A.
107 "Visitors are received": Ibid, p. 136.
107 "a strange kind of": Ibid., p. 136A.
108 "the night soil": Ibid.
108 "however disgusting": Ibid.
108 "The substance is dried": Ibid.
108 "to colour": Ibid.
108 "The visitor": Ibid.
108 "the manipulator": Ibid., p. 137.
108 "This official": Ibid.

108 "Taking the bather's": Ibid.

108 "The operator": Ibid.

109 "a general effusion": Ibid.

109 "a sense of rest": Ibid.

109 "with feelings of": Ibid., p 137A.

109 "a process too": Ibid., p. 138.

109 "of ordinary style": Ibid.

109 "After the cloth": Ibid.

109 whether drinking: Ibid.

109 "I endeavoured to": Ibid.

110 "the violation of": Ibid.

110 "favourable to": Ibid., p. 139A.

110 "The next morning": Ibid., p. 140.

110 "Well," replied Harlan: Ibid.

110 "I shall accompany": Ibid.

110 "Ordering my horse": Ibid.

111 "started with astonishment": Ibid.

111 "thrust the pistol": Ibid., p. 140A.

111 "glowering with displeasure": Ibid.

111 "invocations of vengeance": Ibid.

111 "Of the Persian": Ibid., p. 141.

111 "I was predetermined": Ibid., p. 141A.

111 "in full bloom": Ibid., p. 141.

111 "silently and sweetly": Ibid., p. 143A.

111 "strolled amongst": Ibid.

111 "indulge in the rapture": Ibid., p. 144.

112 "I raised my": Ibid., p. 143.

112 "calmness and gravity": Ibid., p. 142.

112 "I was aware": Ibid., p. 142A.

112 "From his description": Ibid.

112 "with the satisfied": Ibid.

112 "eagerly waiting": Ibid., p. 143.

112 "Get out of the way": Ibid.

113 "as the obligated": Ibid.

113 "joined his entreaties": Ibid., p. 144.

113 "buried beneath": Ibid., p. 149A.

113 "deposited in the bank": Ibid.

113 "presented the bleak": Ibid.

114 "cadaverous faces": Ibid., p. 145A.

114 "the power of": Ibid.

114 "an old negress": Ibid.

114 "Alas the happy days": Ibid.

114 "My good woman": Ibid.

114 "Oh no, my lord": Ibid.

114 "Oh very well": Ibid.

114 "laughed heartily": Ibid., p. 147A.

115 "With the exception": Ibid, p. 150.

115 "his desire to push": Ibid.

115 "the least civilised": Ibid.

115 "I turned my face": Ibid., p. 148.

115 "The scenery is": Ibid., p. 145.

115 "The blossom of": Ibid., p. 150A.

116 "provided with more": Ibid.

116 "Mahomed Ali": Ibid., p. 150.

116 "We all partook": Ibid., p. 151A.

116 "They drew the": Ibid., pp. 151A–152.

116 "Crossing the valley": Ibid., p. 152.

116 "follows his plough": Ibid.

116 "The ascent of the": Ibid., p. 153.

117 "Mahomed Ali refused": Ibid., p. 154.

117 "We hastened our steps": Ibid.

117 "I found it": Ibid., 154A.

117 "the fleas": Ibid., p. 153.

118 "slept soundly and": Ibid.

118 "a passport or": Ibid., p. 154.

118 "I objected as": Ibid.

118 "When they found": Ibid.

119 "on the advice": Ibid.

119 "Here lyes the": Whitteridge, *Charles Masson*, p. 54.

119 "an officer of": Ibid.

7: KABUL, CONSPIRACY, AND CHOLERA

121 "Every year": Cited in Martin Ewans, *Afghanistan: A New History*, p. 19.

121 "the most pleasing": Lamb, *The Sewing Circles*, p. 223.

122 "inlaid with octagonal": Harlan, *Sketches*, p. 155A.

122 "I remained": Ibid.

122 "might not have": Ibid., p. 157.

122 "a man of slender": Ibid., p. 155A.

122 "the ease and urbanity": Ibid., p. 156.

123 "I remarked the": Ibid.

123 "He said he": Ibid.

123 "it exceeded the strength": Ibid., p. 156A.

123 "a very handsome": Ibid.

123 "fat, chubby": Ibid.

123 "the locality of": Ibid.

123 "amateur pretensions": Ibid.

124 "riches, the number": G. T. Vigne, *A Personal Narrative of a Visit to Ghuzni, Kabul, and Afghanistan*, p. 350.

124 "The Sirdar was": Harlan, *Sketches*, p. 156.

124 "I replied they": Ibid.

124 "I explained to": Ibid.

124 "He asked in conclusion": Ibid., p. 156A.

124 "Your Highness": Ibid.

124 "Oh, East is East": Rudyard Kipling, *The Ballad of East and West, Selected Poetry*, p. 101.

124 "offered with": Harlan, *Sketches*, p. 158.

125 "the Saddozai": Ibid.

125 "extensive plains": Ibid.

125 "weeping willows": Ibid., p. 165A.

125 "one vast": Ibid.

125 "The city is a jewel": Ibid., p. 158A.

125 "with flowers and blossoms": Ibid., p. 161A.

125 "sweet assemblage": Ibid., p. 158A.

125 "ornamental trees, apple": Ibid.

126 "In most countries": Masson, *Narrative of Various Journeys*, vol. 2, p. 243.

126 "the elevated": Harlan, *Sketches*, p. 162A.

126 "into Cabul with": Ibid., p. 164.

126 "and so abundant and cheap": Ibid.

126 "the poor live": Ibid., p. 163.

126 "will cause partial": Ibid., p. 164A.

126 "may be eaten": Ibid.

126 "the best of": Ibid., p 162A.

126 "a vast expense": Ibid., p. 164A.

127 "joyously hailed": Ibid., p. 166.

127 "Bird fanciers carry": Ibid.

127 "The demonstrations of": Ibid.

127 "should a stranger": Harlan, *Sketches*, p. 174A.

127 "professional courtezans": Ibid., p. 175.

127 "Many respectable persons": Ibid., p. 159.

128 "We know nothing": Ibid.

128 "Two grandchildren of": Ibid.

128 "in the capital which": Ibid.

128 "annoyed by the": Ibid.

128 "this remark": Ibid., p. 159A.

129 "Let no Christian": *U.S. Gazette.*

129 "ever dissatisfied": Harlan, *Sketches*, p. 159A.

129 "My host, a man": Ibid., p. 160.

129 "I was careful": Ibid.

129 "filled with exaggerated": Ibid.

130 "Nothing is easier": Ibid., p. 161.

130 "in good faith": Ibid.
130 "I might, at that": Ibid.
130 "I preserved": Ibid., p. 161.
130 "protested against": Ibid.
130 "*There* is a principality": Ibid.
130 "started up in": Ibid.
130 "He saw himself": Ibid.
130 "these fine dreams": Ibid.
130 "satisfied that": Ibid.
130 "secluded from": Ibid., p. 161A.
130 "truly, there is no": Ibid., p. 161A.
131 "The voice of": Ibid., p. 162.
131 "Reports reached": Ibid., p. 169
131 "Alarm and wailing": Ibid.
131 "Over the lintel": Ibid.
131 "Very few revived": Ibid., p. 168.
132 "Sooleyman, an": Ibid.
132 "He sent for": Ibid.
132 "I had seen much": Ibid.
132 "became prostrated": Ibid.
132 "submitted to fatality": Ibid.
132 "stimulating prophylactic": Ibid.
132 "I remained at Shennah": Ibid.
132 "I thought the": Ibid., p. 169A.
133 "Fatigue induced": Ibid., p. 170.
133 "Perceiving the horrible": Ibid.
133 "I felt revived": Ibid.
133 "No inhabitant": Ibid.
133 "After 20 sanguinary": Ibid., p. 169.
133 "Festivals and congratulations": Ibid.

8: THE ALCHEMIST

135 "these letters reached": Harlan, *Sketches*, p. 170A.
135 "diplomatick movements": Ibid., p. 171.
135 "As I could": Ibid.
135 "I determined": Ibid., p. 171.
136 "a man of": Ibid.
136 "Kind, affable and urbane": Ibid.
136 "You have, I fear": Ibid.
136 "This functionary informed": Ibid.
136 "Lest your eyes": Ibid., p. 171A.
136 "The Mirza was": Ibid.

136 "The old man sucked": Ibid.

136 "composed his": Ibid.

137 "As the Nawaub's": Ibid.

137 "feasting, promenading, carolling": Ibid., p. 174.

137 "déjeuner à la fourchette": Ibid., p. 175A.

137 "six sheep in the": Ibid.

137 "Of these the": Ibid., p. 176.

137 "wine was a glorious": Ibid., p. 175A.

137 "Several learned": Ibid., p. 176.

137 "The chief musician got": Ibid., p. 176A.

138 "I regretted the": Ibid.

138 "monstrous apparition": Ibid., p. 176.

138 "said to have cut": Ibid.

138 "by hard drinking": Ibid.

138 "in a fit of": Ibid.

138 "a drinking, smoking": Ibid., p. 176A.

138 "I have an": Ibid., p. 177.

138 "The castle stood": Ibid.

138 "Fountains played upon": Ibid., p. 177A.

139 "Dash always accompanied": Ibid., p. 178.

139 "the maxim of": Ibid.

139 "before our pleasures": Ibid., p. 177A.

139 "strengthening his": Ibid.

139 "From this time": Ibid.

139 "I replied with sarcasm": Ibid.

139 "What arrogance": Ibid.

140 "cholic": Ibid.

140 "His kindness and solicitude": Ibid.

140 "all of which": Ibid.

140 "On the presumption," Ibid., p. 178A.

140 "I suggest that no": Letter dated Feb. 3, 1829, Punjab Records, book no. 115, letter no. 49, cited in Grey, *European Adventurers*, p. 254.

141 "The season was": Harlan, *Sketches*, p. 179A.

141 but the nawaub: Ibid.

141 "His perfect knowledge": Ibid.

141 "The transition": Ibid., p. 180A.

141 "We left the mountains": Ibid.

141 "a superior castle": Whitteridge, *Charles Masson*, p. 78.

142 "redolent of flowers": Harlan, *Sketches*, p. 181.

142 "said to be the": Ibid., p. 183A.

142 "a prominent individual": Ibid., p. 181.

142 "He was a native": Ibid.

142 "His ostensible profession": Ibid.

142 "mathematics, magic": Ibid.

142 "was an enthusiastic": Ibid.

143 "secretly introducing": Mohan Lal, *Life of the Amir Dost Mohammed Khan of Kabul*, vol. 1, p. 144.

143 "The Nawaub's weak": Harlan, *Sketches*, p. 182.

143 "renew the vigour": Ibid., p. 187A.

143 "Men devoted to": Ibid.

143 "The common sense": Ibid., p. 182.

144 "fish of a peculiar": Ibid.

144 "With considerable expense": Ibid.

144 "if true, they": Ibid., p. 185.

144 "An inquiry": Ibid.

144 "He would sink": Ibid.

144 "The Moolvie was": Ibid.

144 "This dark practiser": Ibid., p. 187.

144 "sublimely eloquent": Ibid.

144 "A fine voice": Ibid.

145 "I, in return": Ibid.

145 "Upon this point": Ibid.

145 "Circumstances added": Ibid., p. 184.

145 "Results which": Ibid., p. 187A.

145 "These principles I": Ibid., p. 185.

146 "Dost Mohammad": Harlan, *Narrative*, p. 11.

146 "One of the five": Harlan, *Sketches*, p. 186.

146 "hospitable, sincere": Sir Keith A. Jackson, cited in J. Grant, *Dost Muhammud Khan*, p. 17.

146 "the superflous": Harlan, *Sketches*, p. 186A.

146 "noted in cipher": Ibid.

146 "the unfinished process": Ibid.

146 "his eyes flashed": Ibid.

146 "With gold": Ibid.

147 "It was about": Ibid., p. 189.

147 "The reception I met": Ibid.

147 "The vernal equinox": Ibid., p. 189.

148 "respect for the": Ibid., 6-page insert at p. 189.

148 "I preferred retaining": Ibid.

148 "He insisted upon": Ibid.

148 "deliberately placed": Ibid.

148 "retired with an": Ibid.

148 "drugs such as are": Ibid.

148 "discovered the": Ibid.

148–9 "Next morning": Ibid.

9: COURTIER OF LAHORE

151 "impaled the assailant": Macrory, *Kabul Catastrophe*, p. 70.

151 "one of the": Whitteridge, *Charles Masson*, p. 8.

151 "He cared neither": W. G. Osborne, *The Court and Camp of Runjeet Singh*, p. xi.

152 "He has, by his": H. T. Prinsep, *Origin of the Sikh Power in the Punjab and Political Life of Maha-raja Ranjit Singh*, p. 144.

152 "German, French": Khushwant Singh, *Ranjit Singh*, p. 142.

152 "high character": Alexander Gardner, *Soldier and Traveller: Memoirs of Alexander Gardner*, edited by Major Hugh Pearse, p. 315.

152 "in a state of extreme": Ibid., p. 300.

152 "the most noble": Ibid.

152 "turbans of crimson": Ibid.

152 "a miniature Versailles": Khushwant Singh, *Ranjit Singh*, p. 144.

153 "attired from top": Gardner, *Memoirs*, p. 314.

153 "His *wings* are": Emily Eden, cited in ibid., p. 315.

153 "It is very difficult": Honigberger, *Thirty-Five Years in the East*, p. 46.

153 "cross-legged in a": Osborne, *The Court and Camp of Runjeet Singh*, p. 73.

153 "the most ugly": Baron von Hügel, cited in Gardner, *Memoirs*, p. 303.

153 "He is exactly": Emily Eden, *Up the Country*, vol. 1, p. 284.

153 "a complete brigade": Grey, *European Adventurers*, pp. 160–165.

153 "Harlan replied that": Punjab Records, book no. 97, letter no. 68, cited in ibid., p. 255.

154 "invariably consults": Osborne, *The Court and Camp of Runjeet Singh*, p. 110.

154 "The medicine is": Ibid.

154 "seemed to be": Punjab Records, book no. 97, letter no. 68, cited in Grey, *European Adventurers*, p. 255.

154 "should Mr. Harlan": Ibid.

154 "negotiated on and off": Christopher J. Brunner, *A Man of Enterprise: The Short Writings of Josiah Harlan*, p. 7.

154 "Mr. Harlan is still": Punjab Records, book no. 97, letter no. 68, cited in Grey, *European Adventurers*, p. 255.

154 "to marry a native": Khushwant Singh, *Ranjit Singh*, p. 141.

154 "that wonderful, dirty": Gilmour, *The Long Recessional*, p. 28.

154 "heat and smells": Ibid.

155 "The people about": Punjab Records, book no. 97, letter no. 120, cited in Grey, *European Adventurers*, p. 258.

155 "If not, there": Palmer to Claude Wade, June 19, 1829; cited in Lafont, *La présence française*, pp. 64 and 283. See also Bodleian Library, Mss. Eng. Hist. c 110, pp. 127–128.

155 "every species of licentious": Osborne, *The Court and Camp of Runjeet Singh*, p. 150.

155 "indulged without remorse": Ibid.

155 "selected from the": Ibid.
155 "magnificently dressed:" Ibid.
155 "He orders the attendance": Ibid.
156 "His wine was extracted": Ibid.
156 "It is made for himself": Ibid., p. 189.
156 "The only food": Osborne, *The Court and Camp of Runjeet Singh*, p. 190.
156 "Do you drink": Ibid., p. 82.
156 "copious cups of": Masson, *Narrative of Various Journeys*, vol. 1, p. 443.
156 "gentleness to the": Gardner, *Memoirs*, p. 315.
157 "affected with a": Honigberger, *Thirty-Five Years in the East*, p. 53.
157 "ordinarily apparelled": Macrory, *Kabul Catastrophe*, p. 129.
157 "a clever, cheerful": Ibid.
157 "the pleasure he": Honigberger, *Thirty-Five Years in the East*, p. 53.
157 "He hangs a dozen": Ibid.
157 "selling artificial jewellery": Khushwant Singh, *Ranjit Singh*, p. 145.
157 "covered with pictures": Ibid.
158 "relations with the": Lafont, *La présence française*, p. 64.
158 "Allard with his": Cited in ibid., fn p. 231.
158 "a shirt of mail": Lepel Griffin, cited in Gardner, *Memoirs*, p. 302.
158 "riding about": Osborne, *The Court and Camp of Runjeet Singh*, p. 188.
159 "To attest his profound": *U.S. Gazette*.
159 "a title of nobility": Ibid.
159 "Nawaub of Khoorum": Harlan, *Narrative*, p. 143.
159 "consoling himself": Osborne, *The Court and Camp of Runjeet Singh*, p. 208.
159 "I will make you": Wolff, *Researches*, p. 259.
159 "He is himself": Honigberger, *Thirty-Five Years in the East*, p. 48.
159 "His executions are": Osborne, *The Court and Camp of Runjeet Singh*, p. 182.
159 "whose nose, ears": Honigberger, *Thirty-Five Years in the East*, p. 48.
160 "The fact of his": Wolff, *Researches*, p. 259.
160 "two districts then": *U.S. Gazette*.
160 "these two districts": Lafont, *La présence française*, p. 64.
160 "From this period": Harlan, *Sketches*, p. 189.
160 "being of very": Honigberger, *Thirty-Five Years in the East*, p. 52.
161 "a trick": Charles, Lord Metcalfe, cited in Lunt, *Bokhara Burnes*, p. 37.
161 "little elephants": Ibid., p. 48.
161 "nightingale of the": Ibid.
161 "a nightly dose: Ibid., p. 50.
161 "upon his Bible": Lala Sohan Lal Suri, *Chronicle of the Reign of Maharaja Ranjit Singh 1831–1839*, May 1832.
162 "was invested with": *U.S. Gazette*.
162 "I was both": Harlan, *Memoir*, p. 84.
162 "The military commandment": H.M.L. Lawrence, *Adventures of an Officer on the Service of Runjeet Singh*, p. 45.
162 "zeal and ability": Gardner, *Memoirs*, p. 333.

162 "a man of considerable": Lawrence, *Adventures of an Officer*, p. 46.

162 "They chop off men's": Ibid., p. 226.

162 "I have seen": Ibid.

163 "greatly reduced": Sarah Biller to Princess Mestchersky, May 1841, in Chester County Archives, Pennsylvania.

163 "unflinching firmness": Ibid.

163 "filed a suit before": Grey, *European Adventurers*, p. 256.

163 "a letter full of wrath": Ibid.

163 "I found every": Richard Burton, cited in Meyer and Brysac, *Tournament of Shadows*, p. 30.

163 "Down to Gehenna": Rudyard Kipling, *The Story of the Gadsbys*, cited in Gilmour, *The Long Recessional*, p. 39.

163 "the occasional woman": Gilmour, *The Long Recessional*, p. 18.

164 "I do not think": Burnes, cited in Macrory, *Kabul Catastrophe*, p. 48.

164 "A magnanimous name": Ibid.

164 "I have been": Ibid.

164 "the Moolvie became": Harlan, *Sketches*, p. 185A.

165 "this black magician": Ibid., p. 185.

165 "the traditional lore": Ibid.

165 "The Moolvie": Ibid., p. 187.

165 "My refusal to": Ibid.

165 "travel to Europe": Ibid.

165 "We did not slaughter": Gardner, *Memoirs*, p. 44.

166 "clutched his neck": Ibid., p. 281.

166 "I remained a few days": Ibid., p. 183.

166 "It was unfortunate," Ibid., 178.

167 "most curious": Fitzroy McLean, *A Person from England*, p. 17.

167 "His frame appears": Ibid., p. 18.

167 "He argued with Christians": Ibid.

167 "shake with uncontrollable": Ibid.

168 "Bokhara and Bulkh": Ibid.

168 "a considerable town": Wolff, *Researches*, p. 258.

168 "Bibles in various": McLean, *A Person*, p. 31.

168 "to his great surprise": Wolff, *Researches*, p. 258.

168 "I am a free": Ibid.

168 "I was most": Ibid.

168 "played him false": Ibid., p. 259.

168 "He fell in love": Ibid.

168 "tried to make": Ibid.

168 "He speaks and": Ibid., p. 260.

169 "preached in the house": Ibid.

169 "not to think": Lafont, *La présence française*, p. 64.

169 "Ventura's jaghirs": Ibid.

169 "The French": Gardner, *Memoirs*, p. 310.

169 "informed me that": Wolff, *Researches*, p. 260.
169 "managed to keep": Lawrence, *Adventures of an Officer*, p. 22.
169 "Harland [sic] was once": Ibid., p. 23.
170 "join him with": Ibid., p. 45.
170 "risen from bandmaster": Khushwant Singh, *Ranjit Singh*, p. 148.
170 "legitimate monarch": Harlan, *Sketches*, p. 6.
170 "a wayward tyrant": Ibid., p. 32.
171 "vile and incapable": Ibid., p. 11.
171 "Let his name": Ibid., p. 49.
171 "with unabated zeal": Ibid.

10: THE MAHARAJA'S AMBASSADOR

173 "If out of": Khushwant Singh, *Ranjit Singh*, p. 190.
173 "We have broken": Ibid.
173 "I am too poor": G. B. Malleson, *History of Afghanistan from the Earliest Period to the Outbreak of the War of 1878*, p. 357.
173 "fanatic in profession": Harlan, *Memoir*, p. 162.
174 "wanted his money": Mohan Lal, *Life of the Amir*, p. 171.
174 "From Kohistan": Narendra Krishna Sinha, *Ranjit Sing*, p. 95.
174 "50,000 musketeers": Harlan, *Memoir*, p. 158.
175 "Fifty thousand belligerent": Ibid., p. 124.
175 "a fine-looking man": Osborne, *The Court and Camp of Runjeet Singh*, p. 69.
175 "He alone could": Gardner, *Memoirs*, p. 333.
176 "the Sikhs sadly lost": Ibid, p. 188.
176 "not long before": Harlan, *Narrative*, p. 11.
176 "stating the fact of": Masson, *Narrative of Various Journeys*, vol. 3, p. 335.
176 "now the brothers": Ibid.
176 "A day or two": Ibid.
177 "whether the letter": Ibid.
177 "would receive him": Harlan, *Memoir*, p. 159.
177 "He boasted": Ibid.
177 "If the Prince": Ibid., p. 158.
177 "in an exalted": Ibid.
177 "He lost his temper": Ibid.
177–8 "Your appearance": Ibid.
178 "Feeling myself strong": Ibid.
178 "My brother!" Ibid., p. 159.
178 "Civility required": Ibid., p. 162.
178 "hesitatingly declined": Ibid., p. 163.
178 "The Ameer excused": Ibid.
178 "Then commenced": Ibid.
178 "Impossible brother": Ibid.

179 "I drank from": Ibid.

179 "remarked that Mr.": Masson, *Narrative of Various Journeys*, vol. 3, p. 337.

179 "After witnessing": Ibid.

179 "put the wrong": Harlan, *Memoir*, p. 130.

179 "Sikh gold": Harlan, *Narrative*, p. 12.

179 "day and night": Gardner, *Memoirs*, p. 186.

180 "to frustrate the designs": Mohan Lal, *Life of the Amir*, p. 173.

180 "I divided his": Harlan, *Memoir*, p. 125.

180 "the Sikh army": Mohan Lal, *Life of the Amir*, p. 178.

180 "proposed to retire": Ibid., p. 177.

180 "guns, munitions": Masson, *Narrative of Various Journeys*, vol. 3, pp. 343–344.

180 "the old Sikh": Ibid.

181 "It was agreed": Masson, *Narrative of Various Journeys*, vol. 3, p. 343.

181 "promised entire": Ibid.

181 "coarsely reproached": Ibid.

181 "infidels and their agents": Khushwant Singh, *Ranjit Singh*, p. 190.

181 "There his ears": Masson, *Narrative of Various Journeys*, vol. 3, p. 344.

181 "I induced Sooltan": Harlan, *Memoir*, p. 125.

182 "without the beat": Harlan, *Memoir*, p. 125 fn.

182 "No vestige of": Ibid.

182 "No one could": Mohan Lal, *Life of the Amir*, p. 181.

182 "a tissue of": Ibid.

182 "This appalling news": Ibid.

182 "chagrined and mortified": Masson, *Narrative of Various Journeys*, vol. 3, p. 346.

182 "in bitterness": Mohan Lal, *Life of the Amir*, p. 182.

182 "changing position": Harlan, *Memoir*, pp. 158–160.

182 "By this one": Gardner, *Memoirs*, p. 188.

182 "The prey had": Lafont, *La présence française*, p. 170.

182 "When such sure": Cited in ibid., p. 173.

183 "a vain attempt": Bikrama Jit Masrat, *The Life and Times of Ranjit Singh: A Saga of a Benevolent Despot*, p. 280.

183 "the insurrectionist": Ibid.

183 "somewhat anomalous": McGregor, *The History of the Sikhs*, p. 274.

183 "the state of affairs": Grey, *European Adventurers*, p. 259.

183 "reports concerning": Wade to Macnaghten, Feb. 19, 1834, cited in Lafont, *La présence française*, p. 407.

183 "the excesses and": Masrat, *The Life and Times of Ranjit Singh*, p. 182.

183 "Modesty made": Victor Jacquemont, *Voyage dans l'Inde*, p. 41.

183 "He became hesitant": Masrat, *The Life and Times of Ranjit Singh*, p. 183.

184 "constructed a talisman": Suri, *Chronicle of the Reign*, May 1832, p. 112.

184 "Hallen Sahib": Ibid., p. 290.

184 "once the Maharaja fell": Kirpal Singh, *Ranjit Singh*, p. 180.

184 "had been recommended": Ibid.

184 "the exorbitant sum": McGregor, *The History of the Sikhs*, p. 276.

184 "as he did not": Suri, *Chronicle of the Reign*, May 1832, p. 112.

184 "acting on Harlan's": Masrat, *The Life and Times of Ranjit Singh*, p. 184.

185 "After some delay": McGregor, *The History of the Sikhs*, p. 276.

185 "We endeavoured to explain": Ibid.

185 "sired by an": Harlan, *Sketches*, p. 46A.

185 "the cause of important": Ibid.

186 "Runjeet Sing": Honigberger, *Thirty-Five Years in the East*, p. 55.

186 "I could not forebear": Ibid.

186 "to become notorious": Harlan, *Sketches*, p. 182.

186 "the privilege of": Sirdar Ikbal Ali Shah, *Afghanistan of the Afghans*, p. 27.

186 "the very first": Ibid.

186 "by a rolling process": Harlan, *Sketches*, p. 185A.

186 "Harlan was making": Honigberger, *Thirty-Five Years in the East,* p. 55.

186 "in no very": Lawrence, *Adventures of an Officer*, p. 46.

186 "Any regard between": Ibid.

186–7 "beside himself with": Suri, *Chronicle of the Reign*, May 1832.

187 "threatened to wreak": McGregor, *The History of the Sikhs*, p. 276.

187 "After seven": *U.S. Gazette.*

187 "contempt and disgust": Harlan, *Sketches*, p. 94.

187 "Monarch as he": *U.S. Gazette.*

11: THE KING'S NEAREST FRIEND

189 "a conciliatory message": Brennan, *A Man of Enterprise*, p. 12.

189 "Mr. Harlan, who": Major McGregor, Political Assistant at Ludhiana, letter in Punjab Records, book no. 142, letter no. 78.

189 "His declared intention": Ibid.

190 "I was received": *U.S. Gazette.*

190 "Dost Mohamed received": Ibid.

190 "at the head": Lafont, *La présence française*, p. 65.

190 "commander in chief": *Calcutta Journal*, 1838, p. 77.

190 "he did not deceive": Masson, *Narrative of Various Journeys*, vol. 3, p. 336.

190 "a miscellaneous": Grey, *European Adventurers*, p. 259.

191 "Desultory sniping": Ibid.

191 "in all the records": Ibid.

191 "about three thousand": Osborne, *The Court and Camp of Runjeet Singh*, p. 139.

191 "a park of 45 guns": Narendra Krishna Sinha, *Ranjit Sing*, p. 102.

191 "believed him to": Wade to Macnaghten, Apr. 9, 1834, India Office Library and Records, Bengal Secret Consultations, June 19, 1834, vol. 380.

192 "so unceremoniously": Harlan, *Sketches*, p. 169.

192 "The information": Wade to Macnaghten, Apr. 9, 1834, India Office Library and Records, Bengal Secret Consultations, June 19, 1834, vol. 380.

192 "Agent in Kabul": Wade to Masson, Feb. 11, 1835, India Office Library and Records, Masson Collection, Mss. Eur. E.161/2, 632.

192 "imposed": Ibid.

192 "an adventurer": Ibid.

192–3 "A man of extremist": Masrat, *The Life and Times of Ranjit Singh*, p. 280.

193 "so closely was": Masson, *Narrative of Various Journeys*, vol. 3, p. 384.

193 "An opinion has": Sinha, *Ranjit Singh*, p. 101.

193 "like all the Europeans": Grey, *European Adventurers*, p. 263.

193 "a force 8,000–10,000": Ibid.

193 "devastating the plains": Ibid.

193 "could make no head": Gardner, *Memoirs*, p. 192.

193 "That gallant chief": Masson, *Narrative of Various Journeys*, vol. 3, p. 387.

194 "in despair, he": Macrory, *Kabul Catastrophe*, p. 38.

194 "Mahomed Akbar": Masson, *Narrative of Various Journeys*, vol. 3, p. 387.

194 "the proud King": *U.S. Gazette*.

194 "seemed to bear": Osborne, *The Court and Camp of Runjeet Singh*, p. 195.

194 "flower of Sikh chivalry": Sinha, *Ranjit Sing*, p. 104.

194 "cast a gloom over Lahore": Masson, *Narrative of Various Journeys*, vol. 3, p. 387.

194 "the old Prince's infirmities": *U.S. Gazette*.

194 "remorseless cruelty": Gardner, *Memoirs*, p. 316.

194 "When I marched": Khushwant Singh, *Ranjit Singh*, p. 146.

195 "He acts as a savage": Gardner, *Memoirs*, p. 319.

195 "As the Ameer's": Harlan, *Memoir*, p. 148.

195 "I was instructed": Harlan, *Sketches*, p. 185A.

195 "offering to coin": Ibid.

195 "a gold-mounted": Unidentified newspaper clipping, Sept. 12, 1878, Chester County Archives, Pennsylvania.

196 "touching the forehead as": Harlan, *Memoir*, p. 147.

196 "a long official wand": Ibid.

196 "About 11 o'clock": Ibid., p. 148.

196 "Fiddlers huddled": Ibid., p. 149.

196 "The standing dish": Ibid.

197 "I have frequently": Grant, *Dost Muhammud Khan*, p. 10.

197 "nocturnal orgie": Harlan, *Sketches*, p. 175.

197 "too drunk to": Ibid., p. 175A.

197 "listened to the charge": Ibid.

197 "To avoid the": Ibid.

197 "a young Cashmerian": Harlan, *Narrative*, p. 138.

197 "My proceeding was": Ibid.

197 "In the summer": Harlan, *Memoir*, p. 156.

198 "passed their time": Ibid., p. 151.

198 "repeatedly sat up": Ibid., 152.

198 "When His Highness": Ibid.

198 "occasionally someone": Ibid., p. 153.
198 "He was much": Ibid., pp. 153–154.
198 "Ridicule was": Ibid., p. 154.
198 "one of the essential": Ibid., p. 162.
198 "the manners and": Ibid., 153.
199 "In conversation he": Ibid., p. 128.
199 "The Ameer is": Ibid., pp. 126–127.
199 "Loud and vociferous": Ibid., p. 129.
199 "When the Ameer": Ibid.
199 "by breaking through": Shakespeare, *Henry IV*, part 1, act 1, scene 2.
199 "The Ameer": Harlan, *Memoir*, p. 130.
200 "acquisition of": Ibid., p. 132.
200 "He is no believer": Ibid.
200 "His eyes had a": Ibid., p. 126.
200 "while a large": Harlan, *Narrative*, p. 127.
200 "Hundreds of these": Ibid.
200 "From the frontiers": Cited in Peter Hopkirk, *The Great Game: On Secret Service in High Asia*, p. 192.
201 "ground between": Harlan, *Sketches*, p. 69A.
201 "The field of my": Cited in Macrory, *Kabul Catastrophe*, p. 46.
201 "My friend, you": Ibid.
201 "watch more closely": Ibid.
201 "to interfere": Ibid.
202 "We were received": Alexander Burnes, *Cabool*, pp. 139–140.
202 "As we passed": Ibid., p. 142.
202 "remarkable for his": Harlan, *Memoir*, p. 16.
202 "the Afghans were": Masson, *Narrative of Various Journeys*, vol. 3, p. 445.
202 "The utter and deplorable": Harlan, *Memoir*, p. 19.
202 "ought not to": Macrory, *Kabul Catastrophe*, p. 52.
202 "a breach of etiquette": Harlan, *Memoir*, p. 138.
202 "adapted only": Ibid.
202 "They consisted": Ibid., p. 139.
203 "His Highness was": Ibid.
203 "Dost Mahomed observed": Ibid.
203 "almost caused an": Ibid., p. 141.
203 "To the English he held": Ibid., p. 19.
203 "Dost Mohammed is our": Cited in Lunt, *Bokhara Burnes*, p. 182.
203 "Our first feeling": Macnaghten to Burnes, Sept. 11, 1837, Parliamentary Papers, vol. 25, 1859.
203–4 "taking part in": Lafont, *La présence française*, p. 407.
204 "Every subterfuge that": Harlan, *Memoir*, p. 139.
204 "a strict system": Ibid.
204 "black eyed damsels': Masson, *Narrative of Various Journeys*, vol. 3, p. 453.

204 "I asked where": Ibid.

204 "hardly large enough": Ibid.

204 "represented himself": Harlan, *Memoir*, p. 19.

205 "He was a gentlemanly": Cited in Lunt, *Bokhara Burnes*, p. 184.

205 "We are in a mess here": Cited in Macrory, *Kabul Catastrophe*, p. 56.

205 "abandoned himself": Masson, *Narrative of Various Journeys*, vol. 3, p. 463.

205 " 'This is just my position' ": Harlan, *Narrative*, p. 156.

205 "an immediate remedy": Burnes to Auckland, Dec. 23, 1847, Parliamentary Papers, vol. 25, 1859.

205 "You must desist": Cited in Meyer and Brysac, *Tournament of Shadows*, p. 85.

206 "so dictatorial and": Archibald Forbes, *The Afghan Wars 1839–41 and 1878–80*, p. 9.

206 "Dost Mahomed was": Harlan, *Memoir*, p. 170.

206 "The document was": Ibid., p. 171.

206 "There is no": Ibid.

206 "An official note": Ibid.

206 "referring to the": Ibid.

206 "refusal to recommence": Ibid., p. 172.

206 "The reply I received": Ibid.

207 "paraded him in triumph": Macrory, *Kabul Catastrophe*, p. 57.

207 "The English agent": Harlan, *Memoir*, p. 139.

207 "Their fears were": Ibid., p. 140.

207 "which should certainly": Ibid., p. 170.

207 "had furnished": Masson, *Narrative of Various Journeys*, vol. 3, p. 478.

207 "Fool that I was": Harlan, *Memoir*, p. 140.

207 "The greatest": Ibid., p. 140.

12: THE PRINCE OF GHOR

209 "all the petty": Harlan, *Narrative*, p. 26.

209 "This robber annually": Ibid., p. 28.

210 "fortunate adventurer": Ibid., p. 37.

210 "this princely robber": Ibid., p. 28.

210 "A great bear": Lunt, *Bokhara Burnes*, p. 106.

210 "The Indian Caucasus": Harlan, *Memoir*, p. 37.

211 "The country is": Ibid.

211 "a strong, enduring": Harlan, *Narrative*, p. 53.

211 "His services were": Ibid., p. 101.

212 "a lad of about": Ibid.

212 "an avaricious and": Harlan, *Narrative*, p. 140.

212 "councilor and aide-de-camp": Ibid., p. 101.

212 "The young man": Harlan, *Memoir*, p. 141.

212 "If half you": Macrory, *Kabul Catastrophe*, p. 76.

212 "no very high": Ibid.

212 "an old man in": Henry Havelock, *Narrative of the War in Affghanistan in 1838–39*, p. 93.

213 "were not expected": Suri, *Chronicle of the Reign*, p. 467.

213 "It merely requires": Cited in Macrory, *Kabul Catastrophe*, p. 75.

213 "He avowed schemes": Ibid., p. 79.

213 "His Majesty Shah Soojah-oll-Moolk": Cited in ibid., p. 80.

213 "The Afghans": Cited in ibid., p. 82.

214 "His Highness": Harlan, *Memoir*, p. 170.

214 "Beautiful orchards": Mohan Lal, *Life of the Amir*, p. 147.

214 "the route of Alexander": Harlan, *Narrative*, p. 16.

214 "Bulkh is called": Ibid., p. 28.

214 "the savage Bactrians": Harlan, *Memoir*, p. 62.

214 "about the thickness": Ibid., p. 63.

215 "the tutelary deity": Ibid., p. 64.

215 "The bold and scientific": Ibid.

215 "the ruggedness of": Harlan, *Narrative*, p. 105.

215 "would foil an": Harlan, *Narrative*, p. 106.

215 "broken by steep": Ibid.

215 "wild and broken": Ibid.

215 "huge fragments": Ibid.

215 "large storks could": Ibid., p. 56.

215 "winter residence": Ibid., p. 71.

215 "The yelling of": Ibid., p. 55.

216 "I have known": Ibid.

216 "support the muscles": Ibid., p. 129.

216 "a closely fitting": Ibid., p. 130.

216 "We ascended passes": *U.S. Gazette*.

216 "I surmounted": Ibid.

217 "cashmere shawls": Harlan, *Narrative*, p. 71.

217 "sixteen hundred camels": Ibid.

217 "the plain of Pamezan": Ibid., p. 103.

217 "Mahomedan historians": Ibid.

217 "back to Cabul": Ibid., p. 101.

217 "the elephant parks": Lane Fox, *Alexander the Great*, p. 293.

217 "a strong, hardy": Harlan, *Narrative*, p. 101.

218 "They have large": Ibid.

218 "The hair is black": Ibid.

218 "They are a": Ibid., p. 154.

218 "That prince seizes": Ibid., p. 59.

218 "All unprotected": Ibid., p. 67.

218 "lying in wait": Ibid., p. 62.

218 "diabolical contrivance": Ibid.

218 "To oblige the": Ibid.

219 "The corrupt and": Ibid., p. 69.

219 "Muraad Beg is the": Ibid., p. 82.

219 "The traffic in Toorkistaun": Ibid., p. 45.

219 "half sunk into": Ibid., p. 114.

219 "Wolves, foxes and": Ibid., p. 110.

219 "A noble animal": Ibid.

219 "The gallstone is": Ibid., p. 111.

219 "It has the": Ibid., p. 110.

219 "gold-digging ants": Herodotus, *The History of Herodotus*, book 3, p. 97. See also Michel Peissel, "Address to the Royal Geographical Society," Dec. 1996, and Ben Macintyre, "The gold-digging ants of Herodotus," *The Times of London*, Dec. 4, 1996.

219 "as they burrow": Ibid.

220 "It is a sociable": Harlan, *Narrative*, p. 110.

220 "becoming familiar": Ibid.

220 "The position is a": Harlan, *Narrative*, p. 145.

220 "The appearance": Ibid.

220 "a practical demonstration": Ibid.

220 "letters of a": Ibid., p. 142.

220 "The Ghorian princes": Ibid., p. 87.

220 "Undisguisedly ambitious": Ibid., p. 140.

220 "by matrimonial": Ibid.

221 "who had been invited": Harlan, *Narrative*, p. 141.

221 "three hundred": Ibid., p. 143.

221 "clad in elegant": Ibid., p. 140.

221 "Their arms are a": Ibid.

221 "Persian daggers": Ibid., p. 143.

221 "all men of athletic": Ibid.

221 "the Prince of Cabul": Ibid., p. 142.

221 "three marches away": Ibid.

221 "I readily shared": Ibid.

221 "The chief and his": Ibid.

222 "In person he is": Ibid., p. 140.

222 "A man of vigorous": Ibid.

222 "He is anxious": Ibid.

222 "the resources": Ibid., p. 141.

222 "from an origin": Ibid.

222 "This Hazarrah prince": Ibid., p. 142.

222 "acquainted only": Ibid., p. 143.

222 "promiscuous bodies": Ibid., p. 63.

223 "I speak of them": Ibid.

223 "a six pound": Ibid., p. 130.

223 "seldom miss their": Ibid.

223 "Each one lies": Ibid., p. 136.

223 "Silent and thoughtful": Ibid., p. 143

223 "These Hazarrah princes": Ibid.

223 "I suggested that": Ibid., 137.

223 "proud of their": Ibid., p. 131.

224 "The pantaloons are wide": Ibid.

224 "The government is": Ibid., p. 136.

224 "The occurrence of": Ibid., p. 137.

224 "a rude condition": Ibid., p. 120.

224 "They are by": Ibid., p. 118.

224 "They are the": Harlan, *Memoir*, p. 11.

224 "The mountains are": *U.S. Gazette*.

224 "coined money": Harlan, *Narrative*, p. 133.

224 "a gourd and": Ibid., p. 154.

224–5 "Intoxicating liquors": Ibid., p. 150.

225 "The men display": Ibid., pp. 121 and 150.

225 "The men address": Ibid., p. 122.

225 "indifference and contempt": Ibid., p. 121.

225 "unshod horses": Ibid., p. 150.

225 "Hazarrah ladies have": Ibid., p. 120.

225 "Smiling cupids were": Lane Fox, *Alexander the Great*, p. 317.

226 "horses, slaves, felts": Harlan, *Narrative*, p. 147.

226 "marriage celebrated": Ibid.

226 "In the remotest": Harlan, *Memoir*, p. 152.

226 "Men of ambitious": Harlan, *Narrative*, p. 137.

226 "regular military system": Ibid., p. 143.

226 "a splendid perspective": Ibid.

227 "transferred his": *U.S. Gazette*.

227 "The Prince of Ghoree": Ibid.

227 "I, who am the": Document handwritten in Persian, with two impressions of an oval seal bearing the legend: "His slave Mohammed Reffee, 1255 (A.D. 1838)," in Chester County Archives, Pennsylvania. Translation by A. H. Morton. (Sayyid Najaf appears to have misdated the document by a year.)

228 "Our views contemplated": Harlan, *Narrative*, p. 144.

228 "A firm footing": Ibid., p. 137.

228 "a sovereign prince": Gardner, *Memoirs*, p. 336.

13: PROMETHEUS FROM PENNSYLVANIA

229 "a tall, robust": Harlan, *Narrative*, p. 36.

229 "His eyes are dark": Ibid.

229 "originally well-shaped": Ibid.

229 "finely levigated": Ibid., p. 78.

230 "These subsisted": Ibid., p. 102.

230 "one of the horse": Ibid., p. 89.

230 "perilous even for": Ibid.

230 "through a stony": Ibid., p. 91.

230 "over which it": Ibid., p. 92.

230 "Soofey Beg": Ibid., p. 70.

230 "Many of them": Ibid.

231 "In the storming": Ibid., p. 155.

231 "the best soldiers": Ibid.

231 "released from": Ibid., p. 70.

231 "Surmounting this": Ibid., p. 94.

231 "converted what remained": Ibid., p. 42.

231 "Every remnant of": Harlan, *Memoir*, fn, p. 81.

232 "the subjugation": Ibid., p. 83.

232 "Bulkh is the": Ibid., p. 80.

232 "Possession of the": Harlan, *Narrative*, pp. 29–31.

232 "no different in": Lane Fox, *Alexander the Great*, p. 308.

232 "Coal and wood": Harlan, *Narrative*, p. 47.

232 "a bad man": Ibid., p. 33.

232 "The place is": Ibid., p. 95.

232 "The citadel": Harlan, *Memoir*, p. 34.

233 "The Uzbecks are": Harlan, *Narrative*, p. 63.

233 "They are all": Ibid., p. 85.

233 "Little attention is": Ibid., p. 52.

233 "A melon of this": Ibid., p. 51.

234 "there is nothing so": Ibid.

234 "The Uzbecks have a great": Ibid., p. 61.

234 "a few individual": Ibid., p. 60.

234 "the barrier of political": Ibid., p. 90.

234 "relinquished the": Ibid., p. 39.

234 "a duty of two and": Ibid., p. 40.

234 "the younger brother": Ibid.

234 "control in the politics": Ibid.

234 "His power was": Ibid.

234 "he has in great": Ibid.

234 "he fell sick": Ibid., p. 41.

235 "The punishment of": Ibid., p. 17.

235 "By my expedition into": Harlan, *Memoir*, p. 80.

235 "Commanding a": Ibid.

235 "the direct route": Harlan, *Narrative*, p. 95.

235 "Upon the whole": Ibid.

236 "revolting cruelties": Ibid., p. 96.

236 "The cry was": Ibid.
236 "these remarks refer": Ibid.
236 "A more drastic substance": Ibid., p. 151.
236 "This is drawn into": Ibid.
236 "The ascent": Ibid., p. 96.
237 "This is a most": Ibid.
237 "We crossed the pass in": Ibid., p. 97.
237 "During the height": Ibid.
237 "Three men, two": Ibid.
237 "literally means Hindoo": Ibid., p. 104.
237 "Snowdrifts of an": Ibid., p. 97.
237 "in many places": Ibid.
237 "from a Jew in": Ibid., p. 80.
237 "I kept my footing": Ibid., p. 97.
237 "Our eyes were": Ibid.
237 "Opium moistened with": Ibid., p. 98.
238 "The feet are": Ibid., p. 129.
238 "fled to their": Ibid., p. 103.
238 "the natives had": Lane Fox, *Alexander the Great*, p. 295.
238 "seasoned with the": Ibid.
238 "Our only remedy": Harlan, *Narrative*, p. 103.
238 "instinctively dig": Honigberger, *Thirty-Five Years in the East,* p. 63.
238 "Cave of Prometheus": Harlan, *Narrative*, p. 98.
238 "along with the nest": Lane Fox, *Alexander the Great*, p. 296.
238 "to Alexander's officers": Ibid.
239 "one hundred men": Harlan, *Narrative*, p. 100.
239 "after five days": Ibid., p. 99.
239 "the worst of all": Ibid., p. 100.
239 "Eight or ten": Ibid.
239 "with gold": Ibid., p. 81.
239 "long frock made": Ibid., p. 129.
239 "a white cat's": Kennedy, *Narrative of the Campaign*, p. 118.

14: A GRAND PROMENADE

241 "a grand military": Macrory, *Kabul Catastrophe*, p. 102.
241 "You are an": Ibid.
242 "The Khan declared": Ibid., p. 92.
242 "feelings very": Ibid., p. 88.
242 "mortifying indifference": Letters of Capt. James Douglas, part letter, British Library, undated Mss, Eur c. 181.
242 "generalissimo of": *U.S. Gazette*.
243 "he concluded": Macrory, *Kabul Catastrophe*, p. 96.
243 "Runjit insisted": Masrat, *The Life and Times of Ranjit Singh*, p. 184.

243 "a curious and interesting": Henry Lawrence, *Calcutta Review*, no. 2, p. 476.
243 "By a slight turn": Ibid.
244 "both by nature": Macrory, *Kabul Catastrophe*, p. 97.
244 "produced a moral": *U.S. Gazette*.
244 "indignantly rejected": Macrory, *Kabul Catastrophe*, p. 103.
244–5 "In their audacity": Harlan, *Memoir*, p. 6.
245 "You have": Macrory, *Kabul Catastrophe*, p. 105.
245 "He resumed his serenity": Ibid.
245 "I can no longer": *U.S. Gazette*.
245 "With a countenance": Ibid.
246 "turned his horse's": Kaye, *History*, vol. 1, p. 471.
246 "You may throw": Macrory, *Kabul Catastrophe*, p. 114.
246 "retreated precipitately": *U.S. Gazette*.
247 "dazzling in a coronet": Macrory, *Kabul Catastrophe*, p. 147.
247 "the most complete indifference": Ibid.
247 "a pack of dogs," Ibid., p. 95.
247 "The city is": Letters of Capt. James Douglas, part letter, British Library, undated Mss, Eur c. 181.
247 "It must be admitted": Ibid.
247 "A tall, manly figure": Kennedy, *Narrative of the Campaign*, pp. 119–20.
247 "a free and enlightened": Kennedy, *Narrative of the Campaign*, pp. 119–20.
248 "astonished to find": Ibid.
248 "would have been": Ibid.
248 "It will not be creditable": Ibid.
248 "There was no law": Ibid.
248 "I made no effort": Harlan, *Narrative*, p. 145.
248 "addressed alike": Harlan, *Sketches*, p. 32.
248 "harsh barbarity": Ibid.
248 "Everyone is commanded": Ibid.
248 "self-conceited gentleman": Harlan, *Memoir*, p. 12.
248 "of sedate deportment": Harlan, *Sketches*, p. 186.
249 "issued a conciliatory": Harlan, *Narrative*, p. 144.
249 "the Nawaub": Ibid.
249 "trusting to English": Ibid., p. 145.
249 "The government": Harlan, *Memoir*, p. 9.
249 "If the English": Ibid., p. 8.
249 "imprisoned many who": Ibid., p. 11.
249 "The English": Ibid.
250 "Honours of knighthoods": Harlan, *Memoir*, p. 2.
250 "the extinction of a free nation": Ibid., p. 3.
250 "The temptations": Macrory, *Kabul Catastrophe*, p. 122.
250 "Bad ministers": Burnes, cited in ibid., p. 119.
250 "He oppressed the": Ibid.
251 "Cabul, the city": Harlan, *Memoir*, pp. 151–152.

251 "I have seen this": Ibid., p. 152.

251 "I could not": T. E. Lawrence, cited in Lane Fox, *Alexander the Great*, p. 295.

251 "Something I owe": Kipling, "The Two-Sided Man," cited in Gilmour, *The Long Recessional*, p. 54.

252 "They had not been": Harlan, *Memoir*, p. 151.

252 "Maintaining him": Macrory, *Kabul Catastrophe*, p. 94.

252 "I can place": Ibid., p. 123.

252 "I repossessed": Harlan to G. H. McGregor, superintendent of police, Kabul, Oct. 19, 1839, letter in Chester County Archives, Pennsylvania.

253 "I am": Ibid.

253 "To compare": Ibid.

253 "consider the horse": Ibid.

253 "102 books, 77": Undated list of items left "on trust" to Yusuf Khan, document handwritten in Persian, in Chester County Archives, Pennsylvania. Translation by A. H. Morton.

253 "for the time postponed": Harlan, *Narrative*, p. 144.

253 "This irruption": Ibid.

253 "Harlan was sent": Grey, *European Adventurers*, p. 263.

254 "Plans were": Harlan, *Narrative*, p. 145.

254 "to conquer": Ibid., p. 5.

254 "and no condition": Ibid.

254 "To subdue and crush": Ibid.

254 "Vainglorious": Ibid.

15: CAMEL CONNOISSEUR AND GRAPE AGENT

255 "found the": Josiah Harlan, *Importation of Camels*, U.S. Congress, Executive Document no. 27, part 2, 33 Cong., 1st session, p. 63.

255 "Mr. H. proposes": N. Rogen to F. Baddeley, letter of introduction, March 25, 1840, Chester County Archives, Pennsylvania.

256 "Col. J. Harlan": John Newton et al., Ludhiana, to Anon., letter of introduction, March 2, 1840, Chester County Archives, Pennsylvania.

256 "sallow skin": Passport dated Nov. 1840, Chester County Archives, Pennsylvania.

256 "In referring to": Harlan, *Memoir*, p. 23.

256 "an intelligent and": Sarah Biller to Princess Mestchersky, May 16, 1841, Chester County Archives, Pennsylvania.

257 "You are so interested": Sarah Biller to Madam Vasiltchikoff, May 16, 1841, Chester County Archives, Pennsylvania.

257 "Your peasants": Ibid.

257 "knew of no": Cited in Meyer and Brysac, *Tournament of Shadows*, p. 106.

257 "Our distinguished fellow-citizen": *U.S. Gazette*.

258 "looks upon kingdoms": Ibid.

258 "Our worthy compatriot": Ibid.

258 "General Harlan": Ibid.

259 "The country is": Cited in Macrory, *Kabul Catastrophe*, p. 133.

259 "What will this": Cited in Lunt, *Bokhara Burnes*, p. 201.

260 "See Friends": Ibid.

260 "fiercely bristling": Harlan, *Memoir*, p. 16.

260 "an old invalid": Ibid.

261 *Az barae Khodda*: Macrory, *Kabul Catastrophe*, p. 195.

261 "We are to depart": Florentia Sale, cited in ibid., p. 205.

261 "A universal panic": Ibid., p. 209.

262 "When you're": Rudyard Kipling, "The Young British Soldier," in *Selected Poems*, p. 113.

262 "Our worst fears": Cited in Hopkirk, *The Great Game*, p. 271.

263 "profound regret": Harlan, *Memoir*, p. 3.

263 "the retributive justice": Ibid., p. 9.

263 "A king has been": Ibid., p. 8.

263 "The Avghaun people": Ibid.

263 "a nation whose": Ibid., p. 12.

263 "Sir William Macnaghten": Ibid.

263 "the utter and deplorable": Ibid., p. 19.

263 "frivolity, stupidity": Harlan, *Sketches*, p. 179.

264 "impeached, degraded": Harlan, *Memoir*, p. 12.

264 "oppressed and plundered": Ibid., p. 65.

264 "Have the arts": Ibid.

264 "British executive": Ibid., p. 74.

264 "famines, discontent": Ibid., p. 66.

264 "The clouds have": Ibid., p. 21.

264 "the destruction of every": Ibid., p. 20.

264 "British power in India": Ibid.

264 "a saviour": Ibid., p. 54.

264 "Should a Russian": Ibid., p. 38.

265 "it is pervaded": *The New Books of the Month*, New York, May 1842, p. 219.

265 "extraordinary concoction": Grey, *European Adventurers*, p. 240.

265 "anglophobia": Ibid.

265 "His *Memoir*": Lafont, *La présence française*, p. 66.

265 "the deliberate lies": Grey, *European Adventurers*, p. 242.

266 "everything was done": Lafont, *La présence française,* p. 67.

266 "the English officers": Ibid.

266 "poorer than he anticipated": Frank Ross, introduction to Harlan, *Narrative*, p. 19.

266 "I had money sent": Deposition of Mary Harlan, March 26, 1848, Chester County Archives, Pennsylvania.

266 "a great manorial": *Chester County Place Names*, anonymous document in Chester County Archives, Pennsylvania.

267 "a device for": Frank Ross, introduction to Harlan, *Narrative*, p. 19.

267 "I propose to myself": Josiah Harlan to "My dear Mr. Hoffman," undated, Chester County Archives, Pennsylvania.

267 "Somewhat to": Frank Ross, introduction to Harlan, *Narrative*, p. 20.

268 "a stranger among": Ibid.

268 "unreliable, mendacious": Whitteridge, *Charles Masson*, p. 163.

268 "My natural inclinations": McLean, *A Person*, p. 108.

268 "the rulers of so": Cited in Meyer and Brysac, *Tournament of Shadows,* p. 106.

268 "Everything": cited in Macrory, *Kabul Catastrophe*, p. 273.

268 "may still be": Harlan, *Narrative*, p. 144.

269 "In any place": Kipling, "The Man Who Would Be King," p. 118.

269 "had again": Mordecai Rickets to Josiah Harlan, Paris, June 18, 1844, Chester County Archives, Pennsylvania.

269 " 'sighing his soul' ": Osborne, *The Court and Camp of Runjeet Singh*, p. 208.

269 "Other travellers": Frank Ross, introduction to Harlan, *Narrative*, p. 7.

269 "The introduction": Harlan, *Importation of Camels*, p. 61.

270 "compelled to cross": Ibid.

270 "unlike the": Ibid.

270 "the demand for": Ibid.

270 "Patient under his": Ibid.

270 "As sure footed": Ibid.

270 "renders his breath": Ibid.

270 "great national project": Ibid.

270 "unless government": Ibid.

270 "the camel tribe": Ibid.

270 "to some highly": Ibid.

271 "for the purpose": Laws of the State of New York, 1854, chapter 229, pp. 514–516.

271 "valuable paper": G. P. Marsh, *The Camel, His Organization, Habits and Uses* (1856), pp. 35–36.

271 "The American horses": Frank Ross, introduction to Harlan, *Narrative*, p. 21.

271 "where they wandered": Ibid., p. 21.

271 "I by no means intend": Josiah Harlan, *On the Fruits of Cabul and Vicinity, With a View to the Introduction of the Grape-Vine of that Region into the Central Climate of the United States*, U.S. Senate Executive Document, no. 39, 37 Cong., 2nd session, pp. 526–537.

271 "But is not": Ibid.

272 "Numberless productive": Harlan, *On the Fruits of Cabul*, pp. 526–37.

272 "of mammoth size": Ibid.

272 "cherries, apricots": Ibid.

272 "seedless pomegranates": Ibid.

272 "millions to the": Ibid.

272 "Another discovery": Ibid.

272 "The acclimation of": Ibid.

272 "I propose myself": Ibid.
273 "Great personal danger": Ibid.

16: HARLAN'S LAST STAND

275 "most of the men": Frank H. Taylor, *Taylor's Philadelphia in the Civil War, 1861–1865*, Three Year Regiments, part 4, p. 902.
276 "The cold and rain": National Archives Record Group 153, Records of the Judge Advocate General's Office (Army), entry 15, Courts-martial Case File, file II 703.
276 "also caused many": Ibid.
276 "no requisitions": Ibid.
276 "I was convalescent": Ibid.
276 "I did not report": Ibid.
276 "he had never attended": Thomas P. Lowry, *Tarnished Eagles: The Courts-Martial of Fifty Union Colonels and Lieutenant Colonels*, p. 144.
276 "What in hell": Courts-martial Case File.
277 "What is your": Ibid.
277 "All of you": Ibid.
277 "Stables and Quarters": Taylor, *Taylor's Philadelphia*, p. 903.
277 "consequently the formation": Ibid.
277 "harsh and ungentlemanly": Courts-martial Case File.
277 "If any more": Ibid.
277 "a sedition existed": Ibid.
278 "he is the damned fool": Ibid.
278 "habitual neglect": Ibid.
278 "Charges and specifications": Lowry, *Tarnished Eagles*, p. 145.
278 "a mass meeting": Ibid.
278 "gruff": Courts-martial Case File.
279 "conduct unbecoming": Ibid.
279 "six different": Ibid.
279 "in a very": Ibid.
279 "unofficerlike and ungentlemanly": Ibid.
279 "unusual cheerfulness": Ibid.
279 "steady himself by": Ibid.
279 "I judged from": Ibid.
279 "these promulgators": Ibid.
279 "During the whole": Ibid.
279 "The space in": Ibid.
280 "Did you think": Ibid.
280 "My reputation": Ibid.
280 "Is my condemnation": Ibid.
281 "I have patiently": Ibid.

281 "fighting not against": Ibid.
281 "If in this volunteer": Ibid.
281 "The greatest and": Ibid.
281 "Gentleman, you who": Ibid.
282 "good order and": Ibid.
282 "disrespectful and ungentlemanly": Ibid.
282 "suspended from Command": Ibid.
282 "by invisible enemies": Ibid.
282 "A combination was": Ibid.
282 "It is indeed": Ibid.
283 "as a token of respect": *Virginia Recorder*, Aug. 3, 1862.
283 "To receive from": Ibid.
283 "We have left our": Ibid.
284 "engaged in picketing": Taylor, *Taylor's Philadelphia*, p. 903.
284 "A sabre charge": Ibid.
284 "debilitated from": Lowry, *Tarnished Eagles*, p. 147.
284 "the country's funds": Frank Ross, introduction to Harlan, *Narrative*, p. 23.
284 "The man who": Khushwant Singh, *Ranjit Singh*, p. 146.
285 "soi-disant relations": Gardner, *Memoirs*, p. 325.
285 "English that was": Ibid., p. 383.
285 "visitors to the": Ibid.
285 "Everything in the": W. W. Huston to Josiah Harlan, Oct. 1, 1867, Chester County Archives, Pennsylvania.
285 "iron horse": Harlan, *Importation of Camels*, p. 61.
285 "Harlan, Josiah": Brunner, *A Man of Enterprise*, p. 18.
285 "Harlan, Gen., USA": Ibid.
285 "which put his name": Ibid.
285 "had used it to start fires": Unidentified newspaper clipping, Nov. 11, 1950, Chester County Archives, Pennsylvania.
286 "the lack of": Frank Ross, introduction to Harlan, *Narrative*, p. 23.
286 "Harlan, J., physician": San Francisco City Directory, 1871, p. 305.
286 "phthisis": Mortuary Record of the City and County of San Francisco, entry no. 1102.

EPILOGUE

288 "To subdue and": Harlan, *Memoir*, p. 5.
289 "I will do whatever": Zahir Shah, interview with the author, Kabul, Nov. 12, 2002.
289 "I will go back": Ibid.
289 "I was a": Kipling, "The Man Who Would Be King," p. 139.
289 "I'll make an Empire": Ibid., p. 128.
289 "inspired by": Gilmour, *The Long Recessional*, p. 37.

290 "You'll be turned back": Kipling, "The Man Who Would Be King," p. 119.

290 "Dravot he was": Ibid., p. 126.

290 "He took half an hour": Ibid., p. 138.

290 "You behold now": Ibid., p. 139.

291 "may be seen": Gilmour, *The Long Recessional*, p. 38.

291 "Oh, East is East": Kipling, *Selected Poems*, p. 101.

291 "returned to an office": Kipling, "The Man Who Would Be King," p. 139.

SELECTED BIBLIOGRAPHY

Adams, Henry. *History of the United States of America During the Administrations of Thomas Jefferson*. New York, 1986.

Allen, Charles. *Soldier Sahibs: The Men Who Made the North-West Frontier*. London, 2000.

Ambrose, Stephen E. *Undaunted Courage: Meriwether Lewis, Thomas Jefferson, and the Opening of the American West*. New York, 1997.

Bidwell, Shelford. *Swords for Hire: European Mercenaries in Eighteenth-Century India*. London, 1971.

Brunner, Christopher J. *A Man of Enterprise: The Short Writings of Josiah Harlan*. Occasional paper for the Afghanistan Forum, no. 27. New York, 1987.

Burnes, Sir Alexander. *Cabool: A Personal Narrative of the Journey to, and residence in that City in the Years 1836, 7 and 8*. London, 1830.

Chaffin, Tom. *Pathfinder: John Charles Frémont and the course of American Empire*. New York, 2002.

Cunningham, Joseph Davey. *A History of the Sikhs*. Oxford, 1918.

Eden, Emily. *Up the Country*. 2nd ed., London, 1978.

Elphinstone, Mountstuart. *An Account of the Kingdom of Caubul and its Dependencies in Persia, Tartary, and India*. London, 1815.

Ewans, Sir Martin. *Afghanistan: A New History*. London, 2001.

Eyre, Lieutenant Vincent. *The Military Operations at Cabul*. London, 1843.

Forbes, Archibald. *The Afghan Wars 1839–41 and 1878–80*. New York, 1892.

Gardner, Alexander. *Soldier and Traveller: Memoirs of Alexander Gardner*. Edited by Major Hugh Pearse. Edinburgh and London, 1898.

Gilmour, David. *The Long Recessional: The Imperial Life of Rudyard Kipling*. London, 2002.

Grant, J. *Dost Muhammud Khan*. London, 1842.

Grey Charles. *European Adventurers of Northern India 1785 to 1849*. Lahore, 1929.

Harlan, Josiah. *Central Asia: Personal Narrative of General Josiah Harlan, 1823–1841*. Edited by Frank Ross. London, 1939.

———. *A Memoir of India and Avghanistan*. Philadelphia, 1842.

———. *Oriental Sketches*. Handwritten document in Chester County Archives, Pennsylvania, dated A.D. 1841.

———. *Importation of Camels*. U.S. Congress. Executive Document no. 27, part 2, 33 Cong., 1st session. Washington, D.C., 1854.

———. *On the Fruits of Cabul and Vicinity, With a View to the Introduction of the Grape-Vine of that Region into the Central Climate of the United States*. U.S. Congress. Senate Executive Document No. 39, 37 Cong. 2nd session. Washington, D.C., 1862.

———. *The United States Gazette*. "General Harlan's Eighteen Years' Residence in Asia," including extracts from his journal. Philadelphia, January 20, 1842.

Havelock, Henry. *Narrative of the War in Affghanistan in 1838–39*. London, 1840.

Herodotus. *The History of Herodotus*. Chicago, 1988.

Honigberger, Martin. *Thirty-Five Years in the East*. London, 1852.

Hopkirk, Peter. *The Great Game—On Secret Service in High Asia*. London, 1990.

Jacquemont, Victor. *Voyage dans l'Inde*. Paris, 1836–41.

Kaye, W. J. *History of the War in Afghanistan* (2 vols.). London, 1890.

Keay, John. *The Honourable Company: A History of the English East India Company* (2 vols). London, 1993.

Kennedy, Richard Hartley. *Narrative of the Campaign of the Army of the Indus, in Sind and Kaubool, in 1838–9*. London, 1840.

Kipling, Rudyard. *Selected Stories*. London, 1996 (first published 1888).

———. *Selected Poems*. London, 1986 (first published 1889).

Lafont, Jean-Marie. *La présence française dans la royaume Sikh du Penjab, 1822–1849*. Paris, 1992.

———. *Maharaja Ranjit Singh: Lord of the Five Rivers*. New Delhi, 2002.

Lal, Mohan. *Life of the Amir Dost Mohammed Khan of Kabul*. London, 1846.

Lamb, Christina. *The Sewing Circles of Herat*. London, 2002.

Lane Fox, Robin. *Alexander the Great*. London, 1973.

Lawrence, H.M.L. *Adventures of an Officer on the Service of Runjeet Singh*. London, 1845.

Lowry, Thomas P. *Tarnished Eagles: The Courts-Martial of Fifty Union Colonels and Lieutenant Colonels*. Mechanicsburg, Penn., 1997.

Lunt, Major General James. *Bokhara Burnes*. London, 1969.

MacDonald Fraser, George. *Flashman and the Mountain of Light*. London, 1999.

Macrory, Patrick. *Kabul Catastrophe: The Invasion and Retreat of 1839–1842*. London, 1966.

Malleson, G. B. *History of Afghanistan from the Earliest Period to the Outbreak of the War of 1878*. London, 1878.

Marsh, G. P. *The Camel, His Organization, Habits and Uses*. Washington, 1856.

Masrat, Bikrama Jit. *The Life and Times of Ranjit Singh: A Saga of a Benevolent Despot*. Lahore, 1977.

Masson, Charles. *Narrative of Various Journeys in Balochistan, Afghanistan and the Panjab* (3 vols.). London, 1842.

McGregor, W. L. *The History of the Sikhs*. Delhi, 1870.

McLean, Sir Fitzroy. *A Person from England*. London, 1958.

Meyer, Karl, and Shareen Brysac. *Tournament of Shadows: The Great Game and the Race for Empire in Asia*. New York, 1999.

Osborne, W. G. *The Court and Camp of Runjeet Singh*. London, 1840.

Poullada, Leon B., and D. J. Leila. *The Kingdom of Afghanistan and the United States 1828–1973*. Lincoln, Neb., 1995.

Prinsep, H. T. *Origin of the Sikh Power in the Punjab and Political Life of Maha-raja Ranjit Singh*. Calcutta, 1834.

Sale, Lady Florentia. *The First Afghan War*. Edited by Patrick Macrory. London, 1969.

Scharf, J. Thomas, and Thompson Westcott. *History of Philadelphia 1609–1884* (2 vols.). Philadelphia, 1884.

Shah, Sirdar Ikbal Ali. *Afghanistan of the Afghans*. London, 1989.

Singh, Khushwant. *Ranjit Singh*. London, 1962.

Singh, Kirpal. *Ranjit Singh*. London, 1996.

Sinha, Narendra Krishna. *Ranjit Sing*. Calcutta, 1933.

Suri, Lala Sohan Lal. *Chronicle of the Reign of Maharaja Ranjit Singh 1831–1839 A.D.* Translated by V. S. Suri. New Delhi, 1961.

Taylor, Frank H. *Taylor's Philadelphia in the Civil War, 1861–1865*. Philadelphia, 1913.

Vigne, G. T. *A Personal Narrative of a Visit to Ghuzni, Kabul, and Afghanistan*. London, 1843.

Vogelsang, Willem. *The Afghans*. Oxford, 2002.

Whitteridge, Gordon. *Charles Masson of Afghanistan: Explorer, Archaeologist, Numismatist and Intelligence Agent*. Warminster, U.K., 1986.

Wolff, J. *Researches and Missionary Labours among the Jews, Mohammadans and other Sects*. London, 1835.

ACKNOWLEDGMENTS

I am grateful to many people in several countries for their help with this book: Jean-Marie Lafont, Pam Shenk, Barbara Rutz, Katie Ruane, Ahmad Shaheer, Peter Nichols, Philip Howard, Martin Fletcher, Sandy Morton, Sandra Parsons, Christina Lamb, His Majesty Zahir Shah, Ron Nash, Michael Jay, Juliette Brightmoor, Richard Moore, Roland Philipps, Mary Clare Lithgow, Kate Lithgow, Jeevan Deol, Tina Gaudoin, Peter Hopkirk, Martin Ewans, Ford Ennals, and Karine Tachdjian. I would also like to thank the staff at the Chester County Historical Society, the Rudyard Kipling Society, the Tri-County Historical Society, the British Museum, and the Imperial War Museum for guiding me to a wealth of obscure sources.

I owe a great debt to Ed Victor, my superb agent, and to John Glusman and Aodaoin O'Floinn of Farrar, Straus and Giroux, and Michael Fishwick and Robert Lacey of HarperCollins, for their support and professionalism. My love and gratitude, as always, go to Kate Muir, for her endless insight, good humor, and encouragement.

INDEX